# PHILOSOPHY, HISTORY AND CIVILIZATION

Interdisciplinary Perspectives on R. G. Collingwood

# Philosophy, History and Civilization

## Interdisciplinary Perspectives on R. G. Collingwood

*Edited by*
DAVID BOUCHER, JAMES CONNELLY
and TARIQ MODOOD

UNIVERSITY OF WALES PRESS
CARDIFF
1995

© The Contributors, 1995

Rex Martin's article, 'Collingwood's Claim that Metaphysics is a Historical Discipline', was previously published in a slightly different form in *The Monist*, vol. 72 (1989). Copyright © 1989, *The Monist*, La Salle, Illinois 61301. Reprinted by permission.

All rights reserved. No part of this book may be reproduced, stored in a retrieval system, or transmitted, in any form or by any means, electronic, mechanical, photocopying, recording or otherwise, without clearance from the University of Wales Press, 6 Gwennyth Street, Cardiff, CF2 4YD.

**British Library Cataloguing-in-Publication Data**

A catalogue record for this book is available from the British Library.

ISBN 0-7083-1308-6

B
1618
.C74
P45
1995

Published in association with
The R. G. Collingwood Society
Registered Charity No. 1037636
University of Wales, Swansea SA2 8PP

Jacket design by Design Principle, Cardiff

Typeset at the University of Wales Press
Printed in Wales by Gwasg Dinefwr, Llandybïe

To

W. H. Rieckmann,
President of Industrial Plastics Inc.,
Honorary Fellow of the University of Wales, Swansea,
and Trustee of the Collingwood Society

# Contents

| | |
|---|---|
| Notes on the Contributors | ix |
| Acknowledgements | xii |
| List of Abbreviations | xiii |
| Introduction | xv |
| The Life, Times and Legacy of R. G. Collingwood<br>*David Boucher* | 1 |
| Collingwood and the Idea of Philosophy<br>*Tariq Modood* | 32 |
| Aesthetics and Philosophical Method<br>*T. J. Diffey* | 62 |
| Faith and Reason in the Philosophy of Religion<br>*D. M. MacKinnon* | 79 |
| Art Thou the Man: Croce, Gentile or de Ruggiero?<br>*James Connelly* | 92 |
| Croce and Gentile in Collingwood's *New Leviathan*<br>*H. S. Harris* | 115 |
| Vico, Collingwood and the Character of a Historical Philosophy<br>*B. A. Haddock* | 130 |

Croce, Gentile and Collingwood on the Relation between
History and Philosophy
    *Rik Peters*      152

Collingwood's Theory of Historical Knowledge
    *Leon Pompa*      168

Metaphysics and History in Collingwood's Thought
    *Adrian Oldfield*      182

Collingwood's Claim that Metaphysics is a
Historical Discipline
    *Rex Martin*      203

Collingwood on the Ideas of Process, Progress and Civilization
    *Jan van der Dussen*      246

The Place of Education in Civilization
    *David Boucher*      269

Civilization and the Open Society: Collingwood and Popper
    *A. J. M. Milne*      300

A Baconian Revolution: Collingwood and
Romano-British Studies
    *Margot Browning*      330

Of Mice and Men: Collingwood and the Development
of Archaeological Thought
    *Ian Hodder*      364

Index of Persons      384

Index of References to Collingwood's Writings      387

# Notes on the Contributors

David Boucher is a reader in Politics at the University of Wales, Swansea, a senior associate of Pembroke College, Oxford, a fellow of the Royal Historical Society, a member of Oxford University Press Collingwood Committee, and chairman of the trustees of the Collingwood Society. He is the author of *Texts in Context*, *The Social and Political Thought of R. G. Collingwood* and *A Radical Hegelian: The Political and Social Thought of Henry Jones* (with Andrew Vincent). He has edited *The Social Contract From Hobbes to Rawls* (with Paul Kelly) as well as R. G. Collingwood's *Essays in Political Philosophy* and *The New Leviathan*.

Margot Browning is a post-doctoral Harper instructor in Humanities, and associate of the History Department at the University of Chicago. She is currently a co-chair of the Fishbein Seminar on the History of the Human Sciences at the University of Chicago. Her publications include articles on the history of British archaeology.

James Connelly is a principal lecturer at the Southampton Institute of Higher Education. He has written a number of articles on Collingwood in such journals as *History and Theory* and *Storia, antropologia e scienze del linguaggio*, and contributes to *Collingwood Studies*.

T. J. Diffey is reader in Philosophy and has been dean of the School of Cultural Studies at the University of Sussex. He is the editor of the *British Journal of Aesthetics* and the author of *Tolstoy's What is Art?* and *The Republic of Art and Other Essays*.

Jan van der Dussen is Professor of History and Philosophy at the Open University, The Netherlands. He is the author of *History as a*

Science: The Philosophy of R. G. Collingwood, and has edited Objectivity, Method and Point of View (with Lionel Rubinoff) and R. G. Collingwood, The Idea of History, revised edition. He has published two books and numerous articles in Dutch. He is a member of the Oxford University Press Collingwood Committee.

B. A. Haddock is a senior lecturer in Politics at the University of Wales, Swansea. He is a fellow of the Royal Historical Society, trustee of the Collingwood Society, member of the Oxford University Press Collingwood Committee, and the author of *An Introduction to Historical Thought* and *The Political Thought of Vico*.

H. S. Harris is Distinguished Research Professor of Philosophy at York University, Canada. He is best known for his seminal studies of Hegel; *Hegel's Development towards the Sunlight* and *Hegel's Development: Night Thoughts*. He has also published *The Social Philosophy of Giovanni Gentile* and edited Gentile's *Genesis and Structure of Society*.

Ian Hodder is reader in Prehistory and a fellow of Darwin College, Cambridge University. He is the author of numerous books, including *Symbols in Action*, *The Present Past*, *Reading the Past*, *The Domestication of Europe* and *Theory and Practice in Archaeology*. Among his edited volumes are *The Meanings of Things* and *Archaeological Theory in Europe*.

The late Donald M. MacKinnon was a fellow of Keble College while R. G. Collingwood was Waynflete Professor of Metaphysics at Oxford. He was emeritus professor at Cambridge University where he had held the Norris-Hulse chair of Divinity. He published a number of books, among them *The Problem of Metaphysics*, *A Study of Ethical Theory*, and *Creon and Antigone: Ethical Problems of Nuclear Warfare*. Professor MacKinnon also published three volumes of his collected papers. A collection of essays has been written in his honour, *The Philosophical Frontiers of Christian Theology*, edited by Brian Hebblethwaite and Stewart Sutherland.

Rex Martin is professor of Philosophy at the University of Kansas and professor of Political Theory and Government at the

University of Wales, Swansea. He is a member of the executive committee of the International Association for the Philosophy of Law (IVR) and president of its American section (1993–5). He is a member of the Oxford University Press Collingwood Committee and author of *Historical Explanation, Rawls and Rights*, and *A System of Rights*. He has edited Gerald C. MacCallum Jr., *Legislative Intent* (with Marcus G. Singer) and is currently working on a revised edition of Collingwood's *Essay on Metaphysics*.

A. J. M. Milne is emeritus professor of Political Theory and Institutions at the University of Durham. He has been a Harkness fellow in the USA at Berkeley and Princeton from 1952 to 1954. He is the author of *The Social Philosophy of English Idealism*, *Freedom and Rights*, *The Right of Dissent* and *Human Rights and Human Diversity*.

Tariq Modood is a senior fellow at the Policy Studies Institute, London, and an honorary fellow of University of Wales, Swansea. He combines his current research in race relations with an older interest in philosophy. He is the author of *Not Easy Being British* and co-author of *Changing Ethnic Identities*.

Adrian Oldfield is a senior lecturer in politics at the University of Salford. He has published widely in international journals including *History and Theory*. He is the author of *Citizenship and Community: Civic Republicanism and the Modern World*.

Rik Peters is a teacher of Economics and Music in Holland. He has published articles in *The Bulletin of the Hegel Society of Great Britain*, and *Collingwood Studies*. He is currently working on a full-length study of Collingwood's relation to Italian philosophy.

Leon Pompa is professor of Philosophy at the University of Birmingham and has twice been the dean of the Faculty of Arts there. He is a member of the Oxford University Press Collingwood Committee and the author of *Vico*, and *Human Nature and Historical Knowledge*, and has edited *Substance and Form in History* (with W. H. Dray) and *Vico: Selected Writings*.

# *Acknowledgements*

Although most of the essays were especially commissioned for this collection, some have been previously published. The editors have included them in order to give a more complete presentation. The editors would like to thank Peter Lang for permission to reproduce T. J. Diffey, 'Aesthetics and Philosophical Method', in T. J. Diffey, *The Republic of Art and Other Essays* (New York, Peter Lang, 1991); Professor Luciano Dondoli the editor of *Storia, antropologia e scienze del linguaggio,* for permission to reproduce the chapters by H. S. Harris and Leon Pompa; Dr Glyn Richards for permission to reproduce D. M. MacKinnon's contribution to *Scottish Journal of Religious Studies,* 13 (1992); and John Hospers for permission to reprint Rex Martin's contribution to *The Monist,* 72 (1989). Jan van der Dussen's chapter is a much revised and extended version of 'Collingwood and the Idea of Progress' first published in *History and Theory,* Beiheft 29 (1990).

We are indebted to Sue Irving, Pat Yates, Christine Roberts and Phyllis Roberts of the Department of Political Theory and Government, University of Wales, Swansea for helping to get this volume into shape.

# *Abbreviations*

| | |
|---|---|
| A | *An Autobiography* (1939) |
| EM | *An Essay on Metaphysics* (1940) |
| EPM | *Essay On Philosophical Method* (1933) |
| EPP | *Essays in Political Philosophy* (1989) |
| FR | *Faith and Reason* (1968) |
| IH | *The Idea of History* (1946 and 1993) |
| IN | *The Idea of Nature* (1945) |
| NL | *The New Leviathan* (1942 and 1992) |
| PA | *Principles of Art* (1938) |
| RP | *Religion and Philosophy* (1916) |
| SM | *Speculum Mentis* (1924) |

All the above books are published by Oxford University Press with the exception of *Religion and Philosophy* (Macmillan) and *Faith and Reason* (Quadrangle Books).

# *Introduction*

It is a little over fifty years since the death of R. G. Collingwood and over twenty years since Michael Krausz edited *Critical Essays on the Philosophy* of R. G. Collingwood (Oxford, Oxford University Press, 1972). The purpose of the present volume is not to bring Krausz up to date, but instead to reassess, from the points of view of authors with a diversity of disciplinary affiliations, some of Collingwood's fundamental doctrines. The chapters by Modood, Diffey, MacKinnon and Hodder, for example, emphasize what they take to be enduring in Collingwood's contribution to the subjects they discuss, namely philosophy, theology, aesthetics and archaeology. The chapters on Collingwood's debt to Italian philosophy provide a fitting prelude to the discussion of his ideas on the philosophy of history and metaphysics. The Italian connection has not before received such systematic consideration, and Collingwood's sources of inspiration are meticulously identified. Connelly argues persuasively that we must more readily acknowledge the degree to which de Ruggiero figures as a significant influence upon Collingwood, while Harris characterizes what Collingwood was trying to achieve in writing *The New Leviathan*, and identifies the precise points at which Croce and Gentile's contribution, both positive and negative, acted as a stimulus to the formation of his own thought. Furthermore, Harris maintains that the philosophy of religion articulated in *The New Leviathan* is highly original and does not have its roots in Idealist philosophy. Knox's uncorroborated claim that Collingwood always maintained that he had learnt more from Vico than from anyone else is given credence by Haddock's tracing of the elements in Vico's thought that surface in one guise or another in Collingwood. Peters explores the influence of Croce and Gentile upon aspects of Collingwood's philosophy of history. In particular he shows how Collingwood's answer to the question of the possibility of historical knowledge is the encapsulation theory that the two Italians developed, and that the theory of re-enactment is implied in Gentile's version of it. What is particularly illuminating is Peters's account of the debate between Croce and Gentile on the rapprochement of history and philosophy, and how the differences between the two Italians helped Collingwood to come to his own understanding, which rejected those aspects of Gentile that Collingwood thought had a tendency to lead to fascism. The following chapters by Pompa, Oldfield and Martin directly or indirectly take up many of the themes which arise in the Italian discussions, especially in the contributions by Haddock and Peters, and take issue with Collingwood himself or with well-established interpretations of him. Pompa's short and lucid chapter discusses the way in which we acquire historical knowledge, and maintains that Collingwood's theory lacks a crucial element that his conclusions require, namely a theory of how our knowledge of the past is socially inherited. Both Oldfield and Martin address themselves to disputes that have arisen out of Collingwood's claim that metaphysics is a historical discipline. Oldfield wants to deny Toulmin's claim that Collingwood is a strong relativist, and suggests that the version that Collingwood holds may at best be described as soft relativism. Martin tries to dispel the idea that the theory of re-enactment must be applicable to historical knowledge of absolute presuppositions by showing that Collingwood did not wish to posit an identity of method between history and metaphysics. Martin contends that it is not what Collingwood said about re-enactment, but what he said about processes that provides the key to understanding the claim that metaphysics is a historical discipline.

The three following chapters by van der Dussen, Boucher and Milne serve to highlight how important the idea of civilization was to Collingwood's whole way of thinking. Van der Dussen examines some of the less well explored ideas of Collingwood's philosophy of history. Following on from Martin's discussion of process, he tries to show the relations between the ideas of process, progress and civilization. Boucher's contribution shows how crucial

Collingwood thought education was to sustain civilization by passing on its fundamental principles and practices, both emotional and intellectual. The content of that education included the conclusions reached in his philosophical discussions of aesthetics, religion, science, history and philosophy, which would in his view stem the tide of irrationalism in its many modern manifestations, including fascism and nazism. Milne's chapter is a fitting extension of the political philosophy implied in the previous chapter. It critically compares Popper's and Collingwood's responses to the revolt against civilization, pointing out the significant differences and similarities in their theories. Milne shows how Popper's idea of a rationalist attitude to politics and Collingwood's dialectical attitude to resolving disputes are in fact different names for the same idea. It is this idea that is lacking in Popper's 'closed society' and Collingwood's 'non-social community'. Milne contends that both Collingwood and Popper fail adequately to come to terms with the question of the moral requirements of a society.

The chapters by Browning and Hodder are complementary: both in their different ways deal with the relationship between Collingwood's archaeological practice and his philosophy of history. Browning wants to relate Collingwood's reflections on archaeology and contemporary history to his philosophy of history, via an exploration of his overall view of science. The selective excavation method which Collingwood practised united the technical revolution in archaeology with the revolution in historical method. Both were Baconian in putting the evidence to the question. In this respect she claims to have restored an empirical aspect to Collingwood's philosophy of history. The method of question and answer, applied to the practice of selective digging, did, however, have its shortcomings in the hands of such a stridently confident archaeologist as Collingwood, as Hodder shows in his example of the excavation of Arthur's Round Table. Hodder's point, nevertheless, is well taken, that Collingwood's own application of the theory need not undermine the theory itself. Hodder argues that Collingwood's philosophy of history has a real contribution to make to five ongoing debates among archaeologists.

The collection in total provides a fresh look at familiar aspects of Collingwood's thought, and sheds new light on our understanding of the interrelatedness of his thought by exploring aspects that have either been neglected or little discussed. The implication then, is that it is timely to bring together a volume that re-examines some of the standard issues in Collingwood studies, and which breaks new ground by exploring aspects of his thought that have suffered relative neglect, but which nevertheless have potentially important contributions to make in our understanding of philosophy, history and civilization.

# The Life, Times and Legacy of R. G. Collingwood*

## DAVID BOUCHER

### I

This chapter serves the purpose of sketching a portrait of the man, his place in contemporary Oxford and his intellectual relations with his colleagues. Furthermore, I want to give an account of the range of his historical and philosophical interests and selectively trace the resonance of his ideas in the works of some of the leading thinkers in a variety of fields of study. The selection is meant to illustrate the pervasiveness of Collingwood's ideas, and by no means claims to be exhaustive. His influence in the philosophy of history and aesthetics is so well known that it needs no reiteration here, and I therefore concentrate upon the less well known areas that have succumbed to his influence. Throughout I will indicate how the chapters in this collection relate to the concerns discussed.

William M. Johnston contends that it was from John Ruskin, mediated through W. G. Collingwood, Collingwood's father, that R. G. Collingwood inherited the passion for breadth of learning which is so characteristic of the younger Collingwood's works.[1] Irrespective of the source of this predilection it is undeniable that Collingwood was of the opinion that a necessary prerequisite to thinking clearly about a subject was a complete immersion in the practice of the activity about which one philosophized.[2] What was, then, the experience which Collingwood could reflect upon, to formulate his own philosophical theories? Born at Coniston in 1889, Collingwood was educated at home until the age of thirteen, principally by his father, with his mother and sisters making a contribution. Two or three hours were set aside each morning for formal lessons, including Greek, Latin and ancient and modern history. For the rest of the day Collingwood appears to have been left to his own devices to pursue, individually or in the company of the other members of the family and friends, whatever he felt inclined to do. With his three sisters, for instance, Collingwood produced a weekly family magazine, examples of which are still extant and in the possession of his daughter Mrs Teresa Smith.[3] The magazine included family news, short serial stories, illustrations and maps, written or drawn by the children themselves.

The foundations of Collingwood's many talents were laid during his thirteen years of education at home. Under the auspices of his father Collingwood became proficient in reading and writing ancient and modern languages. He was taught to sing, play the piano, draw and paint – all skills which he put to good effect in his adult years. Collingwood's father was a particularly good sailor and passed on his enthusiasm for the sport to his son. It was during these early years that Collingwood developed his passion for philosophy. His interest both in philosophy and the natural sciences appears to have been self-motivated (A, 7–8). Collingwood introduced himself to Kant's theory of ethics at the age of eight and felt ashamed at not being able to understand it. He also interested himself in natural scientific theories, which taught him that science is less like a cumulative body of truths and more like a dynamic body of knowledge undergoing continuous change.

Most of this is familiar to Collingwood scholars, and I need not labour the matter further. The point is this: the family atmosphere; the example of talented parents; the judicious balance of formal lessons and self-motivated activity, all served to encourage the widest possible practical and intellectual interests.

These were for Collingwood happy days which abruptly came to an end when his education became more conventionally institutionalized. Rugby School proved to be a great disappointment to him. Instead of stimulating natural inquisitiveness, education at Rugby seemed designed to stifle it. With very few exceptions, he found the quality of the teachers low and their lessons boring. The timetabling of subjects took no account of considerations of continuity and depth, thus devaluing further the intellectual worth of the curriculum. Rugby, far from stimulating independence of thought, appeared to Collingwood to be actively hostile to it. In devoting himself to independent study in, for example, medieval Italian history and early French poetry, he became something of a rebel. In sum, the formal institutional education to which he was becoming accustomed worked directly against the spirit and ethos of the education he had received at home.

Gaining a classical scholarship in 1908 enabled Collingwood to go up to University College, Oxford, where he regained the freedom to indulge his insatiable appetite for learning. Such was his desire for knowledge that he lived the life of a semi-recluse, reading all day and most of the night on any subject which took his fancy. It was during these days, Knox suggests, that Collingwood first became acquainted with his lifelong enemy, insomnia, and possibly the severe strain to which he subjected himself contributed to his later ill-health.[4] In 1910 he took a first in Classical Moderations and in 1912 a first in *Literae Humaniores*, after which he was elected to a philosophy fellowship at Pembroke College, where he became College Librarian and tutor. In 1927 he became University lecturer in Philosophy and Roman History. Between the years 1924 and 1933 Collingwood was the joint editor of *Transactions of the Cumberland and Westmorland Antiquarian and Archaeological Society*, of which he was also president, and did not resign until 1939. He was elected a fellow of the British Academy in 1934 and in 1935 he was appointed Waynflete Professor of Metaphysical Philosophy, a position which he resigned because of failing health in 1941 to return to his late father's home in Coniston with Kathleen Edwardes, who became the second Mrs Collingwood in 1942, and to whom a daughter, Teresa, was born.

The extent of the energy that Collingwood devoted to archaeology has only recently become clear with the discovery of his notebooks, card indices and correspondence among the papers of I. A. Richmond, M. V. Taylor and the Haverfield Foundation in the Ashmolean Library, Oxford.[5] Not only did he travel extensively abroad, which is well known, he also visited Roman sites in Britain, often three or four times. He travelled throughout England and Wales, and parts of Scotland with a heavy and demanding schedule every year, sometimes visiting three sites a day. He would frequently enter into correspondence with the keepers of these sites, and suggest revisions to their information pamphlets and guides.

Collingwood died of pneumonia on 9 January 1943 at

Lanehead, Coniston about six weeks before his fifty-fourth birthday which he would have celebrated on 22 February. Like his father, W. G. Collingwood, but at an earlier age, he drove himself to exhaustion and suffered the same fate, high blood pressure and repeated strokes. W. G. Collingwood had the first of his strokes in 1927, after which his son devoted himself to helping him. Such devotion took its toll on R. G. Collingwood's health. He began to suffer from high blood pressure in 1930,[6] which affected him badly first in 1931 and then again in 1932 after his father's death. In 1931 his condition was quite serious. In a letter to F. Gerald Simpson he reported that he was unable to do any intellectual work without being overcome by exhaustion, and that his doctor warned that unless he rested for several months he would suffer a complete breakdown resulting in 'a permanent loss of strength'.[7] In 1932 he did have a complete breakdown and was forced to seek leave of absence from his university. He never fully recovered, and began to suffer repeated strokes early in 1938 which became increasingly debilitating.[8] The funeral took place on 12 January 1943 in heavy rain with the mountains enveloped in black mist. Canon Wilcox and the Revd R. B. Luard Selby, Collingwood's brother-in-law, presided over the service, which because of the war, weather, transport difficulties and the remote location, was poorly attended. A memorial service in Oxford was not thought appropriate because of family sensitivities.[9]

Collingwood was, by reputation, one of the most gifted teachers of his generation. He took particular care to perfect the technical side of the presentation of his lectures. His diction and elocution, the result of serious voice training, were an example to be emulated. Many of his former philosophy and Roman history students commented on the clarity of Collingwood's presentation. Michael Robbins, who became treasurer and later president of the Society of Antiquaries of London, thought Collingwood's lectures on the philosophy of history 'the most attractive and illuminating' of any he had attended at Oxford.[10] R. B. McCallum claims that Collingwood's 'lectures were models for less methodical, less eloquent, and less audible teachers'.[11] Others talked of his 'extraordinary power of graphic exposition', and his 'faultless delivery'.[12] Throughout his career he made no concessions to the less gifted students attending his lectures.[13] Notwithstanding the difficulty of his lectures, Collingwood attracted many who were not philosophy students, to hear them.[14] Indeed, so popular were his lectures that they were moved from Pembroke to another college with a larger hall in order to accommodate the audience.[15]

Some of his former pupils have claimed that it was 'a privilege' to be tutored by him; 'he was a first-class tutor'; he 'was a great tutor, given to saying much that was unforgettable – and usually right'; 'I have never met anyone since those days who could "grill" a person so kindly'; and 'we all loved him.'[16] The less gifted tended to be overawed by his intellect and brilliance, which made them conscious of their own 'inferiority'.[17] Some of the better students, while impressed by the manner of his arguments, were not always convinced by the conclusions. McCallum, for instance, says: 'In an argument with Collingwood one was nearly always defeated but very often not convinced.'[18]

Many of his books found their first expression in lectures, and it was in tutorials that he clarified many of his thoughts. In addition, Collingwood believed that he was making more of an impression on his students than on his colleagues.[19] It is evident that he much preferred trying out his theories on undergraduates than presenting them to fellow dons (A, 54).

On his death Collingwood left a large number of manuscripts, some of which he authorized for publication, and the decision about the rest he left to his widow and the secretary of Oxford University Press. Collingwood did not designate Malcolm Knox as his editor, although Knox personally thought that he had Collingwood's blessing.[20] Knox's involvement was fortuitous. Kenneth Sisam, the secretary to the press, and a personal friend of Collingwood, wanted to commission a collection of some of Collingwood's previously published essays with some manuscript material, along with a memoir, to be part of his collected works. Sisam did not want an Oxford man because he thought such a person would be out of sympathy with Collingwood's philosophy. It is therefore ironic that he chose Knox, who proved to be quite out of sympathy with Collingwood's later philosophy. It was R. B. McCallum who recommended Knox, and both Ethel, Collingwood's first wife and Kate Collingwood were consulted. Kate did not know that Knox and Collingwood had been friends, and would have preferred Alexander had he been alive. She suggested two other names, Ernest Barker and C. E. Stevens, a fellow of Magdalen. Stevens was not sufficiently philosophically minded in Sisam's view, and he did not express an opinion on Barker other than to say he was very busy. Ethel thought Knox dull but competent. Knox's role became greater than was at first envisaged. Originally it had been to write a memoir and 'generally supervise the editing of a collected volume'. Knox's judgement, including the overturning of Collingwood's authorization of the publication of *The Principles of History*, prevailed until very recently. As early as 1948 admirers of Collingwood's writings were complaining about Knox's 'complete incapacity to understand him, or to appreciate him'.[21] In more recent times Jan van der Dussen has questioned Knox's judgement in the way he edited *The Idea of History*.[22] The lost portion of *The Principles of History* manuscript has now been found, and Knox's role in editing *The Idea of History* will, in time, become clearer.

## II

Collingwood had a tendency to exaggerate the extent to which he was isolated in Oxford. James Patrick has shown that Collingwood's involvement with theologians and historians in Oxford was considerable. He was particularly friendly with C. C. J. Webb. He was also on very close terms with J. A. Smith, with whom he discussed questions of moral philosophy,[23] and Harold H. Joachim, the second edition of whose *Nature of Truth* Collingwood prepared for the press.[24] Collingwood frequently called upon J. D. Mabbott to play the piano and for conversation.[25] Mabbott, one of the younger generation of Oxford philosophers, who was nine years Collingwood's junior, and who, like Ryle, Ayer and Austin, reacted against the Realism of Prichard, Ross and Joseph, had a high regard for Collingwood. Even Collingwood's philosophical opponents were more accommodating than one would expect. He entered into long and detailed correspondence with a number of them, including Ryle and Prichard.[26] Indeed, many of his opponents were Delegates or advisers to Oxford University Press, as Collingwood himself was, and recommended the publication of his books. *An Autobiography*, for example, which Santayana described as 'strangely conceited but instructive',[27] and in which Collingwood was openly contemptuous of his philosophical opponents in Oxford, passed through the appraisal process relatively unscathed.

While there was some disquiet among the Delegates about the possibility of feelings being hurt, it was the tone of the last chapter on contemporary politics that worried them most, only to agree that it was not the business of the Delegates, among them W. D. Ross, H. H. Price, A. D. Lindsay, G. N. Clark and T. D. Weldon, to censor the political views of the author.[28] Collingwood himself was a valued Delegate from June 1928 to July 1941, and in this capacity met regularly with some of his philosophical opponents, for whom, despite his differences, he had a great deal of respect.

Prichard and H. W. B. Joseph dominated Oxford philosophy in the 1930s, and like Collingwood they had been pupils of Cook Wilson. A. J. Ayer refers to Prichard and Joseph as 'two terrible old monsters'.[29] With Prichard, for example, Collingwood entered into an exchange of letters over the use of the word 'claim'. Prichard seems to be suggesting that a right does not necessarily give rise to a claim and that you and I do not have an obligation to perform it. Collingwood took Prichard to be using the term 'claim' as a synonym for right, and hence making a clear distinction between right and duty. Prichard on the other hand replied emphatically. Right was not a substitute for claim, and ordinarily to say that something is right means that I ought to do it. He accepts Collingwood's criticism that the talk of having a claim upon someone arising out of a particular circumstance is a technical and not an ordinary use of the word, and suggests that so is Collingwood's use of 'right'.[30] Prichard is using the word 'right' to refer to what is morally correct, and not in the sense that one may, for example, have a right to freedom of association. By right Collingwood means something quite different. It is for him action according to rule, and many rules may apply to a given situation, but only one right action is possible to perform at a given time. We cannot therefore have an obligation to perform the other right actions. In Collingwood's view only one action can be your duty in a given circumstance, being the kind of person you are, and therefore rights and duties are quite different.

Collingwood admired Ross for almost succeeding in differentiating right from duty, a distinction which Collingwood himself tried to sustain in *The New Leviathan*.[31] Although Ross was livid about the *Autobiography*, he thought that the argument of *An Essay on Metaphysics* was quite clever, even though he did not agree with it. *The New Leviathan*, however, he thought better. 'And', Ross says, 'an unusual experience with me, I find myself in agreement with much of what he says.'[32] Similarly, H. H. Price, one of Prichard's most gifted pupils, thought *The New Leviathan* 'a most brilliant piece of work, and in its own way a masterly one'.[33] It was Price, too, who first read *The Idea of Nature* before Knox became editor, and thought it a marvellous work.[34] Of all Collingwood's books this was the most well received by reviewers (aspects of *NL* are discussed by Boucher, Harris and Milne in this volume).

Although Collingwood intensely disliked being labelled an Idealist,[35] he learnt a great deal from Croce, Gentile and de Ruggiero (as the contributions of Harris, Peters and Connelly illustrate). He did, however, pride himself on being open to the influence of all he read and heard. Aspects of his philosophy certainly have affinities with the ideas of a number of his contemporaries, among them A. J. Ayer, Ludwig Wittgenstein, J. L. Austin and Gilbert Ryle. Collingwood praises Ayer for characterizing metaphysical statements as pseudo-propositions, incapable of verification with reference to fact. Unlike Ayer, however, Collingwood does not dismiss them as nonsense statements. Ayer identified statements such as 'there is a non-empirical world of values' and 'men have immortal souls' as pseudo-propositions,[36] whereas for Collingwood these same statements were Absolute Presuppositions which provided the foundation of thought. In Collingwood's view, Ayer had correctly exposed metaphysical statements for lacking the features of propositions, but Ayer did not go on to determine what sort of statements they were. Since metaphysical statements were not analytic because they were not true by definition, nor empirical and hence could not be validated with reference to fact, they fell, for Collingwood, into a third category of statements, the philosophical, to which the question of truth and falsity is inapplicable. Absolute Presuppositions are absolutely presupposed, or they are not. They are not like propositions, that is answers to questions, and therefore whether they are true or false cannot logically arise (see Martin and Oldfield for further discussion).[37] We do not derive Absolute Presuppositions from experience. They are, Collingwood maintains, 'catalytic agents which the mind must bring out of its own resources to the manipulation of what is called "experience" and the conversion of it into science and civilization' (EM, 197).

Gilbert Ryle, Ayer's tutor and Collingwood's successor to the Waynflete chair of Metaphysical Philosophy, published *The Concept of Mind* in 1949. Ryle like Collingwood was avowedly anti-Cartesian. Ryle's main purpose was to explode the received orthodox doctrine of mind-and-body dualism, or 'the ghost in the machine'.[38] He does so by maintaining that it is a category error to conjoin or disjoin statements about mental and physical processes as if they are of the same logical type, or as if they are species of a genus called experience.[39] We cannot describe mental occurrences as psychic experiences manifesting themselves as effects in observable actions and statements. The mind is inseparable from its 'overt acts and utterances'.[40] Ryle does not mention Collingwood in *The Concept of Mind*. Ryle's inaugural lecture, however, pays more than a polite compliment to his predecessor for contributing to the exorcism of the ghost in the machine:

> Professor Collingwood saw more clearly, I think, than did his more eminent predecessors in the philosophy of history that the appearances of a feud between Nature and Spirit, that is to say, between the objects of the natural sciences and those of the human studies, is an illusion. These branches of inquiry are not giving rival answers to the same questions about the same world; nor are they giving separate answers to the same questions about rival worlds; they are giving their own answers to different questions about the same world.[41]

From his first to his last book Collingwood was determined to show that the mind is indistinguishable from its activities. In *Religion and Philosophy* he maintains that the dualism between thought and action is false, 'the mind *is* what it *does*' (RP, 34). In *The New Leviathan*, like Ryle, Collingwood traces the problem back to Descartes. Collingwood argues that the mind does not inhabit a body as a person inhabits a house. It is thinking that a person is part body and part mind that gives rise to the unanswerable question of the relation in which they stand to each other. The person is wholly mind, or wholly body, depending upon whether the mode of understanding employed is the order of inquiry predicated by the natural or human sciences. It is the relationship between the two modes of understanding, and not between mind and body, that constitutes the legitimate, as opposed to the bogus, philosophical problem (NL, 2.1–2.74).

Ryle's friend Wittgenstein was known in Oxford until the late

1930s only for the *Tractatus*. Wittgenstein was obsessive about restricting his post-*Tractatus* thoughts to a small group of Cambridge confidants. One or two copies of lecture notes, the Blue and Brown books, circulated among a select group in Oxford towards the end of the decade, but there is no evidence that Collingwood had sight of them. Wittgenstein's *Philosophical Investigations* was not published until 1953, yet a number of writers have remarked upon similarities between his much acclaimed theories of language and those of Collingwood.[42]

Wittgenstein's view of the task of philosophy is to expose the difficulties that perplex us, not to resolve contradictions in our practices, but to make clear how the rules relating to them have become tangled, and how the understanding is injured by its collisions with the limitations of language. The metaphor that Wittgenstein uses is that of getting inside the fly bottle to show the fly the way out.[43]

The acquisition of a language for both Collingwood and Wittgenstein is not a matter of imparted definitions which in themselves give little indication of what they might mean in any particular instance. The meanings of words are in their use. To speak a language is inseparable from the activity or form of life integral to it.[44] As Collingwood maintains, 'One does not first acquire a language and then use it. To possess it and to use it are the same. We only come to possess it by repeatedly and progressively attempting to use it' (PA, 250; cf. 227–8, 239–41). In Collingwood's view, words are social customs and their definitions are discernible only in relation to the types of occasion on which they are used (see appendix I, NL, 399, 403). Collingwood does, however, disagree with Wittgenstein's characterization of language and its concepts as instruments[45] or tools.[46] Collingwood emphatically states that language 'is a mode of conduct, an activity . . . not an instrument, it does not exist save in being used'.[47] Words are, in effect, not tools or instruments but actions.

It is, of course, Wittgenstein's view that philosophy describes language and has no business interfering with its use.[48] Because Collingwood was convinced that theory and practice overlap, philosophy had to do more than describe current usage. Examining current usage is the preliminary stage in defining a concept. The aim of philosophy is to know better something that is already understood (EPM, 10, 11, 100, 161, 163, 164, 205).

Collingwood practises philosophy with a practical intent. All of his philosophical books are designed not only to illuminate, but also to contribute to the conduct of the practices about which he theorizes. This does not mean that he offers prescriptions for conduct; that would be to absolve the individual of responsibility for his or her own actions. Philosophy is normative in so far as it articulates the ideals and criteria by which a man or woman can judge his or her conduct successful or unsuccessful (EM 109).[49]

## III

What was Collingwood's intellectual project, and to what extent have his ideas been a source of inspiration to modern writers? Since his unpublished manuscripts were deposited in the Bodleian Library, Oxford in 1979 interest in Collingwood has escalated. The proliferation of work about and inspired by Collingwood since then serves to disguise the steady impact that his philosophy progressively had in the decades after his death, particularly in aesthetics and historical studies.[50]

Collingwood himself distinguished his writings into three categories: philosophical essays, philosophical principles and studies in the history of ideas. While writing *An Essay on Metaphysics* Collingwood came to see it as volume 2, and *An Essay on Philosophical Method* as volume 1 of the philosophical essays. *Speculum Mentis* became *de facto* the first in the series, with subsequent reprintings of it and *An Essay on Philosophical Method* having one and two stars respectively on their spines to denote their place in the series. The relation between the first and second is reasonably clear. Collingwood himself suggests that the first provides an introduction to philosophy, while in the second the philosophy has begun to take shape.[51] The first illustrated a scale of forms analysis by means of a dialectical exploration of experience in which art, religion, science and history were shown to have false conceptions of themselves and to be related to each other in a linked hierarchy of overlapping forms. *The Essay on Philosophical Method* examines the logic of a scale of forms and constitutes a move from the dialectic of experience to the dialectic of concepts (see Modood). The relation between the second and third in the series is extremely problematic. *An Essay on*

*Philosophical Method* assumed a clear distinction between philosophy and history in the course of establishing the differentiae of the philosophical concept. *An Essay on Metaphysics*, on the other hand, is famous for its characterization of metaphysics as a historical science whose purpose is to articulate the absolute presuppositions operating in any particular epoch. The relationship between the two essays is the problem that Rex Martin addresses in this volume. Collingwood himself saw no lacuna between them. They were part of his lifelong endeavour to effect a rapprochement between philosophy and history (see Peters). Each of the two books in its turn he described as the most important that he had written (A, 117–18).[52] Martin contends that the identity that Collingwood posits between metaphysics and history is not one of method. They do not rely upon re-enactment as their point of identity. Alternatively, if history is conceived as a process, of which Absolute Presuppositions are an integral part, the business of identifying and articulating that process is wholly consistent with the scale of forms analysis presented in *An Essay on Philosophical Method*, and avoids the charge of relativism to which the *Essay on Metaphysics* has given rise.

Collingwood's philosophical essays have proved to be a source of inspiration for many distinguished scholars in a variety of academic disciplines, which testifies to the pervasiveness of his influence. The philosophical task that Collingwood set himself in Speculum Mentis, namely the critical examination of the postulates of the forms of experience and their claims to the attainment of knowledge, was taken up in 1933 by Michael Oakeshott in Experience and its Modes. The nature and style of their inquiries are remarkably similar even though their conclusions differ considerably, most significantly in the relation of the forms of experience to each other and to the whole. Collingwood's overlapping hierarchy of forms of experience was rejected by Oakeshott in favour of co-ordinate modes of experience, each independent of the others. The most radical implication of this is a complete disjunction between theory and practice, and consequently a rejection of the practical purpose of Collingwood's philosophy of history.[53]

Joseph Levenson, Andrew Linklater and M. J. R. Healy have found *An Essay on Philosophical Method* particularly fruitful in pursuing their own inquiries in very different fields of research.

Collingwood's principle of concrete affirmation permeates the whole of Levenson's study of Chinese philosophy.[54] A philosopher, Collingwood argues, never merely affirms an idea, nor indiscriminately denies the range of ideas to which it is fortuitously opposed. Concrete affirmation implies the negation of definite doctrines that the philosopher regards as fallacious (EM, 106–7) In the case of Oakeshott, for example, the concrete affirmation that the modes of experience are co-ordinate and autonomous species of a genus was meant to deny that they overlap in a superordinate relation. For Levenson, explicitly following Collingwood, 'An idea . . . is a denial of alternatives and an answer to a question.'[55]

Linklater's philosophy of international relations is an avowed philosophical history along Collingwoodian lines. In an attempt to resolve, or overcome the conflict between the obligations of citizens and cosmopolitan obligations, Linklater constructs a scale of forms of conceptions of international relations whose generic essence is the idea of freedom. Each specification in this scale embodies the generic essence to a greater degree than that which it supersedes. In other words, the scale of forms is a unity of differences in degree with differences in kind, developing first through a tribal stage where communities are estranged and human powers are limited, through the stage of state formation and the overcoming of inter-community estrangement in a higher unity which increases human powers and capacities. Kinship is replaced by citizenship as the mode of social cohesion which nevertheless still posits an internal conception of obligation. Linklater's specification of the forms of international relations concludes 'with the move beyond the particularism of the state to the universal society of free being with rights and duties expressive of their identification with humanity'.[56] Collingwood's own theory of international relations, however, precludes such a conclusion (NL, 30.8–30.99).

Further evidence of Collingwood's pervasiveness is to be found in the work of the statistician M. J. R. Healy, for whom Collingwood is one of his 'culture heroes'. It is the Fallacy of Precarious Margins and the Fallacy of Identified Co-incidents, aptly characterized by Healy 'according as how we try to draw precise boundaries where no precise boundaries exist, or assume in the absence of precise boundaries that no distinctions can be made' (cf. EPM 106–11).[57] In questioning the comprehensiveness of Popper's description of scientific activity as the search for truth by the application of tests to hypotheses, Healy wants to show that science and technology overlap, and that the question and answer complexes appropriate to each differ. While undoubtedly related to science in the use of significance testing, statistics in its question and answer complexes is more closely allied to technology. It is failure adequately to conceptualize the overlap between science and technology, or to understand the identity in difference, that made the Dainton report on the future of the research councils and the Rothschild report on research and development paradigmatic examples of Collingwood's two fallacies.[58]

To extend the scientific connection further, Collingwood's theory of constellations of Absolute Presuppositions, expounded in *An Essay on Metaphysics* and *An Autobiography* stands at the centre of Toulmin's discussion of conceptual change. For Toulmin the originality and significance of Collingwood is that he posed and confronted the most important question about conceptual changes: why and on what occasions do they happen? These questions were to be taken up independently over twenty-five years later by Feyerabend, Kuhn and Hanson. Toulmin contends, however, that in ascribing the changes to 'unconscious thought' Collingwood denies rational choice and lapses into a relativism that deprives us of the possibility of giving rational descriptions of conceptual change.[59] In Toulmin's opinion, Collingwood fails to see the difference between historical relativity, the need to take account of different contexts in making rational comparison, and historical relativism, which confines judgements to the relations internal to these contexts (an interpretation which both Oldfield and Martin contest in this volume). We can avoid relativism, Toulmin suggests, and do justice to the relativity of contexts by distinguishing between the theoretical principles which guide a discipline, and the general disciplinary aims. Changes in the former, resulting in conceptual revolution while the latter remain sufficiently the same, enable such developments, in principle, to be discussed in rational terms. Furthermore, Toulmin wants to suggest that each intellectual activity is not a system of propositions, but a conceptual population comprising numerous co-existent and logically autonomous theoretical elements.

Changes within one population of such concepts will have implications for some, but not for all the historical populations of concepts associated with a particular activity.[60] In this respect there is continuity throughout change (a conclusion with which, on Oldfield's and Martin's interpretations, Collingwood would not radically differ).

*The Principles of Art* and *The Principles of History* were to comprise volumes 1 and 2 in the philosophical principles series. In the former Collingwood modified his earlier view that art is pure imagination,[61] and argued that art is the expression or (what is the same thing) consciousness of our emotions. To deny or suppress these emotions is a corruption of consciousness, and sends distorted and false signals to the intellect upon which it builds a false conception of the self and its activities.

There was a time when Collingwood's *Principles of Art* was required reading in aesthetics, but the rejection of the history of the subject in the 1960s and 1970s rendered Collingwood a casualty. This is not to say, however, that he does not have insights which may profitably be developed. Ted Cohen, for example, has recently argued that Collingwood, more than any other philosopher, tried to understand why anyone should care whether or not something was art. One of the implications of Collingwood's theory of art as the expression of emotion is that 'whenever a person has articulated his feeling sufficiently to make it accessible to others, by way of showing it to them in themselves, the person has indeed produced a work of art'.[62] Both Diffey and Modood, in this volume, confront the Wittgensteinian charge of essentialism levelled at Collingwood, and suggest that it is irrelevant. The philosophical specification of a concept as a series of overlapping forms, a unity of differences in degree and kind, as well as of opposites and distincts, not only enables us to identify an example of a species of a genus, but also to evaluate the extent to which it fails to live up to the ideal. In the philosophy of art for example, as Diffey argues, Collingwood offers a criteriological aesthetic by which to judge success or failure in the production of a work of art, something which Wittgensteinian aesthetics has avoided of late.

*The Principles of History* was never completed, but parts IV and V of *The Idea of History* and much of *An Autobiography* provide discussions of what Collingwood intended to cover. Here we have the doctrine of the logic of question and answer in which it is argued that the meaning of a statement can only fully be grasped in relation to the question it was meant to answer. It followed for Collingwood that no two propositions could be pronounced contradictory unless they were meant as answers to the same question. The logic of question and answer was at the heart of Collingwood's claim that there are no perennial problems in philosophy. Furthermore, it is under this category that Collingwood bases the possibility of historical knowledge upon the theory of re-enactment of past thought, and the possibility of distinguishing our own thoughts from those we re-enact upon the theory of encapsulation (for discussions of various aspects of the principles of history see van der Dussen, Martin, Haddock, Peters, Pompa and Browning).

It would be difficult to overestimate the importance of R. G. Collingwood in the emergence of the philosophy of history in the English speaking world. No discussion of the philosophy of history appears to be complete without some reference to Collingwood. He is used as a foil by some philosophers like Leo Strauss and Karl Popper to develop their own positions; as a source of inspiration by post-Marxists like Agnes Heller, or as a catalyst by such writers as Dray, Pompa and Martin.[63]

Collingwood's work has also been extremely important, however, in the fields of the history of ideas, hermeneutics and theological hermeneutics. Behind the demands of W. H. Greenleaf, J. G. A. Pocock, John Dunn and Quentin Skinner that the study of the history of political thought must become more genuinely historical is the impetus of Collingwood. Skinner, to take the most prominent example, has repeatedly acknowledged his primary debt to Collingwood. It is Collingwood's logic of question and answer and concomitant denial of perennial problems that informs Skinner's 'fundamental assumption as an intellectual historian: that the history of thought should be viewed not as a series of attempts to answer a canonical set of questions, but as a sequence of episodes in which the questions as well as the answers have frequently changed'.[64] Collingwood's emphasis upon the purposive and intentional character of action was supplemented by Skinner with Austin's theory of Speech Acts. Skinner argued that the idea of an illocutionary force was equivalent to the intention an author had in writing the text. It is significant that both Collingwood and Austin understood the use of language as a form of action, and that Skinner himself saw Austin 'as an exemplification of what Collingwood called the "logic of question and answer"'.[65]

Collingwood's impact upon the continental hermeneutic tradition has been considerable, and its susceptibility to his influence may be explicable by Gadamer's observation that the Englishman was really not a foreigner at all, but more like someone residing abroad who never forgets his 'spiritual home'.[66] John P. Hogan goes as far as to suggest that Collingwood 'had a seminal influence on the development of hermeneutics in the twentieth century'.[67] Certainly a formidable array of intellectual giants in the theory of hermeneutics can be invoked to testify their indebtedness, among them Bultmann, Gadamer, Pannenberg, Lonergan and Ricoeur. Like any theorist using the work of another there is a certain amount of misunderstanding and misrepresentation. Bultmann, for example, contends that you could find nothing better said about the problems of history than is to be found in Collingwood's *Idea of History*. While Bultmann endorses Collingwood's theory of re-enactment, he accuses him of unduly restricting history to human affairs and hence excluding the influence of natural occurrences.[68] While it is true that Collingwood believed that all history is the history of thought, thought includes our conception of the situations in which we find ourselves. A natural occurrence cannot be in itself the cause of human action, but the natural occurrence and our conception of it together constitute an efficient cause (EM, 290 and IH, 370).

Gadamer credits Collingwood fully for the service that the theory of question and answer gave to formulating his own theory of hermeneutics. He rejects the theory of re-enactment, however, on the grounds that it is too closely allied to recovering purposes and intentions. Such a theory, Gadamer contends, 'can never do justice to the experience of history in which our plans tend to shatter and our actions and omissions tend to lead to unexpected consequences'.[69] His view of re-enactment is, I think, too literal. Collingwood himself did not, in his theory or in his practice, restrict history to purposive and intentional activity, although he often gives the impression of doing so. He was quite unambiguous in suggesting that the historian puts the evidence to the question, asking of it questions which the authors or participants did not ask, with a view to knowing more about a period than those who lived in it (A, 67). In direct contravention of Gadamer's charge Collingwood contends that 'the recognition that what happens in history need not happen through anyone deliberately wishing it to happen is an indispensable precondition of understanding any historical process'(IH, 269).

Collingwood's theory of re-enactment, like Gadamer's hermeneutics, is best understood not so much as a method, but instead as an account of what happens to us each and every time we attain historical knowledge. Understood as a method, it has been too easily associated with an intuitionist epistemology and dismissed out of hand. Ricoeur and Lonergan are the most perceptive hermeneutic interpreters of Collingwood in recognizing that re-enactment cannot be dissociated from the evidential nature of historical thinking, and the imaginative interpretation of that evidence. As Ricoeur suggests, 'The theme of re-enactment must be maintained in third place, in order clearly to indicate that it does not designate an alternative method but the result aimed at by documentary interpretation and by the constructions of the imagination.'[70]

*The New Leviathan*, it appears, was originally to be the subtitle of a book called *The Principle of Politics*.[71] *The Principles of History* (that is, what survives of it) and *The New Leviathan* are related to each other much more intimately than is generally conceded. History, for Collingwood is self-knowledge of the mind, and *The New Leviathan* provides an account of the development of the mind that history seeks to know. History is described in *The New Leviathan* as the highest form of theoretical reason. *The New Leviathan* is principally concerned with the levels of practical reason, and their relation to society and civilization. Duty, the highest level of practical reason, is the counterpart of history:

> 18.52. The consciousness of duty means thinking of myself as an individual or unique agent, in an individual or unique situation, doing the individual unique action which I have to do because it is the only one I can. To think historically is to explore a world consisting of things other than myself, each of them an individual or unique agent, in an individual or unique situation, doing an individual or unique action which he has to do because, charactered and circumstanced as he is, he can do no other.

Freedom is the essence of mind cultivated by reason gradually eliminating caprice from rational choice. Anything that hinders free rational choice, or self-determination, betrays the existence of force. While force can never be entirely eliminated from the body politic, the ideal of civility assumes its gradual reduction among members of the same community, between communities, and between ourselves and nature. Collingwood's political philosophy falls squarely within the social-contract tradition in so far as it is a conscious attempt to provide the social contract with a historical dimension. He wants to show that at a certain level of cognitive competence, the level differing from community to community, a continuous process of conversion from the non-social to the social condition occurs within the body politic, that is, a constant replenishment of the ruling class by the ruled.

Even though it is a historical philosophy, it is not relativist. Reason defined as the gradual elimination of caprice, freedom as the capacity for rational choice, and civility as the gradual elimination of force, constitute universal criteria by which to judge civilizations and the degree to which barbarism, that is, the conscious subversion of these ideals, is present in them (see Boucher, van der Dussen and Milne).

Collingwood's political philosophy has been relatively neglected until recently. Knox succeeded in attaching a certain stigma to it in intimating in the preface to *The Idea of History* that *The New Leviathan* was to be disregarded as the unreliable thoughts of a dying man. As a work of grand theory in the classical tradition, it was a style sorely out of favour in post-war Oxford. Yet Knox himself drew freely upon the first part of *The New Leviathan* and the unpublished lectures on moral philosophy, to which he had access, in writing his Gifford Lectures on action. Knox is not merely being sentimental about his late tutor when he confesses that it is to him 'indeed I owe more than I could ever express, even were I Chrysostom himself'.[72]

With the publication of Collingwood's *Essays in Political Philosophy*, a number of leading philosophers have indicated that Collingwood's political ideas may genuinely be commandeered in order to understand better some of the perplexing problems of our age. Such philosophers as Simon Blackburn, Colin McGinn and James M. Buchanan, in their brief remarks, may be prophetic about the direction that further interest in Collingwood may take.

Blackburn suggests that there is much in *The New Leviathan* that is 'seminal' and 'astonishingly modern'. Collingwood is commended for a healthy distrust of the *a priori*; for seeing that truth is the result of a process; and for his 'profound respect for the place of ritual and emotion in our dealings with ourselves'.[73] Colin McGinn praises Collingwood for developing an important thesis about the relationship between education and liberal democracy: rational government by majority rule presumes rationality and 'the prime duty of a democratic state is the provision of sufficient mass education to satisfy its own precondition'[74] (see pp. 341–79 for the importance of education). It is in relation to contractarianism that Buchanan sees Collingwood making an important contribution: 'Collingwood's insights on the necessary existence of a non-social community, that must exist alongside but outside of the society that can be organized to allow its own members to rule themselves, may possibly be helpful in fleshing out aspects of the generalized contractarian model that have seemed deficient.'[75]

Milne's chapter compares Collingwood's political philosophy with that of Popper. While both have their deficiencies, each complements the other. Collingwood, for example, is used to modify Popper's idea of an open society. On Collingwood's theory a body politic could never be completely open because of the existence of a permanent, though changing, non-social element incapable of self rule. This is the aspect of Collingwood that Buchanan finds so suggestive, and which McGinn highlights as Collingwood's special insight in seeing the imperative responsibility of society to provide sufficient education to raise them to the level of cognitive competence.

The third of the categories, studies in the history of ideas, Collingwood saw exemplified by his projected books *The Idea of History* and *The Idea of Nature*, both of which were edited by T. M. Knox and published posthumously. Although neither is a self-evident application of a scale-of-forms analysis to the history of ideas, a plausible case could be made to suggest that this was Collingwood's intention. Leon Goldstein has argued that *The Idea of History*, for instance, was supposed to have presented the development of history as a scale of forms, but that the detailed research needed for such a project was not available to be drawn upon.[76] Perhaps some of the accounts Collingwood provides of such theorists as Dilthey have become outmoded and superseded because of the availability of a greater range of the German's work, but the early part of *The Idea of History* is still valuable in that most of the key doctrines developed as historical principles in the latter part surface during the course of his discussion of the development of historical thought.

*The Idea of Nature*, Knox suggested, was Collingwood's attempt to apply the principles of *An Essay on Philosophical Method* to natural science and cosmology (IN, v). In effect, *The Idea of Nature* articulates the constellations of Absolute Presuppositions and their implications in the Greek, Renaissance and modern concepts of nature. Each conception rests upon an analogy. For the Greeks nature is an intelligent organism on the analogy of the individual person projecting his own self-consciousness upon the world of nature. The Renaissance idea of nature is based upon the analogy of God as its Creator with man the creator of machines: nature is a vast complex mechanism. The modern conception of nature is based on the analogy of natural and historical processes. He says: 'Modern cosmology could only have arisen from the widespread familiarity with historical studies, and in particular with historical studies of the kind which placed the conception of process, change, development at the centre of their picture and recognized it as the fundamental category of historical thought' (IN, 10; cf. the slightly different account offered in NL 18.1–18.92). It is this aspect of history as process, development and change that Rex Martin emphasizes in the relationship between the two philosophical *Essays*, and which could be extended further to incorporate *The Idea of Nature* and *The New Leviathan*.

It was perhaps predictable that in investigating the idea of nature Collingwood would treat the problem historically, and that nature itself would become resolved into history. Understanding nature, he argued, requires an understanding of history. The modern idea of nature was historical in that change was conceived as progressive rather than cyclical; nature was no longer mechanical but teleological; in both history and the evolutionary view of nature structure, or substance, was resolved into function; and, the principles of minimal space and time were asserted. The function is perceived as movement, and each movement requires space and happens over time. Any given substance is 'not infinitely divisible'. There will be a limit to the smallest amount of it that can exist and the minimum space it occupies. For the substance to exist, that is to perform its function, requires minimum time. These principles, Collingwood claims, have their counterparts in history (IN, 17–27).

Although *The Idea of Nature* was an exemplification of *An Essay on Philosophical Method*, it failed to account for the transition from one view of nature to another, as the theory of overlapping forms would require it to do. In this respect it does not provide the missing elements in *An Essay on Metaphysics* that would enable us to give an answer to the question he left unresolved, that is, upon what occasions and for what reasons does one constellation of Absolute Presuppositions replace another?

It is evident from his studies in the history of ideas that the changes he identified in the idea of history and the idea of nature were progressive. When changes in the concepts of ethics and metaphysics are looked at historically they too appear to be progressive. The modern conceptions of nature, metaphysics and ethics are more adequate than their predecessors because they have become identified with history. Nature is dependent upon history, metaphysics is a historical discipline, and consciousness of one's duty is identical with the historical consciousness. We should not be deceived by this tendency to resolve everything into history, as Knox was, into believing that Collingwood was necessarily a relativist. He was a historicist in believing that in the context of a complex of circumstances the historical understanding must conclude that things could not be other than they were, but as is evident from his own studies he was not prepared to reserve judgement on whether one set of circumstances was better than another.[77]

Collingwood did, of course, write important works that fall outside his own categorization. He wrote a great deal on the philosophy of religion, and his list of archaeological publications is immense. *Philosophy and Religion*, Collingwood's first book, attempted to extricate religion from all types of irrationalism, not only emotivism and mysticism but also sociological and psychological reductivism, by understanding the Christian creed as the answer to philosophical problems. Collingwood contends that upon the historical facts a true philosophy of life can be built. History and philosophy are shown to be interdependent, and the relation between religion and philosophy one of identity. In essence, he is trying to discern the identity in difference between religion and philosophy, but as one perceptive reviewer remarks, 'Mr Collingwood must surely pay the word identity extra wages for the work that he makes it do.'[78] It was theologically orthodox and a spirited defence of Christianity, to the extent that the Revd F. Relton wondered why its author had not taken Orders.[79] On the flyleaf of his own copy, in the possession of his daughter, Collingwood repudiates the point of view he had expressed and describes it as a 'childish essay'. Collingwood continued to write on religion in a persistent attempt to bring about a rapprochement between faith and reason. He affirmed that religion was as vital to a healthy mind and equally as philosophical as art, science and history (see pp. 100–15).[80] Maurice Cowling in a chapter on Collingwood in *Religion and Public Doctrine in Modern England* testifies to the contribution of the Oxford don:

> Through repeated affirmation of religion's importance and idiosyncrasy in his early writings and through the identity that was asserted in his later ones between religion and metaphysics, he left his distinctive mark on the belief that religion lies at the root of all the thoughts and works of men.[81]

MacKinnon, in this volume, argues, in agreement with Rubinoff, that Collingwood's importance in the philosophy of religion is to have highlighted once again the central issues and confusions of the ontological argument in relation to religion and metaphysics.[82] Anselm's famous ontological proof of the existence of God was significant, in Collingwood's view, because it refused to accept the distinction of the Middle Ages between faith as knowledge of the infinite and reason as knowledge of the finite. Faith, Anselm maintained, is a prerequisite for understanding. His argument, however, at once asserts the priority of faith and the priority of reason in demanding proof of God's existence (FR, 134–5). There is, in Collingwood's view, an interplay between faith and reason. Reason reveals to faith what it cannot otherwise understand, the character of the objects of faith. Collingwood concludes that 'reason is nothing but faith cultivating itself' (FR, 121). The parallels with the doctrine of Absolute Presuppositions are obvious. We accept on faith the indubitable foundations of our beliefs. Reason converts them into a whole edifice of rationally related implications, serving to strengthen the faith itself.

Cowling, Rubinoff and MacKinnon do not pay any attention to

the theory of religion as it emerges from the pages of *The New Leviathan*, but it is this theory, Harris suggests in this volume, that is Collingwood's most original contribution to the philosophy of religion. Harris contends that Collingwood's views on Christianity are both theologically unorthodox, and also unusual in the tradition of Hegelianism.

Collingwood made a significant contribution to archaeology during his lifetime. His excavation of the Roman fort at Ambleside and the published findings were widely acclaimed. His explanation of the purpose of Hadrian's Wall as an elevated sentry-walk, and the hypothesis that further signal stations without an elevated walkway would have been needed along the Cumberland coast were largely corroborated by subsequent research. His collection of the Roman inscriptions in Britain, each drawn with painstaking accuracy, and published posthumously, is never likely to be surpassed. He was widely praised for his remarkable powers of synthesis in piecing together the results of numerous archaeological excavations into coherent accounts of life in Roman Britain, and was responsible for the leading archaeological textbooks for a whole generation of students.[83] M. V. Taylor thought that he was incomparable as a consultant on archaeological problems because of his logical and incisive mind.[84]

His archaeological brilliance was, however, erratic and seriously flawed. His adoption of F. G. Simpson's method of selective excavation, theorized in the form of the logic of question and answer, often led Collingwood to find exactly what he was looking for with fatal precision, and entirely to ignore alternative hypotheses. The most notorious example of this was his selective excavation of Arthur's Round Table (1938), the results of which were exposed as a travesty only two years later. Furthermore, Collingwood's imaginative re-enactment of archaeological evidence in his general syntheses was often a little too imaginative. Even his close friends complained of his tendency to present subjective and imaginative inference as objective interpretation.[85] Margot Browning shows in this volume how Collingwood's Baconian revolution in the theory of history has to be seen in the context of practical historiographical developments, particularly in archaeology. This, of course, adds a further dimension to the question of the sources of inspiration for Collingwood's theory of history. As opposed to the theoretical inspiration of the Italians upon Collingwood's philosophy of history (Connelly, Peters and Haddock) we are asked to consider the view that 'historical contextualization restores an empiricist dimension to Collingwood's philosophy of history.' Hodder complements Browning's discussion by suggesting that it was not so much Collingwood's theoretical programme, but the suspicion that surrounded his resultant interpretations that led archaeologists for more than thirty years after his death to turn away from his theories. Hodder contends that there has been a considerable revival of interest among archaeologists in Collingwood's theoretical insights. Collingwood is of continuing relevance for archaeologists in discussing the relation between historical and natural science; in characterizing human volition, or action; in what he has to say about the use of generalization; and, on the question of validity in interpretation (on validity see Pompa in this volume).[86]

What has been suggested, then, is that Collingwood's early life and education contributed significantly to his broad range of interests which he pursued with an energy which was seriously to damage his health. Although he made it clear in late 1939 that he did not wish anything to be published that was not authorized by him, he changed his mind just before his death and gave his wife and the Secretary of Oxford University Press the right to decide what was of more than ephemeral interest. Knox's involvement was fortuitous and it is therefore ironic that he should have had the final say. Furthermore, Collingwood's isolation was not as severe as he liked to portray it. He had a good many friends in Oxford, including many of his philosophical foes among the Delegates of Oxford University Press. Of the younger generation, such people as Mabbot, Ayer and Austin, while disagreeing with his philosophy, nevertheless liked him personally. It has been suggested that his influence has been extensive in many unlikely fields of study, and continues to grow with the availability of his unpublished manuscripts.

*Notes*
\* I am indebted to W. H. Rieckmann, Rex Martin, James Connelly and Tariq Modood for their comments.
[1] William M. Johnston, *The Formative Years of R. G. Collingwood* (The Hague, Nijhoff, 1967), 28–30, and 64–65.

2 R. G. Collingwood, *Speculum Mentis* (Oxford, Clarendon Press, 1970), 12; 'one must spend much time and trouble in the actual practice of the arts, or at least one of them, and learn to reflect on the experience so gained. The same applies to other forms of thought . . .'
3 See item 1.179 in Donald S. Taylor, 'A Bibliography of the Publications and Manuscripts of R. G. Collingwood, with Selective Annotation', *History and Theory*, Beiheft 24, vol.24 (1985), 28. In *An Autobiography* Collingwood says that it was a monthly magazine. If the title 'The Weekly Cat of Puffapatam' can be relied upon, Collingwood made a mistake.
4 Knox, *Dictionary of National Biography*, 168–9.
5 The papers were discovered by Stein Helgeby under the auspices of the Collingwood Society. I am grateful for his efforts in bringing to light such a rich source of material for Collingwood scholars.
6 Letter from Ethel Collingwood to Malcolm Knox dated 31 December 1941, Knox Papers, St Andrews.
7 Letter to F. Gerald Simpson, 3 June 1931, now deposited in the Bodleian Library.
8 Memoir written by M. V. Taylor, among her papers in an envelope marked 'COLLINGWOOD: an Autobiography', Ashmolean Library.
9 See the letters from G. A. Varty to W. B. Cannon and Kenneth Sisam to W. B. Cannon, dated 12 and 29 January 1943 respectively, file PB/ED 001549.
10 Letter to Grace Simpson, 18 February 1982, now deposited in the Bodleian Library.
11 R. B. McCallum, 'Robin George Collingwood, 1889–1943', Proceedings of the British Academy, XXIX (1943), 466. J. D. Mabbott corroborates this when he says: 'his lectures and Paton's were the only philosophical lectures which had a real style and finish' (*Oxford Memories* (Oxford, Thornton, 1986), 76).
12 T. M. Knox, 'Prof. R. G. Collingwood, F.B.A.' *Nature*, 3823, 6 February 1943, p.164; C. H. L. Bouch, 'In Memoriam', *Transactions of the Cumberland and Westmorland Antiquarian and Archaeological Society*, 43 (1943), 212.
13 R. G. Collingwood, 'Goodness, Rightness, Utility: Lectures delivered in H.T. 1940', Collingwood MS DEP 9, Bodleian Library, fol.10.
14 Responses to a questionnaire distributed by Pembroke College to former students in order to discover their reminiscences of the 1920s and 1930s in the College. The respondents' names are confidential and identified as m. 1921 and m. 1927. I would like to thamk Mrs van Loo, deputy librarian of the McGowin Library, Pembroke College, for being so kind as to let me have copies of those responses which make reference to Collingwood.
15 Tom Hopkinson, *Of This Our Time: A Journalist's Story, 1905–1950* (London, Hutchinson, 1982), 85.

16 Pembroke College Survey, 1983, m. 1920, m. 1927, m. 1930, m. 1930, m. 1924, respectively.
17 Ibid., m. 1928.
18 R. B. McCallum, 'Robin George Collingwood 1889–1943', *Proceedings of the British Academy*, XXIX (1943), 466.
19 Letter to de Ruggiero, 20 March 1921, Collingwood MS DEP 27.
20 In a letter to Sisam, Knox quotes a letter that Collingwood sent to him on 3 September 1939 describing him as his only 'real pupil'. The whole of this account of Knox's involvement is based on the contents of file PP6061, 'R. G. Collingwood, *Philosophical Works*', Clarendon Press Archives. I am grateful to Stein Helgeby and Peter Foden for their hard work in tracking down the Collingwood material that the Press holds.
21 Letter from T. Addis to Ethel Collingwood, dated 11 July 1948, Knox Papers, St Andrews. MS 37524/443(a).
22 R. G. Collingwood, *The Idea of History*, revised edn, ed. Jan van der Dussen (Oxford, Clarendon Press, 1993).
23 For illustrations of their discussions see the J. A. Smith papers, Magdalen College, Oxford.
24 Published by Oxford University Press, 1939. The second edn includes a preface by Collingwood.
25 J. D. Mabbott, *Oxford Memories* (Oxford, Thornton, 1986), 75.
26 See the photocopied correspondence between Ryle and Collingwood on the ontological problem, and between Prichard and Collingwood on right and duty in the Collingwood Papers.
27 Cited in John McCormick, *George Santayana: a Biography* (New York, Knopf, 1987), 396. I would like to thank W. H. Rieckmann for supplying this reference.
28 See file LB8083 relating to R. G. Collingwood, *Autobiography*, Clarendon Press Archives.
29 A. J. Ayer interviewed by Ted Honderich in *A. J. Ayer Memorial Essays*, ed. A. Phillips Griffiths (Cambridge, Cambridge University Press, 1991), 210.
30 See the Correspondence of H. A. Prichard 1925–44, MS ENG. LETT. d. 116, Bodleian Library, Oxford, fols.20, 21–32, 33–5 and 36–45.
31 R. G. Collingwood, *The New Leviathan*, revised edn, ed. David Boucher (Oxford, Clarendon Press, 1992). Ross is mentioned on p.123 of the original edition, and discussed extensively, along with Carritt, Prichard, Joseph and Moore in the 1940 moral philosophy lectures appended to the second edition.
32 Letter from W. D. Ross to K. Sisam, 24 July 1941, file PB/ED 001 549.
33 Letter from H. H. Price to K. Sisam, 10 July, 1941
34 See file PP6061, Clarendon Press Archives.
35 He writes to Ryle, for example, that : 'I am afraid I resent both the label and the irresponsible manner of attaching it' (letter to Gilbert Ryle, 9 May 1935, Collingwood MS DEP 22).

36 A. J. Ayer, *Language, Truth and Logic* (London, Gollancz, 1936), 12. See ch.1 for his discussion of metaphysics. When Prichard and Joseph complained that such a book should never have been published Collingwood is reported to have said, 'Gentlemen, this book will be read when your names are forgotten' (Ayer interviewed by Honderich, *Memorial Essays*, 210).

37 In his memoirs Ayer says of Collingwood's theory of Absolute Presuppositions that, 'there is more to it than I then admitted, but I was impressed by the use which he made of it in his book *The Idea of Nature*, and I admired the style of all his books, whether or not I agreed with their contents' (A. J. Ayer, *Part of My Life* (London, Collins, 1977), 79).

38 Gilbert Ryle, *The Concept of Mind* (Harmondsworth, Penguin, 1970), 17.

39 Ibid., 23–4.

40 Ibid., 26.

41 Gilbert Ryle, *Philosophical Arguments* (Oxford, Clarendon Press, 1945), 4. Cf. Allan Donagan, *The Later Philosophy of R. G. Collingwood* (Oxford, Clarendon Press, 1962), 292, and Richard Sclafani, 'Wollheim on Collingwood', *Philosophy*, 51 (1976), 358.

42 See W. von Leyden, 'Philosophy of Mind: an Appraisal of Collingwood's Theories of Consciousness, Language, and Imagination', in *Critical Essays on the Philosophy of R. G. Collingwood*, ed. Michael Krausz (Oxford, Clarendon Press, 1972), 28–31; Richard Sclafani, 'Sensations, Feelings and Expression', in *A Symposium on Gilbert Ryle*, ed. K. Kolenda, *Rice University Studies*, 58 (1972). Simon Blackburn also compares Collingwood with Wittgenstein. See his review in *Times Literary Supplement*, 6–12 April 1990, p.370.

43 Ludwig Wittgenstein, *Philosophical Investigations* (Oxford, Blackwell, 1978). My account is based on §119, 125, 126 and 309.

44 Ibid., §23, 28–43.

45 Ibid., §569.

46 Ibid., §16, 23

47 R. G. Collingwood, 'Observations on Language', Collingwood MS DEP 16, pp.1–2.

48 Wittgenstein, *Philosophical Investigations*, §124.

49 Cf. NL, appendix I, 402 where he argues that the purpose of moral philosophy 'is to enable you to improve your own practice; and its appeal is an appeal by confirmation or disproved by reference to your practical experience'. There are remarkable similarities between Wittgenstein's description of the foundations of a language game as logically ultimate, unverifiable and not analytically true, and Collingwood's doctrine of Absolute Presuppositions. See Ludwig Wittgenstein, *On Certainty* (Oxford, Blackwell, 1977), §199–205, 411.

Cf. Rex Martin, *Historical Explanation* (Ithaca and London, Cornell University Press, 1977), 203–11.
50 Major studies published since 1979 include W. J. van der Dussen, *History as a Science: the Philosophy of R. G. Collingwood* (The Hague, Nijhoff, 1981); James Patrick, *The Magdalen Metaphysicals* (Atlanta, Mercer University Press, 1985); Donald S. Taylor, *R. G. Collingwood: a Bibliography* (New York and London, Garland, 1988); John P. Hogan, *Collingwood and Theological Hermeneutics* (Lanham, University Press of America, 1989); D. Boucher, *The Social and Political Thought of R. G. Collingwood* (Cambridge, Cambridge University Press, 1989); Michael Hinz, *Self-Creation and History: Collingwood and Nietzsche on Conceptual Change* (Lanham, University Press of America, 1994). Three special issues of journals have been dedicated to his work: *The Monist*, 72 (1989); *History and Theory*, Beiheft 29 (1990); *International Studies in Philosophy*, XXIII (1991). New material from the manuscripts has been published, for the first time since Knox effectively prohibited further publication, in R. G. Collingwood, *Essays in Political Philosophy*, ed. David Boucher (Oxford, Clarendon Press, 1989); R. G. Collingwood, *The New Leviathan* revised edn, ed. David Boucher (Oxford, Clarendon Press, 1992); R. G. Collingwood, *The Idea of History*, revised edition, ed. W. Jan van der Dussen (Oxford, Clarendon Press, 1993).
51 Letter from Collingwood to Chapman, 9 March 1933, Clarendon Archives, file 824123.
52 Letter from R. G. Collingwood to Sisam, 3 June 1939, Clarendon Archives, file 824121 PP509Y.
53 Michael Oakeshott, *Experience and its Modes* (Cambridge, Cambridge University Press, 1933). Oakeshott's popularity is such that it is now available in paperback.
54 Joseph R. Levenson, *Confucian China and Its Modern Fate* (London, 1958), two vols.
55 Ibid., 15.
56 Andrew Linklater, *Men and Citizens in the Theory of International Relations*, second edn (London, Macmillan, 1990), 167.
57 M. J. R. Healy, 'Is Statistics a Science?', *Journal of the Royal Statistical Society*, series A (General), 141, part 3 (1978), 387.
58 Ibid., 388. Both reports are to be found in *A Framework for Government Research and Development* (London, HMSO, 1971).
59 See Stephen Toulmin, 'Conceptual Change and the Problem of Relativity', in *Critical Essays on the Philosophy of R. G. Collingwood*, ed. Michael Krausz (Oxford, Clarendon Press, 1972), 201–21; and Stephen Toulmin, *Human Understanding*, 1 (Oxford, Clarendon Press, 1972), 66–85.
60 Toulmin, *Human Understanding*, 74, 91, 128–30.

61 'The artist does not judge or assert, he does not think or conceive, he simply imagines' (SM, 61).
62 Ted Cohen, 'Reflections on One Idea of Collingwood's Aesthetics', *The Monist*, 72 (1989), 585.
63 Leo Strauss, 'On Collingwood's Philosophy of History', *Review of Metaphysics*, 5 (1952), 559–86; Karl Popper, *Objective Knowledge* (London, Routledge, 1992); Agnes Heller, *A Theory of History* (London, Routledge, 1982); W. H. Dray, *Philosophy of History*, second edn (Englewood Cliffs, Prentice Hall, 1993); Leon Pompa, *Human Nature and Historical Explanation* (Cambridge, Cambridge University Press, 1990); Rex Martin, *Historical Explanation* (Ithaca and London, Cornell University Press, 1977).
64 James Tully, *Meaning and Context: Quentin Skinner and His Critics* (Cambridge, Polity, 1988), 234.
65 Ibid., 275. For a discussion of Skinner's relation to Collingwood and Austin see my *Texts in Context* (Dordrecht, Nijhoff, 1985), ch.5.
66 Hans-Georg Gadamer, introduction to the German edition of *An Autobiography*. Introduction translated by G. Barden and N. MacCormick and published in the *Collingwood Journal*, 1 (1992), 10.
67 Hogan, *Collingwood and Theological Hermeneutics*, 1.
68 Rudolph Bultmann, *History and Eschatology* (New York, 1962), 130–40.
69 Hans-Georg Gadamer, *Reason in the Age of Science* (Cambridge Mass., MIT, 1981), 46. Cf. Hans-Georg Gadamer, *Truth and Method* (New York, Crossroad, 1982), 333–41, and 467–9.
70 Paul Ricoeur, *The Reality of the Historical Past* (Milwaukee, Marquette University Press, 1984), 6.
71 See file PB.ED 001 549, Clarendon Press Archives, on which appear the words 'Professor R. G. Collingwood, Principles of Politics – New Leviathan'.
72 T. M. Knox, *Action* (London, Allen and Unwin, 1968), 16. Cf. 33, 45, 51, 66, 197.
73 See 'Against False Division', *Times Literary Supplement*, 6–12 April 1990, p.370.
74 Colin McGinn, 'Homage to Education', in *London Review of Books*, 16 August 1990, p.16.
75 *Southern Economic Journal*, 57 (1991), 863. A. J. M. Milne has also been influenced by Collingwood in his writings on political philosophy. He applies a scale of forms analysis to the concept of rationality in *Freedom and Rights* (London, Allen and Unwin, 1968), ch.3.
76 Leon Goldstein, 'The Idea of History as a Scale of Forms', *History and Theory*, Beiheft 29 (1990), 45.
77 The series was conceived differently by Oxford University Press some time later with SM, EPM, EM, PA and NL having one to five stars on

their spines repectively. The stars have inexplicably disappeared from more recent reprints.

78 Anonymous review of *Philosophy and Religion*, *Times Literary Supplement*, 25 January 1917, p.41, col.c.

79 Reader's report on *Religion and Philosophy*, Macmillan Archives, Part One, third series, MCCVII, fols.88–9.

80 Lionel Rubinoff has collected most of Collingwood's religious essays in *Faith and Reason* (Chicago, Quadrangle, 1968).

81 Maurice Cowling, *Religion and Public Doctrine in Modern England* (Cambridge, Cambridge University Press, 1980), 167.

82 Lionel Rubinoff, *Collingwood and the Reform of Metaphysics: a Study in the Philosophy of Mind* (Toronto, University of Toronto Press, 1970), 194–212.

83 R. G. Collingwood, *Roman Britain* (Oxford, Clarendon Press, 1923 and 1932); *The Archaeology of Roman Britain* (London, Methuen, 1930); and *Roman Britain and the English Settlements* (with J. N. L. Myers) (Oxford, Clarendon Press, 1936 and 1937).

84 M. V. Taylor papers, memoir of R. G. Collingwood.

85 See, for example, R. E. M. Wheeler, review of *Roman Britain and the English Settlement* in *Journal of Roman Studies*, 29 (1939), 87–8; and I. A. Richmond, 'Appreciation of R. G. Collingwood as an Archaeologist', *Proceedings of the British Academy*, XXIX (1943), 478.

86 Collingwood's work on anthropology, intimated in *The Principles of Art*, and evident in the folk-tale manuscripts, is finding an audience among anthropologists in Great Britain and Italy. Some years ago John Beattie acknowledged the importance of Collingwood's theory of incapsulation – how a conception of the past is encapsulated in the present and has a bearing upon current activities – for anthropological investigations. John Beattie, *Other Cultures* (London, Cohen and West, 1964), p.24. Adam Kuper's thesis that anthropologists took their own societies and invented primitive society as distorted mirror images of them, although developed independently of Collingwood, makes exactly the same points that Collingwood made over forty years earlier in the folk-tale manuscripts. Adam Kuper, *The Invention of Primitive Society* (London, Routledge, 1988). The Oxford anthropologists Wendy James and Douglas Johnson both believe that Collingwood has a great deal to offer the modern field-worker.

# Collingwood and the Idea of Philosophy

## TARIQ MODOOD

During his lifetime Collingwood was seen by contemporary professional philosophers, especially those at his own university, Oxford, as an uninteresting relic of an earlier style of philosophy. He was seen as aspiring to grand theory when such theory had been proved worthless and metaphysics had given way to analysis along the lines of propositional logic. The following generation partly rescued him from this dismissal. They noted that his general philosophical approach, at least in his later works, was not radically different from the dominant school of their generation, namely, ordinary-language analysis; moreover that he was an ally against positivism and therefore on both of these counts a suitable candidate for rehabilitation. This rehabilitation was based on the view that he had more interesting things, and more historically and culturally informed things, to say about particular areas of philosophy than the ordinary-language philosophers, especially in aesthetics, philosophy of history, history of philosophy and methodology of history of ideas. Moreover, it was thought that Collingwood had a further relevance, for he had flirted with a relativism which, while rarely made explicit, was implicit in much of the philosophizing of the third quarter of the twentieth century.

I believe that to see Collingwood in terms of interesting piecemeal analyses and questions of relativism is to distort and diminish his philosophical achievement and certainly his ambition. Those who derided him as too grand or too speculative were closer to the mark.[1] They were wrong to reject him because of it but they more accurately recognized the character of his philosophizing. For Collingwood was very much a philosopher in the grand manner – one of the few native English philosophers of this century to be so – and the object of his concern was not propositions or theories, nor scientific methodology or social-economic systems. He was not simply interested in philosophical puzzles nor specially in the analysis of a particular area of life but in philosophy as the search for a systematic framework for evaluating all human activities. His was a view of philosophy which included the possibility of deriving a general description of the highest achievement of mankind: namely, of a life in which a man or a woman, through the various forms of understanding and culture available to them, can be said to be in contact with reality.

# I

The roots of this conception of philosophy, I believe, lie in late eighteenth-century German intellectual life in which the idea of such an inquiry, as a development out of and away from the epistemological empiricist-rationalist arguments, suggested itself in the following way. Though Hegel may be regarded as its most typical and greatest exponent, the point of departure for this grand view of philosophy as an evaluative inquiry into the ultimate status of the various forms of experience is Kant. For this view Kant's epistemology is accepted as a successful critique of both phenomenalism and transcendental realism, and also as a resolution of the problem of the proper role of the subject and object of knowledge in experience. Kant is taken as having successfully established the need to go beyond the one-sidedness of empiricism and rationalism to a recognition of the inter-dependence, the mutual implication, of the subject and the object in cognition. It is accepted that all human experience has a determinate character and can never merely be an experience of which all that can be known by the subject is that he is having it: it cannot be pure subjective phenomena. On the other hand, for an object of experience to be identified, recognized, compared and classified – for it to be known in any detail whatsoever – presupposes an organized intellectual framework which objects themselves cannot provide but which the subject must find;

perhaps not out of its individual resources but certainly from the activities of subjects. Reality and experience are correlative terms: there is no reality outside all possible experience and no experience which does not have some form of reality or other. An important conclusion of this epistemology is that there is in principle no reason why anything that exists (for us) is unknowable. All real objects are knowable by subjects, for (phenomenal) reality implies knowability. Experience is not a random series of sensations or a stream of consciousness or knowledge of pure objects confronted in isolation: it is experience of an organized world. And it is the active subjective element in experience or Mind which makes an organized world possible. For without the structure of categorical organization which is Mind there would be no world to be experienced, but a chaos – at best – the material for a possible world. To organize such material, to create a world, is to unify what would otherwise be without order into experience, into a knowable reality. Mind, then, is the organizing principle of reality. This is the answer to the epistemologist's question of how reality is knowable.

Objective reality is thus brought within the (possible) grasp of the rational mind. However, if the possibility of objectivity or reality is derived from system in experience then there can only be a genuine triumph over scepticism where we have some method of differentiating between different kinds of systematicity or forms of experience, between those in which reality is actually to be found and those which are, so to speak, empty possibilities or, at least, inadequate. This would not be a genuine problem if Mind consisted in or presented a self-evident principle of organizing experience. Yet the history of metaphysics (or even that of mathematics or science) reveals how (what is assumed to be) the same experience is presented in quite different, often radically different though perhaps internally consistent, conceptual systems. The eighteenth century was an age acutely conscious of this history and troubled by the scepticism which it engenders. Even if we assume, as Kant did, that there is a single universal system of axioms, categories and postulates which can be rationally demonstrated to be uniquely appropriate to the empirical world, there is still a problem as Kant himself recognized of finding some unity amongst the different forms of rational activities such as science, moral life and aesthetic appreciation.

Indeed, this diversity of reason follows from the view that reality, the object of rational apprehension, is to be found nowhere else but within experience. If truth is not that which survives a test of correspondence with a reality independent of the rational subject, then it can only lie in the rationality of the organizing principle of any given experience. Yet there seems to be no single principle of ordering experience which is self-evidently a standard by which all forms of experience may be tested. Rather, the different conceptual systems, the different ways of thinking about or expressing the nature of reality seem to set up or assume quite different tests of what is to constitute knowledge and truth; they embody different – and perhaps incommensurable – forms of rationality. Hence the diversity in conceptions of reality presented by the presence of a full and developed cultural life forces itself on the philosopher's attention and stands as a critical test of his or her epistemology. The philosopher can no longer assume that reason is to be found in or to be identified with any one form of understanding or that its unity is unproblematic. If knowledge of reality depends upon there being an order in experience then religion, morality, politics, art, besides common sense, natural science, mathematics and metaphysics, too, become candidates for forms of knowledge. The rejection of transcendental realism and empiricism seems naturally to suggest that the mind is involved in all activities, and not just those that epistemologists have been typically concerned with. Hence the first step in meeting the new sceptical challenge is to broaden our concepts of reason and truth. We need to develop a theory of rationality sufficiently comprehensive both to accommodate the pluralism implied in the epistemological claims that wherever there is ordered experience there is the possibility of a rational apprehension of reality, and to elucidate the (*prima facie*) distinctive forms of knowing present in a sophisticated culture.

A theoretical recognition of a diversity of distinct, perhaps autonomous, systematic modes of reasoning is, then, a necessary step in an argument against scepticism, but it is not by itself sufficient. The next step is the development of a criterion for evaluating all forms of experience and their claim to be ways of understanding an objective reality. This is really another way of saying that the claim to knowledge implicit in all ordered experience must be shown to be justified in each particular case;

the claims made by religion, morality etc. must not be uncritically accepted at their face value. Philosophy[2] must develop from the resources available within experience a method of differentiating between what is genuine and what is illusory in the organizing concepts and categories of the various forms of understanding. As the supremely reflective activity it surveys the variety of rational activities in order to identify and construct principles of knowledge which will satisfy the sceptic that the distinction between appearance and reality can be made without recourse to a transcendental criterion excluded by Kantian epistemology. A claim to be a form of knowledge presupposes the possibility of testing this general claim; the need for such a test is the logical outcome of epistemology and thus points the way which philosophy must take. No other form of experience is able to evaluate the claims of other forms of experience to the satisfaction of the thoroughgoing sceptic; indeed, each is only imperfectly aware of its own claim to be rational, of its own epistemology. Philosophy, thus, must claim for itself a special position in relation to other forms of experience: it becomes a judge and critic of their constitutive principles and the context for determining claims about the nature of reality. In order for this claim to be accepted, philosophy must demonstrate that it is capable of a more critical and a more comprehensive framework of evaluation than any other form of experience. It must show that it is able to criticize and incorporate the rational elements of all forms of experience while no other form of experience has the reflective sophistication.

Ultimately, this leads philosophy to a search for a perspective in which all other possible forms of experience are fully elucidated, their distinctive principles of reality fully evaluated, each shown to have a place in the search for knowledge and systematically connected and contrasted with all the others. Philosophy must at least explore the possibility of such an ultimate systematic understanding of the possible and necessary forms that reality can and must take. Indeed, rationality, the ability to create order and unity in experience and thereby to give meaning to fragmentary experience, demands that an attempt must be made to pursue the search for unity to its ultimate point; ideally, this ultimate point would be a system which encompasses and systematizes all possible experience into a single self-aware whole, thus transcending or rendering otiose all lesser forms of understanding. If such an ambition is beyond the powers of reason to achieve, reason must satisfy itself that this is so and why. This, then, must be the task for a post-Kantian philosophy, but if so it offers not only the means to rout epistemological scepticism but also the promise of a wider cultural need.

Concurrent with the development of this view of philosophy was the appearance of a profound cultural crisis, originally in Germany and later much more widely. There was a sense of alienation from inherited culture, which no longer seemed to be imbued with a sense of meaning which it was presumed to have once had, most typically in ancient Greece and in medieval society. Religion, art, morality, science, politics and so on all seemed disconnected from each other and to have nothing profound enough to say to stir sensitive, intelligent persons to give themselves up to any of these activities or to find oneself in them.[3] What was particularly wanted was a frame of reference or an overview by means of which the currently hidden meaning of the various aspects of human activities could be discovered or rediscovered and, hopefully, without dependence on simple Christianity, no longer intellectually tenable, or on any other simple childlike faith in miracles, the supernatural and the afterlife. A philosophy which demonstrated the impossibility of knowledge of a transcendental world; the possibility of the human mind coming to an understanding of itself, of establishing the essential principles of the distinctive ways of experiencing the world; of evaluating the claims of knowledge implicit in such principles; and, finally, which sought a unity in this diversity, seemed to offer exactly what was needed to rediscover a meaningful cultural life. What, then, comes to be sought from philosophy is not merely an account of what it is to experience a world but of the potentialities available in one's own cultural world. Thus the question 'what is real?', already linked to the question 'what is mind or reason?', comes to be thought of as dependent upon and a contributor to the answer of the further question 'what is culture?'

*Speculum Mentis* is Collingwood's attempt to sketch a system of philosophy in accordance with the view of philosophy as the principle of cultural unity. He understands the problem of disunity in terms of the alienation of individuals from the activities valued by others and ultimately from even those valued by themselves.

He sees this alienation as a product of the excessive specialism produced by viewing cultural activities as ends in themselves, resulting from the Renaissance quest for autonomy and excellence in each sphere of life. So that culture, which seemed initially to offer a prospect of human development while demonstrating remarkable development on all fronts, seems to be no guide as to how to live a fully active human life.

> Each [mode of culture], cut off from the others, tended more and more to lead its followers into some desert where the world of human life was lost, and the very motive for going on disappeared. Each tended to become a specialised activity pursued by specialists for the applause of specialists, useless to the rest of mankind and unsatisfying even to the specialist when he turned upon himself and asked why he was pursuing it. (SM, 34)

While Collingwood insisted that there could be no return to the cultural unity of an earlier age – such as medieval Christendom when individuals found self-fulfilment in the institutions which nurtured them and where the spheres of fulfilment were understood to be aspects of a single whole – he believed that philosophy's contribution was to create a new cultural unity appropriate to the modern world. For what was needed was a philosophy which could demonstrate that the intellectual and creative aspects of persons were linked with the rest of their personality and society. The conviction that these were appropriate demands to make upon philosophy and were vital to social well-being was summed up in the slogan: 'All thought is for the sake of action.'[4]

Having elaborated the philosophical perspective within which Collingwood's philosophy, particularly *Speculum Mentis*, exists I shall not here try to illustrate how he tried to achieve his task in SM. Principally because Collingwood was soon dissatisfied with the analysis that he there gave of the principal forms of experience, and the cultural unity that he there adumbrated was dependent upon those analyses. I shall instead examine some of the methodological implications of this idea of philosophical perspective as my interest here is in this idea of philosophy rather than in a particular use of it. While any particular use may be unsatisfactory, the important question is whether we are even talking about a possible enterprise. This is especially so as the central idea of SM, the idea that it is the job of philosophy to arrange experience in a hierarchical order, will trouble many who otherwise find attractive the idea that the primary focus of philosophy ought to be with the possibilities and difficulties of contemporary forms of cultural life. Finally, the focus on philosophical method is facilitated by the fact that Collingwood explicitly analysed and defended the method of *Speculum Mentis* in *An Essay on Philosophical Method*.[5] The remainder of this chapter, therefore, will be concerned with this text.

## II

Collingwood is emphatic that philosophy grows out of experience and is about experience. Yet philosophical understanding is not mere descriptive analysis. The simplest way to express the relationship between philosophy and experience, and at the same time to locate the point at which philosophy could be said to begin, is by recognizing that while concepts of ordinary experience confine themselves to limited empirical phenomena to which they seem to be exclusively attached, the same concepts in a philosopher's hand aspire to explain as wide an area of experience as possible. Thus, water is a concept of ordinary experience; in the hands of Thales it becomes an explanatory feature of not just where it is empirically observed but of the nature of the phenomenal world as such. Philosophy is thought not content with knowledge of a part, but to relate that part to a wider whole in order to grasp it more fully. An empirical concept which becomes philosophically employed no longer respects the distinctions of empirical classification but 'leaks or escapes out of these limits and invades the neighbouring regions, tending at last to colour our thought of reality as a whole' (EPM, 35). This description of philosophical concepts conforms to our understanding of art, science, history and so on as forms of experience which claim to be not a part or a limited class of experience but the correct bases of the organization of experience as such, and perhaps also of a satisfactory human life.[6] These cultural forms of experience are (like water etc.) double-aspected: in their empirical aspect they are specialized activities confined to a limited class of phenomena, perhaps with blurred boundaries but respecting the presence of other specialized disciplines with their own separate concerns; in their philosophical aspect they contest these empirical distinctions in their ambition to understand the cultural life of which they are a part within a single system of concepts.

The point to note is that it belongs to the character of a philosophical concept to explain a wide area of phenomena, an area which *prima facie* seems too diverse to be comprehended within a single intellectual framework; it must unite these phenomena. This 'unity' is not an empirical one, and therefore, we have to be open to the suggestion that the methods of philosophy will differ from those of empirical science despite the fact that both arise out of the same experience. According to Collingwood the traditional theory of classification as expounded by philosophers and logicians may be an accurate description of the logic of scientific and mathematical concepts but is wholly inaccurate as a description of philosophical concepts.[7] The traditional theory is that a concept, such as colour, is a genus divisible into separate species, red, blue, orange etc., such that all particular instances of the concept of colour, say a red hat, a blue book etc., are instantiated through one and only one of the species of the genus. A hat can be blue or red or orange etc. but not red and blue at the same time: a coloured object cannot have more than one species of colour. Collingwood points out, however, that the concepts of a philosophical science do not obey this rule: that an action is dutiful does not prevent it from also being to my advantage. Similarly, an expression can be both beautiful and true. Hence, he concludes that the rule 'every concept must have a group of instances to itself' does not apply to philosophical concepts.[8]

In this part of Collingwood's argument there is, however, an ambiguity. Though the quotation in the last sentence may (taken by itself) suggest otherwise, Collingwood clearly does not hold that the scientific theory of classification suggests that no object can be an instance of more than one concept. That idea is absurd: a red hat is an instance of red and of hat. Collingwood's point is that scientific classification excludes the possibility that an instance of one species can also be an instance of another species of the same genus: red objects are not exclusive to red *vis-à-vis* the genera of hat, book etc., but only *vis-à-vis* blue, green etc. It may be countered that Collingwood is still oversimplifying the principles of classification. It may be argued that while it is true that no object can be red and blue all over at the same time, nevertheless, other empirical examples can be found where such simple exclusion does not hold, and without embarrassment to the traditional theory of classification. If, instead of red we take colour as our representative species we will find that a different situation prevails. Presumably, colour is a species of the genus sensory data of which the other co-ordinate species would be smell and sound and so on; and yet this does not, the objector may conclude, prevent an object from being an instance of colour and, say, smell. And how, the objector may ask, is this different from an action which is both dutiful and self-advantageous?

This objection, however, confuses instance with object. Collingwood's point is that on the principle of scientific classification no instance can be shared by co-ordinate species, not that several species may not be instantiated in the same object. A red hat may be perfumed but it is not the redness in the hat that smells. What then, the objector may ask, is the difference between a red perfumed hat and an action which is both an instance of duty and expediency? The difference may perhaps be expressed by saying that while a colour cannot have a smell or sound, a dutiful act may also be expedient. I can imagine my hypothetical objector protest that once again a contrast is being achieved only by not comparing like with like. She may say that what is being compared is an action with a colour and that these are not similar levels of generality, for a colour is but an aspect of a physical object and cannot be found by itself, while an action is not an aspect but the human object of which duty and expediency are aspects. Hence in my saying that a colour cannot be a smell but a dutiful action can be expedient I am not contrasting colour with duty but with action; and while it is true that an action encompasses several aspects in the way that colour does not, it does not follow that the relation between the aspects of duty and expediency in an action is any different, any less exclusive, than between the aspects of colour and smell in an object.

I think we have to concede the objector her objection but are still able to draw an important contrast between empirical and philosophical concepts. The fact that part of that contrast was due, as the objector has discovered, to the levels of generality, i.e., that colour is a relatively simple concept concerned with limited phenomena compared to action, is not a cause for embarrassment. For it is, as we have seen, one of Collingwood's claims that philosophical concepts begin as empirical concepts with aspirations to generality.

We may even take the objector's point further by saying that once we know that we have an instance of colour we also know that, as colour is only found in objects, we have an object of which it makes sense to ask whether it has, and if so, what kind of, smell. I say that this takes the objector's point further because it creates an even closer parallel with the case of duty and expediency. For it is Collingwood's contention that it is characteristic of philosophical concepts like action that consideration of one aspect or species leads to questions about another; that, for example, questions of expediency rationally lead to an evaluation of the goals of action and hence to questions of duty. And, moreover, I do not think that we could (on Collingwood's behalf) rightly restrict this parallel by arguing that while pure thought could lead one from the category of expediency to duty, empirical thought alone could lead one from one empirical species to another because the latter movement of thought presupposes knowledge of how the world actually is (in our example, knowledge about what sensory organs human beings have). This restriction would not do for, as we know, philosophy for Collingwood is not pure thought but grounded in experience: only a thinker steeped in considerations of human action and not a pure thinker could raise questions of duty out of perplexities concerning expediency. Even if we were to accept these several qualifications and conclude that the distinction between the empirical and the philosophical was not (in this limited respect) as clear-cut as initially stated, a relevant point of contrast still remains.[9]

For species of a philosophical concept can be said to 'overlap', in a way not allowed by the traditional theory of classification and not found in ordinary empirical concepts, because no one species of such a concept can make its contribution to human understanding without calling upon and being qualified by other species of that concept. Questions about colour can be satisfactorily investigated without raising questions about smell and vice versa; and the total understanding of the empirical genus, sensory-data, is simply an amalgam of the knowledge within each of its species. We can fully understand colour without reference to smell (though of course we cannot fully understand an object without reference to both and to much else), but we cannot fully understand expediency or self-advantage without reference to duty. As Plato's *Gorgias* and *Republic* part I superbly demonstrate, to claim that the good is self-advantage raises questions about who or what the self is, about how we can be sure what is to its advantage, about the relations between one self and another – in short, that questions about the value of expediency can only fail to give rise to questions of morality, and the latter prevented from impinging on the former, if rational inquiry is arbitrarily arrested. Collingwood, of course, argues that this kind of 'overlap' and competition holds amongst the forms of understanding. If this is so then we must expect from cultural life both a greater variety and – paradoxically – a more integrated unity than is to be found within a narrowly scientific or intellectualistic framework: forms of experience will not fall into place in a neat system of classification and deny analysis into discrete units.

## III

Besides overlap or interdependence, hierarchy was a further feature of the system in *Speculum Mentis*, and we must now consider how Collingwood justifies this feature. The idea of hierarchy or a scale of forms rests on the observation that not only is there a logical relation of overlap between different species or aspects of a genus but that the genus is differently related to each of the species that constitute it. Collingwood explains that there is not, as the theory of classification presupposes, a uniform relation between the genus and each of the species in a philosophical concept because the species of such a concept do not differ merely in kind, nor merely in degree, but both. Temperance, fortitude, wisdom, etc., for example, as species of virtue are different kinds of virtue. Yet, at the same time, they also differ in degree: they are not equally examples of virtue but form a scale in which the higher embodies more of the generic essence than the lower examples. The idea of a scale of forms, that a sufficient difference in degree amounts to a difference in kind, is not in itself peculiar to philosophy. The varieties of $H_2O$ could be said to form a scale: vary the heat and you get progressively different forms of $H_2O$ – ice, water, steam. None of these forms of $H_2O$ are, however, any more or less $H_2O$ than the others. This is so because the variable in this example, heat, is not itself a feature of $H_2O$. In a philosophical scale, on the other hand, Collingwood argues, the variable is not external to the genus; it is the genus itself that varies through one form to another. It varies in kind and in degree with the result that 'every form, so far as it is low in the scale, is to that extent an imperfect or inadequate specification of the generic essence, which is realised with progressive adequacy as the scale is ascended' (EPM, 61). The forms of cultural experience or, say, of moral life give rise to each other not because of external influences in the way that heat is external to $H_2O$ but because of their own internal relationship to each other. Each new conceptually more complex form is an attempt to realize the generic essence more successfully than the existing or conceptually more simple, generically more limited, species. A species is only a part of a genus because it contributes something to the genus not available in other species. Hence, new forms of philosophical concepts arise because existing forms are inadequate and they arise out of the inadequacy and not for some reason external to the concept itself. Each more complex species is the product of the quality of experience within the other species as judged by reference to the common genus; each is an attempt to realize the essence further than the point reached by the other species or at least those less complex than itself.

This, then, is what Collingwood means by a philosophical scale of forms. Let us consider it a step at a time in order to bring out some of its implications. Firstly, then, the simplest addition the discussion of the idea of a philosophical scale of forms makes to the idea of overlap of species is that a concept becomes philosophically interesting when its species or aspects are as significant as the genus, when the discussion of the genus is incomplete without a discussion of the species. For it is recognized that the species are not just examples of a genus which is already understood. Rather, philosophy involves the recognition that the species contribute to the character of the genus. Collingwood expresses the point thus:

> if the distinctions between the various virtues . . . temperance, fortitude, wisdom, and justice . . . are merely specific ways of behaving well or being well-disposed, differing among themselves only in kind, philosophers in general would recognise that to insert a discussion of each into a theory of virtue would be to load the theory with empirical detail. (EPM, 56)

Philosophers are not interested in mere empirical variety and detail; and the merely contingent is philosophically insignificant, not recognized as part of the concept under study but an unremarkable feature of interest only to collectors of fact, which all theories may safely ignore. Yet philosophers are interested in different forms of experience and action, and do not regard them as mere species of what they already understand and of which they have an adequate theory. Their theories are dependent on and challenged by reference to what is encountered amongst the variety. The philosophical consideration of each form of experience, such as art or religion, makes for a re-evaluation of the concept of culture and the unity of experience.

Philosophical theories and definitions must adapt to take into account the distinctiveness of the species. Thus in *Speculum Mentis* the theory of experience proceeds not by imposing a common generic essence on each example but builds the notion of human experience and mind through a sensitivity to variety, expanding and transforming the theory under pressure from each of the varied forms. The species, then, of a philosophical concept, are not merely of empirical interest but are constitutive of the genus and hence necessarily of interest to anyone interested in the genus. The forms that a philosophical concept exhibits are intrinsic to its logic; and conversely new species do not simply expand a genus, they alter its character.

The point just made is very similar to Wittgenstein's critique of essentialism by the deployment of the notion of a 'family resemblance'.[10] Yet the next step of the argument, namely that a concept can be found, amongst its species or instantiations, in greater or lesser degree is diametrically opposed to the idea of 'family resemblance'. For that notion implies, a Wittgensteinian might argue, that species are not closer to the genus than other species *simply by virtue of their logic*: for no member of a family is more a member of that family than any other, though the family would not be the one that it is if any one member was other than he or she is. He might argue that Collingwood's contention seems to be equivalent to the view that the more active members of an actual human family are more familial because they are living much more up to the ideal and so embody more of the concept of the family in themselves and their lives. What is wrong with such an inference, my hypothetical Wittgensteinian may argue, is that to be a better family member is not to be more of a family member; it is not to have more of a genus. The question of falling under a genus is whether the individuals are members of the family, and in this respect both the active and the negligent are equal. A criticism of this sort has been made by C. J. Ducasse (who perhaps is not a Wittgensteinian). He argues, in response to Collingwood's suggestion that university degrees are an example of a scale of forms, that

> it would obviously be false to say that the lowest, viz. the bachelor's is only slightly an academic degree. What is true is that the degree of scholarly equipment (not of academic-degree-ness) which this species of academic degree represents is lower than that represented by the other degrees, and is possibly too low for certain purposes.[11]

Now, while it may be true that a person with an MA has not more academic-degree-ness than one with a BA it, however, is not true that she does not (*prima facie*) embody more of the generic essence, academic knowledge; an essence without which the notion of a university degree does not make sense. What the criticisms of the above sort fail to appreciate is that the genus or concept is relevant not merely in identifying an example but also in evaluating whether an example lives up to its ideal or generic character.

Take the concept of a teacher. Someone fulfils the criterion of being a teacher if he or she has, say, a job at a school, but not all those who have a job at a school equally fulfil the criteria which constitute the full concept of a teacher. The minimal criteria needed to identify someone as a teacher, to satisfy whether he or she falls under the generic term 'teacher', do not exhaust the concept of a teacher. Moreover, the minimal criteria presuppose the wider criteria: we cannot identify a person as a teacher and know what we have identified them as unless we have some notion of what makes a good teacher. It is only because we have notions such as learning, knowledge, guidance, instruction, communication etc., as well as some empirical knowledge about our society, that we can say that a person with a certain kind of job at a school is a teacher. If a teacher lacked (a certain amount of) knowledge and failed (to a sufficient extent) to communicate with his or her pupils or constantly misinformed them (for a non-pedagogic reason), they may continue to exhibit some family resemblance to other teachers but this would be no grounds to say that they fulfilled the genus 'teacher' to the same degree as any other example within that family of cases.

Similarly, to return to the example of the family, a brother who actively lives up to being a brother and whose life is (deliberately, perhaps) centred on his siblings is more of a brother than one for whom brotherhood means little in terms of affections, loyalties, duties and a shared life. And, as a brother is a species of the genus 'family', a person who is more of a brother than his brother also embodies more of the genus 'family' in his person than his more negligent brother. Philosophical concepts, being much wider and more internally complex than teacher or family, are not a narrow set of absolute criteria, such as those which define mathematical properties or scientific entities or legal relationships, and hence it is possible to satisfy them sufficiently to fall within a philosophical concept and yet not sufficiently fully to embody that concept. Indeed, most ordinary concepts, such as teacher or brother, but also citizen, comedian, friend, home, nation, as well as artist, scientist, historian etc. have this feature. The concept is constituted both by criteria of the minimal qualities needed in the object before the relevant description can be attributed to it and *also* by the criteria of defining its own distinctive kind of excellence.

What is important to understand here in order to appreciate what I have chosen to make a second stage in the logic of Collingwood's scale of forms is that these two sets of criteria, the minimal and the maximal, those necessary for identifying mere instances and those for identifying instances of excellence, form a unified concept. There is no logical break between the minimal and the maximal sets of criteria: the first are presupposed by the second, and the first are selected in the light of their relationship and contribution to the second. Rational inquiry or even simply intelligent application of the minimal set of criteria will naturally lead to questions of the sort pertaining to the criteria of excellence. Questions about what is a teacher or a brother or a citizen or an artist may (depending upon how much we already know) start with the search for minimal criteria but will logically proceed through their own internal momentum (hence not in the way that water turns to steam through the interference of heat) to criteria of excellence. And when one reaches this later point one will still be discussing what is a teacher or a brother or a citizen etc. The discussion will have become evaluative, about better and worse teachers and so on, and yet however many aspects and distinctions may have entered the discussion, it will still be within the same genus. The movement from the lower (the more descriptive) to the higher (the more evaluative) is a rational process and does not require any special contrivances or assumptions; on the contrary, the movement can only be stopped for some extraneous and limited purpose of our own, e.g., we have to decide to whom to pay teachers' salaries.

We have seen then that it cannot be a principle of philosophical logic that all instances of a concept necessarily equally instantiate it. In particular, we have also seen that an instance which exhibits a greater degree of a species than another instance may also embody a greater degree of the genus. A person who is more of a brother than another person also embodies the genus 'family' to a greater degree. The question now arises whether some species embody the generic essence more than other species. For, if it is true that by embodying more of a species one also embodies more of the genus one may wonder whether one can have more of the genus, not simply by having more of a species, but by having one species rather than another. With this question we have reached Collingwood's notion of a scale of forms proper. It will readily be seen that this step is crucial to the argument of *Speculum Mentis* and to the aspiration of an evaluative philosophy.

As before, I shall consider this third stage of Collingwood's argument by considering an objection. The objection I have in mind is as follows. It might be said that a person engaged in living a dutiful life, such as, say, Mother Teresa of Calcutta, is a superior example of the category of morality and closer to the generic essence of moral action than a calculating egoist who operates almost exclusively at the level of expediency. This judgement, however, according to the objection, is a judgement from within the context of morality. The superiority of the moral exemplar over the moral defective may be a genuine superiority to which we may all wish to pay tribute but it is a moral and not a logical superiority. As simply logical examples of actions or lives within a certain evaluative context the failure is equally an example of that evaluative context as the success is. For both the failure and the success equally depend for their identity as failure and success of the relevant kind on the application of the same norms and concepts. If our interest is in the logic of these norms and concepts, then a judgement acknowledging failure is as good as a judgement acknowledging success, as long as both manifest the same norms. The objector may express the point by saying that the genus 'good' is really a shorthand for the genus 'good-bad'; hence, though a morally good example must be acceptable as an example of this genus, it is no better as an example; logic, therefore, is neutral between the different constituent elements of a genus. Though this conclusion contradicts Collingwood, it is falsely derived from the substance of the objection which I think is quite compatible with the idea of a scale of forms. The objection is based on the recognition that success of a certain generic kind and failure of that same generic kind (morally good and morally bad acts, for example) may, depending upon the extent of the success or failure, be governed by identical criteria. If, then, the conceptual equipment needed to pick out a morally good act is the same as a morally bad act why is moral goodness considered by Collingwood to embody more of the genus than a morally shabby act? Let us note, however, that Collingwood's view is not that wicked acts are no part of the genus, good. Just as the objector wants to expand the genus, good, to good-bad so Collingwood wants to expand it to utility (or expediency) – right – duty.[12]

If the objector's point is that bad acts cannot be identified with a particular *kind* of actions, viz. expedient actions, but are to be found amongst all different kinds of actions, at the level of, say, duty, as well as expediency; that moral failure is not a level of (moral) action, and, hence, not merely a lower-level type of action, but is to be found amongst all kind of actions and is as varied as the field of human action; that moral failure is not a species of goodness and, therefore, no more distant from the common genus than morally superior actions – if this is the criticism then it is one with which Collingwood need have no quarrel. Collingwood is far from the opinion that expediency is all bad.[13] On the contrary, he believes it is a necessary dimension of all actions and therefore a relevant consideration in all moral choices. He thinks that expediency and duty are not simply opposites.[14] What Collingwood is arguing is that the goodness or badness of expediency cannot be judged by expediency itself but by another species of the same genus as expediency, by one which as a species is truer to the generic essence, to the fullness of the genus. The logical asymmetry between expediency and duty in the genus 'good-bad' is that the badness of an expedient act cannot be recognized till we have a more sophisticated notion of good-bad than is available within the species, expediency.

Knowledge of expediency presents us with an awareness of its goodness but not of its badness unless we have a superior awareness of goodness than is available in the notion of expediency. This is the reason why expediency is – not just morally but logically – an inferior species of good than, say, right or duty. The morally insensitive egoist is a logically poorer example of goodness than Mother Teresa because the understanding available to him is not sufficient to appreciate the full goodness and badness in his actions. Should the hypothetical moral scoundrel be of not just a simple sort but truly dastardly and on the scale of a moral hero, then it is true that his life, if properly depicted, would, logically, be as good an exemplar of the genus 'good-bad' as the life of the Reverend Mother herself. But – and this is important – such a scoundrel would no longer be acting within a world of expediency. His stature depends upon his having the same kinds of understanding as the Reverend Mother.[15] And this, I submit, is sufficient to establish the coherence of Collingwood's idea of a scale of forms and to demonstrate that the concept of the good is an example of it. Some species of the genus 'good' are a poor example of that concept and are dependent upon other species in order to highlight the good-bad in them. We have to reach the higher levels of the genus before we can truly appreciate in what way a bad person is bad. If they confine themselves to a narrow conception of the good, such as expediency, within which what we deem to be their badness does not register as such but, on the contrary, appears as good, then they have a logically inferior understanding of the good than we do. If they wish to act in accordance with the genus 'good' and not just one of its species, they must, in addition to the knowledge they already have, seek other species which take them to the heart of the matter. The exclusively expedient person is a bad person but cannot appreciate his or her badness from his or her limited standpoint, but only from a higher or logically less simple standpoint. 'Higher', because duty presupposes expediency: as duty often conflicts with expediency and qualifies it, a person who lacked a concept of expediency could not have a concept of duty. This logical relationship, however, is one-way. Expediency does not depend upon our having or not having a concept of duty.[16] 'Higher', then, in a logical and not merely moral sense. Duty can encompass and judge expediency and give it its due place but not vice versa. Duty and expediency, then, are members of the same conceptual family but not equally so.

And if it happens that the example, the concept of the good, or its presentation is in some way flawed, at least the justification of the idea of a scale of forms stands.

## IV

Each species of a philosophical genus, then, is a stage in the development of a concept. It has a place in the development of our understanding of an aspect of the world. Each species, in a way, negates the species immediately below it (or, what is the same thing, all the species up to that point) simply because it opposes an existing understanding. It offers new criteria of evaluation. Its newness and its superiority lies in highlighting the deficiencies of the known species of the genus. Each species claims to be a more adequate conception of what the other species assert. It claims to offer what the lesser species seek, though, characteristically, the lesser species have only an imperfect understanding of what they seek. Hence, though expediency is the pursuit of self-interest, it consists in a very limited understanding of the self and what is good for it. It cannot, therefore, fully succeed in its pursuit until a wider understanding is partly found in the notion of social utility where the self is seen as part of a wider society, the conditions of which affects the self and for the sake of which the self must learn to curb short-term expediency. Social utility thus opposes expediency. But it does not reject it altogether; rather, it consists in selecting and ranking the goals which the self should seek to be expedient about. Again, the idea of duty, too, consists in similarly redefining what counts as social advantage by bringing in extra considerations. These considerations are a development of the same questions to which expediency and social utility can be seen as possible answers. More specifically, the idea of duty arises out of the internal difficulties which manifest themselves in a serious application of the concept of social utility. The attempt to practise social utility raises questions as to whose preferences should be counted in the utilitarian calculations and whether everyone is owed the same by all the others, or whether our obligations to some are greater than to others and whether perhaps some are more deserving than others; questions are also raised as to the limits of collective programmes of welfare and felicity, while issue is taken over whether all preferences are as rational as each other. Hence arise further species of the genus 'human good' to specify in detail and to overcome the difficulties of a life lived in accordance with the principle of social utility. A new species, thus, develops out of an existing stock in order to fulfil the inquiry or project embodied in the existing species.

To understand the significance, then, of any one of the species is not merely to understand it as one amongst several species of a genus but as one in a logically interconnected and progressive series. To take a species at its face value or as a self-contained unit is to fail to appreciate what it is trying to do and what it achieves. It must be understood in terms of the strengths and weaknesses implicit in the other species and in terms of its contribution to the aims and the difficulties in them. For 'each term, which in itself is simply one specific form of goodness, has also a double relation to its neighbours: in comparison with the one below, it is what that professes to be; in comparison with the one above, it professes to be what that is' (EPM, 87). The character of a species cannot be understood apart from this need to move to a higher species when it is recognized that an existing species does not exhaust the genus, that what it takes to be the whole and absolutely true is only a part of something wider.[17]

Though Collingwood does not use the term 'dialectic' in *Essay on Philosophical Method* to describe his own ideas, probably so as not immediately to alienate the new schools of analytical and positivistic philosophers of the kind who dismissed *Speculum Mentis* as 'the usual idealistic nonsense'(A, 56), it is obvious that the kind of series I have just described is a dialectical one.[18] A dialectical series is a movement of thought from a lower to a higher level, or a process of conceptual development by combating the error that has manifested itself at the lower level; an error which arises in the context of a line of inquiry. Hence, in overcoming that error or difficulty we (to some degree) achieve the goal that the lower level had set for itself. Of course, in the process of overcoming that error by developing our conceptual resources we become sensitive to new imperatives and, consequently, each advance heralds new problems which seem as insoluble as those of the level before and, indeed, can only be solved by new species within that general line of inquiry.

Though Collingwood chooses not to use the term 'dialectic' no other term is more suited to describing the process in, for example, the following passage: 'The higher . . . negates the lower, and at the same time reaffirms it: it negates it as a false embodiment of the generic essence, and reaffirms its content, that specific form of the essence, as part and parcel of itself' (EPM, 88). That this describes the movement from one cultural form to another as depicted in *Speculum Mentis* is all too clear. There, Collingwood presented each cultural form as arising out of the contradictions of another and in turn giving rise to a third till a level of experience was reached that was free of all necessary contradictions. It should be clear now what Collingwood means by 'contradiction' in this context and, more generally, in the assertion that cultural experience is a logical system. The contradictions within the view of experience and reality implicit in art, and which need religious understanding to overcome them, are not those of formal logicians. The conflict in question is typically not even one between two statements or propositions. It is a conflict between theory and practice; a debilitating discrepancy between what the mind thinks it is doing and what it is doing.[19] Opposition and resolution are possible here because experience for Collingwood is always an expanding system. A distinct form of experience such as, say, religion, viewed from within, may be perceived as a self-sufficient system of categories and concepts.[20] For Collingwood, however, such closedness is only a primitive phase in the life of a form of experience, for they always seek to be not just a species of understanding but the genus itself. The result, however, is, sooner or later, a breakdown of that form of experience as a theoretical whole. Its practice leads it into areas which it cannot theoretically allow exist, let alone explain, and hence the construction of a new theoretical whole to account for the new practice becomes a necessity. The new theory, however, usually goes to some extent beyond current practice and thus guides practice by suggesting new possibilities. This to-ing and fro-ing process is aptly imagined as a dialogue for thought, and can sometimes respond to first-order problems within a practice, and at other times a practice can be seen to follow rationally the lead of theory, which, after all, is always in part an idealization of an existing practice. This relation between theory and practice adds a further point of clarification to how we have to understand the idea of 'overlap'. It is an overlap which not only denies the irrelevance of second-order theorizing to first-order experience but which exists in the dynamic tension between the two.

## V

The open-mindedness of true philosophy can be appreciated by reference to two further features of philosophical reasoning. One is that it is non-axiomatic or reversible and the other is that the idea of finality is foreign to it. Collingwood explains the first by a contrast with mathematics. Euclidean geometry, for example, proceeds by deducing conclusions from premises in accordance with its own or general logical axioms, such as that two straight lines cannot enclose a space (EPM, 151–2). These axioms are presupposed absolutely; they cannot be considered within Euclid and are evaluated by philosophy, a separate discipline. It follows that geometrical reasoning is irreversible or asymmetrical: the axioms are not logically dependent on the conclusions in the way that the conclusions are dependent on the axioms; we cannot argue back from the conclusions of our investigations to query or confirm our axioms. Philosophy, on the other hand, cannot accept a principle of reference or a criterion of valid experience and simply proceed forward from that point. It cannot accept its principles on trust; nothing in philosophy can have the status of a Euclidean axiom – nor, indeed, of an axiom the evaluation of which depends upon a separate intellectual discipline. However we are to understand philosophical reasoning, it must not be on the model of deduction, for we have to allow for the possibility that philosophy can turn back to question and criticize and revise its presuppositions in the light of what is learnt by trying to think (and act) in accordance with those presuppositions.[21] Philosophy is neither limited by nor can suspend judgement on its starting point; it must justify it. Its starting point, as we have seen, is non-philosophical experience, the claims of the various forms of cultural experience. It cannot, then, take an uncritical or hypothetical attitude to these claims, and the fact that it is an intellectual development out of these claims is not an argument for saying that it ought to. Its rejection, vindication or critical modification of these claims must be seen as a necessary part of its character, for such an examination of its critical roots is a necessary part of its self-vindication. By pursuing its own critical character it is in this way able to open what would otherwise be closed conceptual systems.

A similar qualification needs to be made to the idea of philosophy culminating in a single final Truth. The idea of cultural forms as sharing a single common reality necessarily must have a use for the idea of a system, but just as that system is not to be understood in terms of a scientific methodology, so too it has been implicit all along that what is 'permanent and essential is not this or that system, for every particular system is nothing but an interim report on the progress of thought down to the time of making it, but the necessity of thinking systematically' (EPM, 198).[22] Finality, it is argued in *Speculum Mentis*, is the goal that history pursues but which it cannot achieve in practice, and hence collapses in a contradiction the resolution of which is the adoption of a philosophical attitude to experience. The idea of the world as a system of facts which can be known in their entirety is superseded by the idea of the world as a continuously recreated product of the mind. The idea of knowledge as a definitive and final system of propositions was there argued to be one of the inadequacies of history. In his very last work, *The New Leviathan*, Collingwood expressed the same point by saying that the mind is such that the effort to ensure completeness only guarantees that one has not succeeded, for the mind becomes more aware of deficiencies and omissions (NL, 9.33).[23] In that work he also emphasized what had always been implicit, that the next or higher level in a scale of forms, though logically related to and superior to existing knowledge, could not be predicted in advance: there is an irreducibly contingent element in the development of the mind (NL, 9.48).[24] It is part of the nature of human experience that there is always scope for the development of new concepts and categories. The idea that experience can be exhausted and that such exhaustion marks the peak of fulfilment of rationality has no place in the thought of Collingwood. Indeed, the idea of experience coming to an absolute logical end makes no sense, for in any field of human experience we can always imagine further dialogue and inquiry, criticism and counter criticism.[25] As Gadamer, whose thought on this point is very close to Collingwood, puts it:

> Just as the individual is never simply an individual, because he is always involved with others, so too the closed horizon that is supposed to enclose a culture is an abstraction. The historical movement of human life consists in the fact that it is never utterly bound to any one standpoint, and hence can never have a truly closed horizon.[26]

And if experience has this open-endedness then the idea of a philosophical system must reflect this.

## VI

It is apt to conclude this discussion on philosophy by noting that Collingwood had emphasized the historicity of philosophy from his earliest period, from the time when he was committed to grand theory. Most readers of Collingwood have held the view that in his later works he emphasized this historicity to the point where philosophy as an intellectual activity simply became an aspect of historical inquiry. I have argued elsewhere on the falseness of this view and have no space to summarize those arguments except to say that I believe this view has largely arisen because his readers have not sufficiently noticed his different levels of concern.[27] These can perhaps be schematized in the following way:

A (i) Grand theory, e.g. *Speculum Mentis*, *The New Leviathan*
  (ii) Logic of grand theory, e.g. *Essay on Philosophical Method*
B (i) Philosophy of X, e.g. *Principles of Art* and *The Idea of History* (Part V)
  (ii) Logic of philosophy of X, e.g. 'Preliminary Discussion. The Idea of a Philosophy of Something, and in Particular, a Philosophy of History' (1927 unpub. MS, Bodleian Library)
C (i) Intellectual history (the empirical materials out of which the philosophical exercise emerges), e.g. *Idea of Nature*, *The Idea of History* (parts I–IV)
  (ii) Logic of intellectual history, e.g. *Essay on Metaphysics*, *Autobiography*, chapters 5, 7, 8 and 10.

Once it is appreciated that Collingwood had these different levels of concern, there is less reason to conclude that 'like Croce, he came to think that 'philosophy as a separate discipline is liquidated by being converted into history' (IH, x). Indeed, I think we are in a much better position to appreciate Collingwood's pioneering contribution to the discipline of the history of ideas (though we are not helped in this by his sometimes calling it 'metaphysics'). We are also in a better position to see that the mixed empirical-philosophical level of C (i) is not one appropriate for a scale of forms analysis, and therefore the absence of its advocacy at C (ii) level is not a retreat from the arguments of EPM.

The idea of philosophy as the unifier of a fragmented cultural life and the use of scale of forms were central to Collingwood throughout his philosophical career though perhaps not without some modifications or changes in terminology. In his later years he described the mutual interdependence of different forms of experience as rapprochement, and in *Autobiography* rightly wrote of his life-work as being an attempt to bring about a rapprochement between theoretical inquiry and practical life, and within the former between philosophy and history (A147 and 77). While the scale of forms was not appropriate to certain kinds of problems it is not the case that there was a time in his life when he no longer thought that kind of philosophizing valid: it is a constant feature of his moral philosophy lectures given throughout the 1930s and present in his last work, *The New Leviathan*.

*Notes*

[1] The earlier work in particular has thus been derided. For example see A. J. Ayer, *Philosophy in the Twentieth Century* (London: Weidenfeld and Nicolson, 1982).
[2] I write of philosophy as if it was an agent in its own right. I trust that this stylistic convenience is not mistaken for reification.
[3] For a brief account of these sentiments as expressed by Goethe, Schiller, Herder, Hamann, Holderlin and Hegel with particular reference to the social dimension of the problem of cultural fragmentation see Raymond Plant, *Hegel* (second edn, London, Allen and Unwin, 1983), 16–27. For a much more wide-ranging discussion see Charles Taylor, *Hegel* (Cambridge, Cambridge University Press, 1975), ch.1.
[4] This is the opening sentence of the Prologue in SM and reasserted towards its conclusion on p. 35.

5. While Collingwood does not state that EPM is a defence of the method of SM, despite this and Knox's dismissal of SM as juvenilia (*Idea of History*, Editor's Preface, vii) in contrast to his description of EPM as a masterpiece (ibid., xx–xxi), no one can read the two works and doubt it. It is perhaps the one point on which all the subsequent major commentators agree. Hence, *pace* Knox EPM is not merely 'an introduction to a philosophy not yet written' (ibid., xxi). It is equally false to assert that 'the patterns of philosophical thought laid down in EPM do not intrude in Collingwood's later writings' (Alan Donagan, 'Collingwood and Philosophical Method' in M. Krausz (ed.), *Critical Essays on the Philosophy of R. G. Collingwood* (Oxford, Clarendon Press, 1972), 17. As a concrete example cf. EPM with *The New Leviathan*, especially chs.9 and 15–17.
6. Another example, from Lectures on Moral Philosophy, 1933 (unpub. MS), 99, is politics. 'Consequently', Collingwood writes, 'there cannot be a philosophical theory of the state . . . the philosophical theory of politics can only be a theory of the political element which, though people are perhaps readier to discern its presence in the state than elsewhere, is not confined to it but is co-extensive with human life.' This understanding of philosophical concepts is employed throughout the Moral Philosophy Lectures, including the last, written in 1940.
7. Space does not allow me to mention in detail Collingwood's argument on the inapplicability of the logic of empirical concepts to philosophical inquiry. I refer only to those elements of it which assist in sketching his view of philosophy as a whole.
8. EPM, 48. Collingwood's main example of philosophical concepts in the essay are from ethics. This is not surprising as EPM grew out of his methodological introduction to his lectures on moral philosophy, as is apparent from the unpublished manuscripts. See especially the early sections of the 1932 lectures and the explanation of alterations at the beginning of the 1933 lectures.
9. Collingwood did not state that the distinction was a sharp one. He pointed to empirical cases which did not neatly fit the traditional theory and hence did not contrast absolutely with what he claimed for philosophical concepts, EPM, 30. Moreover, if Collingwood is right that the species of philosophical genus are not mutually exclusive but overlap then, since concept is a philosophical genus we must not expect a sharp division between scientific and philosophical concepts.
10. Ludwig Wittgenstein, *The Blue and Brown Books* (Oxford, Blackwell, 1969), 17–20.
11. C. J. Ducasse, 'Mr Collingwood on Philosophical Method', *Journal of Philosophy*, 33 (1936), 95–106, (103).
12. Though slightly different formulations are given at different times this is the basic pattern throughout the 1930s Moral Philosophy Lectures

and elsewhere where he discusses economic, political and moral theory, including NL, chs.15–17. The form and content of the theory is very closely followed in Sir Malcolm Knox's Gifford Lectures, *Action* (London, Allen and Unwin, 1968). For a more independent use of it which integrates it into a political theory see A. J. M. Milne, *Freedom and Rights* (London, Allen and Unwin,1968), especially chs.3 and 4; and for some explicit criticism of Collingwood's ethical and political theory, see Milne's essay in M. Krausz (ed.) *Critical Essays*, where he also defends a hierarchical analysis of practical reason into utility, personal well-being and social morality (p.307). My interest in Collinqwood's ethics is here confined to its hierarchical logic and I do not argue for or against any particular substantive version of this hierarchy.

[13] Not only is expediency an intrinsic species of the genus 'good', but furthermore Collingwood draws the conclusion that pure wickedness is inconceivable, see EPM, 82.

[14] In a scale of forms all forms are in opposition to each other but are not absolute opposites, see EPM, 74–7.

[15] A similar point can be made to defend Collingwood's view that utility is a higher value than pleasure (EPM, 86–8) against the obvious objection that many of the pleasures commonly valued are useless and not readily exchanged for more useful pleasures. The point is that the pleasures must not be harmful: and this is to subordinate them to the category of utility, to determine on which occasions pleasure may be given priority by reference to utility. We are after all in philosophical ethics seeking a criterion for judging whole lives, not particular actions or states of affairs.

[16] More strictly: the minimal concept of expediency does not depend on duty but it is needed to truly know what is expedient. Expediency which follows knowledge of duty is *qua* expediency a species of the genus good (and not on some arbitrary imposed scheme) on a higher level than before. Cf. the idea of the series abc abc abc in SM, 55.

[17] Alan Donagan in Krausz (ed.), *Critical Essays*, 16, fails to appreciate that in this way an abstraction is neutralized for it is unified with what it was abstracted from. His error is that he forces an absolute gulf between the abstract and concrete. No wonder, then, that on his interpretation Collingwood's thought must break down into the scepticism that all thought is incurably abstract. Donagan's whole article seems to be almost a wilful attempt to misunderstand Collingwood in SM and EPM.

[18] Collingwood does, however, use the term to describe the philosophical method of Socrates and Plato whom he believes to be the founders of dialectic, EPM, 10–11. Later he seems to have found the courage to use the term to describe his own views, see, e.g., NL, 22–3, and 326

(also in the draft manuscript, 'What Civilization Means', 26–9). L. O. Mink, *Mind, History and Dialectic: the Philosophy of R. G. Collingwood* (Bloomington, Indiana University Press, 1969) has cogently argued that dialectic is the central idea of Collingwood's philosophy. To avoid some of the most obvious misunderstandings it might be useful to quote his four statements of what dialectic is not: '1. Dialectical thinking does not claim to replace ordinary deductive or inductive logic . . . 2. Dialectic is not a substitute for empirical science nor a theory of any particular subject matter . . . 3. Dialectic is not tied to any simple formula of 'thesis-antithesis-synthesis' . . . 4. Dialectic does not postulate any forces of nature or of history unknown to non-dialectical thought . . .' (22). For a good summary of some of the positive features of dialectic, see Mink in M. Krausz (ed.),123–4; see also W. M. Urban, *Beyond Realism and Idealism* (London, 1949),123–32.

[19] By contradiction, then, Collingwood means dialectical opposition 'using the term dialectic in general as Plato used it to denote the modification of two conflicting assertions by convergence towards an agreement, and more particularly as Kant used it to denote the process by which rules of conduct undergo modification in being applied to actual cases' (Moral Philosophy Lectures, 1932 (though some confusion is present because the lectures are in a binder marked '1920' or '1928'), 71). Cf. NL, 15.74–15.8.

[20] Collingwood's ideas can very interestingly be contrasted with those of Michael Oakeshott for whom a mode of experience is a closed system. See M. J. Oakeshott, *Experience and its Modes* (Cambridge, Cambridge University Press, 1933). For a full discussion of this and other contrasts between these two thinkers on the relationship between philosophy and other activities see my doctoral thesis 'Collingwood, Oakeshott and the Idea of a Philosophical Culture' (University of Wales, 1984).

[21] EPM, 154–5. Donagan, in M. Krausz (ed.), *Critical Essays*, writes that 'this principle, however, is now generally recognised to apply to all branches of inquiry: to mathematics, natural science, and history, equally with philosophy' (17). Collingwood would have welcomed this: his quarrel was not with a description of scientific reasoning but with the suggestion that the description ought to be a model for philosophy; see e.g., EPM, 151.

[22] Cf. Collingwood, *Principles of Art* (Oxford, 1938), p. 297.

[23] Cf. S. Hampshire, *Thought and Action*, new edn (London, Chatto and Windus, 1982), 21ff. on the impossibility of giving sense to the words 'I have identified all the things that are in this room'.

[24] Cf. MacIntyre (1981), 89. It may be that the 'law of primitive survivals' (NL, 9.5–9.58) is a modification of the idea of a scale of forms expressed in EPM.

[25] Cf. my 'Differences in Moral Reasoning', *Philosophical Studies*

(National University of Ireland), xxix (Winter 1982-3), 171-3 where I use this idea to argue that the idea of an absolute breakdown in moral dialogue can be dismissed on *a priori* grounds; cf. R. Bambrough, *Moral Scepticism and Moral Knowledge* (London, Routledge and Kegan Paul, 1979), where it is, quite rightly, argued that this feature of reasoning is not particular to any one form of experience but common to all. Collingwood himself makes this point in 'Reality as History' (1935), unpublished, 19-20.

[26] H.-G. Gadamer, *Truth and Method*, transl. and ed. Garret Barden and John Cumming (New York, Crossroads, 1975), 271; cf. 318-19 where he suggests that Hegel's major shortcoming is that he identified the criterion of self-knowledge with a dialectic which 'must end with the overcoming of all experience'. Collingwood, however, defends Hegel from the charge that his philosophy implies that history must end with the present where this means that future progress is impossible, *Idea of History* (Oxford, Clarendon Press, 1946), 120, and *Idea of Nature* (Oxford, Clarendon Press, 1945), 174

[27] Tariq Modood, 'The Later Collingwood's Alleged Historicism and Relativism', *Journal of the History of Philosophy*, 27 (1989), 101-25.

# Aesthetics and Philosophical Method

## T. J. DIFFEY

The case for taking Collingwood's philosophy seriously is this. Collingwood seeks systematic understanding, that is, he regards philosophy as an ordered inquiry and not the random production of unconnected theses and scattered *aperçus*. He valued truth, he said (and I think it shows in his works), above debate conducted for the sake of victory. He is an uncompromising thinker whose statements, if wrong, are made sufficiently definite for their erroneousness not to have been deliberately hidden away from the critic. Collingwood's writing moreover is mercifully free of that craven subjectivity which infects so much opinion, especially on ethical and aesthetic questions, today. If something is a question of opinion this is not, contrary to current sentiment, a philosophically good excuse or reason to exit browbeaten by the dogma that one opinion is as good as another. Like Plato, Collingwood does not think this, but writes with a Platonic decisiveness, though not of course from a philosophical position at all like Plato's own.

### I

Collingwood wrote on the philosophy of art, or aesthetic, because he had something to say. In *The Principles of Art*, for example, he thought deeply and illuminatingly about a wide range of topics including not only art but also meaning, psychology, art criticism and anthropology. He wrote out of an evident knowledge of art and of philosophy, with a sense of what is important and what is not in any question. Indeed from *The Principles* alone an entire education not merely in aesthetics but in philosophy generally could be had. This education would teach what the methods of philosophy should be; how to go about tackling philosophical problems; and how to take a positive and not merely defensive view of the errors which one will inevitably make in the course of philosophical (or any other) thinking.

In turning to Collingwood's aesthetics, then, one is at the same time still concerned with the central problems of philosophy. So in his aesthetics Collingwood sought to extend and to develop the philosophical tradition from Descartes to Kant, and in particular to take further Hume's distinction between ideas and impressions, which he thought philosophy had never adequately assimilated. Within the framework of a philosophy of mind he offers an acute analysis of the ills of contemporary culture. His account of the decay of magic (in his special sense of that word) and his dismay at the growth of amusement have not lost their relevance in the years since *The Principles of Art* was published, but have, if anything, become more urgent. Collingwood's concept too of the corruption of consciousness is important both for itself and for the light it sheds on the vexed questions of artistic creativity, the evaluation of works of art and the relationship between aesthetics and ethics. *The Principles of Art* then is an unusual fusion of cultural criticism and the philosophy of mind, and indeed could with equal justice have been entitled *A Philosophy of Mind* or even *The Principles of Language*, because for Collingwood mind, art and language are necessarily related.

Collingwood's first contribution to aesthetics or the philosophy of art was his little book, *Outlines of a Philosophy of Art,* published in 1925, though earlier he had also discussed art in his *Speculum Mentis* (1924). The *Outlines* was published in the same year as his article in *Mind* on 'Plato's Philosophy of Art', and when it went out of print some twelve years later in 1937 the Clarendon Press asked him to revise it for a new edition, or to replace it with something new. The outcome of this request was *The Principles of Art.*

Aesthetics is a branch of philosophy in which, contrary to an opinion which possibly lingers still among some philosophers, good work has been done but not much of it at book length. *The*

*Principles of Art* is one of the exceptions. It is one of the few fundamental books in aesthetics, in my view indeed a work of genius, though it has not received its full recognition. It is well known but not taken with sufficient seriousness.

There are external reasons for this. *The Principles of Art* was published shortly before the outbreak of the Second World War and so did not receive the professional discussion it deserved. It was for example never reviewed in *Mind* (though it was reviewed in *Philosophy*).[1] When one recalls, however, what low repute aesthetics was in among philosophers in the English-speaking world in the 1930s, one wonders how far it was the international situation alone which denied Collingwood's aesthetics the serious attention it deserved. By the 1950s, when aesthetics began to be taken more seriously in these circles, Collingwood's philosophical approach was not only out of fashion but was also known *a priori* to be wrong-headed. No scholarship was needed in the 1950s to see that *The Principles of Art* fell foul of the then burgeoning Wittgensteinianism, which was the price aesthetics was then paying for philosophical respectability. Indeed *The Principles of Art*, it was self-evident in those days, was a useful object-lesson in how not to do philosophy.

Nevertheless, in the secondary literature an apparently quite strong though scattered case has been built up against Collingwood's aesthetics over the years. Collingwood, it is maintained, has mistakenly assumed that art is a general term which can be defined by specifying the entity that the term 'art' denotes.[2] He has confused the question, what is art, with the question, what is good art.[3] He has wrongly identified art with language.[4] It is widely held that he distinguishes too sharply between art and craft. His account of art ignores the significance of the medium of art.[5] He makes claims which cannot be right, for example, that the work of art may be 'completely created when it has been created as a thing whose only place is in the artist's mind' (PA, 130); or that the artist cannot set out to create a particular sort of work, e.g. a comedy, a tragedy, an elegy, (PA, 116), that is, that the artist cannot know before creating the work what sort of work it will be.

It seems obvious, therefore, that the case against Collingwood should be examined with a view to determining how decisive it is. Is his aesthetics an edifice reduced to rubble by the successful onslaughts of its various critics? A piecemeal examination of the various criticisms which have been urged against Collingwood is required to answer this question; but to follow that approach is to lose sight of what is to be prized above all, namely the systematic insight which Collingwood has achieved in aesthetics. The crucial point here is that Collingwood's is a systematic aesthetics, which is unusual, and not what is more common, the début of aesthetics in order to round things off and tidy them up for the sake of a systematic *philosophy*.

Of course my praise of Collingwood's systematic aesthetics is worthless if this aesthetics is built out of falsehoods. Is it? I am not convinced by the case against it. That case is based in part upon the failure to take seriously Collingwood's philosophical method. At least some of the criticisms which have been urged against Collingwood can, I believe, be met by a closer consideration than is customarily given of what he was trying to do in *The Principles*. But this consideration must keep prominently in view the nature of Collingwood's philosophical method. We shall never understand him if we try to pick out in piecemeal and seriatim fashion what is true and what is false in *The Principles*. For to seek to identify falsehoods in Collingwood without understanding his principles not of art but of inquiry in general is to overlook what is at the heart of his position; but if that is overlooked we have no assurance that criticism has dealt a fatal blow to Collingwood's *aesthetics*.

## II

The two questions, why is piecemeal criticism of Collingwood unsatisfactory? and what philosophical method is he bringing to aesthetics? are in effect the same question or at any rate have to be answered together. For if we argue that Collingwood is wrong on such and such a point, we overlook his view of the systematic connection which obtains between truth and falsehood in intellectual inquiry, and therefore fail to achieve understanding:

> To a person who knows his business as scientist, historian, philosopher, or any kind of inquirer, the refutation of a false theory constitutes a positive advance in his inquiry. It leaves him confronted, not by the same old question over again, but by a new question, more precise in its terms and therefore easier to answer. (PA, 106)

In his refutation of the technical theory of art Collingwood says:

> An erroneous philosophical theory is based in the first instance not on ignorance but on knowledge. The person who constructs it begins by partially understanding the subject, and goes on to distort what he knows by twisting it into conformity with some preconceived idea. A theory which has commended itself to a great many intelligent people invariably expresses a high degree of insight into the subject dealt with, and the distortion to which this has been subjected is invariably thoroughgoing and systematic. It therefore expresses many truths, *but it cannot be dissected into true statements and false statements; every statement it contains has been falsified; if the truth which underlies it is to be separated out from the falsehood, a special method of analysis must be used. This consists in isolating the preconceived idea which has acted as the distorting agent, reconstructing the formula of the distortion, and re-applying it so as to correct the distortion and thus find out what it was that the people who invented or accepted the theory were trying to say.* (PA, 107, my italics)

If we apply this to Collingwood's own aesthetic theory, as I think we should, we see that the refutation of Collingwood's aesthetics, if such there is to be, must consist not in seriatim arguments that certain particular claims of Collingwood's are false, but rather should proceed by isolating the distorting idea which is supposed to be at work in his aesthetics. What this distorting idea is I do not know, nor have I ever seen it identified by any of Collingwood's critics. It would, I am sure, require an act of philosophical genius to find it, such as Collingwood shows himself to have possessed in his dissection of the technical theory of art. Until Collingwood has been refuted by his own methods I cannot convince myself that in his aesthetics he is mistaken.

## III

One of the main obstacles in recent years to taking Collingwood seriously is the widely held belief, which took root in the 1950s and which so far as I know has not been challenged since, that in aesthetics Collingwood is an essentialist. By essentialism I mean the belief that the word 'art' is a name denominating some common ground or essence which is shared by all works of art and only works of art, and that the task of aesthetics is to understand art by identifying the ground in virtue of which works of art bear the name 'art'. It is not an illuminating criticism of Collingwood to maintain that his aesthetics is committed to essentialism as just defined. It is also a curious charge to bring against a philosopher who in concluding his book said:

> The aesthetician, if I understand his business aright, is not concerned with dateless realities lodged in some metaphysical heaven, but with the facts of his own place and his own time. These, at any rate, are what I have concerned myself with in writing this book. The problems I have discussed are those which force themselves upon me when I look round at the present condition of the arts in our own civilization; and the reason I have tried to solve them is because I do not see how that condition (both of the arts and of the civilization to which they belong) can be bettered unless a solution is found. (PA, 325)

Collingwood believed that what he called 'art proper' could be defined, and if this is essentialism, Collingwood is an essentialist. But this is an uninteresting remark until we know what Collingwood understood by definition in philosophy and what he conceived the problem of explaining 'art proper' to be. By all means let his essentialism be criticized if the objection that he is an essentialist arises in the course of a serious attempt to understand his aesthetics. Without such a study there is no warrant for using Collingwood's aesthetics simply to illustrate what is already known or held on other grounds to be fallacious.

For one thing we should be suspicious of the view that Collingwood naively and unwittingly fell into bad essentialist thinking since he knew no better; because he was for example misled by the grammar of our language into undertaking a necessarily misguided search for the essence of art. On the contrary, he himself warns against versions of essentialism. Scarcely one page into the Preface and he is saying:

> I do not think of aesthetic theory as an attempt to investigate and expound eternal verities concerning the nature of an eternal object called art, but as an attempt to reach, by thinking, the solution of certain problems arising out of the situation in which artists find themselves here and now. Everything written in this book has been written in the belief that it has a practical bearing, direct or indirect, upon the condition of art in England in 1937, and in the hope that artists primarily, and secondarily persons whose interest in art is lively and sympathetic, will find it of some use to them. (PA, vi)

Later he says:

> In modern times there has been a determined attempt on the part of aesthetic theorists to monopolize the word and make it stand for that quality in things in virtue of which when we contemplate them we enjoy what we recognize as an aesthetic experience. *There is no such quality* ... (PA, 38, my italics)

Admittedly Collingwood is here discussing beauty, not art, but he was perfectly capable of seeing the point in connection with art if it needed to be seen. This, however, is superficial skirmishing and we shall not get deeper until we directly address the question of Collingwood's method. In doing so we must keep it in mind that those who have been the swiftest to raise the charge of essentialism in aesthetics have, unlike Collingwood, been followers of Wittgenstein. Collingwood, on the contrary, has his own distinctive view of philosophy.[6] The issue therefore of whether or not Collingwood commits the essentialist fallacy is more properly understood as the question: whose view of philosophy is preferable, Wittgenstein's or Collingwood's? This should not be decided peremptorily in favour of the former without investigating the latter.

## IV

One way to understand how Collingwood understands philosophy is to consider the objection that he is wrong to identify art and language. This seems so obviously wrong that the wonder is how a serious thinker could have thought it. The charge that Collingwood is obviously mistaken is cogent, however, only if we assume that philosophical analysis must leave unchanged that which it analyses. This assumption was made by the ordinary-language philosophy which Wittgenstein's philosophy encouraged, and which the movement against essentialism in aesthetics was part of. A defender of Collingwood will maintain, on the other hand, not that language and art are identical, and are obviously to be seen as so, for if they were it would have been superfluous to have written *The Principles*, but that when art and language are properly understood it will be seen that they are the same. In other words, we should not think of art and language as if they were distinct, but commonly of course we do think just this.

What this shows is not that Collingwood is wrong but that philosophy corrects or revises common understanding, that philosophy has more to tell us than is to be had in the immediate deliverances of common sense. It is Collingwood's teaching here then that there is an identity where we had not imagined there to be one.

We can now see why the consideration of Collingwood's aesthetics cannot be the question of whether he or his critics are right in this or that particular point, but that what is at issue is the entire question of philosophical method. For Collingwood's aesthetics contains theses which nobody could propound by confining himself to an exposition of the logical implications of concepts, the logical facts as it were, without venturing to consider what we can or should mean by the concept under investigation. This account of Collingwood, however, will not appeal to those who believe that a philosopher has no business to explain what the understanding of a concept in its proper sense consists in. For my defence of Collingwood against the criticism that he was wrong to identify art and language rests upon the assumption that it is legitimate to distinguish between, on the one hand, the proper understanding of a concept, and on the other, the understanding of a proper concept. Philosophy as analysis which does not disturb, change or reconstruct the object of analysis opts for the first, Collingwood for the second.

It may be denied that there is any difference here, and asserted that the proper understanding of a concept achieved in philosophical analysis is the same as understanding the concept in its 'proper version'. But I do not think so; for one thing, that I have to resort to scare quotes in talking about the 'proper version of a concept' suggests that the second is going beyond the first by seeking to say something that cannot ordinarily be said, and that therefore there is a difference here. The fact that talk about the 'proper version of the concept', e.g. of art, would worry the Wittgensteinians in aesthetics but not Collingwood, is the very point that must be brought into the open and not foreclosed by the charge that Collingwood is an essentialist. To make that charge is to employ a blocking mechanism against hearing his case. And this case is predicated upon the assumption that philosophy teaches understanding and knowledge through its own methods of systematic inquiry.

How then does analysis of a concept differ from the analysis of a 'concept-proper'? First, analysis of the first kind will not set restrictions on what is to count as art, that is to say, on what art properly is. Defenders of this sort of analysis will think that Collingwood's attending not merely to concepts but to concepts 'in their proper form' violates the philosopher's neutrality regarding questions of substance. Philosophy, as Collingwood practises it, constitutes a substantial addition to or enlargement of our knowledge. So far as aesthetics goes, this means for instance that Collingwood gives the grounds on which our beliefs or judgements about the work of a particular person with apparent claim to the title of artist, say Kipling or Shaw, are correct or incorrect beliefs or judgements.

Secondly, that there is a difference between the analysis of a concept and the analysis of the 'concept-proper' can be illustrated in aesthetics by appeal to those accounts of the concept of art which have recently been gathered under the banner of the 'institutional theory of art'.[7] These proceed without first, or indeed ever, telling us what 'art' ought to mean or what it properly means; for unlike Collingwood's, the account which the institutional theory gives of art is not normative in character. The 'institutionalists', following the Wittgensteinians in aesthetics on this point, purport to tell us how the term 'art' is used; Collingwood tells us how it ought to be used. In explaining what art properly is, he is constructing an account of art, and not, as it were, neutrally reporting from the scene of its usage without making any interventions or judgements of his own. If it is said against Collingwood that this represents an improper use of philosophy because philosophy has no right to intervene in this manner and make a difference to our judgement of substantial questions, then this view of philosophy, from which Collingwood's aesthetics is being criticized, is itself maintaining a view of what the proper task of philosophy is.

## V

If my account is so far correct, it follows that Collingwood cannot be criticized for exercising judgement since no party to the question of how a philosophical account of art is to be undertaken can escape the obligation to exercise judgement *somewhere* on the question of what is proper. We must either propound what philosophy *properly is*, namely (against Collingwood) that philosophy is the normatively neutral analysis of concepts, or (with Collingwood) we must undertake to give an account of what '*art proper*' is. So the question of what is proper appears on one side or other of the equation. Or to put the point another way, the belief that philosophy is the normatively neutral analysis of concepts, that it would be wrong not to undertake normatively neutral analyses of concepts, is itself no less a normative commitment than Collingwood's belief that we should be tackling the question of '*art proper*'.

Philosophy for Collingwood is reflective, or as he calls it, 'thought of the second degree'(IH,1). By this he means that philosophy is thought about thought; in other words, philosophy never simply thinks about an object but also thinks about its thought about that object. In aesthetics this becomes the question of what exactly we are doing when we purport to say what the character of art is. Working out his account of philosophy in relation to history, Collingwood says that philosophy thinks about thought and its object in 'their mutual relation. Thought in its relation to its object *is not mere thought but knowledge*' (IH, 1–2). For the philosopher of history the question is 'How do historians know?' (IH, 3). Notice the emphasis here on 'how' rather than 'what'. Thus for Collingwood a crucial question falling within the ambit of the broader question, what is art?, is the question, *how do artists know that what they are creating is a work of art?* What I am creating may fail to be a work of art, for there is here the possibility of failure, error or delusion. It is the possibility that a claim to apparent arthood may be mistaken that aesthetics as Wittgensteinian analysis has turned its back on in recent years.

The view of philosophy which I am now placing in opposition to Collingwood's is that philosophy is a second-order activity devoted to expounding meanings held to be already implicit in words or concepts (the Wittgensteinians in aesthetics tend to identify these), which themselves are taken as given, taken as the unproblematic point of departure. The analysis is to begin without any reconstitution of the concept to be analysed. Moore's account of 'good' in *Principia Ethica* is an example of this. Moore offers an account of course of what he thinks goodness is when it is *properly* understood, but he is, as it were, *reporting* what goodness is when it is carefully thought about in philosophy; but this is not to analyse 'good' in the sense selected by the philosopher as being the proper sense of 'good'. It is 'good' in the ordinary sense, which, as a result of being subjected to philosophical analysis by Moore, is discovered by him to be the name of a 'non-natural property'. It is not that 'good' in a sense preselected by Moore to be the proper sense of 'good' is that sense of 'good' which designates the so-called 'non-natural property', leaving any other sense of 'good' there may be to fall outside the scope of the analysis or to be rejected as improper uses. For in Moore-type analysis there seem to be no proper or improper uses of concepts, just uses.

One way in which philosophy may be critical, however, is by not beginning from what it presumes to be the given, but to exercise some thought or judgement about what it will accept as the given. Here lies a major difference between what used to be called 'ordinary-language philosophy', which is pertinent here because its interdict on definition in aesthetics *still* holds, and Collingwood's approach to philosophy.

The moral of this is that we should inquire into what Collingwood thinks definition in philosophy is. This we can do best by turning to his *Essay on Philosophical Method*. Collingwood points out here that in mathematics 'definition' carries a special meaning. It is this: 'A person possessing a definition knows the essence of the concept perfectly, one who does not possess it does not know that essence at all'. For in order to know the essence of a concept, this must be something capable of final and exhaustive statement, and an equally sharp distinction must be drawn between knowing something and not knowing it. 'A definition in exact science', Collingwood says, 'states the essence as distinct from the properties; these, which flow logically from the essence, are stated in theorems. The exposition of the concept. . . thus consists of definition and theorems taken together' (EPM, 94). It is because art cannot be defined in this sense that philosophers such as Kennick have asserted that aestheticians, including Collingwood, were mistaken in their attempts to define art. Collingwood made no such mistake, for he pointed out not only that definitions in philosophy do not have that essentialist character which Wittgensteinians have found so offensive, but he went on to characterize what character definitions in philosophy, including I take it the definition of art in aesthetics, must have.

Suppose then a kind of concept, Collingwood says, which cannot be expounded as are exact concepts where we can make a distinction between definition and theorems; suppose rather:

> a kind of concept in expounding which the later part of the exposition, instead of depending upon the earlier as upon a fixed point, serves to qualify or explain the earlier. In the case of such a concept no line could be drawn between definition and theorems; the entire exposition would be a statement at once of its essence, and of its properties regarded as the elements constituting that essence. This would be a definition, for it would state the essence; the concept would remain undefined only in the sense that there would be no one phrase or sentence which could be taken out of its context and called the definition. (EPM, 95)

This, Collingwood says, is the case with philosophy:

> An essay on a philosophical concept like justice does not ordinarily begin with a definition of the concept and go on by deducing theorems about it; it consists from beginning to end of an attempt to expound the concept in a statement which may properly be described as an extended and reasoned definition. (EPM, 95–6)

Collingwood's philosophical exposition of concepts, unlike Moore-type conceptual analysis, offers substantial insights that are unavailable to a method of analysis alone. This claim will create suspicion in the minds of those who believe that philosophy should contain no theses or knowledge-claims, but it would be premature to rule for or against this view of philosophy without first giving a hearing to what Collingwood thinks the nature of philosophical knowledge is. We already know negatively from what has been said above about the essences of concepts (and also from specific doctrines of Collingwood's which are beyond the scope of this essay, such as that of the overlap of classes), that philosophical knowledge must for example be distinguished from, and not confounded with, scientific knowledge. Of course a philosophy that recognized only scientific knowledge to be knowledge, as did the Positivism to which Collingwood was opposed, would have to deny the validity of itself as knowledge. But that is not Collingwood's problem.

## VI

Collingwood's exposition of the concept of art includes an account of what uses of the term 'art' are *improper* uses, so that he differs from the Wittgensteinians not only in envisaging more forms of definition than they do but also in having a broader theory of meaning. He maintains that 'art' is used improperly, for example, when it is used in its obsolete and in its courtesy meanings. The Wittgensteinian aestheticians work with the single idea of meaning as use, or perhaps after all with two ideas, the second being that meaning is not to be identified with naming. Collingwood thinks, however, not only that the term 'art' may be used in various ways but also that it may be misused. To rephrase Collingwood's position in Wittgensteinian terms,[8] Collingwood holds that not all language-games in which the term 'art' occurs are games which should be played:

> The proper meaning of a word . . . is never something upon which the word sits perched like a gull on a stone; it is something over which the word hovers like a gull over a ship's stern. Trying to fix the proper meaning in our minds is like coaxing the gull to settle in the rigging, with the rule that the gull must be alive when it settles: one must not shoot it and tie it there. The way to discover the proper meaning is to ask not, 'What do we mean?' but, 'What are we trying to mean?' and this involves the question 'What is preventing us from meaning what we are trying to mean?' These impediments, the improper meanings which distract our minds from the proper one, are of three kinds. I shall call them obsolete meanings, analogical meanings, and courtesy meanings. (PA, 7)

It is a notable feature of current theories in aesthetics of art that nothing is ruled out as being an improper use of the term 'art'; thus the institutional theory of art is hospitable to all that professes to be art. No phenomenon appears in principle to be excludable. Hence all the fuss in recent years about objects ever more outré offered to the public as works of art such as Carl Andre's firebricks. Here aesthetic theory and the art world unite (or is it conspire?) in their refusal to draw limits to what can count as art.

## VII

A further philosophical difference between Collingwood and the 'ordinary-language Wittgensteinians', who argued that theories of art of Collingwood's kind are impossible, is that for Collingwood philosophical analysis has two stages, not one. Kennick's approach is to ask how the term 'art' is used in the language, and one of the permanent gains of this approach is the discovery that people do not apply the term 'art' under the guidance of a rule learned from some theory of art. But this does not show that every use of the term 'art' is unproblematic and must be allowed its voice in setting the boundaries of aesthetic theory. Rather, we must, Collingwood says, first settle a definite usage for the term 'art', and then secondly proceed to a definition of it. In short, for Collingwood questions of usage and questions of definition are distinct. It is the tantamount denial by the Wittgensteinians in aesthetics of this general philosophical claim which results in Collingwood's theory of art getting dismissed as mistaken or impossible without its ever seeming necessary for contemporary aesthetics to get down to the specific question of what *art* is, or for that matter, to the question of what the proper nature and method of *philosophy* are. The first stage in Collingwood's programme of philosophical analysis is what first he calls 'questions of usage' and later in *The Principles of Art* 'questions of fact'. About these he talks in the manner of Wittgenstein about assembling reminders about what we all know about art; in this first stage, 'We shall be trying as best we can to remind ourselves of facts well known to us all' (PA, 105). But this is not the end of the story, though for aestheticians such as Kennick evidently it does seem to be precisely that.

Collingwood may well agree with Kennick that as speakers of English we know how to use the term 'art';[9] but we might still not know 'to what theory concerning the thing so designated this application might commit us' (PA, 273). It is here in talk of designation rather than in talk of common properties, that if there is an essentialist fallacy, Collingwood may be caught committing it. For the so-called essentialist fallacy is in fact a compound of two beliefs, not one, for one shouldn't be too essentialist about the fallacy. The first mistaken belief is that a substantive term denotes in virtue of a property shared by all its instances and only its instances. The second belief is that the said substantive can only be meaningful because it designates or names. One does not therefore find Collingwood unequivocally committing the fallacy, even if one granted that there is any error here, because his view seems to be that 'art proper' designates or names not a property which works of art share (because for one thing works of art on Collingwood's view are not things that can share properties) but rather 'art proper' designates that complex and corporate activity undertaken by artists and audiences in a reciprocal relationship which is described at length in *The Principles of Art*. There is no attachment to the idea of common properties in Collingwood, then. As for the second idea that the Wittgensteinian anti-essentialists find objectionable, namely the false belief that meaning must be designative in character, this is implicitly criticized by Collingwood himself when he criticizes the belief that a child learns what 'hat', say, means by learning what it names (PA, 227, 228).

In any case the idea that meaning is designation is a venial mistake when made about 'art proper', for 'art proper' is a technical term. (And of technical terms, which are not words in a living language, Collingwood says, 'kindly godparents furnish [them] soon after birth with neat and tidy definitions' (PA, 7).) 'Art proper' is invented, as it were, precisely to be designative, to call attention to that aspect of our engagement with works of art without which art would have no interest or significance, and which the whole of *The Principles of Art* is devoted to elucidating.

Collingwood is interested, then, in the question, why is art important to us? The anti-essentialists in aesthetics on the other hand are interested in the question, what are we doing when we use the term 'art'? These are by no means the same question. Collingwood's interest leads him into a theory about what makes emotion expressed in art truthful. Interest in the second question, however, leads to the sort of case imagined by Kennick in which a person pointlessly and mindlessly is instructed to remove works of art from a warehouse where they are stored with all manner of junk. The person's success in separating works of art from other objects in the warehouse is held to demonstrate his grasp of the concept of art. But *what* concept does success in this curious exercise show him to have grasped?[10]

## Notes

¹ By E. F. Carritt in the October 1938 number of *Philosophy* (X, 52, 492). At the end of an intelligent and interesting review, which deserves to be better known, Carritt speaks of *The Principles of Art* as 'perhaps the most serious attempt at a philosophy of art in our language'.
² In other words, Collingwood is held to have committed the so-called 'essentialist fallacy' which all readers of paragraphs 65 and 66 of the *Philosophical Investigations* know to be a mistake. For a criticism of Collingwood on these grounds see William E. Kennick, 'Does Traditional Aesthetics Rest on a Mistake?', *Mind*, LXVII (July 1958).
³ See Kennick, 'Does Traditional Aesthetics Rest on a Mistake?' and Bernard Harrison, 'Some Uses of "Good" in Criticism', *Mind*, LXIX (April 1960).
⁴ Peter G. Ingram, 'Art, Language and Community in Collingwood's *Principles of Art*', *Journal of Aesthetics and Art Criticism*, XXXVII, No. 1 (Fall 1978).
⁵ Richard Wollheim, *Art and Its Objects: an Introduction to Aesthetics* (New York, Harper and Row, 1968), §23.
⁶ Notwithstanding the fact that Collingwood is no follower of Wittgenstein's, there is, as is well known, some strikingly common ground between Collingwood and Wittgenstein: for example in the attacks both philosophers mount on the idea that ostensive definition is the foundation of meaning, is the means by which words latch on to the world, and that language is acquired and its meaning understood through ostension.
⁷ A large literature has gathered under the 'institutional theory of art'. Prominent in this is the work of George Dickie, who defines 'a work of art' thus: 'a work of art in the classificatory sense is (1) an artifact (2) a set of the aspects of which has had conferred upon it the status of candidate for appreciation by some person or persons acting on behalf of a certain social institution (the art world)' (*Art and the Aesthetic: an Institutional Analysis* (Ithaca, Cornell University Press, 1974), 34). Also see my article 'The Republic of Art', *British Journal of Aesthetics*, 9, 2 (April 1969).The institutional theory of art is an example of a philosophical analysis of a concept which is not an analysis of that 'concept proper', and which does not offer a normative account of the concept of art. This is not surprising since it was developed specifically to take account of Wittgensteinian-inspired criticisms of normative theories such as Collingwood's was held to be. There is nothing in principle that is ruled out from the domain of art by the institutional theory of art, whereas on a theory such as Collingwood's the apparent claims of many works to be works of art do not survive the criticism made against them on the basis of the theory.

8 Though Collingwood warns that use of 'a special "philosophical language" commits the user, possibly even against his will, to accepting the philosophical doctrines which it has been designed to express' (PA, 174).
9 Although according to Collingwood we speak some words not as speakers of English but as civilized Europeans: 'The word [beauty] does not belong to the English language as such, but to the common speech of European civilization (le beau, il bello, bellum; . . .)' (PA 37). And later a similar point is made about 'expressive' and 'imaginative': 'we might know how to apply them (that being a question of usage, or ability to speak not so much English as the common tongue of European peoples) . . .' (PA, 273).
10 For a further discussion of this case see my 'Essentialism and the Definition of "Art" ', *British Journal of Aesthetics*, 13 (1973).

# Faith and Reason in the Philosophy of Religion

## D. M. MacKINNON

Collingwood was a man of something very near genius. But it was genius of a kind that sometimes showed itself most clearly in the brilliant ideas thrown out with dazzling rapidity in the course of essays and articles focused on quite different subjects. He never wrote (apart from the very early *Religion and Philosophy*) a sustained treatise on the philosophy of religion to compare with the later works on method, on politics, on aesthetics, on metaphysics, on nature and on history. Certainly these works are of a different date, and some of them, especially the last, betray signs of great differences in mood as well as in date of composition. But to glean his mind on the nature, in particular, of faith, one has to turn to occasional papers, and in the light of them, go back to the major treatises and extract from them confirmation and redefinition of the views suggested as the writer's own.

It is legitimate to begin by remarking that in his *Autobiography* published in 1939, there is nothing directly to suggest the deep concern with religious belief manifested across the years in many writings, and in lectures, for instance in those on ethics given in the autumn of 1933, and in the version of the later-published *Idea of Nature* delivered a year later, which concluded with the exposition of theological cosmology. In his 1933 course on moral philosophy, the last lecture had dealt quite explicitly with the theme of grace and freedom, with the quotation towards its end of Luther's words: *Dann ich stehe, ich kann nicht anders, so helfe mir*

*Gott*. At such a human climax we had to reckon with an action that, to the agent, seemed determined and inescapable, yet at the same time was altogether his own. But in the *Essay on Metaphysics*, which followed in 1940 the *Autobiography* at less than a year's interval, he returned explicitly to the theme of faith in such a way that some commentators (e.g. his editor, the late Sir Malcolm Knox) found the views it contained anticipated in a pamphlet on *Faith and Reason*, published in 1928 in a series entitled: *Affirmations* (Ernest Benn), explicitly subtitled, *A Study of the Relations of Science and Religion*. This pamphlet had followed an essay, published in the *Hibbert Journal* for 1927 (pp.3–13) entitled: 'Reason is Faith Cultivating Itself', from which in some respects it quite sharply differs. And here one encounters one of the difficulties attending any attempt to define Collingwood's contribution to the philosophy of religion. Although he could write superbly (and his successor in the Waynflete chair at Oxford, Professor Gilbert Ryle, in his own inaugural lecture in 1945 praised his style very highly), he wrote often at speed and disregarded his previous, even quite recent, treatment of the same topic. A glaring instance of this disregard is found in the *Autobiography* when, in the course of his polemic against 'Realism', he denigrated the work of the Oxford philosopher, H. W. B. Joseph, to whose 'great little book' (Collingwood's own words), *Some Problems in Ethics* (1930), he had paid a glowing tribute in the lectures on moral philosophy in 1933. Six years later Joseph's seeming indifference to historical relativity made him a suitable subject for contemptuous dismissal, as one whose philosophical style was narrowly eristic, and who had ended by accepting the metaphysical doctrine of Plato's 'middle dialogues' as substantially true.

The article in the *Hibbert Journal* for 1927 is in my judgement one of Collingwood's most valuable explicit contributions to the philosophy of religion, and I propose to devote some time to analysing it. The first paragraph emphasizes the sharp difference between *pistis* as understood in the New Testament, and the *pistis monimos* mentioned by Plato in the 'divided line' in *Republic* VI. The latter is, for Plato, a *pis aller*, its objects the 'chairs and tables, animals and men' of everyday life, ontologically inferior to the paradigmatic forms on which they depend, themselves to be grasped by pure intellection. And for all the great differences between Plato and Aristotle, Collingwood found a comparable emphasis in the latter.

With Christianity we find 'added to Greek thought — the idea of a higher kind of knowledge, a knowledge in which we apprehend not the finite, but the infinite, not nature but spirit, not the world but God': 'Reason is Faith Cultivating Itself' (p. 5). And this knowledge is called faith. This statement is followed by a paragraph in which boldly and to some extent dismissively, Collingwood contrasts Christianity with neo-Platonism, while emphasizing that both alike sought to satisfy needs left unfulfilled by the intellectual traditions of classical Greek philosophy. His scholarship is cavalier; but he pinpoints the irruptive force of Pauline and Johannine Christianity as they were received in the Hellenistic world of the first centuries of our era.

Collingwood then turns to medieval thought, and in particular to Anselm. Like his very different German Swiss contemporary, Karl Barth, Collingwood remains fascinated by the achievement of that great medieval master. 'Anselm', he writes ('Reason is Faith Cultivating Itself', 7), 'searching for a proof of God's existence that should be absolutely convincing, discerned one which convinced only a person who already believed in God; and the strange thing is that when this was pointed out to him, he does not appear to have been in the least disconcerted.' And in these words Collingwood shows the source of his own later engagement with the ontological argument, the subject of his controversy in 1935 with Mr (later Professor) Gilbert Ryle – a controversy that was at once sterile and extremely illuminating.

With a brief reference to later medieval debate concerning the relations of faith and reason, Collingwood vaults the centuries to Descartes to find in the *Cogito* 'a point in which faith and reason absolutely coincide'. So he continues, 'Reason itself is henceforth seen to depend for its cogency on that immediate and indemonstrable certainty which is faith' ('Reason is Faith Cultivating Itself'). And Kant only takes Descartes further when he makes God, freedom and immortality 'truths of which life itself, all life, not this or that form of experience, assures us'. So indeed one of the great critics of the ontological argument, classically formulated by Anselm, 'abolishing knowledge to make room for faith', bade men and women find in their 'universal and necessary experience' of every day their own 'responsibility and spontaneity', their 'timeless and eternal reality' and 'the existence of an infinite mind upon which our own finite nature somehow depends'. Collingwood characterizes these certainties as being 'of precisely the same kind as Descartes' "cogito ergo sum" '. But if faith is as Kant conceives it, how does it come about that anyone is without it? Here Collingwood makes an important distinction between being certain, and recognizing by reflection that one is certain. Here again the Cartesian *Cogito* is the paradigm. For *fides quaerens intellectum*, we have to substitute a faith that achieves self-conscious possession of its own reality. Yet while acknowledging Kant's work as supremely significant (six years later in the *Essay on Philosophical Method*, Collingwood is to speak of him as 'bestriding the world (of philosophy) like a Colossus'), he goes on to speak of the interplay of faith and reason in a style that is very much his own. Speaking of characteristically religious faith, he suddenly states that 'in Kant and his successors the doctrine of the Trinity becomes a demonstrable and almost fertile logical principle.' Here obviously he is thinking of the Hegelian as distinct from the very different Kantian dialectic. But he concludes with reference again to Anselm; he suggests that from *fides quaerens intellectum* which issues into faith's effort to achieve, through reflection, awareness of its own reality, there will emerge a new understanding of reason as 'faith cultivating itself'.

The article has all Collingwood's brilliance, and reveals his astonishingly wide philosophical culture. Although in the *Autobiography* he pleads the cause of a proper study of the history of philosophy, his own approach to its study remained brilliantly impressionistic. The pages on Kant that I have just considered display remarkable intuitive perception; they raise the question why one of the most drastic critics of the ontological argument shared with its classical medieval exponent an understanding of the relations of faith and reason (the latter term is here used less restrictively than in the context of Kant's Dialectic) curiously akin to Anselm's own. For as Koyré[1] has pointed out, Anselm wrote for his monks in Bec whose faith had been undermined or threatened by the words of the atheists who said in their hearts that God was not. Rather Anselm bade those monks in the *Proslogion* so to conceive God that to deny his existence was to plunge into formal self-contradiction. He sought brilliantly to marry faith and logic by showing that the existence of the One whom his monks praised daily in the sevenfold 'divine office' (the *Opus Dei*) was guaranteed as totally invulnerable to sceptical question inasmuch as his existence could only be denied by an act destructive of the very possibility of rational argument. The inspirational boldness of the enterprise is fascinating; but Anselm does not succeed, or is he prevented from establishing the existence *in re* of *id quo nihil maius cogitari potest* by the logical mistake of treating existence as a characteristic? And here immediately one recalls Collingwood's controversy with Ryle. Professor Lionel Rubinoff[2] has given an account of this controversy which includes extensive quotations from a letter Collingwood sent to Ryle on 9 May 1935, following the appearance of Ryle's article 'Mr Collingwood and the Ontological Argument' in *Mind* for April of that year. Ryle's polemic was of course directed against the account of the ontological argument contained in Collingwood's *Essay on Philosophical Method*, published two years before. But the thrust of Ryle's argument is clear: to accept the ontological argument involves treating existence as a predicate, and failing to recognize that to say e.g. of tame tigers that they exist is something of a different order from saying that they growl. If we affirm that they exist, we are saying that the complex concept of tame-tigerhood is exemplified; we are not characterizing them as we are when we say that they growl. It is impossible to escape the conviction that Ryle is right and that the ontological argument is invalid inasmuch as it obliterates the distinction between characterization and affirmation of reality. Existence is not a characteristic and must not be treated as such.

And yet when one returns to Collingwood's article of 1927, aware that not only Kant, Frege, Russell and Ryle but also Aquinas himself have laid their axes to the argument's tree, one is perplexed – especially when one notes that Kant's *point de départ* is curiously akin to a secularized transcript of that of Anselm's work. Kant certainly saw that this point of departure needed to be secured against destruction by the sort of argumentation he judged to be fatal to much traditional metaphysics. A proper understanding of the complementarity of *Anschauung* and *Verstand* in knowledge of the world around us also imposes upon us acceptance that the categories which make its achievement secure, at the same time bar us from any extension of their role in scaling the heights of the transcendent. Both ontological (and cosmological) proofs of God's existence fail.³ Yet the logically fallacious character of the former at least built on the confused recognition that divine reality must be self-authenticating. And it was of course with the nature of that self-authentication that Collingwood engaged in the article in the *Hibbert Journal* more effectively than in the brilliantly written *Essay on Philosophical Method*.

But in what way did the attention which this theme received in his later writings extract its substance from entanglement in the logical fallacy pinpointed by Ryle? The essay on *Faith and Reason* that quickly followed the article in the *Hibbert Journal* anticipated some of the themes taken up in the *Essay on Metaphysics*; in fact it formed a bridge between the *Hibbert Journal* article and that book. Yet before he published the *Essay* Collingwood had published his brilliant, bitter *Autobiography*, showing that he saw his task as that of bridging the gulf between philosophy and history, attacking many of his immediate predecessors and contemporaries in Oxford for ignoring the range of issues he had opened up in his inaugural lecture as Waynflete Professor in the autumn of 1935, when he had spoken on the historical imagination. His polemic seemed to take for granted a more or less thoroughgoing historical relativism, where the history of philosophy was concerned; but this relativism was defended by way of a frequently effective attack on the school of John Cook-Wilson as historically philistine and incapable of the empathetic effort required to master a classical philosophical text, whether Aristotle's *De Anima* (on which Collingwood had lectured) or Kant's *Critique of Pure Reason*. The logic of question and answer was defended by reference to Collingwood's experience as a working archaeologist; and that experience is also reflected in the accolade he bestowed as an historian on the brilliant student of seventh-century Greek history, Alan Blakeway, whose premature death as acting head of the British School of Athens in the autumn of 1936, had been a most grievous loss to the study of Greek history, especially where archaeological materials could be used to complement the exiguous literary sources. Archaeology was for Collingwood the way into history, and methodological reflections extracted from his field experience were used to help define the historian's proper procedure.

The 'Absolute Presuppositions' that it is the proper task of the metaphysician to define provide the frame of reference for the natural scientist every bit as much as the historian; they help frame the questions the investigator must answer and the ways in which he must seek the conclusions that are his goal. Whether in laboratory, in library, or on a 'dig', we are in creative bondage to assumptions the metaphysician will help us bring into self-conscious awareness, although in the *Essay* Collingwood confines himself to natural science. Even in this summary account of the *Autobiography* and *Essay*, one can catch certain clear echoes of the earlier explicit treatment of the relations of faith and reason: this is so despite the fact that the human sensitivity with which in the *Hibbert Journal* article Collingwood had virtually identified the world of faith with that of the experience of life as it is lived, seems virtually gone. This no doubt is *partly* due to Collingwood's nearly obsessive concentration in his later years on problems of historical method and his tendency to identify philosophical insight with heightened historical self-consciousness.

Professor Rubinoff effectively concludes his excellent book with a long quotation[4] from the final pages of Collingwood's early work – *Speculum Mentis*. In the concluding sentence of this quotation, we read: 'It is God who accepts the burden of error, takes upon himself the moral responsibility for the fall, and so redeems not his creatures but himself' (SM, 303). Here the reference in Hegelian style to the doctrines of the Incarnation and Trinity is clear enough. Again one is reminded of the conclusion of the article on reason as faith cultivating itself. But if faith as Collingwood conceived it finds its ultimate religious definition in Christianity, what of the historical commitment of that faith? What indeed of the problem of the historical Jesus, what of the significance for Collingwood of that great controversy, belonging chronologically to his formative years, between Professor Adolf von Harnack and the Abbé Alfred Loisy? One is tempted to say that for Collingwood, Loisy in *L'Évangile et L'Église* was more nearly a kindred spirit than the learned Berlin Protestant study of Christian origins. What is certainly true is that contemporary writers on the foundations and nature of Christian belief are quick to exploit Collingwood's historical relativism in the interests of a Bultmannian programme of 'demythologization'. Certainly in Collingwood's own writing (for instance in the passage from

*Speculum Mentis* quoted above) one can discern the influence of post-Kantian Idealism for which Jesus' way from Galilee to Jerusalem to Galilee, from life to death to resurrection was a transcript into terms of individual biography of Spirit's recovery of itself: the *Noli me tangere* of Christ to Mary Magdalene emerges as an effective parable of *Aufhebung*. But we have to reckon with the fact that Collingwood attributed to the Christian movement, and by implication to the ministry of Jesus, an explosive intellectual force that was hardly consonant with this sort of diminution of its earthly reality into an acted parable of intellectual reconciliation. One recalls here not only the sharply Kantian orientation of the *Hibbert Journal* article (and between Kant and Hegel a great gulf is surely fixed), but also the *Marxist* tendency not only of the conclusion of the *Autobiography*, but of parts of the unfinished *Principles of History*.

Here again it is the confused, unfinished character of Collingwood's work that daunts any attempt to define in summary terms his contribution to the philosophy of religion. His admiration for Bradley's essay on the presuppositions of critical history,[5] and his often brilliant comments on historical writing and methodology, show that he had it in him to contribute signally to the understanding of hermeneutic activity. But his very sense of the importance of such work (e.g. its crucial significance for the history of philosophy, on which occasionally he could write with a sharpness of perception rivalled only by A. N. Whitehead, whose work he highly esteemed) became obscured by his eagerness to establish clear canons of historical method. Yet his comments, for instance, on Berkeley's criticism of 'the bifurcation of nature' to be found in *Speculum Mentis*, and (in slightly different form) in the *Idea of Nature* show how he had it in him to combine a historically sensitive appreciation of the *Sitz im Leben* of a classical philosophical text with the power to extract lessons of permanent philosophical significance from that appreciation. It is as if the metaphysician (to extend that term to include the philosophically oriented student of the history of philosophy) was at war with the historian in Collingwood's mind, proving in the end incapable of resistance to the latter's claim to sovereign dominion. And the *Essay on Metaphysics* (in spite of the reference to the history of theology) is mainly, though not entirely, the monument to the latter's triumph.

Yet on that work two comments must be made. Collingwood differentiates the nature of the modern metaphysician's concern with 'Absolute Presuppositions' from the concern of traditional Aristotelian ontology with being *qua* being. Now he might have made his meaning clearer if he had recalled explicitly that Aristotle regarded the object of the metaphysician's concern as definable either as being *qua* being or as substance, the latter because it was for him the nuclear, axial realization of being to which quality, accident and the rest were relative. In a perceptive comment in his monograph on Hegel,[6] the British Idealist, Edward Caird, suggested that with Kant, and still more with Hegel, subject had replaced substance as the pivotal focus of the metaphysician's concern. For Collingwood it is the subject who frames the absolute presuppositions as painfully distinguished from propositions, hypotheses etc.: it is the subject who has to undergo the intellectually testing experience of the substitution of one set of such presuppositions for another. Had Collingwood the historian attended more closely to the detail of such substitutions, he might have enlarged at this point his sensitivity to the subject's experience to the point of reaching out towards the way in which he conceived that experience in the more Kantian style of the *Hibbert Journal* article of 1927. For the substitution of one set of presuppositions for another, or the rendering of a set of presuppositions internally consistent with itself, is something that needs to be conceived in a less restrictedly intellectualist style than Collingwood allows in the *Essay on Metaphysics*: it belongs to the world of *fides quaerens intellectum* as Collingwood recharted that world in his own writing.

Secondly, what the student of the *Essay on Metaphysics* notices is the extent to which Collingwood restricts himself there to the discussion of revolutions in natural science. This concentration is focused on the treatment of Kant's deep commitment to the Newtonian mechanical view of the world, and more generally on the treatment of the notion of causality. And here the reference should be made to the more effective presentation of his views on this notion given in a paper to the Aristotelian Society in 1938. Here he has high praise for Russell's well-known paper 'On the notion of cause',[7] and shows himself impressively sensitive to the insights to be extracted from some of its more violent paradoxes. Collingwood sometimes seems nearly obsessed by the adherence of philosophers to old-fashioned styles of illustration in discussing such notions as thing, cause, event etc. as if the Newtonian world-model remained authoritative. If he seems in the *Essay* naturally intellectualist, he is splendidly alert by implication to the need to take stock, at the deepest level, of the revolutions touching our conception of the most elementary yet pervasive features of our total environment – space, time, thinghood, causality, motion and the rest. He saw philosophers as in bondage to conceptions which were obsolete despite their being deeply embedded in the language of every day. He therefore regarded them as incapable of renewing effectively for their own age the kind of deeply critical appreciation of the human significance of the changes taking place, which had been achieved in the eighteenth century by such men as Leibniz, Berkeley and Kant. And here from the at first surprising concentration of the *Essay on Metaphysics* we can extract lessons highly significant for the kind of tasks that confront us as human beings under the sun.

No one who spoke as Collingwood did in the concluding lecture of his course on moral philosophy in the autumn of 1933 could be judged indifferent to the significance of religious experience at its most demandingly paradoxical. Yet as I have said, from his writings it is hard to extract an easily definable philosophy of religion. It is not simply that there is no work in his later period corresponding to the *Principles of Art* or even the unfinished *Principles of History*, treating of religion; it is rather that there are often hardly compatible references to fundamental problems in this area across the years, focused initially less in the very early *Religion and Philosophy* than in the two articles of 1927 and 1928, and in the elusive affirmation of the ontological argument, traceable in the 1935 controversy with Gilbert Ryle. At first sight it seems very strange that a philosopher attracted to a degree of historical relativism should combine with this a readiness to learn from Kant, and still more a deep commitment to what he saw as the core of the so-called ontological proof. But if it seems strange, it may also prove extremely suggestive, and demanding an interpretation that goes beyond the mere recognition of inconsistency. To that interpretation there is surely a key in Collingwood's repeated adherence to the Anselmian rubric *fides quaerens intellectum*.

Whitehead, whom Collingwood greatly admired, remarked that

in the history of metaphysics the modern period was marked by successive attempts to find a substitute for substance, the pivotal notion of the classical Aristotelian ontology. Reference was made above to Edward Caird's suggestive comment that with Kant and Hegel subject had usurped this role. Certainly in Kant substance emerges as one of the three categories of relation (along with causality and reciprocity), whereby the subject is enabled to establish the kind of permanent background necessary for the apprehension of objective change. It is an indispensable condition of the possibility of objective awareness; but it is established as valid only as such. In other words, its significance lies in the context of the subject's active experience.

Collingwood began his *Essay on Metaphysics* with a sharply polemical attack on the classical ontology, and it has been remarked that the presentation does less justice to the theme than the references to the same conceptions in the earlier *Essay on Philosophical Method.* Thus he had nothing to say in *Metaphysics* on Aristotle's insistence that being is analogical. But the Idealist emphasis is clearly discernible, and also the author's awareness that those belonging to that tradition were from one point of view, activating a style of philosophizing that had its source in Augustine and Anselm, and that Kant himself 'bestrode the world like a Colossus' because he had given to this style a new cutting edge. For all the datedness of e.g. his views of causality, he set the subject's experience at the centre, and if he rejected the logic of the ontological argument, he none the less responded to its fundamental impulse – the reach towards the transcendent out of experience.

Collingwood never lived to integrate this underlying commitment of his mind either with his *Naturphilosophie* or with his intense and besetting preoccupation with the problems of historical method. But the 1935 controversy between himself and Ryle (to succeed him in the Waynflete chair ten years later) remains significant inasmuch as it was at the centre of Collingwood's achievement in the philosophy of religion, to pinpoint again the religious and metaphysical impulses behind the confusions of the ontological argument.

One is reminded of Bradley's insistence that the rejection of the religious consciousness as inauthentic is something totally inadmissible.[8] It is also worth recalling here the long paper in which

Professor John Cook-Wilson, whose influence on Oxford philosophy Collingwood so fiercely assailed in his *Autobiography*, defended theistic belief.[9] The influence of this paper can be traced in many places, not least in the strong defence of the ontological argument mounted by Professor C. C. J. Webb in his *Problems in the Relation of God and Man*. It was Anselm's genius to have defined the project of marrying faith and logic. It was Bradley's judgement that metaphysics constituted the attempt to find bad reasons for continuing to believe what we have accepted on instinct. Anselm was convinced that his monks' commitment to their God must be rendered inviolable to any sort of contradiction. It is the continuance of this tradition in Collingwood's concern with the ontological argument, at a new level of sophisticated self-consciousness, that gives his work in the philosophy of religion a significant place in his *oeuvre*.

## Notes

[1] Alexandre Koyré: *L'Idée de Dieu dans la philosophie de Saint Anselm*, still in my view one of the most valuable appreciations of the historical *Sitz im Leben* of Anselm's *Proslogion*, my debt to it in this section of my essay will be obvious to anyone who has read it.

[2] Professor Lionel Rubinoff: *Collingwood and the Reform of Metaphysics* (Toronto, University of Toronto Press, 1970), 202ff. Professor Rubinoff's book is one of the most valuable works on Collingwood I have read, and I am very much indebted to it, for all my differences in judgement from him.

[3] Kant regarded the ontological proof as fundamental to the cosmological and physico-theological proofs which he also discussed. In it for him the essence of metaphysical theism was concentrated, possibly because he had learnt from Leibniz that a God about whose existence there was any element of 'perhaps' was a 'not-God'.

[4] Rubinoff, *Collingwood and the Reform of Metaphysics*, 334.

[5] Bultmann himself discussed admiringly Collingwood's *Idea of History* in his Gifford Lectures, *History and Eschatology* (1957). It should be noted that the aspect of Collingwood's work on history that Bultmann himself found most congenial was its discernibly existentialist implications.

[6] In Blackwood's series of philosophical monographs. This impressive monograph is all the more remarkable in that it appeared before there was any knowledge of Hegel's crucially important *Jugendschriften*.

[7] To be found in *Mysticism and Logic* (London, Allen and Unwin, 1963).

[8] The man who demands a reality more solid than that of the religious

consciousness, seeks he does not know what' (*Appearance and Reality* (Oxford, Clarendon Press, 1930), 398).
[9] John Cook-Wilson, *Statement and Inference*, 2 (Oxford, Clarendon Press, 1926), 835–67.

# Art Thou the Man: Croce, Gentile or de Ruggiero?

## JAMES CONNELLY

Collingwood's philosophical work was influenced by, and displayed many affinities with, contemporary Italian philosophy. In what follows I shall explore some of these links, and I shall argue that the real question is that of affinity, not influence, and that the key figure for Collingwood was Guido de Ruggiero.[1] The most obvious starting point for a discussion of these themes is *An Autobiography*; obvious, but problematic. The book is both on the witness stand and in the dock, where it is accused of serious intellectual misrepresentation: it has always attracted adverse critical attention in respect of its accuracy as an account of Collingwood's philosophical development; in particular, the manner in which he covers his relationship with the Italian philosophers Croce, Gentile and de Ruggiero has cast a shadow over opinions of the book. Generally, I submit, there can be little doubt about its veracity, although it is admittedly incomplete. I shall address Collingwood's relation with these Italian philosophers and try to clarify the important affinities, sympathies and influences.

Neither Croce nor Gentile is mentioned by name in the *Autobiography*; de Ruggiero is mentioned only once, as a friend and recipient of '*Libellus de Generatione*'. Responses to the lack of explicit acknowledgement of influence run the gamut from mild puzzlement to the charge of deliberate concealment. Momigliano, for example, comments on 'the amazement of those readers who were aware of Collingwood's dependence on his Italian friends at not seeing this debt acknowledged'. He explained this by Collingwood's tendency to 'an extravagant exaggeration of his own originality'.[2] This charge of concealment is a serious one. Some critics have even gone so far as to assert that the *Autobiography* cannot be what it claims to be, '*un livre de bonne foi*'.[3] If Collingwood deliberately refrained from openly acknowledging an intellectual debt in the service of promoting his own claims to great originality, then the charge of bad faith is hard to escape. But it is unfair to draw any conclusion without first considering the *purpose* of *An Autobiography*.

Collingwood conceived the book as telling what was worth telling of the story of his thought (A, 18);[4] and what he thought worth telling was principally whatever had some bearing on his current intellectual concerns, especially where he had not yet had the opportunity to expound them. He never promised what the critics chided him for ignoring – an account of the influences on his thought. Perhaps he should have written a different sort of book; but he wrote the book he chose to, and its faithfulness to its own declared agenda is not the same as deliberate deception. Certainly there are many things missing, and it is true that Collingwood failed to mention the Italians; but there are many omissions, as one can only expect in a short book of 167 pages which neither claimed to be, nor could ever have been, fully comprehensive. For example, Collingwood scarcely mentions J. A. Smith, and when he does, it is to accuse him of failing to carry the work of the Idealist school forward. There is no glimpse here of his friendship with Smith or of the mischievous side of their character revealed by the comment that 'if you and I are to be fellow conspirators against the minute philosophers we ought, I suppose, to indulge in a certain amount of conspiratorial correspondence.'[5] The significance of the chapter entitled 'Minute Philosophers' would not have been lost on Smith. But in the book Collingwood is in censorious mood, and the Smith he writes of is not 'Dear J. A.' so much as the Smith who (with others) would not publish and 'failed to avert the collapse of the school to which they belonged' (A, 18). At least his friend Joachim had published *The Nature of Truth*; but Smith, despite being an inspiring teacher and a great scholar never published anything of book length, and when he came to deliver his Gifford lectures in 1930 on *The Heritage of Idealism* he 'meandered on, at last broke down altogether, and nothing was published because there was nothing to publish.'[6] A thin heritage indeed, and one which led Collingwood to despair and to censure his friend sharply. Again, Samuel Alexander receives scarcely a mention, and yet the two were friends, correspondents and frank critics of each other's work.[7] When Collingwood required a testimonial for his election to the Waynflete chair in 1935 he turned to Alexander, deriving great amusement from having the support of one of the leading Realists of the day.

Although neglected within its pages, Croce's influence can perhaps be discerned in the form and title of the book. Just over a decade earlier Collingwood translated Croce's *Contributo alla critica di me stesso* under the title *An Autobiography*; his own followed Croce's in being primarily an *intellectual* autobiography: 'The autobiography of a man whose business is thinking should be the story of his thought. I have written this book to tell what I think worth telling about the story of mine' (A, Preface).[8]

This is later supplemented by the remark that its purpose 'is to put on record some brief account of the work I have not yet been able to publish, in case I am not able to publish it in full' (A, 118). This was to be no Russellian interweaving of life, loves and intellectual crises. Croce writes in a similar vein that 'the chronicle of my life, so far as it contains anything worth recording, is contained in the chronology and bibliography of my written works; and since I have taken no part, either as actor or as witness, in events of another kind, I have little or nothing to say of the men I have known or the things I have seen.'[9] It is hard to believe that Collingwood did not have Croce's autobiography in mind in writing his own. Each was written in its author's fiftieth year and at the onset of war. Croce writes in 1915: 'As I write these lines, the war rages around me, and may well involve Italy' (116); Collingwood's was published at the outset of the Second World War. Much of this is no doubt coincidental, as the occasion of writing the *Autobiography* was convalescence from illness, yet I suspect that he seized the opportunity and relished the parallel.

Collingwood's *Autobiography* was notable for its drive, passion and occasional venom: Croce's was rather more sedate; indeed, one critic was moved to ask 'can it be that there is a fundamental aridity in the Philosopher of the Spirit?'[10] But they shared something more important: each was an account of thought, not memoirs; each was written at the same point in its author's life and was a summary of progress to date. Croce begins with the words: 'Having now reached my fiftieth year, I have determined to employ the ideal pause in my spiritual life which that date brings with it in looking back at the road I have traversed, and trying to fix my eyes on what I still have to traverse in the years of work that lie before me.'[11] Collingwood's intention is similar, but with one marked difference: he knew that his life was drawing to a close. In recognition of this he wanted to record in outline what he might not have time to complete and publish in full. This was an issue of the greatest urgency, and it was perhaps this sense of urgency which generated the book's pace and vivacity. Collingwood died less than five years after writing his *Autobiography*; Croce lived another thirty-seven years after writing his. Although both were interim reports on work done and prospectuses of work to do, Collingwood knew his was one of the last he would produce:

> My life's work hitherto, as seen from my fiftieth year, has been in the main an attempt to bring about a rapprochement between philosophy and history . . . Before [*The Principles of Art*] had gone through the press I was overtaken by the more serious illness which gave me both the leisure and the motive to write this autobiography; whose purpose is to put on record some brief account of the work I have not yet been able to publish, in case I am not able to publish it in full . . . I am nearly fifty and cannot in any case hope for more than a few years in which I can do my best work. (A, 76 and 118)[12]

Collingwood did not want to waste space on what the reader could find elsewhere in his published writings. The book traces certain themes as they developed towards his current views by presenting a summary exposition of those views. Thus we find an account of the development of his philosophy of history, of his political and ethical thought, and of his later views on metaphysics, but nothing on aesthetics or religion or philosophical method. Collingwood was well known as a follower of Croce, as he acknowledged in a letter in May 1921: 'This article is written for England, where I am known as a friend and disciple of your philosophy . . .' In correspondence Collingwood went further than any of his critics in admitting his debt to Croce. Given this debt, in matters of both form and philosophical substance, which he knew would be apparent to attentive readers, the question arises why he never once acknowledged it in his *Autobiography*? One obvious answer is simply that he thought it unnecessary, precisely because it was so well known; the other is that he conceived the subject matter of the book as his own thought, not that of others, and that he left the job of fixing affinity and influence as a task for those with nothing better to do.

To return to the charge of concealment: it should be noted, first, that there were many philosophers, both contemporaries and predecessors, who pass unmentioned; he simply ignored the question of influence. Secondly, within the philosophical world everyone knew (and Collingwood knew that they knew) that he was influenced by the Italians. Indeed he made no secret in the 1920s of his affinities and interests. For instance, in 'Croce's Philosophy of History' he writes candidly of the development of Croce's thought at the hands of de Ruggiero and Gentile, something of which he obviously approves; and in 'Can the New Idealism Dispense with Mysticism?' he sympathetically expounds and defends the views of Gentile. This paper was delivered at the joint session of the Mind Association and the Aristotelian Society in 1923: it would surely have required an impressive feat of philosophical juggling to hide from that audience his philosophical affinities. Again, we find that in his lectures on the philosophy of history he is fully prepared to discuss Croce and Vico at length. Is it really conceivable, then, that Collingwood thought that anyone was likely to be deceived by his not mentioning these Italian philosophers into believing that they had not influenced his thinking?

So why did Collingwood make no references to the Italians? It can hardly be supposed that he wished to deny or hide the relationship from the Italians themselves. There are many occasions on which he freely and gratefully acknowledges his debt to de Ruggiero and Croce and indeed probably credits them with a greater influence than they really had. There are two possible answers: the first is that Collingwood was reluctant to acknowledge openly his debt to the Italians because he was afraid that his contemporaries would be inclined to write him off as being merely a follower of theirs or as a 'New Idealist'.[13] If this was the reason one can only say that it was practically quite useless: from this point of view it would have been better to have acknowledged the debt and gone on to elaborate the points of agreement or disagreement. One of the problems, of course, was that his isolation became self-fulfilling in that the turn to Italy both confirmed and exacerbated the suspicions which Collingwood's Oxford colleagues already had of him.

The second and more general answer is that given in a letter to Croce, where he explains why in *The Principles of Art* Croce's name is

> mentioned hardly at all; but that is in accordance with a method of writing which I inherit from a long line of English philosophers and it will not disguise from you, or from anyone else who knows anything of the subject, the closeness of the relation which connects my thought with your own.[14]

This seems clear, but is he consistent in his practice? As a general rule he mentions people by name only when he is deliberately and explicitly expounding their doctrine or where he is quoting their words with approval. He therefore mentions them by name in the expository parts of his lectures on the philosophy of history, moral philosophy and political philosophy; otherwise he claims that: 'my rule in writing books is never to name a man except honoris causa, and . . . naming any one personally known to me is my way of thanking him for what I owe to his friendship, or his teaching, or his example, or all three' (A, Preface).

Again, in his correspondence with Ryle, we find Collingwood justifying his procedure partly as a question of good manners and partly as a point of philosophical principle:

> It is only in part a question of good manners. But that does enter into it; and there my general rule is that I mention names only *honoris causa*. For example, I owe much to Ross's book on *The Right and the Good* . . . I name him as having, in discussing the relation between pleasure, knowledge, and virtue, explained them . . . as constituting a scale of forms: but in that very passage . . . mentioning Joseph's doubt whether pleasure is a good at all, I do not name Joseph because I differ from him; and where I criticize Ross's calculus of goods, quoting his actual words . . . I do not name him. But, going beyond the question of manners (which no doubt might be called rather a question of cowardice or dislike of coming into the open and saying 'Thou art the man; de te fabula narratur') my real reason is that in the work of any competent philosopher I find that the part played by systematic

fallacies is partial only; repeatedly, when real difficulties arise, his insight into the subject, sharpened by a sense of the difficulty, leads him to reject the fallacy even at the cost of inconsistency and to adopt a better procedure than that which he had followed, wrongly as I believe, when he thought it was plain sailing.[15]

This passage refers to Collingwood's procedure in *An Essay on Philosophical Method*, in which these precepts are followed scrupulously. It is harder, however, to agree that he followed them with the same consistency in *An Autobiography*. In that work we find that Croce (clearly on the side of the angels) receives no mention at all, whereas Prichard and Joseph and the realists (clearly on the side of the devil) receive many mentions, few of them friendly. Collingwood seems to be inconsistent in applying his criterion; one might go further and say that he seems to reverse it so as to mention people only *dishonoris causa*. He has no hesitation there in crying 'Thou art the man' as he points the finger of blame.[16]

At this point it might be helpful to leave *An Autobiography* and reconstruct Collingwood's relationship with his Italian contemporaries independently. He went up to University College in 1908 and by September 1910 had discovered Croce's work. His tutor, E. F. Carritt, had an interest in Croce's aesthetics and Professor J. A. Smith, with whom he later became friendly, had developed an interest in Croce on a trip to Naples and drew on his work in his inaugural lecture as Waynflete Professor of Metaphysical Philosophy in 1910.[17] By this time there was a lot of interest in Croce's work following his successful appearance at the International Congress of Philosophy in Heidelberg in 1908.[18] Given Collingwood's acquaintance with Croce's work, and presuming that he had access to *La Critica* at this time, he must simultaneously have become acquainted with the writings of Gentile and de Ruggiero.

Work in Italian philosophy peaked in 1920–1. His first published book was a translation of Croce's *The Philosophy of Giambattista Vico* in 1913.[19] This was followed in June 1920 by a translation of de Ruggiero's 'Scienza come esperienza assoluta', 'Croce's Philosophy' and 'Croce's Philosophy of History'; the composition of the '*Libellus de Generatione*' in July; the translation of de Ruggiero's *Modern Philosophy* (begun in 1919); and lectures on the philosophy of de Ruggiero in Michaelmas term. In 1921 he wrote and delivered a paper on Croce's aesthetic and revised the translation of Croce's book *Aesthetic*; he also contemplated publishing a translation of de Ruggiero's *Filosofia del Cristianesimo*.[20] In 1923 he delivered 'Can the New Idealism Dispense with Mysticism? In 1925 he was translating Croce's *Autobiography* and in 1926 de Ruggiero's *History of European Liberalism*. In 1928 he translated Croce's article 'Aesthetic'; in 1931 de Ruggiero's 'Science, History and Philosophy' and in 1934 Croce's 'Introduction to Eighteenth-Century Aesthetics'. It is worth noting that it was in November of 1920 that he wrote and delivered 'Reflexions on Realism'; that is, at the end of a year in which he had been entirely immersed in the world of contemporary Italian philosophy. Against this background it is perhaps little wonder that he was moved to describe Realism as 'the undischarged bankrupt of modern philosophy'; a reading of the '*Libellus de Generatione*' reveals similarly forceful language. We can see, therefore, that what the *Autobiography* fails to make clear is that his attack on realism and his preoccupation with the agenda of Italian philosophy were two sides of the same coin. The early 1920s marked both the high point of the Italian influence and the turning point in relations with his Oxford contemporaries. Later, from *Speculum Mentis* onwards, he was developing his own philosophy; he moved on from exposition and sought to develop and adapt and expand the work of the Italians. From this point onwards, generally speaking, he refers to the work of others only when he is deliberately setting out to expound *their* philosophy, not when he is seeking to expound his own.

Collingwood's growing sense of philosophical isolation, especially following the reading of 'Reflexions on Realism', is well documented in his *Autobiography*. Prior to giving the paper, he wrote to de Ruggiero that if he found people willing to listen to him he would consider publishing the '*Libellus de Generatione*', which he had sent to de Ruggiero in the summer of that year.[21] They didn't listen, and he didn't publish: 'I read my paper on Realism last November and no one seemed much interested', he remarked shortly after, and he later recollected that 'So far as my philosophical ideas were concerned, I was now cut off not only from the "Realist" school . . . but from every other school of thought in England, I might almost say in the world.'[22] It was his interest in a historical philosophy, the key point of intellectual affinity with the Italians, which distanced him from both the Realists and the Idealists: 'I find myself rather inclined to react against the English idealists because they imported so much of what was *bad* in Hegelism into England; and I find their present successors a real nuisance and my chief enemies.'[23] Both camps lacked historical awareness and hence 'a historically-minded philosopher here is a *vox clamantis in deserto*.'[24] Thus we can appreciate the sense of isolation he expresses to de Ruggiero when he writes that 'for four months I have been deep in historical studies . . . the return to philosophy means a return to work in which I become more and more conscious of being an outlaw.'[25] Yet his mood was not always so pessimistic: 'I now find that *Speculum Mentis* is exciting a good deal of attention and is regarded as possibly opening a new movement in English philosophy. People, intending praise, say as T. H. Green was to Kant and Hegel, so is R. G. C. to Croce! and Gentile!'[26] His isolation was not, perhaps, so complete as he later reported. John Mabbott described him as a remote and secretive character, but adds that he would drop in to play his piano and 'argue about creative activity'. Mabbott was a friend of Gilbert Ryle's and not an idealist; yet he learnt Italian in order to read Croce and Gentile. Ryle himself remarks in his 'Autobiographical' that 'In 1924 I spent some time acquiring a reading knowledge of Italian and a modest grasp of Italian philosophy by reading some Croce, but more Gentile.'[27] He makes light of this, but none the less it would appear that in the early twenties the gulf between the camps was less extreme than the gloomy picture painted by Collingwood in 1939. Mabbott also provides evidence for the impact of *Speculum Mentis*, which he

> once took as the basis for a weekly college discussion class. I got an artist friend to read the chapter on Art, and the college tutors in Chemistry, History and Theology to read their relevant chapters; and each of them to attend the discussion on his chapter. It worked well. Collingwood's writing is clear and alive; and my colleagues not only understood it, but enjoyed the experience. For the last chapter entitled 'Speculum Speculi', on philosophy, I got Collingwood himself to come along. He was a success with my pupils – we had to get him back for a second session. He was delighted with my application of his principle of first-hand experience.[28]

Despite these friendships and shared interests in unexpected places, Collingwood wanted allies of a sort not forthcoming in England. He wanted to create a philosophy which took the claims of history as a form of human experience seriously, and this wish coincided with what he found in contemporary Italian philosophy. Its historical bent was apparent from Vico onwards, and was manifest in those, such as Croce and Gentile, who had learnt from him. It should be remembered that even where English philosophers took history seriously they rarely engaged in philosophy of history as Collingwood understood it. Bradley had in *The Presuppositions of Critical History*, but this was an exception; there was little else of merit, and what there was, was not written with the benefit of practical first-hand experience of historical and archaeological research. Part of his irritation derived from the fact that while others talked about history, he *practised* history. His reflections on the problems of historical method arose directly out of experience in the world of archaeological digs and Roman inscriptions, and his historical problems derived not from the study but from the field. Thus he approved of the Italians because they approved of history (and practised history) and he took from them what he recognized as valuable in explaining his own experience as a historian.

## Croce

Croce was a friend who visited Collingwood in Oxford in 1923 and wrote movingly of him after his death. Collingwood translated some of his books and articles, and published appreciative, but critical, accounts of Croce's philosophy. His debt to Croce was well known: so well known that there were some who considered Collingwood to be little more than a disciple; this is untrue (and Croce also thought it untrue). However, there was certainly a great degree of philosophical indebtedness, as Collingwood himself was always quick to acknowledge in his correspondence with Croce. For example, in 1921 he wrote, in explanation of his critical comments on Croce in 'Croce's Philosophy of History' that 'I have no time to write about work to which I feel hostile: I only write about the people whom I most closely agree with.'[29] The two men were on friendly terms, but Collingwood's relationship with Croce was always deferential (as the tone of his letters shows); he always considered himself to be very much the junior partner. Croce was the older man by twenty-three years and in many ways a father-figure who was admired and respected, but also rebelled against. The relationship was never one of equals, and this is borne out by the contrast with Collingwood's working relationship with de Ruggiero in which they engaged in the mutual exchange and criticism of ideas. Whereas Collingwood deferred to Croce and always wrote to him flatteringly, with de Ruggiero he was more open and comfortable, and more willing to discuss ideas, papers, books, schemes, projects: everything from a half-baked thought to a fully worked out essay or book. It is hard to imagine Collingwood sending the text of the experimental essay '*Libellus de Generatione*' to anyone but de Ruggiero. Thus Collingwood wrote to de Ruggiero in May 1921 that he was working on a philosophy of conduct showing how the cycle of ethical concepts derive from the concept of becoming; it was to de Ruggiero that he poured out his '*Libellus de Generatione*'; it was to de Ruggiero that he wrote in September 1922 sounding out the ideas and themes he intended to develop in *Speculum Mentis*: 'Somehow there is a real identity and a real distinction between things like art, history, religion, action, science, philosophy etc. How to formulate the identity and the differences'; it was to de Ruggiero that he wrote to say that he had finished the book and that it was 'mostly stolen from Hegel and other people'. While Collingwood wrote deferentially and respectfully to Croce in 1928 saying that 'I have learnt from you to regard philosophy as primarily the methodology of history . . .', it was to de Ruggiero that he later explained that in *The Principles of Art* he was

> recasting the science of mind into the form of history . . . into a new form of history not merely philological but philosophical. The philosophy in it is not, as Croce has said, simply its methodology. The absorption is mutual: the product is not philosophy based on history nor history based on philosophy, it is both these things at once.[30]

In writing to Croce, by contrast, he was deferential, humble and flattering:

> My Dear Croce, The Clarendon Press is sending you a copy of my new book, a treatise on aesthetic called *The Principles of Art*. I hope that you will do me the honour of accepting it in token of the debt (far too great

and too complex to be ever acknowledged in detail) which I owe you in every department of thought and more especially in aesthetic. If you should read the book, you will find the doctrine taught in it is in all essentials your own, as I have learned it from you and reconstructed it in my own mind, in terms of my own experience, over a period of many years: for my central theme is the identity of art and language, and my book is nothing but an exposition of that theme and some of its implications . . .[31]

This slightly Heepish attitude was recognized by Momigliano who remarked that 'what I know of the correspondence . . . shows how little Croce got from Collingwood whose personal attitude to Croce was always reticent and somehow disingenuous.'[32] This remark sums up the one-sidedness of the relationship; with de Ruggiero there was a free exchange of ideas and genuine mutual criticism, as there also was with Smith and Alexander, but with Croce Collingwood seemed to go out of his way to agree, to flatter, and to play the acolyte.

## Gentile

Gentile's influence on Collingwood is less often remarked than Croce's, but none the less well documented: it can be found from *Religion and Philosophy* through to *The New Leviathan*.[33] 'Croce's Philosophy of History' (1921) contains explicit and favourable reference to Gentile and 'Can the New Idealism Dispense with Mysticism?' (1922) presents a concise and sympathetic account of Gentile's philosophy in response to hostile attacks. Croce discerned the 'misguiding influence' of Gentile's actualism in *Speculum Mentis*. The 1936 lecture 'Human Nature and Human History' is Gentilean in spirit, while the preparatory notes for this lecture are Gentilean in statement.[34] In these Collingwood explicitly used Gentilean terminology for the purpose of abstractly stating the basic theses of the lecture; in writing the final version of the lecture he dropped Gentile's language in favour of his own.

But his relationship with Gentile is complicated by politics. Croce and de Ruggiero were both (although in different ways) liberals; Gentile was a fascist. Collingwood was a self-professed liberal, and his sympathy with de Ruggiero's liberalism is demonstrated by his comment on *The History of European*

*Liberalism* that 'The political principles expounded and implied are at every point my own, and expressed with a justness and completeness that leave me nothing to do but express my complete agreement.'[35] His preface to the English translation is laudatory and conveys in a nutshell his own liberal political philosophy. The liberalism of de Ruggiero and Croce was thus compatible with Collingwood's political outlook; but Gentile's fascism most certainly was not, and this influenced their relationship adversely. One could not claim that they were friends, nor, to my knowledge, did they correspond. Collingwood appreciated Gentile's philosophical work and assimilated some of it to his own; but from the moment that Gentile became a fascist Collingwood treated him with the utmost suspicion, spurred on, no doubt, by the principled opposition of both de Ruggiero and Croce. In the year that his translation of the *History of European Liberalism* appeared, Collingwood met Gentile in Rome:

> Gentile ... was very cordial and gave me a copy of the new edition of his *Studi Vichiani*; we spoke mostly of education in Italy and England, of the organisation of elementary schools, and so forth; he asked me whether I had studied the present political situation in Italy, and I replied that a foreigner staying three weeks in a country could not hope to form a just opinion of its political situation; he spoke of you [de Ruggiero], as if to discover my present relation to you, and I said that you were one of my greatest friends and that I was staying in your house. Apart from these matters, we spoke altogether of education and things like that.[36]

Collingwood was polite but refused to be drawn, although there is little doubt of his true opinion of the Italian political situation. This political antipathy spilled over into personal antipathy: in 1928 he refused Gentile's request to translate his *Logic* into English;[37] and in *An Autobiography* he displayed both antipathy and disgust towards the unnamed Gentile: 'There was once a very able and distinguished philosopher who was converted to Fascism. As a philosopher, that was the end of him. No one could embrace a creed so fundamentally muddle-headed and remain capable of clear thinking.'[38]

However, this cannot be taken at face value: first, it begs the question by assuming the complete interpenetration of philosophical theory and political practice: that is, it more or less assumes their identity; and secondly, it implies that Collingwood regarded everything Gentile wrote after his conversion to fascism as devoid of philosophical value. To take the points in turn: it may be that Gentile's actualism committed him to denying the distinction between theory and practice, but it does not follow that Collingwood had to be committed to the same view. However, Collingwood does go a long way towards denying the distinction between theory and practice, although he was searching for a rapprochement between them rather than a reduction of one to the other.[39] But this left him with a problem: if he moved towards a denial of the distinction between theory and practice, he moved towards Gentile's position — but Gentile was a fascist as a consequence of his philosophy, and Collingwood wants to avoid this conclusion. The only philosophical way out would have been either to deny the close relation between theory and practice, which he did not want to do — rather the contrary — or to have reconstructed Gentile's philosophy so that the practical consequences no longer followed. But he finds the issue too uncomfortable to handle openly and evades it by refusing to acknowledge what he owed to Gentile. In so doing he needed to posit an absolute disjunction between the pre-fascist Gentile (who was a good philosopher), and the post-fascist Gentile (who was a bad philosopher), as this was the only way he could rescue his own reliance on some of his key doctrines. But however he tried, he could not hide the fact that he had learnt much from Gentile, and carried on learning from him long after his conversion to fascism. The natural reading of the passage from *An Autobiography* is that all of Gentile's post-fascist writings were philosophically worthless: but this is an unsustainable position. Examples of Gentile's influence on Collingwood's later writings might be considered of little interest if he had been simply recycling the uncontaminated pre-fascist work; but Collingwood also wrote favourably in print of some of his post-Fascist writings, and was influenced by others;[40] given this, it is impossible to deny that the remarks in *An Autobiography* are false and misleading: he was trying to sit on a branch which he had already sawn off the year before.

This occurred in a review of a Festschrift published in 1937[41] in which he singles out Gentile's paper on 'The Transcending of Time in History', and writes that:

> Gentile . . . holds that all reality is historical . . . What is indubitably historical is the life of the human mind . . . mind is the only reality, nature is only a construction of ideas, a product of human thought, existing and therefore developing with the development of the thought that constructs it. Nature, in the scientist's present conception of it, is not historical; but the scientist's present conception of it is only the stage now reached in the historical development of science, and thus not nature itself, but the reality . . . underlying it, is historical, being in fact the scientist's thought. Time is transcended in history because the historian, in discovering the thoughts of a past agent, re-thinks that thought for himself. It is known, therefore, not as a past thought, contemplated as it were from a distance through the historian's time telescope, but as a present thought living now in the historian's mind. Thus, by being historically known, it undergoes a resurrection out of the limbo of the dead past, triumphs over time, and survives in the present. This is an important idea, and I believe a true one. Its importance . . . lies in the fact that, so conceived, history is no longer a 'story of successive events': it is the actual possession by the historian, here and now, of the thought whose history he studies. And a past whose thought the historian is unable thus to make his own, whether through lack of evidence or through defect in his own mental powers, inability to sympathize with it, is a past at once dead and unknowable. This doctrine has a practical bearing on historical method. It implies that in order to understand a certain past event or state of society the historian must not only have sufficient documents at his disposal; he must also be, or make himself, the right kind of man; a man capable of entering into the minds of the person whose history he is studying.[42]

This was written about fourteen years after Gentile joined the Fascist Party. The themes closely parallel the philosophy of history expounded so lucidly in chapters 9 and 10 of *An Autobiography*. Collingwood had already reached these conclusions for himself in his *Die* manuscript ten years earlier; he is using Gentile here to confirm his own thinking. But in so doing he nonetheless identified him as the author of 'important' and 'true' ideas and thereby set a trap for himself, a trap he could not escape. One might argue that Gentile was simply recycling his earlier views and that its philosophical content is unaffected by its re-presentation in a fascist bottle. But this will not do. At the very least, these doctrines have been endorsed by someone who is supposed, now, to be incapable of clear thinking: surely this endorsement by a philosopher tainted with fascism raises questions that should be faced openly and honestly? But Collingwood finds the issue too uncomfortable to deal with and in *An Autobiography* resorts to bombast, denouncing Gentile while remaining silent on the merits of his philosophy.

Collingwood wrote this review at the time he was preparing his British Academy lecture on 'Human Nature and Human History'.[43] As we have seen, the preparatory notes for this lecture were couched in Gentile's terminology; in addition, the lecture as published contains a number of ideas and phrases which come straight out of this review and in many ways it reads as an amplification of its leading ideas. I am not suggesting that he plagiarized Gentile, or simply used his ideas unreflectively; neither am I suggesting that what he said was anything other than the outcome of many years' thought and reflection. But it has to be admitted that Collingwood fails outright in his foolhardy attempt to denounce Gentile whilst simultaneously drawing on his doctrines.

## De Ruggiero

The suggestion canvassed earlier was that Collingwood and de Ruggiero were engaged in a collaborative relationship of the sort found among friendly equals. Evidence of their mutual regard can be found in the fact that Collingwood delivered a series of lectures on de Ruggiero in 1920, and in the dozen pages devoted to *Speculum Mentis* in de Ruggiero's *Filosofi del Novecento*.[44] To see that they were equals who rebelled against Croce, the philosophical father-figure, we need go no further than a letter from 1921:

> Your last attack on the Crocean windmill was excellent, and Croce's reply in the Critica rather amused me. You can't get him to see that the four sails of his windmill aren't somehow a special divine decree: but there is something plaintive and rather pathetic in his references to this rebellious son of his who will go on beating his father, though his father's affection for him remains unchanged.[45]

Collingwood was probably closer philosophically to de Ruggiero than he was to either Croce or Gentile.[46] Croce certainly saw the influence of de Ruggiero in Collingwood's criticism of himself:

Collingwood's criticism was identical to that which had been ringing in my ears and coming before my eyes for ten years or more in Italy . . . These advocates of 'actual idealism', a sublime yet empty philosophy had accused me of not having raised myself to that sublimity, of not having dissolved all distinctions in the act and thereby of being both a realist and an idealist, one in contradiction of the other. Having patiently explained why I could not accept this new revelation I expected it to fade away and fall into oblivion, as was its very nature and as in fact eventually happened. At that time the extreme and very radical theorist of actual idealism was De Ruggiero who having gone to England, informed Collingwood of his opinion and put him on guard against my philosophizing which was old-fashioned, naturalistic, empiricist and so on. Thus Collingwood ended his work with a salute to my two 'successors', that is De Ruggiero and his master and colleague . . . De Ruggiero in the same year opened fire on me by dedicating to Collingwood a work of his in which he replied in amoebean verse to Collingwood's work in the very same way, judging and condemning my philosophy of art.[47]

Croce then goes on to argue that 'Collingwood himself put an end to that kind of criticism and abandoned the concomitant profession of actualism whose misguiding influence is still felt in *Speculum Mentis* . . . I conscientiously criticized this work for its presupposition and particular arguments.'[48]

## '*Libellus de Generatione*'

Collingwood wrote *Libellus de Generatione*: an Essay in Absolute Empiricism between 20 and 23 July 1920, and sent it to de Ruggiero, to whom it was dedicated.[49] This is an important essay for a number of reasons: first it shows something of his thought in the year he was immersed in Italian philosophy and presenting his anti-Realist arguments to his Oxford contemporaries; secondly, it substantiates some of his claims in *An Autobiography* regarding his thinking at the time and his intellectual development; thirdly it illuminates his working relationship with de Ruggiero.

In justification of the subtitle of the essay Collingwood begins by following Hume in denying substance and resolving all reality into the actuality of experience. Here, as so often, he wants to rescue Hume from his professed followers among the Realists and positivists. Briefly stating his conclusion, he writes that: 'My fundamental doctrine is that reality is becoming, that is to say reality not so much *is* as *happens*; which implies that the reality of mind is the process of its experience, its life and nothing else.' He goes on to remark that 'My own philosophy I regard as derived from Hume's annihilating criticism of realism through a chain of interpretation embracing, primarily, the German and Italian idealists, and secondarily the empiricists . . . of the nineteenth century and the new realism of the twentieth.' Unlike his 'absolute' empiricism, however, these others failed to achieve a clear statement of their own principles. His aim in the first part of the essay is to demolish the Realists' account of knowledge and judgement, and in the second to assert the superiority of a conception in which knowledge and judgement are resolved into process or becoming.

The essay's two parts are titled: 'The World of Being' and 'The World of Becoming'. The first chapter is entitled 'The Dissolution of Realism' and contains material which was reworked later in the year in 'Reflexions on Realism'. In *An Autobiography* Collingwood attributed to this paper an argument which showed that the Realists were implicitly claiming to know what they had previously defined as unknown (A, 44). The '*Libellus*' develops this by showing the impossibility of accounting for knowledge on the supposition that subject and object are things simultaneously standing apart as separate items in the world and yet somehow brought into mutual relations in the act of knowing. He argues that the attempt must lead to a dialectic in which Realism bifurcates into either objectivism or subjectivism, both being based on the 'formula of an independent subject and object standing in a knowledge-relation'.[50] Realism is unable to account for knowledge and equally unable to account for error; and its internal dialectic leads inevitably to its dissolution. Within 'the world of being' inhabited by realism, there can be no real distinctions, everything becomes indistinguishable from its own opposite; but in 'the world of becoming' distinctions can be made and held on to. By giving an account of reality and knowledge as becoming it becomes possible to account for both identity and difference and truth and error.

Realism cannot account for becoming and hence cannot account for the possibility of historical knowledge. Collingwood offers an alternative in which, within the idea of becoming

Identity . . . means that the past phase of the process is preserved in the present phase . . . The present affirms the past. Difference means that the past moment is transcended, is superseded, is no longer in existence; the present negates the past. The categories of identity and difference are thus, as interpreted in the world of becoming, the categories of affirmation and negation, positivity and negativity. Take two phases of a process, A and B. At a given moment the phase in existence is A and is not B. But to leave it at this would be to deny the reality of the process, that is continuity, as to assert that I am my present self, and not my past self. Such an assertion cuts the thread of continuity in the process, denies the world of becoming and reasserts the world of being, with the result that *coincidentia oppositorum* is set up and my present self becomes indistinguishable from my past. To reassert the process it is necessary to assert that my past self lives on in my present self, that the present phase is B as well as A, though it is definitely premised that A is not B and B not A – that they are different phases of the process. A truth in the world of becoming can only be expressed by a contradiction, a synthesis of opposites. But in this synthesis each term retains its own meaning, and is not destroyed but rather explained by its opposite. What we mean by saying 'I am my present self and not my past self' is not really expressed till we have added 'I am my past self too'. In being transcended, the past phase is destroyed but at the same time it is preserved. The past is entirely misunderstood if it is regarded either as pure negativity, that is as having been left utterly behind and in no sense preserved, or as pure positivity, that is as surviving entirely unchanged in the present.

This presentation of the ideas of incapsulation and of a living past shows both his closeness to the Italians and his distance from the older British Idealists. Their conception of reality was static; their absolute, he says, is a static Spinozistic absolute which cannot allow for process and becoming; it is a form of Realism, and it cannot provide an account of or accept the reality of history. Collingwood's 'absolute', by contrast, is dynamic: 'There is no whole. Becoming is not a series that can be summed to any number of terms, nor yet to infinity.'[51] This has implications for his views on philosophical method, which were worked out in conjunction with his lectures on moral philosophy and published in *An Essay on Philosophical Method*, but earlier informed the essays 'Economics as a Philosophical Science' and 'Political Action'. These essays echo the view expressed in the Preface to '*Libellus*' that he will not 'admit any dualism between mind and its object such that while mind is wholly process its object can be conceived as a static whole outside it. The object is process too, and these are not two processes but one process.' In studying something philosophically the subject matter of the inquiry has to be conceived as a process or it cannot properly be conceived at all. Thus in the essay on economics he wrote that 'The conceptions of value, wealth, and so forth are not ultimate inexplicables; they can be understood, but only by resolving them into the conception of economic action'; and in 'Political Action' he stated that he was going to put the issue

> in the form of the question "What is political action?" That is to say, I propose to take my stand, not on the category of substance and attribute, but on the category of action; questions which [are] insoluble in terms of substance and attribute, are soluble in terms of action.
> (EPP, 58 and 92–3)[52]

The answer to our question, then, is that de Ruggiero was the key sympathetic spirit and influence on Collingwood's philosophizing; an influence profound because reciprocal. And it seems to me that in *An Autobiography* Collingwood quite clearly pointed to de Ruggiero in this respect. When he wrote that he sent a copy of the '*Libellus*' to 'my friend Guido de Ruggiero', this was no idle comment, and indeed the influence of the '*Libellus*' itself is palpable within the book.[53] In this light his decision to ignore Croce and Gentile attains added significance and points to the conclusion: 'De Ruggiero, *thou art the man.*'

## Notes

[1] For further discussion of Collingwood's affinities with Italian philosophy and philosophers, see the chapters by Bruce Haddock, H. S. Harris and Rik Peters in this volume.

[2] Arnaldo Momigliano to Croce; it is worth noting that Croce did not accept this account. In Commemoration of an English Friend, a Companion in Thought and Faith', in *Thought, Action and Intuition*, ed. L. M. Palmer and H. S. Harris (Hildesheim: Georg Olms Verlag, 1975), 57.

[3] H. S. Harris in the Introduction to Gentile's *Genesis and Structure of Society* (Urbana, University of Illinois Press, 1960), 15.

[4] *An Autobiography* (Oxford, Clarendon Press, 1939), Preface.

[5] Letter to J. A. Smith, 27 June 1932.

[6] T. M. Knox in a letter to James Patrick, cited in *The Magdalen Metaphysicals* (Macon, Mercer University Press, 1985), 47.

7 See *An Essay on Metaphysics*, 172–8. The two men corresponded frequently, mostly on aesthetics, from the 1920s until Alexander's death in 1938.
8 Perhaps he also had Vico's *Autobiography* in mind.
9 B. Croce, *An Autobiography* (Oxford, Clarendon Press, 1927), 22.
10 Middleton Murry, quoted in C. Sprigge, *Croce* (Cambridge, Bowes and Bowes, 1952), 10.
11 Croce, *An Autobiography*, 19.
12 Collingwood, *An Autobiography*, 76, 118.
13 This whole question touched a nerve: see, for example, *An Autobiography*, 56 where he complains of a reviewer of *Speculum Mentis* dismissing it in a few lines as 'the usual idealistic nonsense'. Collingwood remarks that it might be nonsense, but it was neither 'usual' nor 'idealistic'. Similarly in correspondence with Gilbert Ryle he objects to Ryle's description of him as, 'for what such labels are worth, an idealist' and insists that he has 'nowhere in this essay or any other publication or lecture so described myself'. He goes on to remark that 'I protest allegiance to nobody; I regard myself as free to learn what I can from all the philosophers whose writings I can read' letter to Gilbert Ryle, 9 May 1935. Collingwood's objections to labels are identical with those expressed by Croce in his *Autobiography*.
14 Letter to Croce, 20 April 1938.
15 Letter to Gilbert Ryle, op. cit. Ryle himself scarcely refers to anyone by name in *The Concept of Mind*; Oakeshott, to take another example, is equally parsimonious with references.
16 It is worth pointing out, however, that relations were, and remained, cordial in many respects. For example, he wrote to Joseph thanking him for sending a copy of F. H. Bradley's *Presuppositions of Critical History* and remarks that 'It is very good of you to have lent me this rarity, which I have long wanted to see & have never seen before.' Even after the blunt speaking of *An Autobiography* he had a copy of *An Essay on Metaphysics* sent to Joseph and received a reply in gratitude.
17 J. A. Smith was Collingwood's immediate predecessor as Waynflete professor and supported his application for the chair.
18 See James Patrick *The Magdalen Metaphysicals*, 53.
19 Collingwood used to say, according to Knox, that Vico had influenced him more than anybody else (Preface to *The Idea of History*, viii).
20 Collingwood's activity in this field took place against a background of other work on contemporary Italian philosophy: for example, J. A. Smith's paper on 'The Philosophy of Giovanni Gentile' (1920), the appearance of Gentile's *The Theory of Mind as Pure Act* in an English translation in 1922, the work of H. Wildon Carr and much critical work by Bosanquet both in book reviews and in his *The Meeting of Extremes in Contemporary Philosophy* (London, Macmillan, 1921). In a critical

review for the *Oxford Magazine*, Collingwood suggests that Bosanquet failed to distinguish the views of Croce and Gentile and also to understand their central doctrines.

[21] Letter to de Ruggiero, 4 November 1920.
[22] Letter to de Ruggiero, 20 March 1921; *An Autobiography*, 53.
[23] Letter to de Ruggiero, 20 March 1921.
[24] Letter to de Ruggiero, 9 January 1931.
[25] Letter to de Ruggiero, 4 October 1927.
[26] Letter to de Ruggiero, 16 September 1924.
[27] In *Ryle* edited by Oscar Wood and George Pitcher (London, Macmillan, 1971), 3.
[28] John Mabbott, *Oxford Memories* (Oxford, Thornton, 1986), 75-6.
[29] Letter to Croce, 29 May 1921.
[30] Letter to de Ruggiero, 12 June 1937.
[31] 20 April 1938.
[32] Arnaldo Momigliano, in *Thought, Action and Intuition*, ed. Palmer and Harris, 5.
[33] See the chapters by H. S. Harris and Rik Peters in this volume.
[34] In the preliminary notes for the lecture written on 9 March 1936 as part of 'Notes on the History of Historiography and Philosophy of History', Collingwood states that 'what is falsely called human nature is really human history . . . [and] the fundamental theses of such a view would be something of this kind: 1) Human nature is mind . . . 2) Mind is pure act. Mind is not anything apart from what it does . . . 3) The pure act posits itself and its own presupposition at once . . . 4) Past time therefore is the schema of mind's self knowledge.'
[35] Letter to de Ruggiero, 18 September 1926. de Ruggiero's work was a spur to his own, and he later wrote that 'I am trying to write an essay on the fundamental conceptions of political thought, which bring me into constant touch with many ideas on that subject which I have learnt from you. When it appears I hope you will feel that I have been a good pupil' (letter to de Ruggiero, 22 November 1928).
[36] Letter to de Ruggiero, 16 April 1927.
[37] I owe the story to Rik Peters.
[38] *An Autobiography*, 158.
[39] Ibid., 147, and in his letter to T. M. Knox on 2 November 1937, 'I don't know how far you would go in your repudiation . . . of a dualism between a "theory" and "practice". I would go a terrible long way, myself.'
[40] E.g. *The Philosophy of Art*, 1931.
[41] Review of *Philosophy and History: Essays Presented to Ernst Cassirer* (Oxford, Clarendon Press, 1936), *English Historical Review* (January 1937).
[42] Ibid., 143.

43 He footnotes the Cassirer Festschrift twice in the lecture.
44 Bari, 1934.
45 Letter to de Ruggiero, 21 September 1922.
46 This suggestion is developed by Clementina Gily Reda in her work on Collingwood and de Ruggiero.
47 Croce, 'In Commemoration of an English Friend', 52–3. The reference is to Collingwood's article 'Croce's Philosophy of History' (1920). Croce, like Collingwood, cannot bring himself to mention Gentile's name.
48 Ibid., 53. The idea that Collingwood abandoned Gentile and de Ruggiero is convincingly refuted by H. S. Harris and Rik Peters in this volume.
49 In *An Autobiography*, 99, he claimed to have sent de Ruggiero a typescript and to have destroyed the original. It now appears that he sent the original MS to de Ruggiero; whether he kept a copy for himself we do not know. The copy in the Bodleian Library is a photocopy.
50 '*Libellus de Generatione*', 16.
51 Ibid., 61.
52 The essay was first published in 1925, and the second in 1928.
53 We find it either directly or indirectly in chapters 9 and 10 on the philosophy of history, and also in chapter 11 on Roman Britain (see pp. 141–3 and compare with the passage quoted above from '*Libellus*').

# Croce and Gentile in Collingwood's New Leviathan

H. S. HARRIS

In April or May of 1958 I borrowed *Religion and Philosophy* from the University of Illinois library, set it beside the other books of Collingwood (which I had owned since the late forties) and began to read Collingwood's works in their chronological order, for the purpose of including him in my survey of 'The Study and Influence of Gentile in the Anglo-Saxon World'.[1] There is hardly anything in that survey that I would now wish to change. But this present essay will illuminate it, and provide a contrasting context. I intend to examine the problem of intellectual influence from Collingwood's side, and from the end rather than from the beginning.

I mean also to proceed, as well as I can, in Collingwood's own mature way. At the beginning of chapter 9 in *The New Leviathan* he says that he is following Locke's 'historical plain method' in his construction of the 'modern European mind'. I shall use Collingwood's conception of that same method to observe the influences (so far as I can plausibly identify them) in the formation of Collingwood's own mind. Indeed, Collingwood's 'historical plain method' has been, not the whole, but still the main – and the distinctive – component in my own active career as an intellectual historian. I cannot say that I owe it to Collingwood himself, for I believe that I was applying it to the study of Gentile in a fairly self-conscious way before I embarked upon any serious study of Collingwood. But I think that I derived it myself from much the same sources as those that moulded Collingwood's mind. It is that belief that gives me the confidence to offer my surmises here as serious historical observations. Some of them are no more than plausible working hypotheses: and all of them must be checked (and confirmed, modified or discarded), by others who use the Collingwood papers, and concern themselves with the intellectual world in which Collingwood grew up, in other directions and in greater detail than I have done or can do.

What I propose to do here is to run through the theory of 'Man' expounded in the first part of *The New Leviathan*, and identify all of the 'influences' – especially the Italian influences – that can plausibly be detected both in the form, and in the matter of the theory. Some things – especially, for instance, the example set by Hobbes, as the original model of the 'classical politics', I shall largely take for granted. For obvious reasons of space, I shall expound nothing in detail. But I hope that what I say will be clear enough to guide anyone who wants to go deeper. For what I call the 'primacy of ordinary discourse' is basic to the 'historical plain method'. *The New Leviathan* anticipated some of the positions and methods associated with the name of J. L. Austin. The 'primacy of ordinary discourse' (clearly laid down in NL, 3.15) is a fundamental characteristic of Collingwood's reformulation of the 'speculative idealist' tradition of Germany and Italy. It was from Collingwood's younger contemporaries Price and Ryle (and from Austin himself) that I imbibed the project of 'thinking with the learned and speaking with the vulgar' as Berkeley, the only Anglophone speculative thinker of the 'modern classical period' put it. Since I have been by choice an interpreter of the speculative tradition myself – Berkeley's Muse is an appropriate one to invoke.

With that much of a preamble, we can begin. The first chapter of *The New Leviathan* is entitled 'Body and Mind'. The relation that Collingwood sets up between the two concepts is exactly that which Gentile establishes between the *logo astratto* and the *logo concreto*. 'Body' is what the abstract sciences of nature concern themselves with, while 'mind' is the concern of the philosopher and the cultural historian. It is the 'sciences' that tell us all that we know of their 'objects' – so we cannot use the supposedly more primitive 'objects' to define the sciences. Thus, at the very beginning the principal novelty of this 'new' Leviathan is established. Hobbes was a materialist: he took the primary reality to be 'body' – which is unconscious. Collingwood is an Idealist, i.e. one who takes the primary reality to be 'mind' or consciousness; and the conceptual means by which Collingwood is able to establish a direct relation between his work and that of his great predecessor was provided by the most radical of the modern Idealists. We ought to notice also – because it is so typical of them both – that Collingwood writes of physics and physiology with a much more vivid appreciation than Gentile could ever muster. But at 1.84 we read, 'Man as mind is whatever he is conscious of being.' Later on (at NL, 9.17) Collingwood refuses to commit himself categorically to the assertion that 'what mind is resolves itself without residue into the question what mind does.' But we have only to read 1.84 together with 9.16 and 9.17 to see that methodically Collingwood is – and he knows that he is – an 'actual Idealist'. Hence when we find the echo of Augustine at the end of the first chapter: 'The general form of answer [to the question 'what man is as mind'] is: "*In teipsum redi*"', we need not hesitate to conclude that Collingwood is linking Gentile with Hobbes. For it is Gentile who quotes this tag incessantly: and Hobbes (as we are all expected to remember) says at the end of his Introduction: 'He that is to govern a whole nation, must read in himself, not this or that particular man; but mankind . . .'[2]

The 'proper object' of simple 'consciousness' in Collingwood's theory is 'feeling' (NL, 4.19). The English Idealists had made 'feelings' fundamental in varying ways. But in attaching himself to that tradition as he did, Collingwood was definitely siding with Gentile against Croce; and the fact that he first developed his evolutionary theory of 'consciousness' in *The Principles of Art* strongly suggests that the Italians were at least as influential as Bradley here. Collingwood himself worked on the greatly improved second edition of the translation of Croce's *Estetica* (1922);[3] so when he was studying Gentile's *Filosofia dell'arte* ten years later,[4] he could not fail to be mindful of Croce's view that 'feeling' was only a 'confused' concept – and certainly not a fit foundation stone for the philosophical theory of 'experience'. Probably he was dissatisfied with Gentile's own account of the concept (even when he had the *Introduzione alla filosofia* to back it up in 1933).[5] But I feel sure that both the urge to show that Croce was mistaken, and the desire to improve on Gentile's simple-minded 'enlightenment theory' of pleasure and pain, lie behind the fascinating elaboration of the concept which Collingwood gave in *The Principles of Art* and *The New Leviathan*.[6]

The whole theory of 'feeling' as the 'object' of consciousness, and 'knowledge' as the result of 'reflection' upon consciousness has a Kantian family resemblance to Croce's theory of aesthetic 'intuitions' and logical 'concepts'; and we know (from *Speculum Mentis*) that Collingwood's own meditation began in that general context. But it is now the differences that are important. I feel sure that the whole theory of 'attention' as the mental function by which we make a 'here-and-now feeling' into a definite perception owes more to Collingwood's direct observation of his experience as a painter (NL, 4.55, 5.71–5.72), and to his literary observation (NL, 5.73), than it does to any philosophy book.[7]

Already, in Collingwood's account of the 'selective attention' which creates the 'edges' that make our employment of a two-valued logic possible, we encounter the negative concept of 'repression' (NL, 4.51). Here we can recognize the great shadow of Freud. Collingwood's attitude to the science of psychology was even more violently bi-modal than the science itself in his time. Croce and Gentile were as placidly indifferent as they were ignorant about experimental psychology; and they were confidently contemptuous (though not much better informed) about 'depth psychology'. Collingwood was respectably well informed (for a layman) about both schools. But whereas he was hostile to the experimental school, almost to the point of actual irrationality (EM, chapter 11) he was critically appreciative of Freud and his followers. Whatever faults (of abstraction etc.) they might be guilty of were no greater than – and essentially no different – from those that could be found in Hobbes; and it was easy to show that their method and results were a development of the great tradition of 'scientific introspection' of which Hobbes was the founder. Collingwood's theory of the 'unconscious' shows that, and it is one of the most noteworthy achievements of his *Principles of Art* and *The New Leviathan*. He built a bridge between Freud's theory and the work of someone like William James.[8]

Together with our empirical world of knowledge built on selective attention to 'feeling', there comes to birth the 'philosophy of common sense'. In Collingwood's England the most redoubtable champion of this philosophy was G. E. Moore. I am not an expert on the Anglo-Idealists' response to Moore, but it seems to me that Collingwood's 'Cartesian' view that 'the question which Berkeley answered in one way ("sensa are mind-dependent") and

Moore ... in the opposite way ("sensa are not mind-dependent") is a nonsense question' (NL, 5.36) is distinctively Gentilian.[9] The claim that 'no possible answer is right because the question arises logically from an assumption that is not made' follows directly from the methodological principle that 'mind is what it does'; and Collingwood gives his answer as a 'methodological negative' (NL, 5.39). There are no 'objects' of feeling. Feelings themselves are the 'objects' of thought. We might say therefore that, as Gentile is the Hegelian 'Actual Idealist', so Collingwood is the Kantian (or 'critical' practitioner) of the 'method of immanence'.

The theory of language as 'any system of bodily movements, not necessarily vocal, whereby the men who make them mean or signify anything' (NL, 6.1) was surely inspired originally by Croce's theory of art as 'linguistica generale'. It had been advanced first (in a form almost exactly like that which Collingwood gives it) by C. S. Peirce; and the social psychologist G. H. Mead was interpreting human behaviour in the same spirit in Collingwood's own time. But there is no reason to suppose that Collingwood knew Peirce's early work (any more than I did, when I first waxed eloquent about 'the body is all a language' in Gentile's *Genesis and Structure of Society*);[10] and the insularity of British academic life suggests that he would not have read G. H. Mead.[11] This is a case, I think, where Collingwood anticipated Gentile – and both of them were stimulated by Croce.

When we come to the primacy of practical consciousness (and practical reason) in Collingwood, it is certain that his inspiration is Italian (rather than Anglo-Hegelian) but we cannot say decisively that it is more Gentilian than Crocean. The wisest course when we are faced with the definition of conceptual thinking as an 'act of practical consciousness' is to refer back to Vico's *verum/factum* doctrine as the common source for all three of them. But it is only right to emphasize that methodically Collingwood is closer to Gentile than to Croce. The whole progression of his 'phenomenology of mind' depends on the actualist doctrine that 'mind is what it does'. When Collingwood himself claimed that Vico had influenced him 'more than anyone else', he was probably thinking of the historically conditioned character of Vico's theory as what distinguished his own 'methodical' actualism from Gentile's 'metaphysical' (or 'absolute') doctrine. One reason for his agreement with Croce in assigning to philosophy the humble journeyman role of doing the historian's methodology, was his vivid awareness that it is pre-philosophical felt experience that makes abstractions concrete. Thus he does not see himself, like Locke, as an 'underlabourer' for the scientists. But he does see himself as the 'servant of servants' in the scientific community – and not just as the servant of historians. One cannot imagine that either Croce or Gentile would have thought that the 'Idea of Nature' was worth writing a series of lectures about. But it came naturally enough to the man who could say 'The life of thought is a symbiosis of immediate consciousness with abstractions' (NL, 7.65). That 'abstractions' are alive (as the word symbiosis implies) was fairly explicitly denied in the logical theories of both of the Italians. In this respect, the evolutionary gradualism of Collingwood's theory of mental development made him a better Hegelian than either of them.

The concept of 'appetite' (in chapter 7) is Aristotelian, but the bifurcated theory of 'hunger' and 'love' is explicitly Platonic in its inspiration (cf. NL, 10.53). 'Hunger' is, of course, the Hobbesian 'perpetual and restless desire of power after power' (NL, 8.25); but the primitive modification into 'love' transforms the Hobbesian evolution of rational selfishness into a religious quest for a higher form of selfhood altogether. Thus *The New Leviathan* turns the old *Leviathan* upside down and makes it the vehicle for a Hegelian version of Plato's tripartite soul which owes more to Bradley than it does to the Italians.

But as a religious theory *The New Leviathan* is, properly speaking, independent of both traditions. Bradley (whose mysticism is laughed at in NL, 7.66) would probably be shocked at the pagan suggestion that the 'hungry' self wants to be God (NL, 8.26). But this apparent anticipation of Sartre is the primitive love-modification that gives rise finally to the Christian 'God of Love'. Collingwood's initial rejection of the thesis that 'fear made the gods' (NL, 8.27–8.28) is certainly biased in historical terms. But this is the modern bias; and it sets Collingwood at the opposite pole from Gentile – whose theory of God as the 'absolute object' (i.e. the source of *authority* and *law*) was certainly the negative stimulus of Collingwood's view here that Divine authority breeds human tyranny; for Collingwood, that was the lesson of Gentile's fascism. Both of them were one-sided Hegelians – for Hegel's own theory unites the poles; but

Hegel himself would certainly agree that Collingwood chose the 'higher' side – the one that belongs properly to our modern world. Also – as we shall soon see – Collingwood does not really deny the role of fear in the making of the gods.

The human love of God – like Hegel's 'Unhappy Consciousness' – is a lost soul. But in Collingwood's view this questing love becomes the origin of the experimental method, because it does not – cannot – know what it is looking for. Collingwood would probably have said that Hegel's Unhappy Consciousness, belongs to the phenomenology of 'civilization' rather than that of 'man'. But it is interesting to note that in Hegel's theory the singular Unhappy Consciousness leads us to 'Observing Reason'. Of course, 'consciousness' is never really 'unhappy' according to Collingwood (NL, 12.6). In its Hobbesian restlessness it is always trying something.

Collingwood's comments about Christianity are strikingly unorthodox – both theologically and within the Hegelian philosophical tradition. I cannot even verify my ascription of the doctrine that 'God is Love' to him – though I think it is implied by his comment about 'Christian Love' in 11.56; and further that it is the logical justification for siding with 'Civilization' against 'Barbarism'. But the whole doctrine of Barbarism is both shockingly prejudiced as history, and conceptually incoherent as philosophy; so I do not want to found any judgements upon it. Collingwood's implicit theory of the evolution of Christianity may be mirrored in it, but we must work the theory out from the first three parts of the book. Collingwood's philosophy of religion is quite original with him (as far as I can make out). It deserves to be studied and worked out properly (and as far as I know this has not been done yet).

What is visible on the surface may have been influenced by Freudian theory in a general way, but not by any philosophical tradition that I can identify. Primitive Judaism, says Collingwood, was a 'fear religion'. Christianity was originally an 'anger religion' (NL, 10.6). In the fall of Adam, God let us down. He must be punished for this, and must 'atone'. 'Love' as a proper 'desire' (rather than as the primitive modification of 'appetite') can only come into being after the experience of 'anger' (Collingwood's 'anger' is the Freudian 'frustration'. That is why it seems legitimate to see the influence of Freud here). Fear – the 'fear of the father' – is an important phase in the evolution of religion; but the narcissism of the infantile ego came first. Hegel gave the love-principle its primitive Mother-identity; but Collingwood, we may notice, was as patriarchal as Freud and Hobbes.

When he comes to 'happiness' Collingwood claims to be restating Aristotle. But his theory of 'good' is too modern for that to be more than an appearance. The goal of human life cannot be summed up as 'happiness', because there is nothing simply 'good' in the world, and hence no final 'felicity' (to use the name that Hobbes employed). Tam O'Shanter's drunkenness is not (as both Aristotle and Mill would have said) a 'life suitable for pigs', but an experience of bliss that makes life real and vivid again. As we said already, Collingwood denies that there is a state of 'Unhappy Consciousness'. But he defines 'sin' very aptly as the inability to stand comparison with one's God (NL, 12.68); and he rightly claims that it is the saved soul that remembers its sinful condition as 'unhappy' (NL, 12.72). This is an application and development of Gentile's doctrine that 'error' and 'evil' exist only as sublated (or as the 'abstract logos'). Collingwood claims to be putting Hegel right at this point (NL, 12.6) – and I suppose Gentile would have said the same. Needless to say, Hegel's full doctrine of Unhappy Consciousness is far too complex to be susceptible of any such simple correction – and in some of its shapes it is not phenomenally experienced as a present 'unhappiness' at all. 'We' can observe it as philosophers. (But I must not let myself be seduced into putting the 'reformers' right!).

If it were not for the doctrine of 'symbiosis' I should be tempted to say that Collingwood was betraying his commitment to the primacy of ordinary discourse when he calls 'unhappiness', 'badness' and 'weakness' abstractions (NL, 12.60–12.63). Both pain and grief are real experiences as far as I can see, and one has to be a *metaphysical* actualist to get round this. That is to say, one has to substitute the *a priori* truth of 'thinking' for what is 'felt'. This is one place where the influence of Gentile is very obvious, and it is not certain that Collingwood can escape all of the problems to which this gives rise. But his integration of depth psychology and the resulting doctrine of 'corruption of consciousness' provide some grounds for thinking that his doctrine that unhappiness is always 'a mixed emotion of happiness and unhappiness' (NL, 12.64) can be consistently and plausibly worked out. If it can, however, we shall almost certainly find that just as 'in fact we are happier than we know' (NL, 12.65), so Plato and Hegel will be right also in claiming that in some outwardly 'happy' states we are much 'unhappier' than we know (and that, of course, will come as no surprise to students of Freud).

Modern environmental consciousness has taught us that perhaps the concept of nature 'crushing us' can be 'clearly worked out', and that Collingwood's own theory offers a way of showing that NL, 12.83 is only a half-truth. But that is the sort of fruitful 'error of historical perspective' that Collingwood's basic historicism *predicts*; so we must not tax him with it. It is more to the point to praise the insight involved in his recognition of Hobbes as our first defender against what Toynbee called the 'Intractableness of Institutions' (NL, 12.9 and 12.93). If there is an Italian influence here it is that of de Ruggiero's *History of Liberalism* (my memory does not serve me well enough to decide this, but I am inclined to doubt it). Croce certainly never thought of Hobbes like this; and Collingwood's aversion for fascist dictatorship – and for Gentile's idealistic defence of it – makes his evaluation of Hobbes's *Leviathan* a most remarkable achievement of dialectical comprehension on his part.

I do not know why Collingwood makes such a 'mystery' out of free will. It was open to him to point out, as Schiller did, that whenever the human organism is not under the pressure of 'appetite' it is 'free' to play with its conscious capacities. This is readily observable in other mammalian species; and one would have thought that Collingwood's own education (which certainly guides his thoughts about the topic in part III) would recommend this view to him. Instead, he follows Kant in arguing that we must 'deny ourselves' ('accept unhappiness') in order to be free; and it was apparently Freud who convinced him that there is an element of Augustinian perversity in our nature that leads us to do this. (He is right to say that the 'death instinct' does not explain anything, but he seems to think that it describes something – NL, 13.39.) Even though he did not like the 'play theory' of education – which was much in vogue in the 1930s – it is still astonishing that he ignored the Hegelian theory that the free self demands to be 'recognized' – since this is easily grasped as a 'modification' of the Hobbesian appetite for power. The Christian theology of 'disobedience' seems to be what triumphed in his mind here.

Since 'liberation' comes by 'naming', the element of 'self-denial' involved in our freedom is hardly great enough to be noticeable; and Collingwood's doctrine is that before we can really notice our freedom, our 'self-respect' must be aroused. The language is Kantian, but I think the inspiration comes from Plato's guardian-educators – who were the first play-theorists. But it is quite likely that Collingwood is not mindful of any canonized philosophers here, for it is fairy-tale magic to which he appeals in defence of his 'naming' theory (NL, 13.46); and we now know that fairy tales were a special interest of his. (We might say that – at least in this connection – he looked to them as Freud did to free association and dreams as a way of recovering our 'repressed consciousness'.)

The appeal to Spinoza (NL, 13.45), however, is at least partly a cloak for Gentile. Spinoza does indeed say that our liberation from the bondage of 'passion' is through the 'strength of the intellect'. But in Collingwood's theory the action into which passion is transformed is the 'pure act' of *thinking*. And because thinking – even as 'naming' – is already action Collingwood needs the different language of 'fact' and 'deed' for his theory of 'action' in the ordinary sense of the word. When our practical reasoning culminates in actual choice and decision, 'thought' turns into 'deed' (NL, 13.86). Gentile himself uses 'act', and 'fact'; but the double vocabulary of 'act' and 'deed' enables Collingwood to superimpose the Crocean theory of the 'distinction' between theory and practice onto Gentile's doctrine of their essential identity. He would rightly have said himself that the real inspiration of this combination came from Vico's *verum/factum* principle.

He would have been right in this, because his commonsensical reliance on language as a social construct enables him to avoid all the problems of the 'transcendental ego'. There is no 'transcendental Adam' who 'names the animals' (and everything else). We become 'free' by giving things their right name – the name that our common language supplies (NL, 13.42). What an African witch doctor calls things may be very different from how an educated European names them in 1940 (or 1993). But we cannot transcend our place and time. (*The New Leviathan* was conceived as a response to the great witch doctor who wrote *Mein Kampf*. But I have no time and space to explain why I think Collingwood's critical historicism fails to respond adequately to that terrible challenge. I mention Hitler only to remind you that 'magic' of language can be black as well as white.)

Collingwood himself refers to Croce when he comes to state his theory of 'utility' as the first form of practical Reason (NL, 15.16). But he has already indicated that he does not accept the *dichotomous* approach of the two Italians by thrusting 'rightness' in between 'utility' and 'duty'. Croce, as we know, regarded both 'law' and 'right' as 'economic' (i.e. in Collingwood's terminology 'utilitarian') concepts. Gentile, on the other hand, regarded social law and the state as 'ethical'. But we do not need to worry about that, because it is clear that Collingwood was only *negatively* influenced by it. He stands firmly in the English tradition of liberal opposition to the Germanic evil of 'herd-marching' (NL, 33.21.– 33.79); but that does not make him a Crocean here.

Because he insists that he has simply found his three forms of practical reason in the discourse of modern civilized Europe, we might be misled into believing that the methodologically progressive development of 'consciousness', in part I has now come to a halt. But that would be a mistake. We can easily discover why 'Utility' must come first, and how 'Right' and 'Duty' are 'modifications' of it. Utilitarian reasoning accepts its 'end' as a simple datum. No further reason need be given for it (NL, 15.42); and it is concerned with *indefinite* individual goods (NL, 15.72) which become more determinate when we have to decide what is 'right'. Even the 'right' thing is not determinate 'in every way', however. Only in the consciousness of 'duty' do we reach an end that is *omni modo determinatum*. This 'progressive determination' is something that we find in Hegel's *Phenomenology*. When Collingwood says 'I do not know what [Tell the truth] does mean' (NL, 16.75) he is making exactly that point that Hegel makes against 'Reason as Lawgiver'. But it is Bradley's *Ethical Studies* that is guiding his thought, rather than Hegel.

He tells us this himself (NL, 16.15). His whole account of 'right' – correcting the older English Utilitarians on one side, and Sir David Ross on the other – is inspired by Bradley. When rules conflict (as in Kant's famous problem about telling a lie from benevolent motives) Collingwood says exactly what Bradley would say: 'It depends upon what kind of man you intend to be' (NL, 16.72). It is this dialectics of the rules of conduct that drives us on to the concept of 'duty' as the perfectly determinate deliverance of my conscience. Just as Bentham wanted to stand still at the level of Utility, so Kant (and W. D. Ross as well) is fixated at the level of Right. But it was truly shameful on Collingwood's part to suggest that 'herd-marching' was the root of Kant's problem (NL, 16.75n.). This was obviously an afterthought. In reality Collingwood understood the influence of Newtonian science on Kant better than that. He does proper justice to Kant's theory in his chapter on Duty (NL, 17.62–17.7); and it was from Vico (I am sure) that he got the contrast between the Kingdom of Ends as 'Plato's Republic' and the phenomenal world as 'the sewage of Romulus'.[12]

Collingwood's theory of 'duty' is Crocean. What he says about Bradley's 'My Station and its Duties' being a 'Kantian regularian morality' (NL, 17.17) is rather inaccurate; and although his own ultimate reliance on 'religion' was certainly inspired by Bradley (and other Anglo-Hegelians), this mistake about Bradley's ethics shows how the later influence of Croce prevailed in his mind (and his memory) as far as the concept of 'duty' was concerned (cf. NL, 17.80).

At this point my examination of the influences detectable in part I is complete; and this is a good place to stop. For although I could find more evidence of Italian influence – and specifically of Gentile's influence[13] – in part II, and even in part III, I should only be reinforcing points that have been well enough established already; whereas it is the last point offered by part I that forms our proper climax. When Collingwood says in NL, 18.51 that 'History is to duty what modern science is to right', he is pointing to Croce's concept of 'ethicopolitical history' as the context with which all 'modern' philosophical analysis is to be done. This is not only an appropriate summary of what he owes to the Italians; it points also to what is original and different in Collingwood's work. Even as a philosopher of historical methodology and historical interpretation, he is more of an empirical scientist than his Italian mentors. Neither of them could have produced the systematic theory of 'experience' that Hobbes inspired him to write. It involves techniques of introspection, and experimental observation (e.g. the observation of fairy tales) which they regarded as beneath the dignity of the philosopher. Freud was even less worthy of notice, in their eyes, than Hobbes. It might occur to Croce (not Gentile) to remind us of Panurge telling Pantagruel who he is in fourteen languages (NL, 16.61). But it is Peirce deciding whether to pay his fare with five pennies or a nickel whom we remember when Collingwood discusses the problem of how he is to pay for his tobacco (NL, 15.71). Collingwood and Peirce were both of them as far removed from the Olympian Don Benedetto and from the hyper-enthusiastic Professor Gentile, as they were from the pedantic Kantian, H. A. Prichard, who can solemnly discuss 'shouting to revive a fainting man' as a possible 'duty'.

There is no need, therefore, for those who feel that Collingwood has been underrated and undervalued to be shy about recognizing his debt to the Italians. He was shy about it, because those who were not 'idealists' themselves, used it as an excuse for dismissing him unheard. But times have changed, and it is those who were at the door ready to carry him out for dead while he was yet alive, who have now perished. Now they are buried, and he is still with us. We can even recognize him now as a forerunner of J. L. Austin and the dictionary readers. But he was not that kind of Baconian observer either. In fact there is nothing better calculated to show us the humbly systematic 'moral scientist' that he aspired to be (in the tradition of Hobbes, Locke, Hume and Bradley) than a close examination of what he did with the work of his Italian masters. It was by 'naturalizing' them (and by studying the latest introspective psychology) that he became the genuinely original philosopher of mind that he really is.

## Notes

[1] See G. Gentile, *Genesis and Structure of Society* (Urbana, 1960 (paper 1966)), 7-41. The discussion of Collingwood runs from 14 to 20.

[2] Compare Gentile, *Sommario di pedagogia*, I, 3, note (for example); *Leviathan* (Oakeshott), 60. Collingwood himself quotes the conclusion of Hobbes' 'Introduction', This makes the substitution of *in teipsum redi* for the Hobbesian *nosce teipsum* more striking.

[3] See David Boucher, *The Social and Political Thought of R. G. Collingwood* (Cambridge, Cambridge University Press, 1989), 251, n.85.

[4] The Oxford Idealists were very excited about the appearance of this book (1931). The best evidence for this is that Collingwood's erstwhile tutor, E. F. Carritt, began to translate it into English almost at once. The students of J. A. Smith, Collingwood, and H. J. Paton (and others whose names I do not know) would have had a translation at hand by 1932 if the publisher had not gone bankrupt – see *Genesis and Structure* (1960), 54, item 8.

⁵ See ch.3. This essay was first published in the *Giornale critico* in 1928 (it can be found now in Gentile, *Opere complete*, 36).
⁶ Whether Croce's theory of a dialectic of distincts lay behind the distinction between thoughts as 'constituents' of mind and feelings as 'apanages' ( NL, 4.17–4.19) I cannot say. There may be no reason to postulate Italian influence here. There is need for more work on the theory of 'feeling' in the British Idealists generally; and Collingwood's theory would be the right focus for it, because he took account of Freud (who was unknown to earlier British thinkers, and haughtily dismissed by the Italians).
⁷ I am deliberately ignoring the influence of Hegel's *Phenomenology* because of Collingwood's anti-German bias in his last years. His serially progressive development of the thesis that 'mind is what it does' certainly has its inspiration in the *Phenomenology*, and the progression from sensation, through perception to understanding is certainly modelled on it. But we need more evidence before we can discuss Hegel's direct influence fruitfully. The influence of the other 'phenomenology' (Husserl etc.) does not seem to have been studied yet. Perhaps (like myself) Collingwood was virtually untouched by it. But we must wait for someone who has examined the papers to tell us the answer here.
⁸ If I am allowed a blind guess, I will hazard the opinion that it was the *Principles of Psychology* which helped Collingwood formulate his own 'painter's experience' as he does (compare the *Principles of Art* as an evidential foundation for this hypothesis).
⁹ I have to point out that I am not an 'expert' here, because I do not know what the Anglo-Idealists untouched by Italian influence said about this either before or after the appearance of Moore's 'Refutation of Idealism'.
¹⁰ All of the discussions of Peirce, Royce and Mead in my *Social Philosophy of Giovanni Gentile* arose from the comments and suggestions of M. H. Fisch, when he read the first draft of the Ph.D. thesis in 1953.
¹¹ This may be a prejudiced judgement. It was through observing the bookshelves of H. H. Price that I myself first realized that G. H. Mead was someone whom I ought to know more about. (But Price could read more widely in his chosen field, because he did not try to read in as many fields as Collingwood.)
¹² He got his classical reference (Cicero speaking of the younger Cato) by looking into the *Oxford Dictionary of Quotations*, I expect (that is how I found it). But the tag fixed itself in his mind (just as it did in mine) through Vico's use of it in *Scienza nuova*, 131. Vico has not arrived even in the 1979 edition of the ODQ.
¹³ Thus Collingwood's theory of 'dialectic' is Hegelian – not simply

'Platonic' as it might appear (and as Collingwood wants to pretend – see NL, 24.61 and 29.3–29.5). But when he insists that dialectic is between contradictories (NL, 29.52) we can go further and say that he is consciously siding with Gentile against Croce.

# Vico, Collingwood and the Character of a Historical Philosophy

## B. A. HADDOCK

That Vico exercised a profound influence on Collingwood's thought is by now something of a commonplace. Indeed, we have it on Knox's authority that Collingwood regarded Vico as the philosopher from whom he had learnt most (IH, viii). And yet the account Collingwood offers of his own intellectual development in the *Autobiography* curiously omits Vico.[1] Whatever problems the *Autobiography* might pose for a reconstruction of Collingwood's intellectual biography, it is clear from publications spanning his career that he was by no means anxious to obscure Vico's seminal contributions to traditions of thought which had nurtured his own conception of philosophy. In *Speculum Mentis*, for example, Vico's contention that 'poetry is the natural speech of children and savages' is described as 'the clue to the solution of all the problems of aesthetic'; while Croce's aesthetic theories, fashionable at the time and largely endorsed by Collingwood, are seen as closely dependent on Vico (SM, 58, 74). Nor does Collingwood's regard for Vico's contribution to philosophy of art diminish in his later writings. In the *Principles of Art* Vico's portrayal of the childlike quality of art is again alluded to; and he is described as the originator of 'the philosophical theory of art as imagination' (PA, 80, 138).

References to Vico's significance in philosophy of history are both more fulsome and more elaborate. In *Speculum Mentis* we find Vico accorded pride of place as one of the pioneers of 'the revolution in historical thought which took place in the eighteenth century' (though Collingwood adds the rather curious claim, presumably suggested to him by his study of Croce's radically reconstructive monograph on Vico, that 'even Vico thought that historical facts could be deduced a priori in the absence of positive evidence') (SM, 216).[2] By 1930 Collingwood had come to identify Vico with one of the crucial turning points of modern thought. In his Historical Association pamphlet on the philosophy of history he describes Vico as having 'laid the foundations of the modern philosophy of history in much the same sense in which Descartes . . . laid those of the modern philosophy of science'.[3] In his discussion of Vico in *The Idea of History* (his fullest account of Vico's thought in print), Collingwood attributed two seminal innovations to Vico. In the first place, he had exploited the advances in critical method made in the seventeenth century in order to show that 'historical thought can be constructive as well as critical, cutting it loose from its dependence on written authorities and making it genuinely original or self-dependent, able to recover by scientific analysis of data truths which have been completely forgotten' (IH, 70–1). And, secondly, he had 'developed the philosophical principles implicit in his historical work up to a point' which demanded a reappraisal of philosophy itself (IH, 71).

What Collingwood has here attributed to Vico assumes a larger significance in the context of his own thought. In his mature work he saw the elaboration of an autonomous theory of historical knowledge as the burning task confronting modern philosophy. And he was quite clear that establishing a proper epistemological foundation for history would have radical implications for the character of philosophy as a whole. When, in the *Autobiography*, he described his life's work as having 'been in the main an attempt to bring about a *rapprochement* between philosophy and history', he was consciously setting his own achievement in the context of a group of concerns which he had always traced back to Vico (A, 77).

Vico, then, can be seen to have been an abiding presence throughout Collingwood's career. His very first publication had been his translation of Croce's *La filosofia di Giambattista Vico*.[4] And Croce himself saw Vico as a key influence in Collingwood's shift from a youthful adherence to Idealism to a later adoption of a version of 'absolute historicism'.[5] Croce's claim, however, needs to be treated with some caution. He assumes that Collingwood's mature thought agreed in all essentials with his own. Croce sees the work of Collingwood's youth (down to *Speculum Mentis* in 1924) as the product of Gentile's influence.[6] He endorses Collingwood's own reservations about *Speculum Mentis* recorded in the *Autobiography* (A, 56). And a comparison of Collingwood's position in his early essay on 'Croce's Philosophy of History' with his view in *The Idea of History* certainly supports Croce's contention that Collingwood had moved towards a conception of philosophy as the 'methodological moment in historiography'.[7] In the early essay Croce had been criticized, and Vico with him, for treating philosophy as 'a mere subordinate moment in history'.[8] Yet Collingwood's strategy in *The Idea of History*, concerned to explore 'the philosophical problems created by the existence of organized and systematized historical research', was cast very much in the Crocean mould (IH, 6). Whether or not Croce's interpretation of Collingwood's development is defensible (and he can appeal for further support to Collingwood's admission in a letter of 5 January 1928 that 'I have learnt from you to regard philosophy as primarily the methodology of history'), it certainly confounds the task of charting Vico's influence upon Collingwood.[9]

We are faced with two related problems. On the one side, while it would be absurd to deny that Croce exercised an important and possibly decisive influence on certain aspects of Collingwood's thought, it would be misleading to identify their views, especially on the larger question of the character of philosophy. Collingwood might choose to explain his debt to Croce in a private letter in terms of a common conception of philosophy as the methodology of history; but in his mature work this was never more than one aspect of an endeavour to specify the historical dimension in experience. Collingwood's *Essay on Philosophical Method*, belonging as it does to the same period as the letter cited above, becomes a crucial text in any evaluation of his development. He is preoccupied there not with the way historians, or even historians of philosophy, go about their work but rather with the relation of philosophy as a whole to its past. And even in *The Idea of History*, where his approach is more narrowly methodological, he specifically identifies as a further task for philosophy a 'general overhauling of all philosophical questions in the light of the results reached by the philosophy of history in the narrower (methodological) sense', issuing in 'a complete philosophy conceived from an historical point of view' (IH, 6–7).

The other side of our problem concerns Croce's role in fostering Vico's reputation in the early decades of the twentieth century. Croce had been a leading influence behind the definitive edition of Vico's works.[10] And his own monograph did much to bring Vico to the forefront of philosophical attention.[11] But he had never cast himself in the role of the modest commentator. His reading of Vico had a fierce polemical edge. Vico had been appropriated by a succession of critics to bolster their own philosophical positions.[12] When Croce turned his attention to Vico, his wider interest in discrediting the remnants of positivist and Marxist history was very much in mind. Vico was valued precisely in so far as he could be seen to sustain the fundamental tenets of Croce's own philosophy. Croce was clear that his reconstruction of Vico's thought was a partial operation. Whatever in Vico's *Scienza nuova* might be cited in support of the idea of a science of society was left on one side, with attention fixed instead on the gulf which separated history and the humanities from the natural sciences.[13] Collingwood, coming to Vico through Croce, cannot but have found Croce's interpretation persuasive. Just how far Vico can be said to have influenced him independently of Croce remains to be established.

Collingwood follows Croce in his detailed discussion of Vico in *The Idea of History*, focusing on the epistemological and methodological ideas in the *Scienza nuova* which might serve as the foundation for an autonomous theory of history. He sees Vico's crucial contribution as the extension of a conventionalist theory of mathematics in his early writings to the larger view of institutions as artefacts in the *Scienza nuova*.[14] If Vico is right in his contention that men can only know that which they have made (*verum et factum convertuntur*), it follows not only that Descartes and his followers have misconstrued the paradigmatic status of mathematics for the natural sciences but that the historical world (as a human artefact) can be rendered intelligible in ways that are always foreclosed with regard to nature.[15] Attempts in seventeenth- and eighteenth-century thought to fashion a science of human nature after the example of the physical sciences were thus doubly mistaken. Not only had the special characteristics which distinguished the human world been disregarded but the epistemological basis of natural science had itself been misconceived. The best that could be achieved in the natural sciences were hypothetical reconstructions of processes which might be supposed to be akin to the workings of nature. Nature itself, as God's artefact, would be fully intelligible only to him. Human institutions, however, as the product of agents pursuing their various ends, could be reconstructed from the inside. Collingwood could thus see in Vico's theory of historical knowledge an intimation of his own view that a proper explanation of human conduct required both objective behavioural description and internal understanding (IH, 213). And he claims that Vico's view of history as 'emphatically something made by the human mind', with its stress on the piecemeal development of institutions and practices, represents the first 'completely modern idea of what the subject-matter of history is' (IH, 64-5)

Yet Collingwood's identification of Vico's view with his own was always fraught with difficulties. In the first place, he claims more for the *verum/factum* principle in the sphere of institutions than seems warranted. Collingwood argues that, for Vico, 'the fabric of human society is created by man out of nothing, and every detail of this fabric is therefore a human factum, eminently knowable to the human mind as such' (IH, 65). But making out of nothing was always something that Vico reserved either for God in his creation of the world or for men in purely conventional contexts.[16] Geometry remained a paradigm case of human knowledge precisely because all its elements were under (definitional) control. In extending the *verum/factum* principle to the human world, Vico was not committed to arguing that men make history in precisely the way that geometers invest surfaces, lines and figures with certain properties. In an important respect, men do not know quite what they are doing as they struggle to do the best they can for themselves in the difficult circumstances of practical life. Their actions have unintended consequences which thwart the achievement of their ends. And their ignorance of the myriad hopes and ambitions of other agents renders their grasp of the wider social context necessarily imperfect. It remains the case, however, that when men act in the world they are contributing to the creation of languages, practices, customs, institutions etc. They certainly make their own history but not (as Marx was later to reiterate) exactly as they choose.[17] Indeed Vico is committed to the view that what men have made (a world of civil institutions) will only be intelligible to them retrospectively, through the application of the sorts of methodological principles defended in the *Scienza nuova*. What he cannot allow is that a historian bent upon reconstructing an episode in civil history should restrict himself to grasping the thought in the mind of the agent. Collingwood's contention that a 'historian of a certain thought must think for himself that very same thought, not another like it' would thus be applicable only in special cases (such as an account of Euclid's proof of Pythagoras) (A, 111). Vico's concern is rather to understand both an agent's view of the world and the wider developmental context which lends significance to what was actually said or done.

What we encounter here is more than a technical disagreement over a specialized issue. Collingwood had specifically insisted in the Introduction to *The Idea of History* that his own view of philosophy of history should not be confused with the speculative systems of Voltaire or Hegel or the nineteenth-century positivists which sought a substantive pattern in history. He conceived the philosophy of history, instead, 'as thought of the second degree', exploring 'the philosophical problems created by the existence of organized and systematized historical research' (IH, 3, 6). For Vico, on the other hand, a distinction between (what might be called) speculative and critical philosophy of history could not arise. Reflection on the methodological problems confronted in reconstructing past human conduct involved not simply formal questions about the historian's practice (the nature of evidence, judgement etc.) but substantive questions about the kinds of agents whose conduct was under scrutiny. It was precisely because human nature had undergone such dramatic transformations in the course of its development that historians required more than critical reflection on their own methods in order to correct misleading judgements. Sensitivity in the portrayal of the customs and traditions of remote cultures could certainly be encouraged. What historians had somehow to grasp, however, was that reason itself was a product of history. And hence the application of the criteria of rationality of a civilized society to distant or obscure periods would necessarily engender distorted accounts of the past. Scholars, according to Vico, had judged the origins of humanity 'on the basis of their own enlightened, cultivated, and magnificent times', when they should have devoted all their efforts to understanding the vastly different thinking of early peoples who interpreted the world in imaginative rather than rational terms (SN, 123). What the *Scienza nuova* offered was not only an account of why historical thinking might go wrong but also an explanation of how general patterns of thought had developed. Indeed Vico would argue that without the support of a substantive developmental theory, his specific methodological recommendations would be inapplicable.

Collingwood's distance from Vico on this point is evident when we turn to the terms in which he sought to establish the autonomy of history from natural science. History, concerned as it was with 'actions of human beings that have been done in the past', finds itself committed by its very subject matter to methods and procedures that have no parallels in the natural sciences (IH, 9). Observation and experiment had transformed the natural sciences since the seventeenth century. But (*pace* Hume) such methods could not be applied to the social world because human action comprised a dimension which was not open to empirical observation or generalization of the usual kind. An action (according to Collingwood's celebrated distinction) involved not simply a behavioural dimension ('everything belonging to it which can be described in terms of bodies and their movements') but an 'inside' which 'can only be described in terms of thought' (IH, 213). What made an action meaningful was not the bodily movements which happened to accompany it but the thought it was intended to express. Men made history in the sense that they 'enacted' intentions. They acted the way they did because they had the ideas they had. And a historian could (in principle) understand a past action because an idea once 'enacted' could always be 're-enacted' in the historian's own mind.

So far Collingwood might be supposed to be pursuing a Vichian theme. He could insist, with Vico, that historians had access to an insider's understanding of the civil world which was different in kind from the hypotheses and laws of natural science. But a closer examination of his methodological comments on how that insider's knowledge might be unearthed reveals a fundamental rift in their positions. Collingwood's strategy is to focus on the individual agent. His central contention is that history should be seen not as a succession of 'mere events', connected only by constant conjunction, but as a *Zusammenhang* of intentions. A historical inquiry would not be complete with the enumeration of the sorts of occasions on which events of a specific kind might be expected. A historian would want to know why A did B. His answer would state a logical rather than contingent connection between the thoughts in the mind of an agent and the actions he performed. Faced with a puzzling piece of evidence, the historian had to establish what a man in particular circumstances could logically be up to. His solution to the dilemma would be an inference from the documents at his disposal, and historical knowledge would be demonstrable because the historian could show at each stage of his argument how he was led to relate questions to answers as intentions to actions.

Collingwood's crucial claim here is that an acceptable account of a past action should be in terms which the agent in question could (in principle) have recognized. Agents must be presumed to have been trying to do something from the evidence of the traces which their conduct has left behind. What Collingwood leaves out of account, however, is the problematic nature of instrumental rationality itself. Vico's specific criticism of the historical practice of his contemporaries had focused on the naive belief that critical criteria prevalent in advanced societies could be presumed to have been current at more primitive stages of development. But the thinking of early cultures had been quite otherwise. Vico describes the first societies as 'small, crude, and quite obscure', peopled by creatures whose world was a projection of their imaginations (SN, 123). The rules and conventions which governed their conduct were fantastic rather than rational. Accordingly, it was 'beyond our power to enter into the vast imagination of those first men, whose minds were not in the least abstract, refined, or spiritualized, because they were entirely immersed in the senses, buffeted by the passions, buried in the body' (SN, 378). To apply a logic of question and answer to these men would presuppose that one had already established what (in principle) they could be trying to do. Collingwood's methodology, in fact, hinges on the assumption that thought is 'an eternal object', unaffected by 'the fact of its happening in time' (IH, 218). Vico's point, however, was that forms of argument, no less than specific moral or political principles, were transformed in the course of historical development. Indeed, it was disregard of the historical character of ideas that rendered accounts of early societies anachronistic.

Vico's case against anachronism depended not simply on awareness of the snares which might entrap the hasty historian, leading him to interpret evidence in the light of his own settled assumptions, but on a wider conception of history as a succession of necessary stages of development. His celebrated division of history into successive ages of 'gods', 'heroes' and 'men', each endowed with a distinctive set of ideas, attitudes and institutions, constituted an ideal scale of development (an 'ideal eternal history traversed in time by the history of every nation in its rise, development, maturity, decline, and fall', SN, 349). It was not supposed that the detailed histories of different nations would be identical, nor that the 'natural' sequence might not be interrupted by contingent circumstances (war, conquest, famine etc.). But Vico felt that he had established a model which would enable obscure ideas or artefacts to be understood in relation to the cast of mind of the society from which they had originally issued.

It is not difficult to see why Collingwood should have ignored this dimension of Vico's thought. The implication of his distinction between critical and speculative philosophy of history was that confusion of the two kinds of inquiry would issue in serious conceptual muddles. And yet we find Vico insisting that sound methodological practice requires the support of a substantive theory of historical development. Nor is the model for Collingwood's selective approach to Vico far to seek. The centrepiece of Croce's monograph on Vico had been an attempt to apply distinctions to the *Scienza nuova* that had been left confused in the original text. Thus Vico's pure philosophy was distinguished analytically from an associated mass of historical and empirical material.[18] Whether or not Croce's procedure is justified (it is, of course, difficult to reconcile with the approach to past ideas recommended in *The Idea of History* and the *Autobiography*), Collingwood had himself adopted a radically reconstructive technique in his treatment of individual thinkers. His concern was to chart the emergence of a defensible conception of history from confused beginnings; and at each turn his own philosophy served as the criterion of what that defensible view might be.

It could not be expected, then, that Collingwood would present a balanced picture of Vico in *The Idea of History*. He was interested in Vico only in so far as his arguments could be seen to provide a foundation for later (more satisfactory) accounts of the character of historical knowledge. And, as we have noticed, he chose to focus on Vico's contribution to epistemology rather than his wider conception of the pattern of the past. When he turned to Vico's specific methodological proposals (his use of language and myth as evidence, his conception of tradition as a 'refractive index' which distorts the transmission of ideas to posterity, and his advocacy of a comparative method to highlight the broad features of societies at similar stages of development), he disregarded the speculative philosophy of history which underpinned them (IH, 70). Yet Vico saw the substantive theory of the way societies change as crucial to his whole project. The simple claim that men make their own history would be bereft of methodological implications without it. Vico had never argued that we could understand the historical world from the 'inside' simply because we shared with men of the past a capacity for 'making' ideas, institutions, artefacts etc. Indeed he claimed that the gulf which separated the primitive and civilized worlds was so great that we moderns lacked the 'power to enter into the vast imagination' of the first men (SN, 378) But while we 'cannot at all imagine' how the founders of humanity thought, we can make efforts to 'comprehend' them (SN 378).[19] And it is the model of historical development (the *storia ideale eterna*) which furnishes us with an interpretative framework.

What had seemed to unite Vico and Collingwood, an insistence that problems of historical understanding could not be resolved by adopting the methods and procedures of the natural sciences, thus conceals a fundamental methodological divide. But it would be rash to assume that Vico's influence upon Collingwood extended no further than Croce's suggestive misreading. Collingwood had always seen his treatment of conceptual problems which arise in the conduct of historical research as a preliminary stage in a larger enterprise, the exploration of the historical dimension in experience as a whole. This project, involving as it did a reappraisal of the nature of mind and language, was somewhat swamped in *The Idea of History*. Yet it is arguable that Collingwood's views on the character of history have been misinterpreted through neglect of his wider philosophical interest.[20] And it is certainly the case that he is closer to Vico in his conception of the role of philosophy than in his detailed treatment of specific methodological issues. In what follows attention will be focused on two related claims: (1) that philosophy, like human nature itself, is a product of its history; (2) that reflection on that history is not a prolegomenon to the pursuit of philosophical questions but the very substance of the discipline.

It should be clear from the outset that Vico and Collingwood both rejected the view of philosophy as a self-contained discipline, generating its own problems and employing methods unique to itself. Philosophy should attend, instead, to the characteristics which distinguish the different modes of understanding and practice given in concrete experience. Where traditional philosophy had gone astray was precisely in its procedures. What purported to be a pursuit of a universal truth could be no more than a description of how we happened to see things for the moment; and the methods we employed would similarly presuppose that what was currently taken to be sound argument could be presumed to be applicable in any context.

Collingwood focuses his criticism in the *Autobiography* on the universalist assumptions of traditional philosophy. He specifically takes issue with the supposition, crucial to the practice of his contemporaries, that philosophy is concerned with a central stock of 'eternal problems' which had been handled more or less adequately by the philosophers of the past. Such a view presupposes an abstract criterion of truth. Collingwood argues, however, on both logical and methodological grounds, that an abstract criterion is not only unattainable in practice but inconceivable in principle. When we explore a philosophical problem, he suggests that we must initially establish which question or questions a given argument is designed to answer. When we go on to ask whether or not an argument is true, we must mean true in relation to a specific question. To argue that we should appraise an argument outside a context of question and answer is to deceive ourselves by our own subtlety. We would be presupposing as a criterion of truth simply the standards which we would have employed had the argument been one we had elaborated for ourselves in response to our own dilemmas. Yet it is only through historical inquiry that we can establish which questions have actually been posed. The philosopher who disregards the historical dimension of his work is, according to Collingwood, in the position of trying to argue that Plato was right (or wrong) without having ascertained what he was trying to say (A, 29–43, 53–76).

Vico's specific target was the anachronism at the heart of the social and political thought of his day. The fashionable theories of natural law and social contract each presupposed that basic interpretative criteria remained unaffected by historical development, enabling assumptions about the nature of rational argument or reasonable behaviour to be transposed from one epoch to another without detriment to either historical accuracy or prescriptive force.[21] Here was an obvious source of historical confusion. Vico had discovered in the course of his detailed historical studies that sense could not be made of (say) the early history of Roman law or Homeric poetry without taking the radically different ethos of a primitive society into account.[22] But his larger concern was with the chronic misconception of the character of philosophy which followed from the adoption of anachronistic categories. Philosophy as a pursuit was itself the product of historical development. Yet natural-law theorists saw no need to appeal beyond the natural light of reason in order to specify the proper relations between individuals in any society. Vico insisted, instead, on a distinction between the 'natural law of the peoples' and the 'natural law of the philosophers'.[23] It was the fact that certain practices had emerged (within the 'customs of the nations') which made the subsequent philosophical understanding of natural law possible.[24] Without an awareness of the antecedent developments which enable philosophical questions to arise, philosophers would find themselves perpetuating a series of myths that obscured any understanding of either formal argument or the past. The point to stress here, however, is that Vico had come to his reappraisal of the role of philosophy not simply through criticisms of the shortcomings of other philosophers but through reflection on the implications of assumptions embodied in the work of historians, jurists and literary critics.

The picture we see emerging, then, is of philosophy as an exploration of the presuppositions of such fields as art, history, natural science etc. Unlike the logical positivists, however, whose stress on philosophy as a second-order inquiry might seem to be strikingly similar to this position, both Collingwood and Vico held that a philosophical account of what made a particular mode of discourse possible also had implications for the way that mode of discourse should be conducted. Collingwood's contention that philosophy is 'thought about thought', reiterated throughout his career, involved the clear implication that a principal means of improving the substantive work of a discipline was to clarify the conceptual confusions which practical work had thrown up (IH, 1 and EPM, 160–70). The continued flourishing of historical studies, for example, would thus depend, at least in part, upon the sorts of investigations which occupied Collingwood in *The Idea of History*. And in the *Autobiography* and *An Essay on Metaphysics* he argued the stronger case that the well-being of a civilization was linked to the capacity of philosophy to expose and eradicate muddled thinking (A, 147–67 and EM, 133–42, and 338–43). Vico, too, saw the *Scienza nuova* not simply as a response to philosophical error but as a foundation for a surer understanding of the beginnings of human history. Indeed he regarded the exercises in historical reconstruction which constitute the body of the text as practical illustrations of the implications of his theories.[25]

But it is not only that philosophy should concern itself with other (historically given) modes of experience; rather that philosophy requires an account of the significance of its own past if it is to be thoroughly self-critical. Problems generated in concrete fields are thus not only a logical, but also a historical presupposition of philosophical inquiry. Vico makes the point in terms of his distinction between 'poetic wisdom' (*sapienza poetica*) and 'esoteric wisdom' (*sapienza riposta*) (SN, 363, 364). A set of purely expressive concepts (*universali fantastici*) are seen as a necessary presupposition of an intelligible world (SN, 209). Vico portrays the first peoples as entirely devoid of rational concepts. Yet they require some sort of conceptual framework in order to think and act. Vico's response to this dilemma (common to all theorists who try to explain the historical emergence of civil society from a state of nature) was to seek the genesis of civilization in the intellectual destitution of the first men. Without the assistance of rational discourse or revelation, 'the first men of the gentile nations, children of nascent mankind, created things according to their own ideas' (SN, 376). Unable to conceive the world in rational terms, 'they gave the things they wondered at substantial being after their own ideas, just as children do, whom we see take inanimate things in their hands and play with them and talk to them as though they were living persons' (SN, 375). An initial conceptual order accordingly emerges not through critical reflection but through a species of 'poetic wisdom'. Imaginative distinctions would be made from the data of immediate experience, linking different objects or activities together as a class. And though such distinctions might appear to be fanciful or even absurd when judged according to the standards of later (more sophisticated) times, they at least provided the foundation for a meaningful world.

The crucial contrast is between a 'rational and abstract' metaphysics ('like that of learned men now') and an imaginative metaphysics which projects properties and possibilities upon the external world (SN, 375). Vico is not simply making a point about the style of thinking which happened to be characteristic of early societies. His contention is that primitive culture ('by a demonstrated necessity of nature') had to assume a 'poetic' form (SN, 34). He couples his empirical claim about the character of the first phases of civilization with a logical claim about the necessary priority of a purely expressive mode of thought. Early men cannot be portrayed as taking stock of their situation and acting in their best interest because (quite literally) they had nothing with which to take stock. The world around them and their (somewhat haphazard) relations with one another were interpreted in terms of images they had conjured from their unrestrained imaginations. The intelligible world was a fantasy; and it was only very much later that men began to reflect on the relative merits of this or that conception. What must be emphasized, however, is that critical reflection (described by Vico as the 'esoteric wisdom' of the philosophers) would not have been possible without a prior body of unreflective images and ideas as a basis for deliberation (SN, 363, 1043). A theory of knowledge which failed to account for the 'poetic' roots of understanding, according to this view, should be regarded as seriously defective.

Collingwood endorses a comparable position in the *Principles of Art*. His principal target is the view of art as some kind of optional extra, an embellishment or amusement or means of gratifying repressed desires. What such views miss is any conception of art as a necessary mode of experience, indispensable both as a reference point for reflection and as a means of attaining any degree of self-knowledge. Without some sort of interpretative framework, experience would be literally inconceivable. We would be passive creatures to whom things simply happened, unable even to distinguish one experience from another. Raw, undifferentiated experience is transformed into something meaningful precisely through the exercise of capacities associated with the world of art. We become aware of our emotions, for example, only by giving expression to them (PA, 105–24). And this involves two related activities: selecting an aspect of our experience for particular attention and projecting that experience in a symbolic guise which enables it to serve as a focal point in our subsequent experience. In imagining a state of ourselves and a sphere in which to operate, we are actually giving ourselves an identity. Our feelings, which had been merely 'impressions of sense', are raised to a higher plane as 'ideas of imagination' (PA, 222). Where we had previously been dominated by fleeting sensations, we are now able to dwell upon a sensation or feeling at will, lending a settled quality to our inclinations. And though imagination alone would not be enough to enable us to make abstract judgements about our conduct, we would (at least) have acquired sufficient self-consciousness to see ourselves as creatures demanding distinctive kinds of satisfaction.

Collingwood follows Vico and Croce, then, in attributing an epistemological significance to the imagination. The fact that we can make relational judgements presupposes a world of concepts and objects; and these can only originate in our ability to focus attention and project qualities (PA, 223–87). He follows his sources, too, in contrasting the universal judgements of philosophy and science (the former categorical, the latter hypothetical) with the singular assertions of the imagination (cf. SN, 209, 219). When philosophers reflect on the nature of categorical or hypothetical judgements, however, they must give some account of the antecedent conditions which make such judgements possible. And, because the roots of philosophical understanding lie outside philosophy itself, this can be achieved only by engaging in a species of inquiry which involves both philosophical and historical dimensions. A phenomenology of forms of experience (such as Collingwood had attempted in *Speculum Mentis*) is thus a central philosophical desideratum. What is at issue here is precisely philosophy's relation both to other modes of experience and to its own past. Disregard of the wider context renders philosophy dogmatic, an application of certain methods to a designated array of problems without a grasp of why such problems should arise. A self-critical philosopher requires the skills of a historian. And in exercising those skills, he is not providing a foundation for philosophy but doing philosophy itself. As Hegel had long ago observed, 'the way to science is itself already science, . . . the science of the experience of consciousness.'[26]

To argue that the pursuit of philosophy presupposes an elaborate cultural inheritance, and that an account of the significance of that inheritance is a central philosophical task, does not commit one to any particular view of the way a historically orientated philosophy should be conducted. Yet the role of imagination in constituting a meaningful world of experience has far-reaching implications for our understanding of ideas, symbols, artefacts etc. We are dealing here not simply with a constructivist view of culture but with what might be described as a constructivist view of human nature itself. Collingwood had always insisted that 'mind is what it does', a product of successive attempts to understand its own nature and to act in the world in accordance with its various conceptions (IH, 226). Vico, too, had seen men as essentially self-creative, acting and reacting in relation to other men and circumstances, moulding their characters in ways which only historical awareness would disclose. Men had (collectively) created an identity for themselves through their thoughts and deeds. What they had done or could do, what they judged to be true or false, significant or trivial, depended upon a social context which their own actions would be instrumental in changing. Vico's specific objection to the natural-law theorists (Grotius, Selden and Pufendorf) had been that they failed to take account of the transformation wrought in human nature in the course of its development.[27] They assumed that their own moral and political ideas were universally valid, applicable in the evaluation of arguments and practices in any age or context. Vico's contention, however, is that philosophy, no less than other cultural artefacts, is a product of a particular mode of social life. Its judgements reflect the dominant concerns and styles of argument within a culture. Nor is it simply a subtle ideological 'colouring' that is in question here. Vico insists on the logical point that arguments make sense only in a given framework. When that framework is disregarded, and attempts are made to transpose criteria from one context to another, arguments are rendered either meaningless or absurd.

Collingwood himself addressed precisely these issues in *An Essay on Metaphysics*. He was concerned specifically with the logical problem of what is presupposed by the fact that we can formulate arguments, ask questions etc. Just as he had stressed the importance of locating a text in an appropriate context of question and answer, so he now seeks to identify the presuppositions which enable questions to arise (A, 29–43, 53–76). To ask a question presupposes a state of affairs that makes the question meaningful. To use Collingwood's example, to ask a man whether he has stopped beating his wife presupposes that he had been in the habit of beating her (EM, 25–6). And the presupposition will itself be dependent upon other presuppositions concerning the conventions surrounding the relations between men and women in a particular society. These presuppositions Collingwood calls 'relative', in the sense that they can be shown to be related to other presuppositions in a chain of question and answer (EM, 29–30). We cannot, however, ask questions about the presuppositions of presuppositions without end; ultimately we will be faced with a presupposition which it makes no sense to question, what Collingwood calls an 'Absolute Presupposition' (EM, 31–3). 'Absolute Presuppositions' constitute the 'hinges' without which the rest of our questioning activity would be meaningless. For the metaphysician who knows his business, it is not a question of establishing which 'Absolute Presuppositions' are true, but rather of finding out 'what absolute presuppositions have been made by this or that person or group of persons, on this or that occasion or group of occasions, in the course of this or that piece of thinking' (EM, 47). A historical mistake about which absolute presuppositions have in fact been made on a given occasion necessarily distorts our understanding of an argument. And in explaining the natural sources of anachronistic judgements Collingwood adopts something very like Vico's analysis of the 'conceits' of nations and scholars, each intent upon interpreting a remote body of ideas in terms of their own basic assumptions (see EM, 56–7, 86, 160, 203; cf. SN, 122–8). For Collingwood, then, 'all metaphysical questions are historical questions, and all metaphysical propositions are historical propositions (EM, 49). As a historical science, metaphysics is conceived as an exploration of the presuppositions of particular modes of thought. The traditional aspiration to depict a 'timeless' reality is set aside in favour of an account of the way patterns of thought have changed in the course of historical development. And the clear implication is that arguments presupposing radically different assumptions are in fact incommensurable.

The parallel with the *Scienza nuova* is manifest. Vico's *storia ideale eterna* furnished a set of criteria which enabled the artefacts of a particular society (ideas, institutions, symbols etc.) to be interpreted without recourse to anachronistic assumptions. The historical ages of 'gods', 'heroes' and 'men' were essentially distinct *Weltanschauungen* whose nodal assumptions gave a particular character to a way of life. Ideas and utterances couched in the idiom of one *Weltanschauung* would be unintelligible in the idiom of another; but each idiom would nevertheless constitute a necessary phase in the cycle of historical development. Whatever men had thought or done could be located on a scale of development which combined a contextual reading of the practices within a given age with an awareness of the changes that had made a particular action (mode of thought, expression, procedure etc.) possible. Only a historically conceived philosophy, in Vico's view, could disclose both the original meaning of a given argument and its larger significance in an evolving history of ideas.

But Vico is not simply concerned with the (straightforward) question of historical accuracy. His interest is principally in the philosophical question of what it means to understand anything at all. His point is clear. Utterances (arguments etc.) do not make sense in isolation, like crystals of meaning complete in themselves, but have to be set in the context of the network of assumptions from which they had issued. The appropriate response to a puzzling utterance is not to treat it as a suitable case for analytical dissection but simply to try to reconstruct the attitude of mind which might make an utterance of that sort intelligible. What might appear to be a special requirement for the historian of remote ideas is actually a *conditio sine qua non* for understanding as such. A remark addressed to a colleague over coffee, no less than an obscure text, will presuppose a determinate linguistic context. A philosopher who neglects that context when he explores past ideas will in fact have failed to comprehend precisely why he finds his colleagues so readily intelligible.

What links Vico and Collingwood together is a concern to explore the historical dimension in philosophy. Both rejected the view of human nature as a fixed phenomenon, awaiting adaptation in response to external circumstances. They looked, instead, to the gradual disclosure of human identity in the course of historical development as men sought to make themselves at home in an inhospitable world. Any general characterization of what it means to be a human being would necessarily involve an account of the significance of change through time. To ask philosophical questions about knowledge or conduct presupposed a foundation in what men had actually sought to do or say. And this could be achieved only through patient reconstruction of the original cultural context which made actions or ideas meaningful.

Vico expressed the point in his characterization of the roles of philosophy and philology in the *Scienza nuova*. In the traditional view, philosophers would be occupied exclusively with abstract and universal ideas, perennial in their appeal and unaffected by the local circumstances which might have coloured their original formulation; while philologists (among whom Vico included 'all the grammarians, historians, critics, who have occupied themselves with the study of the languages and deeds of peoples: both at home, as in their customs and laws, and abroad, as in their wars, peaces, alliances, travels, and commerce') would be intent upon the detailed specification of texts, artefacts and traditions, oblivious to wider theoretical questions about the agents whose thoughts and deeds were under scrutiny or the philosophical and methodological problems which might be encountered in studying the past (SN, 138, 139). But, according to Vico, the conventional opposition of philosophy (as the study of the universal) and philology (as the study of the particular) would not do. Philosophers could not ignore the different meanings which (apparently similar) ideas had borne in different cultures, nor could philologists disregard the changes in human nature which had obscured the original significance of artefacts from early periods of history. Philosophers and philologists needed one another's skills if they were to perform their tasks properly. Philosophers had 'failed by half in not giving certainty to their reasonings by appeal to the authority of the philologians, and likewise . . . the latter failed by half in not taking care to give their authority the sanction of truth by appeal to the reasoning of the philosophers' (SN, 140). A culture, with all its distinctive characteristics, was the product of transient events and would in time give place to a vastly different network of rules, conventions, modes of thought, feeling and behaving. Historical change pervaded all aspects of human life; the point of philosophy was to make its impact intelligible.

When Collingwood looked back on his career in the *Autobiography*, it was the 'attempt to bring about a *rapprochement* between philosophy and history' which struck him as a unifying theme (A, 77). He had endorsed an essentially Vichian conception of history as the key to a science of human conduct. He not only insisted that a properly conducted philosophy had necessarily to build upon its own past but also argued that philosophical and historical questions should be treated in similar fashion.[28] What lay behind such a claim was the view of culture as a human construct. Human judgements conferred meaning or significance upon ideas and institutions; and these would change in shifting circumstances. The role of philosophy, in this scheme of things, was twofold: to explain both how original meanings could be recovered and why it was that such methods were best suited to the study of human conduct. Vico, too, had seen philosophy as both a methodological examination of the problems involved in doing history and an analysis of what it is about human conduct that especially lends itself to historical study. Following Collingwood's discussion in *The Idea of History*, critics have tended to focus on more narrowly methodological issues in considering his debt to Vico. Yet it is in terms of the larger conception of human beings as essentially historical creatures that their views might be more profitably compared. It may be, of course, that Collingwood has followed Vico in error in jettisoning so much from the traditional view of philosophy. But an examination of a source of some of his principal arguments at least serves to clarify what he is claiming.

*Notes*

[1] See Joseph M. Levine, 'Collingwood, Vico and the *Autobiography*', *Clio* 9 (1980), 379–92.
[2] And see Benedetto Croce, *La filosofia di Giambattista Vico* (Bari, Laterza, 1911).
[3] R. G. Collingwood, 'The Philosophy of History', in his *Essays in the Philosophy of History*, ed. W. Debbins (Austin, University of Texas Press, 1965), 127.
[4] Benedetto Croce, *The Philosophy of Giambattista Vico*, translated by R. G. Collingwood (London, Howard Latimer, 1913).

5. Benedetto Croce, *Bibliografia vichiana, accresciuta e rielaborata da Fausto Nicolini* (Naples, Riccardo Ricciardini, 1947–8), 2, 823.
6. See, in addition to *Speculum Mentis*, R. G. Collingwood, 'Croce's Philosophy of History', in his *Essays in the Philosophy of History*, 3–22; and 'Can the New Idealism Dispense with Mysticism', *Aristotelian Society, Supplementary Volume* III (1923), 161–75. For discussion of Gentile's influence on Collingwood see Lionel Rubinoff, *Collingwood and the Reform of Metaphysics* (Toronto, University of Toronto Press, 1970), 315–22.
7. See Benedetto Croce, *Teoria e storia della storiografia* (Bari, Laterza, 1973, tenth edn), 140.
8. R. G. Collingwood, 'Croce's Philosophy of History', in his *Essays in the Philosophy of History*, 20.
9. See Alan Donagan, *The Later Philosophy of R. G. Collingwood* (Oxford, Clarendon Press, 1962), 315.
10. *Opere di G. B. Vico*, 8 vols. in 11 (Bari, Laterza, 1911–41). Fausto Nicolini, a close associate of Croce, was the principal editor for the series. Croce assumed responsibility for vol. 5.
11. Benedetto Croce, *La filosofia di Giambattista Vico*.
12. For full bibliographical details see Benedetto Croce, *Bibliografia vichiana*.
13. See Hayden V. White, 'What is Living and What is Dead in Croce's Criticism of Vico', in Giorgio Tagliacozzo and Hayden V. White, eds., *Giambattista Vico: an International Symposium* (Baltimore, Johns Hopkins University Press, 1969), 379–89; and B. A. Haddock, 'Vico and Idealism' (University of Oxford D.Phil. thesis, 1977).
14. See R. G. Collingwood, *The Idea of History*, 64–5; Benedetto Croce, *La filosofia di Giambattista Vico*, 11–40.
15. See Giambattista Vico, *Opere filosofiche*, ed. Paolo Cristofolini (Florence, Sansoni, 1971), 63; and *Scienza nuova*, paras. 331, 349. Henceforth reference to the *Scienza nuova* will be to SN, followed by the paragraph number common to the Nicolini edition (*Opere*, Milan and Naples, Ricardo Ricciardi 1953) and the English translation by T. G. Bergin and Max H. Fisch, *The New Science of Giambattista Vico* (Ithaca, Cornell University Press, 1968).
16. See Giambattista Vico, *Opere filosofiche*, 803.
17. Karl Marx, 'The Eighteenth Brumaire of Louis Bonaparte', in his *Surveys from Exile*, ed., D. Fernbach (Harmondsworth, Penguin, 1973), 146.
18. See Benedetto Croce, *La filosofia di Giambattista Vico*, 41–7.
19. See Leon Pompa, 'Imagination in Vico', in Giorgio Tagliacozzo, ed., *Vico: Past and Present* (Atlantic Highlands, NJ, Humanities Press, 1981), 162–70.
20. See Louis O. Mink, 'Collingwood's Historicism: a Dialectic of Process',

in Michael Krausz, ed., *Critical Essays on the Philosophy of R. G. Collingwood* (Oxford, Clarendon Press,1972), 154–78.
[21] See B. A. Haddock, *Vico's Political Thought* (Swansea, Mortlake Press, 1986), 125, 162–9, 172–82.
[22] See Max H. Fisch, 'Vico on Roman Law', in Milton R. Konvitz and Arthur E. Murphy, eds., *Essays in Political Theory Presented to George H. Sabine* (Ithaca, Cornell University Press, 1948), 62–88; Donald R. Kelley, 'Vico's Road: from Philology to Jurisprudence and Back', in Giorgio Tagliacozzo and Donald Phillip Verene, eds., *Giambattista Vico's Science of Humanity* (Baltimore, Johns Hopkins University Press, 1976), 15–29; and B. A. Haddock, 'Vico's "Discovery of the True Homer": A Case-Study in Historical Reconstruction', *Journal of the History of Ideas*, XL (1979), 583–602.
[23] Giambattista Vico, 'De constantia iurisprudentis', in *Opere giuridiche*, ed. Paolo Cristofolini (Florence, Sansoni, 1974), 673; and see SN, 311–13, 329.
[24] Giambattista Vico, 'Letter to Monsignor Filippo Maria Monti', in *Opere*, 116.
[25] See especially SN, 780–904 for Vico's 'Discovery of the True Homer'; and SN, 1009–19 for a discussion of Bodin. Cf. Collingwood's claim that in his chapter on 'Art' in his Roman Britain he had solved 'a much-debated problem in history, not by discovering fresh evidence, but by reconsidering questions of principle' (*An Autobiography*, 145). See R. G. Collingwood and J. N. L. Myres, *Roman Britain and the English Settlements* (Oxford, Clarendon Press,1936), 247–60.
[26] G. W. F. Hegel, *Phenomenology of Spirit*, transl. A. V. Miller (Oxford, Clarendon Press, 1977), 56.
[27] See Giambattista Vico, *Opere filosofiche*, 175–7; and SN, 329.
[28] 'The study of Plato was, in my eyes, of the same kind as the study of Thucydides' (A, 72).

# Croce, Gentile and Collingwood on the Relation between History and Philosophy

RIK PETERS

## I  Collingwood's Development 1919–1930

In 1939 Collingwood wrote in his *Autobiography*: 'My life's work hitherto, as seen from my fiftieth year, has been in the main an attempt to bring about a *rapprochement* between philosophy and history.' In this paper I would like to discuss some aspects of Collingwood's *rapprochement* between philosophy and history in the light of the debate between Croce and Gentile on the same subject.[1]

In Collingwood's view, the main task of the *rapprochement* between philosophy and history was to explain the principles of the study of history in order to improve historical thinking in all its forms (A, 77–9). A philosophy of history, conceived in this way, would also have its repercussions on philosophy itself. For philosophy would become more historical if philosophers recognized that the historical aspect of their subject matter could not be neglected. This would imply, of course, that they should think about philosophy according to the newly developed principles of history. Towards the end of his life, Collingwood went so far as claiming that all philosophy was to be 'liquidated' by history (IH, x). Besides its theoretical implications, the *rapprochement* between philosophy and history had important practical implications as well.[2] For in Collingwood's view history had to become the science of human mind which could be helpful in promoting the control of human affairs. In this context

Collingwood referred to a historical society in which people would understand each other in a historical way instead of mastering or being mastered by each other.[3] But, of course, first of all the principles of history had to be established. According to Collingwood this meant that two categories of problems had to be solved: 'epistemological problems' to be grouped together under the question 'how is history possible'; and 'metaphysical problems' concerned with the subject matter of history, that is in Collingwood's words, the elucidation of terms like event, process, progress, civilization and so forth (A, 77).

In his *Autobiography* Collingwood mentions that around 1919 he began to think about problems like these and that already in 1920 he had formulated his first principle of history. This was the idea that history should be seen as a process being still alive in the present. As we will see, this idea of history as a process remained the *basso continuo* of Collingwood's philosophy of history (A, 97).

In spite of this achievement in the early 1920s the *rapprochement* between philosophy and history was not yet complete. We can see this from Collingwood's book of 1924, *Speculum Mentis*. In this work Collingwood makes a clear distinction between history and philosophy: history is conceived as the assertion of fact while philosophy is seen as the self-knowledge of mind. History can never reach the stage of absolute knowledge, since the totality of facts is infinite and therefore unknowable. Only philosophy, knowing that all facts are created by the mind, can have insight into the totality of facts and therefore claim the status of absolute knowledge (SM, 208–11, 231, 291ff).

This distinction between history and philosophy did not satisfy Collingwood, however, and after *Speculum Mentis* he kept on working on the *rapprochement* between the two. The most important moment in this development, Collingwood says in his *Autobiography*, took place in 1928, when he registered his conclusions of nine years' thought on the philosophy of history (A, 107). Collingwood summarized his conclusions in three well-known propositions. The first is: 'All history is the history of thought.' The second is: 'Historical knowledge is the re-enactment in the historian's mind of the thought whose history he is studying.' The third: 'Historical knowledge is the re-enactment of a past thought incapsulated in a context of present thoughts which, by contradicting it, confine it to a plane different from theirs'(A, 110–15).

This last proposition, Collingwood says in his *Autobiography*, was the solution to the most difficult problem he had ever solved in his study of historical method, namely the problem of the identity and difference between the past thought and the re-enactment of that thought. Collingwood meant by this the problem that a historian has to rethink a past thought in the same way as it was once thought in order to understand it. But he has to think the past thought also in a different way, for he must be conscious of the fact that it is a past thought that he rethinks. In other words, while re-enacting a past thought he has to be conscious of the historicity of his re-enactment. If he is not conscious of this historicity of the thought he rethinks, the past thought will be 'running away with him', as Collingwood expresses it.[4]

This problem caused him so much trouble that its complete solution came only a few years after 1928 in the form of the incapsulation theory which he summarized in the third proposition (A, 110).[5] This theory accounts for the problem of the difference between the past thought and its re-enactment in the present, the difference being one of context. A historian rethinks the past thought as it was thought in the past, Collingwood maintains, but he always rethinks it in the context of his own present thoughts. For example, I can now rethink Plato's thought but I know at the same time that I am here in England, and that it is 1995 etc. So, one could say that our present thoughts are in contrast with the re-enacted thoughts of the past and in that way keep the latter in their place (A, 112–14). Through his incapsulation theory Collingwood promoted historical thinking to the rank of self-knowledge of the mind. Mind, in his view, is what it does, so in order to know what mind is we have to study what it has done in the past. This is possible because of the contrast between the rethought thoughts of the past and our present thoughts. This contrast enables us to have a better knowledge of the nature of our own thoughts and our mental life in general. Thus self-knowledge, which is philosophy, has become totally historical in character.

We may conclude that after about 1930 Collingwood had completed his theory of history as the re-enactment of past thought being encapsulated by present thoughts. Thus Collingwood showed how knowledge of the past was indeed possible and thereby solved his epistemological problem. Moreover, history became self-knowledge of the mind. In *Speculum Mentis* this position had been reserved exclusively for philosophy. This means finally, that in the period 1928–30 Collingwood developed a theory in which history and philosophy came closer to each other.

Now, what was the role of Croce and Gentile in this development of Collingwood's *rapprochement* between philosophy and history? It is not easy to answer this question, because Collingwood never expressed publicly his debts to the two Italians. This is very surprising since the relation between philosophy and history was, as we will see, one of the most important points of discussion between Croce and Gentile, and Collingwood was very well acquainted with their works. Besides, Collingwood could get a lot of first-hand information from his friend Guido de Ruggiero, a pupil of Gentile. Fortunately, Collingwood expressed his opinion on Croce and Gentile more freely in his letters to de Ruggiero than in his books. In 1926 Collingwood wrote to his friend: 'For myself, I am trying to clear up my conception of History – *helped greatly, but not wholly satisfied*, by both Croce and Gentile, and developing further the view expressed in *Speculum Mentis*. And always pursuing the study of history itself'.[6]

In the last section of my paper I hope to settle the question to what degree Collingwood was 'greatly helped but not wholly satisfied'. In order be able to do this, I will first deal with the discussion between Croce and Gentile on the relationship between history and philosophy. I will not give an exposition of their discussion in all its details, however interesting they may be, but only to the extent that is necessary in order to have a better understanding of Collingwood's relation to both philosophers.

## II Croce and Gentile on the Relation between History and Philosophy

The problem of the relation between history and philosophy is one of the main topics in the discussion between Croce and Gentile. Though from the first letters which Croce and Gentile wrote to each other from 1896 onwards the problem appears in different forms, I will concentrate on the culmination of the discussion as it developed towards the end of 1906.

The occasion of the discussion of that year was afforded by Gentile's review of an article by Windelband. In this review Gentile puts forward for the first time his thesis of the identity of philosophy and the history of philosophy. According to Gentile, every philosophy implies the history of philosophy, and every history of philosophy implies its own philosophy. This applies not only *a parte obiecti*, in which every philosophy is a part of the history of philosophy but also *a parte subiecti*: every creation of a new philosophy implies knowledge of the history of philosophy.[7]

Gentile distinguishes three phases in the development of every new philosophy. In the first, someone has only a vague idea of philosophy, in the second, he comes to know a certain philosophy of a certain philosopher, and in the third, he criticizes the philosophy which he has learnt, thus forming his own philosophy. This last phase Gentile calls the 'historical-philosophical moment'. Gentile emphasizes that these three phases are in fact one single process, beginning with a poor philosophy which enriches itself by studying the history of philosophy.[8]

Croce totally disagreed with Gentile, and for this reason did not want to publish the recension in *La Critica*. Croce wrote to Gentile that he was wholly mistaken in mixing up the historical phase with the philosophical one. In Croce's view, history and philosophy are to be considered as two distinct realms of the mind. Besides this, Croce was of the opinion that the process does not end in philosophy but in history: only when one has judged a certain philosophy historically does the process end. So for Croce there are not three phases, but four, the last being history which presupposes the philosophy obtained in the third phase.[9]

This rejection of Gentile's theory of the identity of philosophy and its history followed the same lines as Croce had expounded in his *Lineamenti di una logica* of 1905. In that work Croce distinguishes two forms of experience: art and philosophy. Art represents reality in its individuality, while in philosophy universal concepts are elaborated. The synthesis between a representation and a universal concept is to be found in the individual or historical judgement. History, which contains both the individual and the universal, represents the most concrete form of knowledge. So, for Croce, art and philosophy are thus logically prior to history and this means that history can never determine the development of either art or philosophy.[10]

Gentile retorted however, that when we read a philosophical work, we are already philosophizing with the author as soon as we begin. This means that the historical moment – that is the reconstruction of the thought by reading it – coincides with the philosophical moment.[11]

From his side, Croce was not convinced by this argument. He maintained that when we read Plato or Aristotle we are not judging their philosophy. This can only be done by an individual judgement in which the intuition of Plato or Aristotle is synthesized with a universal concept as presented by philosophy. Philosophy itself however, is not capable of judging a past philosophy since it lacks the intuitions of Plato or Aristotle.[12]

Gentile's answer to this argument was that the individual moment – the intuition – is resolved into the *filosofia in fieri*. For no philosophy is born in abstraction, he argues. The aspects of the time and life of a philosopher – in other words, the individual circumstances of the philosopher – are determinate for his philosophy. This means that in order to understand someone's philosophy we need to have knowledge of his biography and therefore of the time in which he lived. This is also the case for one's own philosophy. You cannot understand the nature of your own philosophy without knowing the history of your own time and its philosophy. Gentile says that *in abstracto* it is of course possible that someone discovers Kant's *a priori* synthesis without knowing Kant. But, not knowing Kant, he will not be able to understand fully the significance of his own discovery. So, Gentile denies the possibility of a philosophy which is not at the same time a reconstruction of the history of philosophy. Philosophy and the history of philosophy are identical.[13]

After this answer by Gentile, the two philosophers exchanged only a few more letters on this subject, but they never reached agreement. Two years later, in 1909, Croce published a second edition of his *Logic*. The third section deals with the identity of history and philosophy.[14] It seems therefore that Croce had been convinced by Gentile's arguments, but on further consideration it is clear that his version of the identity is in many ways different from that of Gentile. As in his first *Logic*, history is still seen as a synthesis between an intuition and a universal concept. History still contains concepts and therefore presupposes philosophy. A new aspect of Croce's position is, that he considers philosophy to be presupposed by history. For every philosophical judgement is developed in the mind of an individual philosopher as an answer to a certain question. This question presupposes in its turn an individual judgement which is historical by its nature. So Croce comes to the conclusion that every philosophy presupposes history.[15] This prepared the way for Croce's final view, as expressed in his *Theory and History of Historiography*, that historical thinking is the beginning and end of all thinking, philosophy being methodology of history.[16]

Gentile, on the other hand, kept to his view that philosophy should be seen as the beginning and end of all thinking. We have already seen how Gentile claimed that the *filosofia in fieri* resolved the individual moment into itself, which implies that when we read the work of a philosopher we necessarily already philosophize with him. So in reconstructing the thought of a past philosopher we construct our own philosophy at the same time. This view formed the basis of Gentile's theory of the mind as pure act, which was developed by him in the years between 1909 and 1911.[17] According to this theory all reality should be seen as nothing else than our mind in action, or *pensiero pensante*. So past reality is for Gentile past thought or *pensiero pensato*. The past can become real again when it becomes thought in action and to achieve this we have to rethink the past thought.[18] In this dialectical process Gentile makes a distinction between two phases. In the first one, we repeat the past thought by rethinking it as our own thought, thus actualizing the past thought. In the second phase the actuality of the past thought is transcended in a new act of thinking in which the past thought gets a new objectivity: it is absorbed by our thinking in action, forming an organic whole with it. So, while philosophy is history, it is at the same time the surpassing of it. For this reason Gentile claims that the history of philosophy is universal history.[19]

We are thus confronted with two versions of the identity between history and philosophy. In Croce's version history is the beginning and end of all thinking and philosophy is conceived as an aspect of history. In Gentile's version on the other hand, philosophy is the beginning and end of all thinking and history is only seen as an aspect of philosophy.

## III 'Greatly Helped but Not Wholly Satisfied'

'Greatly helped but not wholly satisfied', the first part of Collingwood's statement on Croce and Gentile in his letter to de Ruggiero, has become much clearer by the preceding discussion. In his attempt to bring philosophy and history closer together, Collingwood could draw from the discussion on the relation between philosophy and history as it had developed between Croce and Gentile. Of course, Collingwood was not acquainted with the letters of the two Italians, which were published in the 1970s and 1980s, but he was able enough to grasp the essence of their discussion from their published works. In these works the two Italians prepared the way, one could say, for Collingwood's *rapprochement* between philosophy and history.

The most remarkable point, in my view, is the apparent parallels between Gentile's dialectic of the mind as pure act and Collingwood's re-enactment theory. For the first two propositions of Collingwood's theory, 'all history is the history of thought' and 'all history is the re-enactment of past thought', are in fact implied by Gentile's theory. Even the problem of Collingwood's third proposition concerning the identity and difference between the past thought and its re-enactment in the present can be found in Gentile's two phases of rethinking. For we have seen how Gentile makes a distinction between two phases within the rethinking of a past thought. In the first, the past thought is repeated, in the second, it is surpassed by a new act of thought. This theory shows that Gentile was indeed conscious of the difference between the past thought on the one hand and its re-enactment on the other hand.

We can conclude that Collingwood was indeed 'greatly helped', though it should be added that for his epistemological question it was more by Gentile than by Croce. In fact, the parallels between the theories of Gentile and Collingwood are so striking that the question 'why was Collingwood not wholly satisfied?' even becomes a rather puzzling one.

In this respect it is a pity that Collingwood never fully expressed his debts to the two Italians. During the 1930s he developed a more positive attitude towards Croce, however: the section on Croce in *The Idea of History* is the most favourable Collingwood ever wrote on his philosophy of history (IH, 190–204). Collingwood's attitude to Gentile was two-faced. In a review of 1937 of Gentile's article 'The Transcending of Time in History', Collingwood completely agreed with Gentile's thesis that the historian transcends time by re-thinking the thoughts of a past agent, which is of course wholly in line with Collingwood's own theory of re-enactment.[20] This praise for Gentile's philosophy of history is in sharp contrast with the often cited remark made in his *Autobiography:* 'There was once a very able and distinguished philosopher who was converted to Fascism. As a philosopher that was the end of him' (A, 158–9). From this remark the conclusion can be drawn that Collingwood still valued the pre-fascist Gentile and that he saw some connection between Gentile's fascism and his later philosophy, with which he disagreed. But of course this remark is not sufficient to give an exact indication of the relation between Gentile and Collingwood. It is after all written in 1938 and possibly coloured by Collingwood's political passions. Moreover, it is not the expression of a theoretical criticism of Gentile's philosophy.

Fortunately enough there is one manuscript in the Bodleian Library in which Collingwood expresses his criticism of Croce and Gentile in a more philosophical way. The manuscript was written in 1933 and has the title 'Notes towards a Metaphysic'. The second part of it is called 'Gentile on History'.[21]

This title does not in fact reflect the content, since Collingwood begins this part with a criticism of Croce. Collingwood argues that Croce's polemic with Hegel brought him to the position that an individual judgement can only be concrete when all categories known to philosophy are present in the judgement. This has the consequence, Collingwood maintains, that it becomes impossible to see a development in history; for when all categories are present in the judgement, it is not possible to indicate the difference between one fact and another on the basis of a category.[22]

The theory which Collingwood criticizes is developed in Croce's second *Logic*. In this part Croce argues that the most fundamental concept within the individual judgement is the concept of existence. This concept is involved in every individual judgement, since the fact stated in the judgement must be a real fact; in other words: it must exist. According to Croce the concept of existence is present in the individual judgement in all its universality, singularity and particularity. So the concept of existence involves all existing things and therefore all concepts. For this reason, in judging reality in its individuality, we use all concepts known within philosophy.[23] This means that when we read a past individual judgement in, for example, the history of Rome by Livy we have to know all concepts involved in that narrative. But every concept implies other concepts as well, so in the end all concepts are involved in understanding Livy.[24] The simultaneous presence of all concepts is only possible of course in Croce's dialectic of distincts and not in Hegel's dialectic of opposites, because two opposite concepts can never be present simultaneously in one single judgement. Croce developed his dialectic of distincts because for him historical events are never opposed to each other.

We may conclude from this that Croce did indeed maintain the view which was opposed by Collingwood. Furthermore Collingwood seems to be correct in claiming that Croce's theory of the simultaneous presence of all concepts is the result of his polemic with Hegel.

In this context it is interesting to note that Collingwood defends Hegel against Croce in *The Idea of History*. Collingwood argues there that Croce's criticism of Hegel's dialectic of opposites is only correct when history is seen from the outside. For all events seen from the outside are not opposite to each other, but only distinct. For the 'inside' of an event Hegel's theory of the dialectic of opposites can be used, since ideas can be opposed to each other. For example, the Protestant idea of the papacy and the Catholic idea of it are diametrically opposed to each other (IH, 118–19).

My conclusion concerning the question of Collingwood's relation to Croce is the following. Collingwood was 'greatly helped' by Croce's theory of history considered as individual judgement. But he was not 'wholly satisfied' with Croce's dialectic of distincts. The first reason for this is that it can only be applied to the outside of events. As Collingwood used to maintain, however, that we should always see history from the 'inside' in order to understand it, we may conclude that Croce's dialectic is in Collingwood's view of little use. Secondly, Croce's dialectic of distincts leads to the notion of the individual judgement in which all categories are simultaneously present. This notion impedes the distinction between one fact and another, with the result that history cannot be seen as a development. This view is in contrast with Collingwood's first principle, according to which history should be seen as a process.

On the basis of this criticism of Croce, one would expect that Gentile's dialectic of the thinking act would be received more favourably by Collingwood, because in that theory mind is seen from the inside while it also takes opposition into account. But, to our surprise, Collingwood criticizes Gentile for the same fault as Croce! Because of its relevance, the passage concerned will be quoted in full.

> The past is, on this [Gentile's] view, an abstraction from the present, which alone is actual; history is a projection of thought backwards into time, like a jet of water thrown backwards by some marine animal to push it forwards. There is therefore no real development; only an eternal present, which does not enrich itself by taking up the past, but defecates a past out of itself. This seems to me to be subjective idealism. It follows from the indifference of logical structure between fact and fact; since in everything that matters every fact is identical with every other, all presents are the same present, differing 'merely empirically' i.e. not at all. The past being a mere abstraction from the present, past facts cannot be known in their concreteness, and there is no series of facts; everything is in a timeless present. Gentile seems to me to have concentrated his attention on the epistemological notion of the historian building up his history into the past and so forming his perspective of past time, but to have neglected the problem of the relation between perspectives; and each man's perspective is for him a subjective-idealistic world, in which the object is not spirit (pensiero pensante) but idea (pensiero pensato). The problem of development, which had been pushed out of sight by Croce's polemic against Hegel, has been wholly overlooked by Gentile, with the result that Fascist thought, egocentric and subjective, can rightly be called by Croce *antistoricismo*.[25]

This passage clearly demonstrates that Collingwood stood in a rather ambivalent relation to Gentile. On the one side he mentions Gentile's attention to the epistemological problem of history, but on the other side he criticizes the Italian for not accounting for the aspects of development in history and the relation between perspectives. Collingwood's final judgement is plainly negative: fascist thought is subjective and anti-historicist.

In Collingwood's view, both Gentile's blindness for development and for the relation between perspectives follows from the indifference of the logical structure between one fact and another in relation to the act of thought. The reason for this is that all facts are created by the eternal act of thought. This has as consequence that there is only one perspective, namely the perspective of the eternal act for which all other perspectives are only *pensati*, so they are not any more in action. When there is no real difference between the facts, it is impossible to see history as a process.

We may therefore conclude that though Collingwood in the 1930s was still in favour of Gentile's epistemological view of the historian creating history by his act of thinking, he was not wholly satisfied with Gentile's version of the subjective, monoperspectival eternal act which was characteristic of fascist egocentrism.

Collingwood, however, did not confine himself to criticism but tried to solve the difficulties of their theories. About three years later his solution was complete, as we can see from a manuscript of 1936.[26] As in his manuscript on Gentile of 1933, Collingwood begins with a criticism of the idea of the eternity of the past which, is in his view, nothing but a grandiloquent way of saying that the past can become present by re-enacting past thoughts[27].

The problem is, Collingwood maintains, that the word 'thought' is equivocal. On first sight it may mean the act of thinking (*noèsis*) or the object or content of thought (*noèma*). These two notions of thought are not identical, since you can rethink an object of thought but not an act of thought, every new act of thought being different from the old one.

To clarify his point, Collingwood gives the examples of Pythagoras' thought about the triangle and the thought of William the Conqueror during the Norman Conquest. The thought of Pythagoras about the triangle is a pure content: it is contemplation of an object. Therefore, the thoughts of other people about the triangle were for Pythagoras no necessary part of his thinking about the triangle. But the thought of William the Conqueror during the Norman Conquest is an act of thought about an act of thinking, namely about the thought of his opponent Harold. In other words, William the Conqueror was thinking about a political situation, and this situation was not merely apprehended, but constituted by certain acts of thinking. So for William, knowing what other people thought about the political situation was not only an integral part of thinking about the situation, it was the essential part of it. There was no political situation distinct from what people thought of it, Collingwood says. In this situation Harold's thought is a factor in William's thought. The logical relation between the object and the act of thought is different from the one in Pythagoras' case. For in Pythagoras' case the thinking is about an object, while in William's case the thought of Harold is absorbed in the thinking of William. Pythagoras can therefore never transcend the object in his thought, but William can indeed transcend Harold's thought. In this manuscript Collingwood does not explain how this transcending of a thought is possible. The reason is obvious; for in 1930 he had already solved this problem by the incapsulation theory: a re-enacted thought is contradicted and transcended by present thoughts.

One may consider Collingwood's theory of perspectives as an important modification of Gentile's theory. In 1933 Collingwood had criticized Gentile for not accounting for development and the relation between perspectives. Both problems followed from the logical indifference of the facts to the eternal act. All facts are *pensieri pensati* as recreated by the eternal act. As all perspectives are facts, or *pensieri pensati*, the eternal act cannot account for the relation between perspectives. In 1936 Collingwood concentrated his attention on the problem of the logical relation of the facts to the act. He then argues that the object–act or *noèma–noèsis* relation, is too simple as a theory of historical thought. It can only account for thought which is not original, which is mere repetition, as for example our thought about Pythagoras' thesis. The logical structure between the thoughts of William, Harold and the historian is much more complicated because William's thought is an act of thought about an act of thought. In other words, William's thought is already a re-enactment of Harold's thought. This means in terms of the incapsulation theory that William's thought transcends the thought of Harold by contradicting it. Harold's thought thus becomes a factor in William's thought. For this reason the historian re-enacting William's thought re-enacts at the same time Harold's thought. In this way he can relate William's perspective to Harold's. This means that he can discover the difference between two past thoughts and see the actions of William and Harold as a process. The historian, moreover, continuously contradicts both William's and Harold's thoughts by his own thought. This means that he is not merely repeating their thoughts but transcending them.

According to Collingwood this theory of the re-enactment of re-enactments is crucial for the theory of history. In his view, it also has consequences for the history of philosophy, for it takes into account that the understanding of one's philosophy is already the transcending of it.

We can now see clearly how Collingwood modified Gentile's theory. By accounting for the logical difference between the re-enactment of the thought of a pure object and the re-enactment of past thoughts in action, Collingwood can make a distinction between two types of past thought and their implications for re-enactment by the historian. In this way he is able to see the relation between perspectives and therefore development. In other words, Collingwood modified the one–one relation of Gentile's between the *pensiero pensato* and the *pensiero pensante* or *noèma–noèsis* relation to plurifold relation in which several acts of thought are present in one act of thought. The reason for making this modification is not merely theoretical. For Collingwood was looking for a way of historical thinking which could be of some help for people in understanding each other. This historical understanding was in his view necessary in order to control human affairs in a better way. Collingwood was greatly helped by Gentile's demonstration that historical knowledge is indeed possible as re-enactment of past thought. But it was his dissatisfaction with Gentile's egocentristic fascism that made Collingwood look for a solution in order to save this achievement from these evils. Collingwood was well aware that understanding each other requires that we should be capable of relating our perspectives so that we can learn from each other with the exclusion of all subjectivism. Only this kind of historical thinking could be the basis of Collingwood's greatest ideal: the historical society.

*Notes*
[1] The first inspiration for this article came from D. Boucher, *The Social and Political Thought of R. G. Collingwood* (Cambridge, Cambridge University Press, 1989). I am most grateful to Professor Dondoli and to Professor Harris for their criticism of the main argument and to Professor van der Dussen and Mr Wijsmuller for their critical reading of the whole manuscript.

2 These are thoroughly studied by Boucher, *The Social and Political Thought of R. G. Collingwood.*
3 R. G. Collingwood, Scheme for *The Principles of History*, 1939, cited in van der Dussen, *History as a Science: The Philosophy of R. G. Collingwood*, (The Hague, Nijhoff, 1981), 431–2.
4 W. J. van der Dussen, *History as a Science*, 148–9.
5 Collingwood in 1928 had already formulated a first version of the incapsulation theory: 'To re-enact the past in the present is to re-enact it in a context which gives it a new quality. This context is the negation of the past itself . . .' cited in van der Dussen, *History as a Science*, 146–7.
6 Letter from Collingwood to de Ruggiero, 18 August 1926, cited in van der Dussen, *History as a Science*, 31.
7 G. Gentile, '*Il circolo della filosofia e della storia della filosofia*', La Critica, VII (1909), 143–9. Now in: G. Gentile, *La riforma della dialettica hegeliana* (Florence, Sansoni, 1975 (first edn., 1913)), 138. Cf. Gentile's recension of '*Die Philosophie im Beginn des zwanzigsten Jahrhunderts, Festschrift für Kuno Fischer herausgegeben von W. Windelband*', La Critica, V (1907), 146–51.
8 G. Gentile, *La riforma della dialettica hegeliana*, 142–3. Cf. Gentile, *Lettere a Benedetto Croce, a cura di Simona Giannantoni* II (Florence, Sansoni, 1974), 337–9, Gentile to Croce, 16 December 1906.
9 B. Croce, *Lettere a Giovanni Gentile* (Milan, Mondadori, 1981), 216–18, letter of 14 December 1906.
10 B. Croce, *Lineamenti di una logica come scienza del concetto puro*, (Naples, Gianni, 1905), 57–8, 91.
11 Gentile, *Lettere a Benedetto Croce*, II, 338–9, letter of 16 December 1906.
12 Croce, *Lettere a Giovanni Gentile*, 219–20, letter of 18 December 1906.
13 Gentile, *Lettere a Benedetto Croce*, 348–9, letter of 29 December 1906.
14 Croce, *Lineamenti di una logica come scienza del concetto puro*, 119–47.
15 B. Croce, *Logica come scienza del concetto puro* (Bari, Laterza, 1928), fifth edn (first edn, 1909), 126–8.
16 B. Croce, *Teoria e storia della storiografia* (Bari, Laterza, 1948), sixth edn (first edn, 1917), 136–51.
17 These are the dates of the first actualist articles: G. Gentile, 'Le forme assolute dello spirito', in *Il modernismo e i rapporti fra religione e filosofia* (Florence, 1962), 259–75 (Bari, 1909); G. Gentile, 'L'atto del pensiero come atto puro', in *La riforma della dialettica hegeliana*, 183–96.
18 Gentile, 'L'atto del pensiero come atto puro', 184–5.
19 Ibid.
20 Review of *Philosophy and History: Essays Presented to Ernst Cassirer*, ed. Raymond Klibansky and H. J. Paton, in *English Historical Review*, III (1937), 143–4.

21 Bodleian Library, MS DEP 18, 'Notes towards a Metaphysic II', Peri Phuseoos, B, 8–11; van der Dussen, op. cit., 448. D. S. Taylor, 'A Bibliography of the Publications and Manuscripts of R. G. Collingwood with Selective Annotation', *History and Theory*, XXIV, 4, Beiheft 24 (1985), no. 1.63.
22 Collingwood, 'Notes towards a Metaphysic', 8–9.
23 Croce, *Logica come scienza del concetto puro*, 110–13, and 199.
24 Croce, *Logica come scienza del concetto puro*, 184–5.
25 Collingwood, 'Notes towards a Metaphysic II', 9–11. In September 1930 Croce read a paper in Oxford with the title '*Antistoricismo*' (now in *Ultimi Saggi*).
26 Van der Dussen, *History as Science*, 180–1.
27 Collingwood wrote these notes probably as a preparation for his lecture 'Human Nature and Human History' which he was to give in May 1936 (IH 205–31). It is possible that Gentile played a certain role in the preparation for this lecture. Collingwood had just read and reviewed Klibansky's *Philosophy and History in Honour of Cassirer*. It is to this collection of essays he refers several times in his lecture. One of these essays is Gentile's 'The Transcending of Time in History' (91–107). In this essay Gentile argues that all time in history disappears in the eternal act of thought. This was exactly the theory which Collingwood had criticized three years before as subjective idealism for which it is impossible to see the relation between perspectives. In is in line with this position that Collingwood begins his manuscript about the relation between perspectives with a criticism of the concept of eternity of the past.

# Collingwood's Theory of Historical Knowledge

## LEON POMPA

The particular aspect of Collingwood's philosophy of history which I wish to discuss in this chapter is his account of the way in which we acquire historical knowledge. He is, of course, justly famous for his continued efforts to grapple with this problem. One of his primary concerns was to show that, although our knowledge of history depends upon methods which are very different in kind from those used in the natural sciences, it should be regarded as scientific because the methods appropriate to it are as rigorous as those utilized in the natural sciences and lead to conclusions which are equally justified and defensible. This is a view which, largely as a result of his work, has won wide support among subsequent philosophers. It is not my intention here to attempt to discuss the whole of his account of what this involves. But as a preliminary to what I do wish to discuss, I shall make brief mention of certain fundamental features of his view.

The first is that the subject matter of history differs from that of the natural sciences because history is concerned with human activities and experiences, and these have a thought element which is missing in the natural world with which the physical sciences are concerned. The historian cannot therefore rest content with purely physical descriptions of what has occurred, but must give an account of the context of thought, belief and intention within which human actions occur. On Collingwood's view, indeed, thought is not merely part of the context within which human activity takes place but it is also, in the form of human intentions, irrespective of whether or not they are successfully implemented, partly constitutive of the activities themselves. Hence his well-known claim that once one has discerned the thought within an action one already has the explanation for that action. No further causal account, of the sort which is appropriate in the natural sciences, is required.

The second feature follows almost directly from this thesis. Once it is accepted that historians' primary requirement is to recover the thoughts of historical individuals or communities, a large part of the task is one of interpretation and understanding, for which they must have recourse to the historical imagination. In this respect the historian's procedure, as Collingwood remarks, resembles that of the novelist.

Nevertheless, despite the importance of interpretation and understanding, historians also make truth claims, and it is for this reason that history should be thought of as a science. But since the subject matter of history consists in the intentional activities of past human agents, these truth claims must take account of the thoughts and intentions which those agents had, which, as I mentioned just now, are partially constitutive of the actions themselves. There must therefore be an acceptable way of establishing what these were. Collingwood's claim is that they are established when, by a process of inference from evidence presently available to the historian, we can reconstruct a context within which we can rethink or re-experience the thoughts which the historical agents themselves had.

This brief account of some of the main claims involved in Collingwood's view of historical knowledge, ignores a number of standard difficulties of interpretation. There is, for example, no clear agreement among commentators that re-enactment is, as I have suggested, the goal of historical knowledge rather than part of the method involved. Nevertheless, enough of it is, I believe, uncontentious, to provide the background for the specific set of claims which I wish to discuss. The central point upon which I wish to focus is the thesis that, to arrive at an understanding of the thought of past agents and past societies which can be claimed to be true, historians must proceed by a process of inference from evidence presently available to them, largely in the form of past human artefacts which have been preserved for us. What I wish to suggest is that although this is certainly a part of the historian's procedure, it cannot be all that is involved and that, if it were, history could not be accepted as a genuine form of knowledge. If it were, in other words, Collingwood's claims for scientific history would collapse. My thesis is therefore that, for reasons which I shall try to explain, Collingwood has offered as an account of the whole of historical method a part which could not operate in the absence of something which he has completely overlooked.

To introduce this claim, I would like to begin by looking at some aspects of Collingwood's criticisms of other conceptions of history. Quite early in *The Idea of History*, he indulges in a rather Hegelian line of thought when, after a discussion of Thucydides, he points out that we could not get at historical truth if all we had to go on were the reports of eyewitnesses (IH, 25–6). The question which he raises is, therefore, how we can justifiably go beyond reliance upon such reports. Hegel had raised the same question, of course, when he asked how we could go beyond the work of the original historian who was, if not an actual eyewitness to the events in which he was interested, at least very close to them. The difficulty about reliance upon eyewitness reports is that they are confined to specific events, that they occur within specific historical contexts, and that they therefore offer no guidance as to how to achieve a longer-term viewpoint. Hegel's claim was that the first move towards transcending these limitations lay in a wish to produce universal history, although he had many criticisms of the defects of this sort of history. Collingwood's suggestion is that many historians have tried to avoid the limitations of reliance upon eyewitness testimony by the production of what he calls 'scissors-and-paste' history. 'Scissors-and-paste' history consists in longer-term compilations of the work of earlier historians, i.e. the construction of narratives based upon the work of so-called earlier 'authorities'. But this, Collingwood argues, is an unacceptable form of history. Before the work of earlier historians can be accepted and incorporated into a historical account, it stands in need of judgement by historians themselves. The historical value of the so-called 'authority', irrespective of whether we conclude by accepting his account or by deriving some other knowledge from it, depends, on this view, upon the historian's making a judgement about the authority himself. And to do this justifiably, the historian must do it in accordance with an acceptable criterion. Collingwood ascribes the realization that this is so to Bradley, in his well-known essay 'The Presuppositions of Critical History'. But although Bradley realized that historians do not simply take over what the authority asserts, but frequently use it to argue for some different assertion, he was himself unable to produce a satisfactory version of the criterion required to do this (IH, 240). Bradley's own suggested criterion was, as Collingwood points out, too empiricist: it was simply judgement based upon what experience teaches us to be the case in our own everyday world. Although Collingwood does not himself say so, Bradley's criterion had affinities with Hume's thesis of the uniformity of human nature. But somebody with Collingwood's sensitivity to the ways in which human conceptual schemes may have changed in the past, could not rest content with a criterion which would tend to assimilate all past thought to our own. Collingwood saw that what we need is a criterion which will give us access to systems of belief which may have been quite other than our own, a criterion which will therefore allow us to offer a quite different account of the activities of other periods than that at which we would arrive if Bradley's suggestion were accepted.

I shall return to the question of Collingwood's account of the criterion in a moment. But first I want to concentrate upon a further consequence which he drew from his quite correct rejection of 'scissors-and-paste' history. This is that because historians must subject past authorities to their own historical judgement, they can take nothing whatsoever as given. This comes out particularly clearly in a passage in which Collingwood criticizes a more sophisticated conception of historical knowledge, which he introduces in the course of discussing the role of the *a priori* imagination in constructing a picture of the past. The imagination which he is referring to here is likened by him to the Kantian *a priori* imagination, which introduces principles of necessity to help in the construction of the historian's picture of the past. According to this more sophisticated view, Collingwood writes, '[t]he historian's picture of his subject . . . appears as a web of imaginative construction stretched between certain fixed points provided by the statements of his authorities' (IH, 242). But this more sophisticated conception is also inadequate, for, he continues,

[w]e think of our web of construction as pegged down, so to speak, to

the facts made by the statements of authorities, which we regard as data or fixed points for the work of construction. But in so thinking we have slipped back into the theory, which we now know to be false, that truth is given ready made in these statements. We know that truth is to be had, not by swallowing what our authorities tell us, but by criticising it; and thus the supposedly fixed points between which the historical imagination spins its web are not given to us ready made, they must be achieved by critical thinking. (IH, 243)

So the 'web-between-fixed-points' view, as I shall call it, is unsatisfactory also since, in taking anything at all as fixed, the historian immediately falls back into an unhistorical form of thought. The conclusion to which all this leads, of course, is that historians must take nothing for granted. What they must do, instead, is to put the whole of their conclusions upon a basis of inference from evidence, in accordance with the criterion of historical knowledge. For convenience, I shall refer to the thesis that the historian must take nothing whatsoever for granted as the thesis of historical autonomy.

Before I turn to the question of the criterion itself, there is one further point which must be made in connection with the question of historical autonomy. It may not appear strictly correct to say that Collingwood allows the historian to take nothing for granted. A little later in *The Idea of History* he points out that we cannot use evidence unless we come at it from a basis of historical knowledge. 'The more historical knowledge we have', he writes, 'the more we can learn from any given piece of evidence; if we had none, we could learn nothing . . . It follows that historical knowledge can only grow out of historical knowledge' (IH, 247). But this, as it turns out, still does not mean that historians can simply take over other historians' knowledge. They are entitled to take it over only if they are prepared to endorse the reasoning upon which it is based. Thus there is still nothing ready made, nothing fixed and therefore, as Collingwood goes on to explain, nothing which later historians may not revise or reject. So when he says that historical knowledge can grow only out of historical knowledge, he does not intend to imply that anything is ever fixed in advance of the historian's interpretation of the evidence. He is simply recognizing that the state of historical knowledge is continually changing, and that the different states that it is in at different times will provide different heuristic contexts within which historians can pursue their research. These different states may well enable them to ask different questions and to see different things as evidence in relation to these questions, but they never provide a set of statements which they can take as given. This, of course, is one of the reasons for his Crocean conclusion that every generation must construct history afresh and in its own way.

Arising from his initial rejection of 'scissors-and-paste' history and its 'web-between-fixed-points' successor, therefore, Collingwood arrives at the conclusion that historians are not entitled to accept any statement whatsoever as a historical statement unless they can justify it on the basis of valid inferences used in accordance with a proper criterion of historical knowledge. So firmly, indeed, did he hold this view that he was prepared to assert that if we had access to a statement about the past by two different means, by historical inference and by memory, say, in the former case alone would it be an example of historical knowledge.

It is possible now to turn to the question of the historian's criterion. Here Collingwood appears to offer two different views. This might seem to constitute a difficulty, but I do not think that it does since the two views appear to be complementary. According to the view which is stated most frequently, the criterion of historical truth is the idea of history itself. This, Collingwood says, is akin to a Cartesian innate idea or to a Kantian *a priori* notion. This is the idea of an imaginary picture of the past. In asserting that it is in the Kantian sense *a priori* Collingwood wishes to rule out the suggestion that it might be a chance product of psychological causes. '[I]t is', he writes, 'an idea which every man possesses as part of the furniture of his mind and discovers himself to possess in so far as he becomes conscious of what it is to have a mind' (IH, 248). In addition, he goes on to say, it is an idea which can never be fully satisfied by any historical work, but this in no way detracts from its status.

If, for a moment, we consider this notion of the historical criterion, it is clear, I think, that it amounts to a defence of historians' right to believe that what they are trying to construct is an account of something which is real. In other words, it is a statement of their right to use the present, as we perceive it here and now, as evidence for the past, and to use what look like human artefacts, as we perceive them here and now, as evidence of a specifically human past. It is in this sense alone that it can be thought of as a criterion of historical truth. It is as though Collingwood sees himself confronting the sceptical question, 'why should we believe that the products of historical research refer to anything real, any real past, at all?' And his answer is that we have no option but to believe that it does, because that is necessary to having a mind, or having beliefs, at all. If this is right, then Collingwood's assimilation of this criterion to the Kantian *a priori* is correct.

In this case, however, we must also note that, like Kant's own *a priori*, while it may assure us that the present which we see around us had a past, or that the things which we take to be artefacts really are artefacts, i.e. that they are the remnants of a real human past, it throws no light whatsoever upon the specific content of that past. This criterion, for example, would do nothing to assure us that one determinate account of the past was nearer to the truth, or more worthy of belief, than another. It is, in other words, a purely metaphysical criterion which would have no role to play in determining which of the many accounts of the past that we might create ought to be believed.

For the latter, therefore, we must turn to Collingwood's second criterion. Here what he is most anxious to insist upon is coherence and consistency. In view of the fact that there is, as he has insisted, nothing given to the historian, nothing fixed which may not be unfixed, the only way in which the historian can proceed, he writes, is 'by considering whether the picture of the past to which the evidence leads him is a coherent and continuous picture' (IH, 248). And the historian arrives at this by critical historical thought, i.e. by exercising the *a priori* categories of the imagination upon what is available as evidence. The aim, which is given validity by the first criterion, is to use 'the entire perceptible here-and-now as evidence for the entire past through whose process it has come into being' (IH, 247). The fact that this aim can never be achieved fully in practice is not an obstacle, for it does not detract from its regulative character.

Thus the two criteria are not incompatible. The metaphysical criterion assures the historian that the whole perceptible present has come into being through past processes and is therefore evidence for it. And armed with this conviction, which introduces Kantian principles of necessity into their reconstructive activity, historians must create the most coherent and consistent account of the past and its relation to the whole present that they can. It is the wholeness of the present with the past processes which have brought it into being, which justifies the use of coherence and consistency as the critical criterion which historians must employ.

It is time now to consider this account more critically. Before I say what I think is wrong with it, let me start with something which I think is right in it. This is Collingwood's rejection of 'scissors-and-paste' history. I shall not say anything in defence of this claim since I believe that Collingwood has correctly diagnosed the defects of this kind of history. If I advance one step from here, however, and consider his criticism of the 'web-with-fixed-points' view, the position becomes less clear. This is because Collingwood here takes the fixed points to be statements accepted uncritically on the strength of their authorities. Now, if this is what the fixed points consist in, I think that Collingwood is correct to dismiss them. But it does not follow, as the rest of his account asserts, that there is no necessity for fixed points of any kind at all. It is one thing to deny the necessity for fixed points based upon authority and quite another thing to deny the necessity for any fixed points of any kind whatsoever. And it is this latter claim, which is fundamental to his account of historical knowledge as being wholly the product of critical historical thinking, which I wish to dispute.

As a first step towards explaining why I think that this is unsatisfactory, let me return to the question of the double criterion and the notion that knowledge that the entire perceptible present is a result of the past will suffice to justify coherence and consistency as the practical criterion in historical research. The suggestion appears to be that because we know that everything which now exists had a past, we are justified in using coherence as our criterion of historical truth. But this is surely incorrect. To see this, one must note that not even evidence, which will consist in present artefacts, can be accepted at its face value. Before it can be accepted as evidence it must be interpreted in an appropriate way. If it is interpreted in one way, it will provide evidence for one picture of the past. If it is interpreted in a different way, it will provide evidence for a different, possibly incompatible, picture of the past. It may well be that both of these pictures of the past are internally coherent, but that will certainly not suffice to show that one or the other or, indeed, either, is correct and that we ought to accept it as true. So, before we use anything present as evidence, we must face the prior question of how it should be interpreted. Hence, even if we are armed with the knowledge that the entire perceptible present has come into being as a result of the entire past, this will give us no guidance as to how to interpret the present in order to use it correctly as evidence for the past.

Before I pass beyond this point, let me offer another reason why I do not believe that Collingwood's two related criteria are sufficient to establish his general claim. This arises from the fact, which Collingwood has himself had to admit, that even if it is the case that the entire perceptible present has come into being as a result of the entire past, we do not know the entire perceptible present as a whole. We know it, so to speak, in bits and pieces; we know some bits of it better than others and we are almost certainly completely wrong about some other bits of it. So even if we were confident that the present constitutes a whole, and that, as a whole it has come into being through the past as a whole, we do not know it as a whole. But if this is so, we would not be justified in accepting pictures of the past on the strength of the fact that, as coherent wholes, they could be inferred from the parts of the present that we believe we know. If what we know about the present are fragments of a whole but not the whole itself, we shall certainly not be justified in accepting pictures of the past on the strength of the fact that they are coherent in themselves and can be inferred validly from these fragments. We shall be justified in our inferences to the past only if we know the present as a whole and can infer validly from that to the past as a whole.

The problem, therefore, is that not only is it the case, as Collingwood has argued, that there are no historical statements which historians can accept as given, it is also the case that there is no interpretative scheme which they can accept as certain in order to establish some statements about the past. Collingwood's appeal to the use of inference from present evidence, in accordance with the criterion of coherence, does nothing to resolve this problem. For if we have no justified reason for starting our inferences from one interpretation of the data rather than some other, we shall not be justified in accepting the conclusions reached by one set of inferences rather than some other as true. To use the present somewhat overworked expression, if the data are overdetermined by the possible interpretative schemes and if we lack a rational way of deciding which interpretative scheme to adopt as the basis for our inferences, what passes as historical knowledge will rest upon a purely arbitrary basis.

Now if this problem were put to historians, there is no doubt that they would immediately point out that it is not the case that they have no way of choosing between alternative interpretative schemes. They can, they will say, go quite a long way in dismissing some possibilities simply because accepting them would lead to conclusions about the past which conflict with what they know to be true. In fact, this is so obvious that many of the potential infinity of interpretative schemes are never entertained at all for precisely this reason. It may well be theoretically possible to suggest ways of interpreting present data such that, on the basis of inferences drawn from them, we should have no reason whatsoever to believe in the existence of, for example, a man called Garibaldi or the occurrence of events such as the Crimean War or the French Revolution or of the existence of the Greek or Roman empires. And if we were prepared to entertain such interpretative schemes, our whole picture of the determinate past would be quite other than it is. And this, it should be noted, would be a theoretical possibility even if we hung on to the belief that the entire perceptible present has come into being as a result of the entire past. But even if the use of such interpretative schemes is theoretically possible, no historians would dream of using them. And the reason why they would not, they will point out, is that they already know that there were such things as the Greek and Roman empires, such events as the French Revolution and the Crimean War and such a man as Garibaldi.

The question must therefore be raised whether Collingwood could reply to this challenge in the same way as the historians. At first sight it might appear that he could. For his insistence that historical knowledge grows out of historical knowledge seems to imply exactly the answer that the historians have given. These bizarre possibilities can therefore be rejected because it is already a matter of historical knowledge that there was a Greek and Roman empire and so on, and our further historical knowledge must build upon this already extant knowledge. Upon closer inspection, however, it becomes clear that Collingwood could not reply in these terms. For the thesis of historical autonomy states that a historian can take over already extant historical knowledge only by endorsing the reasoning upon which that is based. But if the reasoning upon which it is based is conducted in accordance with Collingwood's account of historical inference, we simply run up against the original problem of how to make a rational choice between different competing interpretative schemes. And there seems to be no solution to this problem which is compatible with the thesis of historical autonomy. The conclusion of this line of argument must therefore be that if Collingwood's account of the basis of historical knowledge were correct, we could not accept history as a genuine form of knowledge, for we could not justify our belief that it results in historical truth.

If this is correct, then, something has gone wrong in Collingwood's account of this reasoning. To see what this is, I wish to return to one of the conceptions which he rejected, the web-between-fixed-points view. Collingwood's objection to this, it will be remembered, was that historians were not entitled to take over the fixed points. If they wished to take them over, they could do so only if they subjected them to a form of historical reasoning. Now, when I discussed this, I suggested that this was correct if the fixed points were simply the statements of some so-called authority, Suetonius, say, or Tacitus, to mention some of Collingwood's own examples. But I also pointed out that it did not follow from the fact that there were no authorities which could act as fixed points that there were no fixed points whatsoever. And it is this claim which I now wish to defend.

The first thing to be noted is that, despite Collingwood's claim that there are no fixed points which the historian can accept as given, there are a surprising number of things which look very much like fixed points. Some of the very simple examples which I have given already, such as the occurrence of the French Revolution or of the Crimean War, look very much like such fixed points. Everybody with any pretensions to historical knowledge at all accepts statements about these things as statements of historical fact and does so, on the face of it at least, without indulging in any such process of historical reasoning as that which Collingwood offers. Acceptance of these events as being historically true seems very much to be a part of our inherited cultural learning. Of course, it might be possible for Collingwood to explain the wide diffusion of such beliefs, without the diffusion of the form of historical reasoning upon which, he says, they must rest, as a result of a division of intellectual labour. It is the historian's job, he could say, to establish such truths and ours to receive them. But, in the end, the basis for their being truths which it is rational to accept would be that they were supported by the appropriate form of historical thought, even if it were the case that not all of us who accepted them had ourselves judged them to be true as a result of applying this form of reasoning. As a matter of fact, I doubt whether he would have adopted this form of reply, because the thesis of historical autonomy entails that the only truths which are historical are those which the individual has reconstructed through historical reasoning. Thus the argument which concludes that belief in the Second World War is not a historical belief if it is based upon, for example, memory rather than historical reasoning, entails also that none of these beliefs are historical if they are based upon a diffusion of the results of a division of labour rather than upon individual historical thinking. But, in the end, whatever reply Collingwood offered would be unacceptable, since his account of historical thinking would not entitle even the historian to claim that these were truths.

If, therefore, as seems to be the case, there are many fixed points, and if they cannot be explained by Collingwood's account of historical thought, what is our basis for accepting them? The answer which I wish to propose is that we accept them because they have become constitutive within our consciousness as a result of their transmission from the past. We believe them because we are taught to believe them; and we are taught to believe them because they are part of the large body of truths which every society has about itself and which it hands down, by a relatively continuous process of transmission, to later societies, by all the methods, formal and informal, by which knowledge is disseminated. It is the existence of this large body of inherited knowledge of the past which Collingwood overlooked in his account, as a result of which it became impossible for him to show that historical knowledge was a genuine form of knowledge at all.

The point which I wish to emphasize, therefore, is that Collingwood paid insufficient attention to the phenomenon of historical consciousness itself. In the way in which he approached the problem of historical knowledge, he thought of the historian as a rational inquirer, who could take nothing for granted, but, armed with a set of rational methods of enquiry and a body of data, must draw conclusions about the past by applying these methods to this body of data. But this way of thinking about the problem neglects the crucial fact that historians are themselves historical products and that this gives them in advance of any particular inquiries which they wish to make, a determinate picture of the past which provides a framework of fixed points of knowledge which acts as a touchstone both of the truth of their new discoveries and of the adequacy of the methods of interpretation which they use in arriving at them. It is the fact that, as a result of the way in which a body of knowledge about the past has been built up in us historically, we know ourselves to occupy a certain position within a determinate conception of history, which provides us with a determinate criterion by which to interpret new evidence and, on the strength of that, to come to augment our knowledge of the past. But this would be quite impossible if we thought that we could dispense with this historically acquired body of knowledge and replace it by a body of knowledge dependent solely upon the inferential methods advocated by Collingwood. On the latter view historians are presented as though they occupy a vantage point outside history and, from that vantage point, must seek to establish conclusions about what is within history. But, as I have argued, if historians were to occupy such a vantage point outside history, they would be unable to secure a foothold within it. Even if we accepted Collingwood's account of what I have called the metaphysical criterion, and were thus assured that there had been a past of which the present was a consequence, we would be unable to justify a single belief about the determinate content of the past if we had to disregard the fact that we know that we ourselves occupy a particular place in relation to it. But knowing that we occupy such a place is indissolubly connected with knowing many determinate facts about it. What I am claiming, therefore, is that historians could not be historians if they did not already possess a historical consciousness. This means that, as a result of the process of the historical transmission of knowledge, they must already be in possession of a large body of knowledge which outlines the general structure of a determinate past to which their society and they are related. This inherited knowledge provides the fixed points in the web of knowledge which they seek to spin. Without it they would be unable to establish any historical knowledge at all, because they would be unable to justify their interpretation of evidence in such a way as to be able to claim that inferences from that interpretation rather than some other lead to knowledge of a real past rather than to that of an imaginary past.

In advancing this view, I do not wish to imply that Collingwood's account of historical thinking is entirely wrong. On the contrary, I believe that his theory of historical inference is largely correct. His mistake was, however, to present it as the whole of what is involved in reaching historical knowledge, whereas, I believe, its results can be accepted as true only if it operates within a context of known historical facts which cultures acquire in the course of their own historical development and which, as members of those cultures, historians must accept as true in advance of the more specialized research which they carry out as historians. In short, the inferential beliefs about the past which can be reached by Collingwood's methods can be accepted as true only if they can be connected to a prior knowledge of the past which we accept on the basis of cultural inheritance rather than rational inference. Inferential knowledge of the past is possible only for a consciousness in which historical knowledge has already become constitutive as a result of the way in which that consciousness has itself developed historically. This is the point which Collingwood wholly overlooked in his desire to preserve the thesis of historical autonomy.

# Metaphysics and History in Collingwood's Thought

## ADRIAN OLDFIELD

Collingwood's theory of presuppositions has created problems for some commentators who have wished, in however qualified a way, both to endorse his account of historical knowledge, and to account for the kind of conceptual change which Collingwood argues takes place as one set of presuppositions supersedes another. Different sets of presuppositions have been presented as if they created sharp discontinuities between the natural and human worlds of different historical epochs. They thus constitute insurmountable barriers to the understanding of any historical epoch which does not share the same set of presuppositions as the inquirer. On this argument it has been easy to characterize Collingwood as a relativist, as Stephen Toulmin does,[1] or as a sceptic, as T. M. Knox does (IH, xix), and cut the ground from under Collingwood's claims about the possibility of historical knowledge. Knox suggests that some time in the early 1930s, after he had written *An Essay on Philosophical Method*, Collingwood's thinking about history and philosophy underwent a profound change, and that all his later writings, which include *The Idea of History*, *An Autobiography* and *An Essay on Metaphysics*, are suffused by both intemperate passion and an all-consuming epistemological scepticism. His theory of absolute presuppositions – the force of the 'absolute' is dealt with below – as put forward in *An Essay on Metaphysics*, revealed a hitherto absent historicism in which absolute presuppositions are not universal, but are 'always historically conditioned' (IH, xvi). Hence the scepticism about attaching any truth value to historical knowledge claims. The theory seemed to make it impossible to attain historical knowledge.[2] Now Collingwood certainly maintained that historical knowledge was possible, and it will be argued here that his theory of absolute presuppositions, while it does pose difficulties, does not vitiate the possibility.

In considering Toulmin's charge that Collingwood was an epistemological relativist, and that therefore no rational account of conceptual change is possible, a distinction needs to be made between what may be called 'hard' and 'soft' versions of relativism. It is 'hard' relativism that is Toulmin's accusation. The thinking which takes place in any epoch does so within the context of *its* set, or 'constellation,' of absolute presuppositions. Since different sets of such presuppositions are incommensurable, it is not possible for inquirers who do not share the presuppositions of their subjects to 'know' what their thoughts were. Historical knowledge is thus circumscribed by the presuppositions of the historian, and every epoch writes its own history. 'Soft' relativism, on the other hand, merely makes the trivial point that the truth of claims to knowledge is always 'relative' to questions asked. It will be argued that Toulmin has misunderstood the nature of absolute presuppositions, and the procedure whereby Collingwood suggests conceptual change takes place, though he has been helped in his misunderstanding by Collingwood himself. Collingwood is a soft relativist, but he is more accurately described as an epistemological pluralist: there are different modes of knowledge, each with its own criteria.[3]

It is proposed in what follows to show not just that Collingwood's theory of absolute presuppositions and his account of historical knowledge can be reconciled, but that any account of the latter is incomplete without consideration of the former.

# I

Any theory of knowledge must answer three questions: the ontological question – what entities it is possible to have knowledge of; the epistemological question – what the grounds are upon which claims to knowledge of such entities are based; and the methodological question – how one reaches knowledge of such entities. During the course of examining Collingwood's answers to these questions, it is hoped to make clear both what it was that Collingwood thought was involved in making a claim to historical knowledge, and how he accounted for conceptual change. The overall purpose is to refute the charge that he was a relativist in Toulmin's sense.

The first question to be considered is concerned with distinguishing historical knowledge from other kinds of knowledge. It involves a discussion of the content given by Collingwood to the term 'thought.' As Louis Mink has pointed out,[4] nothing is more well known about Collingwood than his arresting claim that 'All history is the history of thought' (IH, 215). When he made this claim, it is important to recognize that Collingwood was not marking out the territory of the historian. He was rather concerned to establish and advance arguments for a mode of thinking distinct from other modes of thinking, especially religious and scientific thinking. This distinct and autonomous mode of thinking, which he called 'historical,' was something which he thought professional historians typically practised, but it was also a mode of thinking practised by anyone who thought self-consciously and reflectively about the actions of both other people and himself. Again he recognized that the territory of the historian was far wider than reflective thought about the actions of other people. It included, for instance, the customs, habits and institutions of the past, and the changes which occur in them over time, not all of which could be traced to the intentions and purposes of the people who may have been ultimately responsible for them.

What content, then, did Collingwood give to the term 'thought'? To begin with, thought is not to be conceived as occurring only at a high level of abstraction, nor as something which is somehow divorced from experience. It has a particularly close and intimate connection with action, and Collingwood's own thinking about this connection was a continuous one. Thus the first sentence of *Speculum Mentis* reads: 'All thought exists for the sake of action' (SM, 15). The last chapter of *An Autobiography* is titled 'Theory and Practice,' where he writes about his concern for a 'gloves-off philosophy'. He did not want 'a philosophy that should be a scientific toy guaranteed to amuse professional thinkers safe behind their college gates . . . I wanted a philosophy that should be a weapon. So far, I was with Marx' (A, 152–3). *The*

*New Leviathan, Or Man, Society, Civilization and Barbarism*, was specifically occasioned by the rise of fascism, and the Second World War. Civilization depended on metaphysical clarity, and it was this which Collingwood was after.

The connection between thought and action is also brought out, more philosophically, in what he has to say about the 'inside' and the 'outside' of an event, where it is thought, the 'inside,' which provides the warrant for calling an event an action. In *The Idea of History*, Collingwood illustrates his meaning with the examples of Caesar's crossing of the Rubicon and his assassination, and writes:

> By the inside of the event I mean that in it which can only be described in terms of thought: Caesar's defiance of Republican law, or the clash of constitutional policy between himself and his assassins. The historian . . . is investigating not mere events (where by a mere event I mean one which has only an outside and no inside) but actions, and an action is the unity of the outside and inside of an event. (IH, 213)

Here, thought is not necessarily something written down, but is something which is discovered by examination of the evidence. Again, though thought is distinct from feeling and emotion, it is not so distinct as to be discontinuous with such concepts. Whereas feeling and emotion are, in their immediacy, unreflective, thought is reflective, and can thus reflect on feeling and emotion. To 'feel' anger, love, ambition is to experience them directly: to 'think' about anger, love, ambition is to experience them only indirectly, to experience them not as feelings or emotions, but as concepts. Feelings and emotions thus survive in thought as concepts, but not in the immediacy of their experience. Thought cannot recapture, or 're-enact,' to use Collingwood's term, feelings and emotions in their immediacy, but only in so far as they can be conceptualized.[5] This is a way of elucidating the term 'thought' by saying that its content is filled solely by that which can be re-enacted. And it is this which defines the scope of *historical* knowledge as a mode of thinking: only something which can be re-enacted is something which can be historically known. Only thought can be re-enacted: only thought can be historically known.

## II

As a preliminary to considering the epistemological question – what is historical *knowledge*? – some attention is required to how knowledge of thought is possible. It has sometimes been thought, more rarely now than a generation ago, that the re-enactment doctrine is a methodological prescription. In advocating re-enactment, it is alleged that Collingwood was overcoming the 'other-minds' problem by an intuitive leap: by an act of concentrated empathy peculiarly gifted people could penetrate the minds of other people and come to know intuitively their thought processes.[6] This is not so: penetrating another's mind, if this is ever possible, is not the first step in the process of re-enactment, but at most the final step. It indicates *what* the historian should be about, not *how* he should do it.[7] Collingwood's methodological approach to historical knowledge is based on twin injunctions: the logic of question and answer;[8] and scrupulous and critical attention to evidence. In his so-called 'logic' of question and answer – for it is not really a logic, and thus a replacement of propositional logic, but a method of inquiry – Collingwood is concerned to dispute a rather crude empiricism whereby facts are gathered in great number, and then inferences drawn from them to form generalizations of explanatory force. Collingwood insists that inquirers do not approach the 'facts' of human existence so blankly, but come to them with problems or questions. Their task is to *establish* facts as they answer their questions and resolve their problems. The remains of the past, that is, documents, artefacts, and so on, do not produce historical facts until they have been duly questioned.

Collingwood's methodological standards were as rigorous as any historian could wish. Just as thought experiences feeling and emotion not directly but indirectly, so knowledge of past thought is gained inferentially. He did not doubt that the past had existed, but argued that it no longer existed. As it *had* existed, the past was inaccessible to the historian. The only past that was accessible was that which present evidence revealed under critical questioning. History, he wrote,

> is a science whose business is to study events not accessible to our

observation, and to study these events inferentially, arguing to them from something which is accessible to our observation, and which the historian calls 'evidence' for the events in which he is interested.

(IH, 251–2)

The achievement of historical knowledge is thus by inferential argument from that which is present: namely, the evidence which the past has left behind, and evidence is anything that can be so used.

Collingwood's recommendation of inferential argument as the procedure for historians is highlighted by consideration of cases where evidence is mean and sparse. His own historical work was on Roman Britain, a period often characterized by patchy evidence. In one passage he calls into being an entire community:

> At Silchester a tombstone was found, with an inscription . . . containing the name of a certain Ebicatos and written in the Irish, as distinct from the British, form of Celtic. An Irishman who died in Silchester and left friends able to make him an epitaph in his own language, must have been a member of an Irish colony in the town.[9]

His conclusion that this colony existed rests entirely upon the discovery of the tombstone: its existence is inferred because otherwise the presence of a tombstone in the Irish form of Celtic is unintelligible.

Elsewhere, Collingwood's concern is with what kind of a wall was Hadrian's Wall: more particularly, why the Romans changed from a Vallum frontier (a broad, flat-bottomed ditch) to a Wall frontier. 'The Wall,' he writes, 'in spite of appearances, was not strictly a fortification.' Its physical characteristics were not such as to make it an effective fighting platform for Roman soldiers, who were equipped and trained to meet their enemies in the open. With no artillery, Caledonian armies could not have been beaten off, but small raiding parties would find it an obstacle. They could indeed have crossed it, but once the alarm had been given, they would have found it 'almost impossible . . . to get back, especially if they were laden with plunder'. Collingwood concludes thus:

> The Wall, therefore, was a police work rather than a military work; and if it seems surprising that continuous lines of so elaborate a type should have been constructed merely for police purposes, it may be well to

remember that no longer ago than 1843 the English in India constructed a continuous barrier 2,500 miles long, made of a thorn-hedge reinforced with stone walls and earthworks, and patrolled it for thirty-five years with 14,000 officers and men, merely for the purpose of preventing smuggling in salt.[10]

What Collingwood presents us with here is the conclusion of an inferential argument, by which he has come to knowledge of the thinking which those Romans did who decided to change the nature of the frontier which separated them from Caledonia. If they had wished to build a military fortification, the Romans, given the state of their military art, would have done something different. They did not: hence they must have intended no more than a police work. In such a way, Collingwood has rethought, or re-enacted the thinking of those Romans involved.

A final example reveals what Collingwood meant when he wrote that 'to know another's act of thought involves repeating it for oneself' (IH, 288). Suppose that a historian

is reading the Theodosian Code, and has before him a certain edict of an emperor. Merely reading the words and being able to translate them does not amount to knowledge of their historical significance. In order to do that he must envisage the situation with which the emperor was trying to deal, and he must envisage it as that emperor envisaged it. Then he must see for himself, just as if the emperor's situation were his own, how such a situation might be dealt with; he must see the possible alternatives, and the reason for choosing one rather than another; and thus he must go through the process which the emperor went through in deciding on this particular course. Thus he is re-enacting in his own mind the experience of the emperor; and only in so far as he does this has he any historical knowledge, as distinct from a merely philological knowledge, of the meaning of the edict. (IH, 283)

Re-enactment is thus the conclusion of an inferential argument.

If the question is raised how we can be certain that we have repeated another's act of thought, then the answer is: only as certain as the evidence at our disposal allows us to be. Taking the case of autobiography, Collingwood argues that mere recollection is insufficient to recover one's own thought: 'If I want to be sure that twenty years ago a certain thought was really in my mind, I must have evidence of it' (IH, 296). What cannot be done is the re-enactment of thought in its immediacy. Thought arises in a context, but it 'is capable of sustaining itself and being revived or repeated without loss of its identity'. It is not repeated *in vacuo*, but always in some new context, and this new context must be receptive to that thought. In order that we may come to knowledge of another's past thoughts, 'we must come to them prepared with an experience sufficiently like his own to make those thoughts organic to it' (IH, 300). Or, as he put it somewhat more accessibly, 'the object must be of such a kind that it can revive itself in the historian's mind, the historian's mind must be such as to offer a home for that revival' (IH, 304). Collingwood expressed a similar thought in his anthropological work. In an unpublished manuscript from 1936–7 on magic, he wrote: 'If magic were a form of belief or custom peculiar to primitive peoples and absolutely foreign to the mind of civilized man, the civilized historian could never understand it.'[11]

The re-enactment doctrine, however, is not without its problems. In relation to the Irish community at Silchester, for instance, it might be thought that Collingwood is making it all up, that he is 'making' history, rather than reconstructing it.[12] In a sense such a thought would be correct; but he is not doing anything beyond inferring the minimum necessary to make intelligible what would otherwise be an unintelligible occurrence, using what evidence he has, and what general information he has about the period. Such acts of 'interpolation' are 'in no way arbitrary or merely fanciful'; they involve 'nothing that is not necessitated by the evidence,' but they are 'essentially something imagined'. This entire activity Collingwood called the '*a priori* imagination,' which the historian uses to bridge 'the gaps between what our authorities tell us,' and which gives 'the historical narrative or description its continuity' (IH, 240–1). But the *a priori* imagination not only acts in this constructive way, it is critical as well. For the 'authorities' of the historian do not tell him anything unless he critically questions them, and the basis upon which the historian does this is, again, the *a priori* imagination.

> It is thus the historian's picture of the past, the product of his own *a priori* imagination, that has to justify the sources used in its construction. These sources are sources, that is to say, credence is given to them, only because they are in this way justified. For any source may be tainted . . . The *a priori* imagination which does the work of

historical construction supplies the means of historical criticism as well (IH, 245).

For Rex Martin, the idea that the historian's criterion of historical construction is 'simply himself' (IH, 139) leads Collingwood into a 'radical subjectivism' which is 'dangerously close to anarchy'.[13] Louis Mink makes a similar point, but goes on to argue that Collingwood's doctrine of the *a priori* imagination was an imperfect attempt to bring out the notion of the absolute presuppositions of history. The doctrine was an attempt to show that 'historical knowledge is not *merely* empirical but is based on an "innate idea" which is "the idea of history itself".'[14] Lionel Rubinoff, in considering the same issue, likewise suggests that the doctrine of the *a priori* imagination is an absolute presupposition of history. The criterion of historical truth, according to which the historian argues from evidence to facts, is not something that can be derived from history alone, nor from the judgements of other historians, nor from our own experience. It must arise from within the latter, and yet not be purely subjective.[15] The historian, after all, as Collingwood was well aware (IH, 251–2, 303), has to defend his conclusions, his inferences, publicly. Knowledge is public. The propriety of his inferences must be something that he can justify, and on the argument that the remains of the past never *speak for themselves*, do not say anything to us until duly questioned and criticized, it is difficult to see whence the criterion of historical truth can be derived, unless it be something internal to the historian as a participant in the 'innate idea' of the 'idea of history itself'.[16]

## III

At this point it is appropriate to introduce Collingwood's theory of absolute presuppositions, and examine the epistemological basis of historical knowledge. The theory is stated in chapters IV and V of *An Essay on Metaphysics*, where it is put forward in terms of a body of propositions and definitions. Absolute presuppositions can be characterized in the following way. The thinking of any society, at any given stage in its development, comprises a system of concepts and principles operating on different levels of generality. Our acceptance of concepts and propositions on the lower levels of generality is 'relative to' those on the higher levels, and such lower-level concepts and propositions are presupposed only 'relatively' to those on more general levels. When we reach the most general level of all, our reasons for accepting concepts and principles cannot be explained in terms 'relative to' any more general considerations, so that those upper-level concepts and principles are presupposed not relatively, but 'absolutely'.[17] Collingwood defines relative and absolute presuppositions as follows:

> By a relative presupposition I mean one which stands relatively to one question as its presupposition and relatively to another question as its answer . . . An absolute presupposition is one which stands relatively to all questions to which it is related, as a presupposition, never as an answer. (EM, 29–31)

He brings out the difference between relative and absolute presuppositions in a characteristically impish way in *An Essay on Metaphysics*, where it is a pathologist who is patiently questioned:

> If you were talking to a pathologist about a certain disease and asked him 'What is the cause of the event E which you say sometimes happens in this disease?', he will reply 'The cause of E is C'; and if he were in a communicative mood he might go on to say 'That was established by So-and-so, in a piece of research that is now regarded as classical.' You might go on to ask: 'I suppose before So-and-so found out what the cause of E was, he was quite sure it had a cause?' The answer would be 'Quite sure, of course.' If you now say 'Why?' he will probably answer 'Because everything that happens has a cause.' If you are importunate enough to ask 'But how do you know that everything that happens has a cause?' he will probably blow up right in your face, because you have put your finger on one of his absolute presuppositions, and people are apt to be ticklish in their absolute presuppositions. But if he keeps his temper and gives you a civil and candid answer, it will be to the following effect. 'That is a thing we take for granted in my job. We don't question it. We don't try to verify it. It isn't a thing anybody has discovered, like microbes or the circulation of the blood. It is a thing we just take for granted.' He is telling you that it is an absolute presupposition of the science he pursues . . .
> (EM, 29–31)

What Collingwood claims for absolute presuppositions is that they underlie *all* systematic thinking: they are the foundation of knowledge, and as such *a priori*. The truth or falsehood of different constellations of absolute presuppositions is a question which does not arise, for absolute presuppositions are not answers to questions, and therefore verifiable, but are the 'yardsticks' by which the truth or falsehood of the propositions to which they give rise is established. It follows from this that different constellations of absolute presuppositions will give rise to different 'yardsticks' of truth or falsehood; and that there is no higher criterion to which the inquirer can refer to judge the competing claims of different yardsticks.

Hence arises the original question: since different epochs have different constellations of absolute presuppositions, and since we, as inquirers, operate within our own constellation, how is historical knowledge possible? Any claim to knowledge would seem to be no more than a claim which can only be justified within one constellation of absolute presuppositions, namely our own. The success of any attempt to rethink past thought will thus be illusory, because our thinking can only take place in the context of a constellation of absolute presuppositions which is different from that of the people whose thought we are studying.

For Toulmin, thus, Collingwood is an epistemological relativist. What Collingwood says about absolute presuppositions is that they change. Any given constellation of them is subject to 'strains' which, if they become great enough, provoke the collapse of one constellation and its supersession by another, 'which will be a modification of the old with the destructive strain removed; a modification not consciously devised but created by an act of unconscious thought' (EM, 48). Toulmin has taken Collingwood to task over this passage. The term 'unconscious thought', for Toulmin, begs the question whether the change is to be accounted for rationally or causally. It cannot be the former without destroying the 'absoluteness' of the presuppositions in question, without, that is, invoking a further, higher, set of absolute presuppositions according to which rational choice can be made. If it is, on the other hand, causal change that is operative, then Collingwood's account leads him to relativism. One way of salvaging Collingwood's thought from this fate is, as Toulmin suggests, first to remark that absolute presuppositions are of disciplines or sciences, rather than of epochs[18] (which, as we shall see, is more consistent anyway with Collingwood's position), and second to distinguish the *theoretical* principles of any science from its *disciplinary aims*. Any amount of substantive change can be allowed in the former, so long as the latter remain constant and invariant. For it is the 'disciplinary principles that are *constitutive of*' any science, whereas its theoretical principles are merely '*operative within*' that science. Toulmin has to acknowledge, however, that 'when there are cross-purposes *both* at the theoretical *and* at the disciplinary level,' then 'communication breaks down inescapably' between different constellations of absolute presuppositions,[19] and the charge of epistemological relativism returns.

Rex Martin also suggests that 'there appears to be a tension, amounting perhaps to an inconsistency . . . within Collingwood's own philosophy.'[20] The inconsistency arises from the demands of the re-enactment theory and the implications of the doctrine of absolute presuppositions. Martin argues for the possibility of cultures where the kind of human agency demanded by the re-enactment theory may simply be absent. His examples are of societies where human behaviour is interpreted in deterministic historical-materialist terms; societies where there is wholesale submissiveness to divine determinism; and Skinnerian societies where 'behaviour was understood wholly cybernetically'.[21] Of such societies, with no conception of human agency, the re-enactment theory can offer no intelligible account. Quite so, it cannot. And Collingwood would clearly recognize that it could not, as his remarks on magic, cited above, indicate. Martin's proposed resolution of the inconsistency does not, however, address the issue which he says gives rise to the appearance of the inconsistency. He argues that the instances subsumed under any absolute presupposition are susceptible of extension, such that any given absolute presupposition may take as one of *its* instances, those which are otherwise subsumed under a different absolute presupposition, so long as they are appropriately redescribed. In such a way, different absolute presuppositions 'interpenetrate' each other to make trans-historical and cross-cultural understanding possible.[22] It is difficult to imagine, however, how an instance of human behaviour subsumed under absolute presuppositions having as their content determinist historical-materialism, the will of God or Skinnerian stimulus-response, could be *redescribed* as an instance of human *action*, explicable according to the demands of re-enactment theory. Collingwood, at least, was clear in the radical distinction he made between *behaviour* and *action*. The status of Martin's examples is, thus, somewhat indeterminate. Be that as it may, Martin's proposed solution is ingenious, even if it has nothing to do with his examples, and even if it is not something that can be found in Collingwood.

Both Toulmin and Martin misrepresent what Collingwood understood by the nature of absolute presuppositions. From the fact that Collingwood said that change between absolute presuppositions could be radical, they have inferred, incorrectly, an incommensurability between different absolute presuppositions, such that trans-historical understanding is problematic. It is not, for either of them, an impossibility; but it is nevertheless a potential problem. In the remainder of this chapter I want to show that the problem does not arise if absolute presuppositions are interpreted dialectically.

Collingwood is an epistemological relativist only on the assumption that constellations of absolute presuppositions exhibit the same 'strainless structure which characterizes a body of propositions in mathematics'. But they are not timeless like the propositions of mathematics: on the contrary, they are historical, and subject characteristically to strain and change. 'Any given constellation of absolute presuppositions [has] in its structure not the simplicity and calm that characterize the subject-matter of mathematics but the intricacy and restlessness that characterize the subject-matter, say, of legal or constitutional history' (EM, 76–7).

What Collingwood exemplifies when, in *The Idea of Nature*, *The Idea of History*, and *An Essay on Metaphysics*, he engages in historical inquiry into the absolute presuppositions of past epochs is first, that absolute presuppositions are of disciplines or modes of thinking; second, that some absolute presuppositions do not, or have not changed since systematic thinking began; and third, that when they do change, the change is not discontinuous but 'dialectic'. And 'dialectic' is to be understood here in the sense of something struggling to become that which it is not, which, when it becomes what it is not, does not lose, but retains a connection with what it was. Collingwood suggests as much as this in the passage already cited from *An Essay on Metaphysics* when he says that the new set of absolute presuppositions will be a *'modification* of the old' (EM, 48, emphasis added).

An illustration of conceptual change may be found in *An Autobiography*, where Collingwood argues, against those whom he calls 'realists,' that Plato's *Republic* and Hobbes's *Leviathan*, so far as they are concerned with politics, are concerned with different problems, for 'Plato's "State" is the Greek *polis*, and Hobbes's is the absolutist State of the seventeenth century.' Nevertheless, there is a connection between Plato and Hobbes, but the connection is not 'the sameness of a "universal", and the difference the difference between two instances of that universal.' On the contrary, the sameness

> is the sameness of an historical process, and the difference is the difference between one thing which in the course of that process has turned into something else, and the other thing into which it has turned. Plato's *polis* and Hobbes's absolutist State are related by a traceable historical process, whereby one has turned into the other . . . Pursuing this line of inquiry, I soon realized that the history of political theory is not the history of different answers given to one and the same question, but the history of a problem more or less constantly changing, whose solution was changing with it. (A, 62)

The objections of Toulmin and Martin are thus misdirected. Radical discontinuity between different sets of absolute presuppositions, such as they suggest, would indeed inhibit the possibility of historical knowledge. But radical discontinuity is not the same thing as radical difference, and it is 'difference' that Collingwood is talking about. The circumstances which Toulmin and Martin indicate as possible are not those which Collingwood is concerned with. As a historian, his concern was with what had happened, not with what it was logically possible to imagine happening.

## IV

But what do absolute presuppositions look like? They have been called, by Mink, 'a priori conceptual systems,' similar to Kant's 'categories of understanding,' and Wittgenstein's conception of a common language;[23] and by David Rynin they have been characterized as 'definitions,' in the sense in which definitions are '*decisions*, commitments, acts, and as such neither true nor false'.[24] Both Mink and Rynin are concerned, at least in part, to rescue Collingwood from the charge of relativism about the possibility and nature of historical knowledge, and I do not quarrel with their views here. If the argument remains at this level, however, then the theory of absolute presuppositions is left to consider statements which, however fundamental they are, have an inescapably trivial appearance. In *The Idea of Nature*, for instance, Collingwood suggests that there are at least two 'indispensable presuppositions of any "science of nature",' namely 'that there are "natural" things,' and 'that "natural" things constitute a single "world of nature"' (IN, 29). No doubt he is correct here, but such observations do not get us very far in any analysis of scientific knowledge.

Collingwood's analysis of the theory of absolute presuppositions is to work backwards from statements to the questions to which they are answers, or from propositions to the presuppositions which underlie them, until we reach rock bottom with presuppositions which are not answers to questions, and which are therefore absolutely not relatively presupposed. If we reverse this procedure, and start with absolute presuppositions working forwards, then we have a much more fruitful way of linking the theory of absolute presuppositions with Collingwood's theory of historical knowledge. If we stand at the mouth of a river, we have only to walk along its bank to find its source: if, on the other hand, we stand at its source, while some courses will definitely be ruled out, there is a variety of courses which might have been taken. A better metaphor would be a temporal, rather than a spatial one. Thus if we are currently in a particular situation – say, a member of the French National Assembly in 1792 – we have some awareness of how we arrived in such a situation, but we do not know precisely what our situation will be in the future, though we may have a fair idea of what situations we will not be in. Questions arise from constellations of absolute presuppositions, but there is no logical entailment between them and the questions which do arise. One constellation can give rise to a number of relative presuppositions.

What I am suggesting here is that for the theory of absolute presuppositions to illuminate Collingwood's theory of historical knowledge, then what has to be incorporated is an analysis of what relative presuppositions have in fact been given rise to by particular constellations of absolute presuppositions. Thus, the arguments of Mink and Rynin need to be supplemented by greater attention than either of them gives to the history of science and the history of history which Collingwood writes about in *The Idea of Nature* and *The Idea of History*. In the light of such considerations I want to advance the argument that constellations of absolute presuppositions, and their attendant relative presuppositions, appear much more as stages in the development of intellectual traditions,[25] or of theories of knowledge. The advantages of characterizing the theory of absolute presuppositions in this way are first, that it emphasizes, in a way that Mink's and Rynin's accounts do not, the dynamic element in bodies of ideas (though it is of course a major part of Mink's argument that constellations of absolute presuppositions form open and dynamic, not closed, systems of thought); second, that it permits the observation, as Collingwood himself recognized, that while some ages may be characterized by a dominant constellation of absolute presuppositions, most ages are characterized by the coexistence of different intellectual traditions; and finally, that 'tradition' is the term used by Collingwood in *The Idea of History*.

Collingwood's concern in the first parts of *The Idea of History*, that is, before the essays which make up the Epilegomena, is to offer an analysis of three traditions of thinking, each of which was in its time inimical to the development of historical knowledge: Greek mathematical thinking of the sixth century; medieval theology; and the concern with natural science from the sixteenth to the nineteenth centuries. At the same time, his concern was to offer an account of the development of a different tradition of thinking which not until the late nineteenth and early twentieth centuries was able to offer a theory of knowledge which did proper justice to historical thought. What hindered its development is best expressed by Collingwood himself.

> Historical thought has an object with peculiarities of its own. The past, consisting of particular events in space and time which are no longer happening, cannot be apprehended by mathematical thinking, because mathematical thinking apprehends objects that have no special location in space and time, and it is just that lack of spatio-temporal location

that makes them knowable. Nor can the past be apprehended by theological thinking, because the object of that kind of thinking is a single infinite object, and historical events are finite and plural. Nor by scientific thinking, because the truths which science discovers are known to be true by being found through observation and experiment exemplified in what we actually perceive, whereas the past has vanished and our ideas about it can never be verified as we verify our scientific hypotheses. Theories of knowledge designed to account for mathematical and theological and scientific knowledge thus do not touch on the special problems of historical knowledge; and if they offer themselves as complete accounts of knowledge they actually imply that historical knowledge is impossible. (IH, 5)

Collingwood's argument is that each of these three traditions of thinking had its period of dominance, when *its* concerns coloured the whole field of intellectual inquiry. But mathematical thinking still goes on, albeit much changed from the time of the Greeks, as does theological and scientific thinking. The changes that have occurred in mathematical thinking – and the same could be argued for theological and scientific thinking – are not such as to cause us to doubt that present-day mathematical thinking traces its inheritance back to Greek mathematical thinking. The same inherited character distinguishes the theory of historical knowledge. It did not just spring from a vacuum, nor was it simply a resolution of strains and antinomies in mathematical, theological or scientific thinking. It sprang from an independent tradition which was at times coexistent, though always uneasily so, with these other ways of thinking; from a tradition which may be traced back to Herodotus. What is significant in Herodotus is that he treated the doings of men as actions for which there were reasons: it being the job of the historian to discover what those reasons were. What is significant in Thucydides, the 'successor' of Herodotus, is that he treated the doings of men as behaviour for which there might be adduced causes in the form of unchanging psychological laws. The achievement of Herodotus was thus 'overlaid and smothered beneath [the] antihistorical' tendency of Greek mathematical thinking, and it stayed smothered for years (IH, 30). It was not revived in any extensive form until Vico, and thereafter the main characters in its development were Kant, Hegel, perhaps Marx, Simmel, Dilthey and finally Croce. By this time there was a fully-fledged theory of historical knowledge – the 'historical' always to be understood as that which can be re-enacted or rethought in the present.

Collingwood's job was to work through this theory for an English-speaking audience in the predominantly hostile environment of positivism and its varieties. His hope was that in the study of man as a thinking, and sometimes rational, being, the theory of historical knowledge, as an autonomous mode of knowledge, would come to supplant theories which denied man the capacity to be a moral agent. Presupposed by Collingwood's theory of historical knowledge is a belief in human agency: a belief that human actions are free, and that human actions make a difference. The purpose of studying history is to learn what man has done, in order to know what man is, and what man can do. But though human actions are free, this freedom is exercised within a context of surrounding circumstances and conditions.

> For a man about to act, the situation is his master, his oracle, his god. Whether his action is to prove successful or not depends on whether he grasps the situation rightly or not. If he is a wise man, it is not until he has consulted his oracle, done everything in his power to find out what the situation is, that he will make even the most trivial plan. And if he neglects the situation, the situation will not neglect him. It is not one of those gods that leave an insult unpunished. (IH, 316)

Collingwood's view here is close to the 'situational logic' of Karl Popper. What is involved in this logic is 'an idealized reconstruction of the *problem situation* in which the agent found himself,' in terms of which we 'make action "understandable" . . . that is to say, adequate to his situation as he saw it'.[26] His view is also close to that of the other Karl, Karl Marx: 'men make their own history, but they do not make it just as they please; they do not make it under circumstances chosen by themselves, but under circumstances directly encountered, given and transmitted from the past.'[27]

The point of this essay has been to suggest that, whether or not Collingwood's theory of historical knowledge is valid, it can only be sustained against the charges of relativism and scepticism if his theory of absolute presuppositions is interpreted on lines such as advanced here. I have tried to show, albeit extremely briefly, that this is how Collingwood himself argued in *The Idea of History*, and the same analysis could be done for *The Idea of Nature*. He stated his position at least as early as 1927 in a review of Oswald Spengler's *Decline of the West*, where he argued vigorously against the idea of cultures being 'self-contained or closed' systems.

> If history is possible, if we can understand other cultures, we can do so only by re-thinking for ourselves their thoughts, cherishing within us the fundamental idea which framed their lives; and in that case their culture lives on within ours, as Euclidean geometry lives on within modern geometry, and Herodotean history within the mind of the modern historian. But this is to destroy the idea of atomic cultures, and to assert not a mere plurality of cultures but a unity of that plurality, a unity which is the present culture, the heir of all its past.[28]

Absolute presuppositions, and their attendant relative presuppositions, are the context within which knowledge is achieved. Different presuppositions will be involved according to whether the object of inquiry is God, nature or man. Just as knowledge of God is not to be dismissed because he is not knowable by the theory of scientific knowledge, so too the presumption is unwarranted that knowledge of man is only to be got by that theory. This is neither scepticism nor relativism: it is, rather, pluralism.

*Notes*

1. Stephen Toulmin, *Human Understanding*, 1 (Oxford, Clarendon Press, 1972), 66–80.
2. I do not propose to deal further with Knox's claim. If the argument stands, which I put forward against Collingwood's account being relativist, then it can equally well operate against the charge of scepticism.
3. In *An Essay on Metaphysics*, and elsewhere, Collingwood in fact makes the point which Toulmin alleges is absent, that absolute presuppositions are of disciplines, or modes of thinking, rather than of epochs. It is the case, though, that in certain epochs one set of absolute presuppositions may dominate. See Toulmin, *Human Understanding*, 79–80, and below for further discussion.
4. Louis O. Mink, *Mind, History and Dialectic* (Bloomington, Indiana University Press, 1969), 157ff.
5. The philosophical arguments here relate to the 'scale of forms' and the dialectical relationship between them which Collingwood first put forward in *Speculum Mentis*, and elaborated in *An Essay on Philosophical Method* (Clarendon Press, Oxford, 1933), ch. III. For discussion of

Collingwood's position here, see Mink, op. cit., and Lionel Rubinoff, *Collingwood and the Reform of Metaphysics*, (Toronto, University of Toronto Press, 1970), chs. V and VI.

[6] Karl Popper, *Objective Knowledge*, (Oxford, Clarendon Press, 1972), 187–9, maintains that Collingwood was a methodological intuitionist, as did W. H. Walsh and P. L. Gardiner soon after *The Idea of History* was published; though Walsh and Gardiner are now said to have abandoned this interpretation. See Margit Hurup Nielsen, 'Re-enactment and Reconstruction in Collingwood's Philosophy of History,' *History and Theory*, 20 (1981), 3–5. Nielsen herself argues that re-enactment *is* a methodological precept, but only when it is seen as a synonym for 'reconstruction by interpretation of evidence' (ibid., 5), a position which is different from, but not inconsistent with the one advanced here.

[7] See Rex Martin, *Historical Explanation: Re-enactment and Practical Inference* (Ithaca, Cornell University Press, 1977), 50.

[8] Collingwood first worked out the logic of question and answer in a manuscript of 1918, *Truth and Contradiction*, which he destroyed in 1938. One chapter remains in the unpublished papers of Collingwood. I owe this information to Peter Johnson, 'Is Collingwood's *Autobiography* Reliable?', *Collingwood Studies*, 2 (1995). In Collingwood's published works, the main sources are *Speculum Mentis*, 76–80; *An Autobiography*, 29–44; *An Essay on Metaphysics*, 23–33; and *The Idea of History*, 269–74, 278–82.

[9] R. G. Collingwood, 'Roman Britain,' in Collingwood and J. N. L. Myers, *Roman Britain and the English Settlements* (Oxford, Clarendon Press, 1937), 316, quoted in Leon J. Goldstein, 'Collingwood on the Constitution of the Historical Past,' in Michael Krausz, ed., *Critical Essays on the Philosophy of R. G. Collingwood* (Oxford, Clarendon Press, 1972), 262.

[10] R. G. Collingwood, *Roman Britain* (Oxford, Clarendon Press, 1934), 32–3.

[11] R. G. Collingwood, 'Folklore, I,' 1936–7, 2, 18, quoted in W. J. van der Dussen, 'Collingwood's Unpublished Manuscripts,' *History and Theory*, 18 (1979), 304–5.

[12] For the view that the terms 're-enact,' 'reconstruct,' 're-create,' and 'rethink' are synonyms in Collingwood's thought, see Nielsen, 'Re-enactment and Reconstruction', 2.

[13] Martin, *Historical Explanation*, 63–4.

[14] Mink, *Mind, History and Dialectic*, 183–7; the quotation from Collingwood is IH, 248.

[15] Rubinoff, *Collingwood and the Reform of Metaphysics*, 274–84.

[16] Lest it should be thought that Collingwood is proposing something eccentric here, he receives some support from fellow historians, as the

following extract makes clear: the historian's 'instinctive familiarity with the evidence results in a useful and necessary sense which extends his range beyond the strict confines of the evidence; even his guesses bear the stamp of truth because they fit the reality of the situation . . . This professional hunch is based on an expert understanding of what can, what must, have happened; more than a guess, it is in the nature of an inspired forecast which often leads to the discovery of evidence supporting it . . . The professional uses his real awareness of what is "right" in a given context in order to fight his way through to an explanation grounded on evidence. It is a tool of selection and divination, not an end to the process of reasoning and discovery. This solid kind of familiarity lies behind everything that is professional about historians' (G. R. Elton, *The Practice of History* (London, Fontana, 1979), 32–3).

[17] This summary is taken from Toulmin, *Human Understanding*, 73.
[18] See above n.3.
[19] Stephen Toulmin, 'Conceptual Change and the Problem of Relativity,' in Krausz, *Critical Essays*, 214–16.
[20] Rex Martin, 'Collingwood's Doctrine of Absolute Presuppositions and the Possibility of Historical Knowledge,' in L. Pompa and W. H. Dray, eds., *Substance and Form in History* (Edinburgh, Edinburgh University Press, 1981), 101.
[21] Ibid., 99.
[22] Ibid., 101–2.
[23] Mink, *Mind, History, Dialectic*, 144ff.
[24] David Rynin, 'Donagan on Collingwood: Absolute Presuppositions, Truth and Metaphysics,' *Review of Metaphysics*, 18 (1964–5), 309.
[25] I have benefited from Andrew Lockyer, 'Traditions as Context in the History of Political Theory', *Political Studies* 27, (1979), 201–17, though he would not necessarily agree with the use to which I have put his thoughts.
[26] Popper, *Objective Knowledge*, 179. For a discussion of Popper and Collingwood, see Peter Skagestad, *Making Sense of History: The Philosophy of Popper and Collingwood* (Oslo, Universitetsforlaget, 1975); and Margit Hurup Nielsen and J. F. G. Shearmur, 'Making Sense of History: Skagestad on Popper and Collingwood,' *Inquiry*, 22 (1979).
[27] Karl Marx, *The Eighteenth Brumaire of Louis Napoleon* (Peking, Foreign Languages Press, 1987), 9.
[28] R. G. Collingwood, *Essays in the Philosophy of History*, ed. William Debbins (Austin, University of Texas Press, 1965), 71.

# Collingwood's Claim that Metaphysics is a Historical Discipline

REX MARTIN

The procedure I will follow in this chapter requires a brief initial note of explanation. Collingwood's texts are opaque at two points. First, he does not make clear what precisely he meant by the claim that metaphysics is a historical discipline. The prevailing interpretation – which I dispute – has been that he had in mind a similarity or identity of certain methods of inquiry or explanation. Second, and more seriously, he does not make clear the relationship of his two main treatises on metaphysics (his *Essay on Philosophical Method,* 1933, and his *Essay on Metaphysics,* 1940). They were written and published only seven years apart and one feels there *ought* to be some connection, if only that of explicit rejection, between them. Their connection is problematic, for they appear, on the surface, very different, rather like the relationship of Plato's *Laws* to his *Republic* (and this difference has been emphasized in the prevailing interpretations of Collingwood). But Collingwood himself is almost completely noncommittal on how they stand, each to the other. He apparently saw in them some sort of continuity (A, 118).[1] But beyond this we have no sense (from his published writings) of what he took their relationship to be.

So, at the very beginning, we confront a formidable problem in interpretation. I have tried to solve this problem, for it needs solving, by triangulation: by going to Collingwood's *other* texts for the development of his ideas. In sum, the mediation between the two metaphysical treatises is there, not directly in the two texts themselves, but in the whole corpus of his published work from that period (1933–42). And it is my belief that the solution to the problem of metaphysical continuity (or its lack) in Collingwood's thought gives us the key to interpreting his claim that metaphysics is a historical discipline. These are not simply two different problems but, rather, two *related* problems – or, if you will, a single problem with two aspects.

Now, let us leave off preliminaries and 'instead of taking now and then a castle or village on the frontier... march up directly to the capital or centre' (in Hume's phrase) of our problem. We turn, then, to Collingwood's account of absolute presuppositions.

# I

That account, as we have it principally in part I of his *Essay on Metaphysics* and also in his *Autobiography*, is very complex. Perhaps Collingwood's central claim is that absolute presuppositions are not propositions at all. But his ostensible reason for saying this was rather eccentric and open to doubt: he claimed that a proposition is always asserted (as true or as false) in a certain context and that it 'arises' and takes its meaning, so to speak, out of the specific matrix that it presupposes. (See in particular his discussion of the logic of question and answer, A, 31–9.) Since it stands to reason that not every matrix can itself depend on a logically prior one, he concluded that there must be some that are simply ultimate: these, by definition, would not be propositions; they would be absolute presuppositions.[2]

Now, it might be useful to consider more fully the account in the previous paragraph. The account does, of course, successfully capture one important part of what Collingwood is saying. Thus, when he said that absolute presuppositions are not propositions, he meant that they can be neither true nor false (see A, 66–7, and EM, esp. 32–3 and also 53–4). And he thought they could be neither true nor false for the simple reason that they hinge on no prior presupposition(s). There are no 'questions' here to which they could possibly be 'answers'.

Since the existence of some such prior context is, in Collingwood's view, a necessary basis for attributing truth values to statements (or to statement-like formulations), we can only conclude that absolute presuppositions, in the absence of these contexts, have no truth value. Thus, his logic of question and answer provides a seemingly neat ground for Collingwood's claim that absolute presuppositions are not propositions.

It is too neat, though. For on the very same basis, we would have to deny that absolute presuppositions, when formulated, could even be meaningful (since meaningfulness for statements is grounded in the very same way as truth values in a question and answer complex). And if absolute presuppositions are not even meaningful, then they cannot, contrary to what Collingwood suggests, be supposed (by anyone who thinks about them) or be presupposed (in some sort of logical relationship) by inferior propositions, or what have you. So, we need some other basis for asserting that absolute presuppositions are not propositional than the so-called logic of question and answer.

Now, Collingwood did identify a certain sense in which an absolute presupposition can be true/false. We might take him here, rather roughly, as distinguishing between our conception of some general feature of the world and our description or formulation of this conception (see EM, 33, 55, 60).

A descriptive formulation can be true or false, for it is an attempt to identify, more or less accurately, what particular conception of things does organize a given universe of discourse. For instance, a person might assert (truly) that most politically active people in Europe and North America, in the things they say when they argue politics, do not hold to the notion of a divine right of kings. Since statements of this sort are characteristically made by historians, Collingwood said that such statements, even when made about absolute presuppositions, are actually 'historical' in nature (see EM, 49, 77, 81, 163). What he was saying here is that so-called metaphysical statements are attempts to convey accurately what was in fact presupposed in a given science or universe of discourse at a given time or place; and metaphysical statements, taken in this way, can therefore be true or false (see EM, 40, 47, 54, 81, 101, 168).

The metaphysical statement is here merely a conceptual representation. But what of the conception it represents, can *that* be true or false?

It was in answer to this question that Collingwood made his claim that absolute presuppositions are altogether incapable of having truth values. There is, his argument goes, no clear way in which such conceptions could be regarded as true or false. For it is difficult to see what they could be referred to in order to determine their truth value: as absolute, they presuppose nothing, nothing is logically prior to them; whereas all of our network of knowledge claims, by which we do determine truth or falsity, for example, by going to the facts of the world, already presuppose them (see EM, 30, 32, 46, 147, 193–4). So, clearly, the way in which we could determine an absolute presupposition to be true or false would have to be vastly different from the way in which a statement *within* the universe of discourse organized by such a conception would be determined to be true or false (see here EM, 147–53 in particular). Once this is said, there seems to be no other way – at least no obvious or accredited way – to assign them truth value at all. Indeed it becomes difficult to identify even a sense in which they could be true or false.

In sum, the description of an absolute presupposition can be, as to accuracy, true or false; but the content itself of the basic conception can be neither true nor false. Absolute presuppositions are not propounded; they are just supposed (EM, 28, 48, 92, 163); and their 'logical efficacy' comes, not from their being true, but simply from their being supposed (EM, 27, 32–3, 39, 42, 52, 101).

Now that we have somewhat clarified Collingwood's contention that absolute presuppositions are not propositions, it might be useful to consider briefly the connection that some have been seen as holding between Collingwood's *Essay on Metaphysics* and A. J. Ayer's *Language, Truth and Logic*. Both Knox and Donagan believe that 'between 1936 and 1938 Collingwood radically changed his mind about the relation of philosophy to history.'[3] Donagan contends, further, that this break stemmed from Collingwood's having read Ayer's book (first published in 1936), with the result that 'he had come to endorse Ayer's view that the propositions of traditional metaphysics are unverifiable . . .'[4]

I think Donagan's insight is very shrewd here. There is clear textual evidence that Collingwood had read Ayer attentively; indeed he devoted an entire chapter of his book to Ayer's critique of metaphysics (EM, 162–71; see also 5 and 19). I do not think we should take Collingwood as *endorsing* Ayer's view, however; rather, we could better regard the *Essay on Metaphysics* as a clever and well-devised attempt to get around Ayer's principal strictures. For the essence of the *Metaphysics* is to deny the exhaustive dichotomizing of all meaningful statements into two exclusive classes, the analytic and the factual-empirical, by arguing that a third class of such statements, the philosophical, exists. At the same time, Collingwood accepts Ayer's thrust that the statements of traditional metaphysics have no truth value.

Let me be more precise. Collingwood did allow that absolute presuppositions, when formulated as statements, were meaningful, for they could be supposed. And, when supposed, they were supposed as true (or as false, e.g. in a *reductio*). So one cannot say in any simple way, then, that they cannot *have* truth values. It follows that one cannot accept (as I made clear earlier) the logic of the question-and-answer account of absolute presuppositions – because to do so would rob them of meaning (of meaningfulness) and any possibility of taking truth values as supposals or even as descriptions. Rather, Collingwood's point here is that absolute presuppositions, when formulated on their own, cannot be *asserted*; for they are unverifiable in the literal sense: there simply is no way to establish their truth value (see EM, 32, 42, 101; also 147–9 and 162).

The differences between Ayer and Collingwood, though, are ultimately as important as the similarities. Ayer thought that because the traditional formulations of metaphysics, conceived as assertions in their own right, were neither analytic truths nor empirical statements, they must be nonsensical and hence, for that reason, could have no truth values. Collingwood's was the very different point that absolute presuppositions can have no independent truth value because, though meaningful when stated, they are not basically assertions at all. In Collingwood's account, these presuppositions are not conceived as *pseudo*-propositions, hence nonsensical, but rather as *non*-propositions to which the application of the term 'nonsensical' would be wholly inappropriate.

In Collingwood's view, every system of inquiry – every science – has some foundation, which is from the standpoint of the practices of that inquiry logically ultimate. It is these foundations that Collingwood referred to as absolute presuppositions. These foundations, respecting any given piece of inquiry or explanation within the practice, are their groundform.

Or, to put the matter more perspicuously, the absolute

presuppositions or basic conceptions of a given system of knowledge are objective standards and conventions to which people conform when they frame and evaluate knowledge claims or hypotheses, when they 'automatically' follow a narrative or a proof, and so on. Absolute presuppositions constitute the nature of our understanding within a particular universe of discourse and they govern the inquiry we undertake and the explanations we give there in individual cases. But if our explanatory practices should prove inadequate, in any of a variety of ways, then we change what we do; and it is through such changes that change can occur in the organizing conceptions themselves. For these basic conceptions are not in our collective unconscious, as shadowy, incipient propositions available for dredging up by psychologists (see EM, 102–3), or out there somewhere in Plato's heaven; rather they are *in* the explanatory practices and knowledge claims themselves. The basic conceptions are objective features, though implicit ones, of any ongoing science. They are a part of the institutional setting, the procedures, of science in a given society (see EM, 194, 196–7).

Collingwood's notion that an absolute presupposition cannot be separated from the statements that presuppose it (contrary to Louis Mink's idea that an absolute presupposition can be treated as an *a priori* concept) leads to the idea that absolute presuppositions are simply a part of scientific practice itself.[5] They are ingredient there as foundation or ground. We exhibit these basic conceptions simply in 'doing' science in the way that we do.

The basic conceptions, in short, are certain general, recurring features of a scientific practice – features of the way we behave when we engage in a particular science. They are not statements but, at best, proto-statements. If we were ever to formulate them explicitly, the formulations would be meaningful but they would not have, except descriptively, any truth value at all. For the foundation statements here are merely more or less accurate formulations, made by the philosopher, of these basic conceptions; they are a way of talking about certain regularities of behaviour (as for example, in the statement of the basic schema of practical inference presupposed in the explanatory re-enactments of historians).

A striking doctrine, then, lies at the heart of Collingwood's distinction between basic conceptions and their formulation.

Absolute presuppositions, the basic conceptions themselves, are not propositions; they are objective patterns and structures in our way of knowing. They are neither right nor wrong, true nor false; they just are. We can, of course, put these structures into words, try to formulate and thereby describe them. Indeed, this is the only way we could come to know that they are there at all, or what they are. And such statements can be, as I've been at pains to emphasize, true or false.

Collingwood himself often called these formulations 'historical,' as we have noted. Certainly they are 'historical' in so far as one strives for accuracy in the rendition of a particular or individual case; but whether they are historical in any other way is something that, by and large, I want to defer discussing until the next two sections. There is, however, one important way in which absolute presuppositions might be described as historical that seems germane to the present section.

For in addition to Collingwood's two main contentions, that absolute presuppositions are not propositions and that they can be rendered (propounded) only descriptively, he suggested a number of other important ways in which absolute presuppositions could be characterized. He claimed that absolute presuppositions are probably culturally delimited (EM, 60, 72), even though the persons who live in a given culture are largely unconscious of them (see EM, 43, 48, 101–2); that these presuppositions are conjoined in a rather loose amalgam, or 'constellation' as he called it (EM, 66–7); that this amalgam is held together under a kind of pressure or strain so that it tends to change over time (EM, 75–7), with the result that the absolute presuppositions themselves are subject to change and always changing (EM, 48n.). But absolute presuppositions cannot be changed directly, for they are held unconsciously (or, if you will, preconsciously).[6] For this same reason they cannot be adopted or discarded directly either. They are not like fashions or fancies that one can capriciously put on or take off (see EM, 48n 193). Rather, absolute presuppositions 'come with the territory,' with the 'doing' of any science. Absolute presuppositions are properly seen as commitments that we have, or are driven to. They are at a far remove from being gratuitous, let alone perfectly gratuitous, as Shalom has claimed.[7]

In sum: (1) any given absolute presupposition will be non-propositional and susceptible of having, other than descriptively, no truth value at all; (2) that presupposition will be, though widespread, culturally delimited; people in that culture will by and large be unaware, though not *necessarily* unaware, that it even exists; it will be the result of earlier – indirect – changes, will be subject to further change, and so on.

Now, much of this is clearly intended to contrast with the Kantian account of the principles of human understanding, with its universal categories and its fixed forms of intuition and its synthetic *a priori* propositions (see EM, 179–80). Moreover, these contentions of Collingwood, just summarized in (2), are all quite interesting – and quite consistent with other things that he said, for example with his criticism of the idea of a science of human nature[8] – but it is worth noting that none of them are *entailed* by his earlier contentions about absolute presuppositions. It is, none the less, possible to hold all these contentions, the initial ones (in 1) and the ones summarized (in 2), as a single, self-consistent view of the nature both of metaphysics and of science. And it is quite evident that Collingwood, basing his claims on work he had done as a historian of scientific ideas (in his *Idea of Nature* and in the *Idea of History*, parts I–IV, in particular), did hold precisely this view.[9]

However, Collingwood did not explicitly restrict his claim that metaphysical propositions are historical – historical, that is, in describing things (absolute presuppositions) that are culturally delimited and subject to change – merely to the negative point that these propositions are not synthetic *a priori* (or are not *a priori* concepts, for that matter).[10] Indeed, his claim that they are historical and that metaphysics is itself a 'historical science' is quite unrestricted (see EM, 49, 163, and 77, 81, for these two claims).

So the question naturally arises whether metaphysics, in being historical, is like the discipline of history or its conventional subject matter in other, perhaps deeper ways as well. We turn to this issue in the next two sections.

## II

The prevailing mood in the interpretation of Collingwood on this point was set early on by T. M. Knox, the editor of Collingwood's two posthumously published philosophical works (IN and IH).

Knox, in his Editor's Preface to IH, focused on 'Collingwood's conceptions of the relation between philosophy and history' (Knox, Pref., vii; see IH, vii–xx). And he claimed that Collingwood came to adopt a 'historicism not unlike Croce's (viii; see also IH, xxi) in which 'philosophy as a separate discipline is liquidated by being converted into history' (IH, x).[11] Knox is referring at this point specifically to Collingwood's doctrine of absolute presuppositions and his conception of 'the purely historical character of metaphysics' in the *Essay on Metaphysics* (Knox, Pref., x; see also xi). The crux of Knox's interpretation here is the idea that for Collingwood the 'practice' of history and that of metaphysics are one and the same (see xvii) and that for all purposes, the two disciplines are identical.

Collingwood's views on the 'practices' of history are well known, for he said, famously, that 'all history is the history of thought' and that 'therefore all history . . . is the re-enactment of past thought in the historian's own mind' (IH, 215). And, given the centrality and importance of re-enactment in Collingwood's account of history, it is perhaps inevitable that some interpreters (in following the lead laid down by Knox) will read Collingwood as saying that the proper method or practice of metaphysics is itself the re-enactment of past thought, specifically of past absolute presuppositions.

Thus, for example, we find this particular motif in Donagan when he equates, on behalf of Collingwood, the recovery of absolute presuppositions with the historian's 'ascertaining' of past thoughts (Donagan, LPC, 268). And we find it more recently in Haddock, in Boucher, in Code.[12]

But there is an interesting twist in these cases as well. They (all or most of them) say that, although Collingwood appeared to believe that re-enactment is the proper goal of metaphysical inquiry (just as it is of history more generally), he should *not* have held this view respecting metaphysics in particular.

Boucher's specific reason for saying this is quite instructive: Collingwood's 'idea that historical knowledge can only be attained by re-enacting the purposeful and intentional thoughts of agents must preclude knowledge of "unconscious thought"'. To put this point differently, we could say that since re-enactment excluded or could not handle so-called unconscious thought, it necessarily excluded those very absolute presuppositions which were the subject matter of metaphysics. This seems a sound criticism of Collingwood because it directly contradicts the *presumed* point of his claim that metaphysics is a historical science.

Behind Boucher's criticism lies, I suspect, a kind of historical realism about re-enactable past thought: for thought to be *re-enacted* (by the historian) it must have a pre-existing, independent existence as thought. This condition is not met by absolute presuppositions. There simply is no past thought to which the metaphysical formulation could stand as the *re*-thinking. Hence, metaphysical inquiry, contrary to Collingwood's view, cannot be a species of re-enactment.

It might be determined, then, that the way to save Collingwood's assimilation of metaphysics to history is to deny historical realism. The doctrine called 'constructionism' mounts such a denial. For the historical constructionist there is not a complex dual agenda, consisting of historians' constructions parallel to and 'about' some independently existing *real* past. Rather, there are simply present data (called 'evidence' when used) and the stories we tell – sometimes in the past tense – to describe and explain these data. On this account historical constructions are not *about* the so-called real past; there is no past for the historian other than what can be constructed on the basis of evidence. The historical past is nothing but the historian's constructed past.

Constructionism allows us to get round the troubling criticism based ultimately on historical realism (the one I attributed to Boucher) by denying that realism. The constructionist says simply that it is *never* true in history that there are or assumedly must be independent past thoughts which are the proper and pre-existing objects of historical inquiry.

One could readily construct a theory (following lines laid down by Margit Hurup Nielsen) that carries the constructionist analysis from Collingwood's concept of history into his conception of metaphysics. It would go something like this. In rejecting historical realism, this constructionist analysis rejects the idea that there is something inherently illegitimate about rethinking 'unconscious' thoughts. For all thoughts (as objects of history) stand on precisely the same footing; none of them are assumed to be pre-existent and independent of the historian's construction. Hence, the analysis continues, it is no objection to using historical constructions in metaphysics to say that metaphysics – in its interest in absolute presuppositions, in 'unconscious thought' – somehow lacks the objects proper to normal historical practice. Of course, the constructionist would have to believe that certain things can count as *evidence* for so-called unconscious thoughts, but this assumption is not eccentric and probably was held by Collingwood himself. Finally, the analysis would have to provide a constructionist interpretation of re-enactment which asserts that re-enactment and historical construction (as based on evidence) are one and the same. For by *identifying* re-enactment with historical construction, the constructionist theorist in effect affirms that Collingwood could consistently and properly hold the re-enactment theory of metaphysical formulation which the earlier critics (Knox, Donagan et al.) agreed in attributing to him.[13]

Now, I do not want to get sidetracked into a discussion of the merits of historical constructionism or of the claim that Collingwood was such a constructionist. I should say, for the record, though, that I doubt the merits of the view at each point.[14]

But this is not the issue. The issue is actually what the putative constructionist theorist and the earlier critics all concur in: that Collingwood, in claiming that metaphysics is a historical science, was intending to assert that re-enactment is proper practice in both history and metaphysics, identically the same in each.

I want to argue here, on the contrary, that the idea of reading re-enactment into Collingwood's account of metaphysics is simply off the point as regards re-enactment, and that the suggested attempt to save this idea (by turning to historical constructionism) is itself off the point for the same reason. Then, after making this argument, I want to turn (in the next section) to developing an alternative account of what Collingwood did mean, in my judgement, in his claim that metaphysics and its propositions are historical.

Collingwood consistently regarded re-enactment as involved with actions. Specifically, the aim of re-enactment was to understand or explain an action by reference to the thoughts – the beliefs and motivations – of an agent.

One of his leading ideas here is that actions typically occur in a context of states of affairs, and that the agent's thoughts about any given state constitute a motivation for his action. Moreover, the agent intends to bring about something with his action, where this something – this end to be achieved or relevant purpose – will help resolve the original situation that motivated his action. The action, in its turn, is thought by the agent to be a means to that end or part of accomplishing it.

Characteristically, then, an explanation by re-enactment would draw on or mention these very points: (1) the agent faced a certain situation, (2) he had a certain end in view (for resolving this situation), (3) $A$ is one of the actions he might take, among others (such as $B$, $C$ or $D$), in such a situation, (4) doing $A$ is judged by him as a means to, or part of, accomplishing his purpose. (And such an explanation would, no doubt, also make use of a few other considerations which we could readily add to our sketch, if need be.)[15]

The basic point of a Collingwoodian re-enactment is to start with a particular situational perception and motivation and a variety of alternative courses of action and, then, by consulting the particulars under the *other* features in the sketch to rule out, in the light of available evidence, all these alternatives but one: the deed performed (called $A$ in the sketch). Thus, an explanation of an individual action by re-enactment is afforded by substituting, under each feature of the sketch, evidentially well-supported statements of fact that satisfy – that exemplify – the terms of those features.

Here the factual filler of any given explanation should not only instantiate one or another of the features of the sketch, but should do so in an intelligible or plausible way. This is provided for when the main points in the sketch – in particular, the deed performed, the situational motivation and the relevant purpose – are satisfied by particular facts which are themselves *intelligibly* connected, in the view of the historian, in the specific relations they have with one another (as spelled out in the sketch).

Or, to put the matter in the way Collingwood put it, we would say that such judgements of intelligible connection allow us, once we have in mind a particular situational motivation and a particular purpose of the agent, to *re-enact* the agent's action. For we can see, with these points in mind and in the light of available evidence, that one of the courses of action – the deed actually performed – makes sense in the situation envisioned and its being done is plausible. Thus, we can successfully get to the deed performed by citing *these* particular thoughts and beliefs that the agent had, and in that sense re-enact it (in imagination).[16]

Re-enactment, as Collingwood conceived it, is directed

specifically to the explanation and understanding of action. Its object is not to explain beliefs *per se*, though it may *use* beliefs in an explanation and may sometimes *add* beliefs to the picture in order to achieve the intelligibility, the capacity to re-enact, at which all such explanations aim.

So, the obvious point at which an absolute presupposition might enter a re-enactment is as one of the thoughts that figure in the thought side of the explanation of an action. Thus, we might look for an absolute presupposition at any of several points: the agent's situational perception, relevant purpose, supposal of alternative courses of action, means/end beliefs, and so on.

But it is rarely the case that historians actually use an absolute presupposition by mentioning it among the thought factors that they employ in a given explanation. It does not seem, then, that the presence of absolute presuppositions at these points (or among these factors) is necessary to the sort of intelligibility Collingwood emphasized in his account of re-enactment.

I grant, of course, that *sometimes* specific mention of the relevant presuppositions (for example, of another and quite different culture) might be necessary to make a given explanation pertaining to behaviour in that culture intelligible to us. And the same might prove true for some explanations in the history of science.

Here the necessity for employing absolute presuppositions is a function of what we don't (yet) understand. But the point is that we cannot make a *general* case for connecting re-enactment with knowledge of absolute presuppositions, along the lines we have been considering, if such presuppositions are used but rarely in actual historical practice.

More important, even when absolute presuppositions are used in historical explanations – and I have allowed that sometimes they are or could be – they are not there themselves in virtue of some *prior* re-enactment. Beliefs may be used in a re-enactment but they are not the object of a re-enactment.

There is, of course, a sense in which a successful re-enactment validates or confirms the evidentially well-supported claim that certain thoughts (that is, the thoughts included in the re-enactment) were the effective thoughts of the agent under study.[17] But these thoughts (certain beliefs, for example) even when they appear in a historical explanation, do so on some basis other than having been previously re-enacted. Thus, when an absolute presupposition appears in a historical explanation (in order to introduce an intelligibility hitherto lacking among the explanatory – the thought – factors) that presupposition (as a thought, albeit un 'unconscious' one) is there on some basis other than having itself been re-enacted.

Let me put my main line of argument somewhat differently now. One cannot responsibly reason from the claim that metaphysics is a historical discipline to the specific conclusion that re-enactment is the way of knowing absolute presuppositions, *unless* we have independent reason either to think that re-enactments standardly figure as our primary criterion for identifying absolute presuppositions or to think that absolute presuppositions standardly figure in re-enactments. As we've seen, neither of these options is at all plausible. And there is no evidence that Collingwood thought they were.

The only way, then, in which one could seriously entertain the idea of an intrinsic or at least general connection between absolute presuppositions and re-enactment is to regard such presuppositions as themselves types of action. Hence, unless absolute presuppositions are actions or can be the more or less direct effects of actions (and thereby the *intended* effect of action), there is little point in making re-enactment the focal point in any Collingwoodian assimilation of metaphysics to history.

Collingwood did not regard absolute presuppositions or changes in absolute presuppositions as something persons perform as actions. The fact that we do not perform them or change them with relevant ends in view, or that we do not do so as a means to such ends (or part of accomplishing them), merely underscores the point that in dealing with absolute presuppositions we are not concerned with actions and thus not concerned with things explainable by re-enactment.

The constructionist should be as affected by this claim as the historical realist (i.e. the person who is a realist about past agents and their beliefs). For the whole point of constructionism is to tell a *suitable* story in the explanation of present data. A re-enactment story about our present or past beliefs – in so far as these were thought to be absolute presuppositions – would simply not be a suitable story. For it would in effect improperly treat as actions things that were not actions by applying to them, inappropriately, categories for the explanation (or understanding) of action.

One final point. I do not want, upon considering the occasions when the historian or the metaphysician *formulates* an absolute presupposition or when a person subsequently self-consciously *supposes* a particular absolute presupposition, to deny that an action of some sort is here occurring. But that which is formulated, the thing that is supposed – that is, the content of the absolute presupposition – is not itself the performance of an action. For the effective having or positing of that content initially (before the formulation or the supposal) is not an action of any sort. Nor do we view the existence or the coming to exist of such a content (or of a change in it – for example, when one absolute presupposition turns into another) as an action performed, or the direct result of one. It may none the less be, through some convoluted chain of connections, the remote and unpurposed effect of actions.

The claim that metaphysics is historical, if it has the precise implication that absolute presuppositions are to be explained or primarily understood by re-enactment, is a deep mistake. It rests on confusing absolute presuppositions with actions performed or on thinking that re-enactment is something other than a standard for the explanation of actions.

But if the re-enactment account of metaphysics is not what Collingwood intended (and I find no evidence that it was), then what did he mean when he said that metaphysics is a historical discipline, that the 'principles and methods' it follows are 'now common form among historians' (EM, 77)? I will turn to the issue raised by this question in the following section.

## III

In his *Autobiography* Collingwood spoke of the need for 'a special branch of philosophical inquiry devoted to the special problems raised by historical thinking'. Here he singled out two kinds of problems: 'Epistemological problems, such as one might group together under the question "how is historical knowledge possible?" [And] metaphysical problems, concerned with the nature of the historian's subject-matter: the elucidation of terms like event, process, progress, civilization, and so forth' (A,77).

It is surprising that, when people have wanted to get clear on what Collingwood meant when he said that metaphysics is historical, they did not turn first to his discussion of what he called the metaphysical aspect of history. It is my view that what Collingwood said about process in history is, in fact, the key to his claim that the subject matter of metaphysics (i.e. absolute presuppositions) and the propositions of metaphysics are historical.

In Collingwood's idea of process, continuities in human thinking exist, and they exist because some temporally later person or group has acquired from an earlier person or group the thought they share. But his notion of continuity does not imply that the whole corpus of acquired thoughts in any given case is acquired from the *same* predecessor or at the same time.

Although continuity in the relationship of predecessor and successor implies a likeness in thinking, Collingwood rejected the idea that such a relationship involves repeated transmission of the same body of thought. The next feature in Collingwood's idea of process is that changes do occur in the body of thoughts acquired from predecessors: a complex of acquired thoughts may be *modified* or some thought may be *added* to it.

A body of acquired thoughts may be modified in any of several ways. An acquired thought may simply fade away and disappear. It may be given more emphasis than it was given by predecessors. Or, finally, an acquired thought may be changed internally: for example, Darwin altered the conception acquired from his predecessors of the permanence of natural kinds by showing that species were not fixed over the long stretch of geological time.[18]

Within internal change, Collingwood particularly emphasized changes that were made along lines already laid down by predecessors. Such lines of alteration could take the form of statements by predecessors of a specific need to change or even of suggested formulas of modification. In each case, here, both the thought that was altered and the reasons or the schemes for modifying it are acquired from predecessors.

In Collingwood's analysis, thought is most commonly modified by being placed in a different context. And this difference in context is usually created by receiving inheritances of thought from diverse predecessors or by letting the same complex of thoughts do work in two quite distinct areas (e.g. in both theology and science). But mere difference in context would not in and of itself modify an acquired thought. For Collingwood an acquired pattern of behaviour or of thinking is usually modified in a new context simply by being thought about in *other* ways, by being itself subjected to new and different ways of thinking.

Collingwood also spoke, as we have noted, of *additions* to a body of acquired thoughts. These additions are novelties, but they always appear in a context of acquired thoughts and have a connection with the thoughts acquired from predecessors. They 'emerge,' as Collingwood put it, in a context appropriate to their appearance; they are emergent additions to a body of acquired thought.[19]

Although Collingwood was interested in change as such, he was primarily interested in modifications and emergent additions in so far as these, in being absorbed into a continuity of thought, affect successors. This consideration leads us to the final feature of Collingwood's account of process: his notion of what might be called cumulative transmission. A cumulative transmission can be said to occur whenever a portion of acquired thought is transmitted to a successor in changed form. Such transmissions can be contrasted with homogeneous transmission, the type of transmission characteristic of intelligent, non-human animals. Collingwood said, for example, that 'cats do not wash by instinct but are taught by their mothers'; however, he pointed out that the feline species exhibits little or no cumulative transmission. People, on the other hand, not only learn but also change what they learn and pass on these changes to their progeny (see IH, 226–7).

The notion of cumulative transmission provides the capstone to Collingwood's idea of process: here process is conceived as a continuum, through a series of predecessor–successor relationships, in which changes occur and are passed on to successors as part of *their* body of acquired thought. Collingwood calls this a 'process of development' (IH, 162).

Such a process has a directional character: the changes passed on to successors are consolidated as part of their ways of thinking and acting; there is no reversion in the thoughts which *they* transmit to their successors back to some ancestral body of thoughts. But the process Collingwood conceived is no mere accumulation of changes: some modified conceptions may fade away completely and others may be modified further in the course of time. For Collingwood, a process of development is one of evolutionary change; there are stages in the process but no *telos*, no ultimate end or goal.[20]

Cumulative development, as we have described it, is an orderly progression of connected stages, each requiring what went before, over time. Sequence and time are, as it were, structural elements in any such process. Collingwood called such processes 'historical.'

'Historical' here does not designate historiography but, rather, a 'process of thoughts' (see IH, 227; also 225). As Collingwood said, 'The historical process is itself a process of thought . . .' (IH, 226). And the 'essence' of history, in this sense, 'lies not in its consisting of individual facts [as some have thought] but in the process of development leading from one to another' (IH, 169; see also 163). In history we have a cumulative sequence, differentiated as earlier and later, wherein 'something is changing into something else. This element of process is the life of history' (IH, 163; see also 162, 164, and A, 97–8).

The term 'history,' in being applied to process, loses its connotation of pastness. As terms, past and present are correlative and can be distinguished; but as stages, they belong to the same process and cannot be sharply separated. In using the word 'history' and its cognates in this way, Collingwood can be taken as denying that any present is isolated from what went before, that it is without essential connection to its past. In a sense the past overlaps the present: since 'the present includes in itself its own past, the real ground on which [the present] rests, namely the past out of which it has grown, is not outside it but is included within' (IH, 229–30; see also 171).

The past, in so far as it exists in any present, is a developed and differentiated past – a past that has been cumulatively transmitted to the present. The living past consists of the end points of various strands of thought which have survived, usually in modified form, through a series of transmissions and which have proceeded from a variety of predecessors.[21] These incapsulated ways of thinking are the culmination of various processes of cumulative development and represent the refinement of these processes into certain definite conceptions and ways of thinking.[22]

Incapsulated past thoughts belong to the present; they are the point of connection between a complex of present thoughts and the historical process of which it is a part. The present – or, to speak more accurately, the present age or civilization – is but a 'focal point' in that process (see IH, 164). And later patterns of thought and behaviour are what they are because of variations in what is now the present (and in subsequent periods) and their cumulative transmission to that later pattern as its 'historic inheritance of thought' (IH, 227).

The human mind (at least in so far as we are concerned with science or with any other comparably high-level universe of discourse) 'lives in historical process' in that activities of thought and of behaviour, when that behaviour is 'determined by thought,' are either constituents of a body of acquired thoughts or derivatives (modifications and emergent additions) from that body. There is nothing in a specific complex of thoughts and behaviour that is extrinsic to one's inheritance of thoughts; such a complex is not separable from specific historical processes. The mind-as-thought here is completely involved in process.[23]

As a special case, then, the metaphysician and his subject matter – whether he studies the absolute presuppositions of the past or of his own day – are themselves wholly bound up in processes of cumulative differentiation and development. Thus, metaphysics as the study of the groundforms of human thought and activity has entirely a historical being.[24]

The implications of Collingwood's view of process are, I think, radical. And they will be radical for metaphysics, as a special case, as well.

Since a thinking mind is the product of various processes of historical development, and since there is no evidence for a single historical process encapsulated by all thinking beings, there is no reason to suppose that any feature of humankind's 'historic inheritance of thought' will be common to all persons. More important, the set of thoughts and actions common to some people at one time will turn into a wholly different set for other people at some later time. Thus, a cumulative process of historical development and differentiation would, in the historical long run, lead to a sheer difference even between widely separated points in roughly the same continuum.[25]

The historical world is 'a world of change, a world where things come to be and cease to be' (IH, 20). The order and structures that we do find in any phase of human life are not immutable, or eternal, or in existence from the beginning; they are produced in process and they change in process.[26]

The negative implication of Collingwood's theory of cumulative process, then, is that no conception – hence, no absolute presupposition – and no action 'determined by thought' can be expected to be common to all men.

We cannot assume that there is or must be a primary and enduring set of thoughts and ways of thinking that runs through the different phases of a historical process. There is no ground except the process itself. Even something so massive as a determinate way of looking at the world (that is, a determinate constellation of particular absolute presuppositions), with its depth and longevity in patterns of thought and behaviour, is transitory and can pass completely away.

These implications exactly capture some of the main features of the 'historical' characterization of absolute presuppositions in the first section of this chapter. I mean such features as that absolute presuppositions are culturally delimited, not common to all times and places, and that they are changeable and changing. These implications, then, would strongly support my contention that the correct way to read Collingwood's controversial claim (about metaphysics being a historical discipline) is in the light of his notion of history as a process of development.

Interestingly, the notion of re-enactment (or of historical construction on the basis of evidence) has no such implications. We cannot infer from it, from re-enactment, to *any* of the so-called historical features of absolute presuppositions described in section I. And this failure gives added substance to my argument that re-enactment is not the key to decoding Collingwood's rather opaque claim about metaphysics.

Indeed, if we take seriously Collingwood's idea of a cumulative process of development, the very fact of differentiation over historical time makes problematic the re-enactment of the actions and the rethinking of the thoughts of earlier people, who are of one cultural formation, by later people, who are most likely of a quite different cultural formation from them. Thus re-enactment (as conventionally understood, as a form of *internal* understanding) is in a kind of conceptual tension with the characterization of absolute presuppositions as 'historical'. The doctrine of re-enactment cannot therefore be expected to help us map at all Collingwood's claim that metaphysics is a historical discipline.[27]

One final consideration. Collingwood, as we noted in section I, said that any given 'constellation' of absolute presuppositions is in an 'unstable equilibrium' in which 'internal strains' are 'taken up' but ultimately without success. If we read further we find him adding that 'where there is no strain there is no history' (EM, 74–5). This remark of Collingwood's about 'strain' is interesting in the present context, for it amounts to a virtual equation of history with change. And that equation provides support, from within the *Essay on Metaphysics* itself, for my argument (in the present section) that a historical process of development is principally what Collingwood had in view when he said that metaphysics and its subject matter are historical.[28]

Now that we have located, correctly I believe, the essential point of Collingwood's claim about metaphysics, we need to face some insistent problems. If we take metaphysics to be a discursive procedure of some sort, a 'science' in Collingwood's rather quaint nomenclature, then we want to know what special goals are set for it by the idea of historical processes of development (processes in which even absolute presuppositions are involved). And we want to know too how metaphysics could go about achieving these goals in a way satisfactory to human reason. I will take up these troubling issues in the final sections of the chapter.

## IV

Here one would expect help, if anywhere, from Collingwood's *Essay on Philosophical Method*, for that work is devoted to identifying the distinctive goals of philosophical inquiry. Its main conclusions could conveniently be summarized in the following propositions: (1) The various theories of a common practice (that is, of a given universe of discourse, of a particular science like physics or history) are assumed to be coextensive or 'overlapping'. (2) The distinctness of each of the competing theories is maintained but not their coequal status, for ideally they will be arranged as subordinate/superordinate. (3) Thus, in a *successful* accounting of a common practice, the various competing theories contain conceptual elements which have been mutually modified in competitive confrontation (or 'opposition,' as Collingwood called it). And what has resulted is an ordering or 'summing up' of all these elements in a single complex whole. (4) Or, rather, it is the *best* theory of the common practice that has all the elements in their right order and, hence, can do the job of 'summing up' properly.

The best theory in effect 'telescopes' our understanding of the common practice; for it is the best account up to that point, given all that went before. And if there is no better theory available or on the horizon, then for all practical purposes, that relatively best theory is *the* proper account of the practice in question.[29]

So conceived, the competing theories constitute a sort of 'scale of forms,' as Collingwood called it. Each such scale is a scale of theories about a single practice (physics, for example), and the constituent theories represent different degrees of adequate understanding of this common practice, with one of them providing the best available understanding.

It is important to bear in mind here that, despite its name, the *Essay on Philosophical Method* does not provide us with a method in the sense of a set of procedures or prescriptions for doing scale-of-forms analysis. Rather, it simply gives us the object or goal which we are trying to attain when our method, whatever it is, is successful.

The resultant schema, a scale of forms (or theories), is useful whenever an institution or a practice is sufficiently complex to allow for arrangement under any of several different patterns or orderings. Collingwood's notion of a scale of forms models one of the ways, perhaps one of the more intellectually satisfying ways, of resolving theoretical disputes that centre on the question of the best or proper understanding of a complex but contested practice.[30]

I want now to suggest that the metaphysical task Collingwood sets with his claim that absolute presuppositions are involved in historical processes of development can be usefully carried out by employing the idea of scale-of-forms analysis. Let me first sketch the appeal of this suggestion and then provide some needed clarifications and amendments that must be added to it.

If we look at scientific practice over time, say, in physics or history (both of which go back a long way, in more or less unbroken continuity to the time of the ancient Greeks), we note that these practices have been viewed differently at different times. Not just the methods, narrowly conceived, and the main substantive theories (which include laws in a natural science) but the very thematics of these disciplines have varied considerably over time. (I mean by thematics such concerns as what constitutes the physical – or the historical – world and what principles must be invoked in order to know about or to explain that world.) But the differences here are not sheer differences; they are *critical* differences. The various thematics have actually confronted one another and competed with one another, just as the methods and the theories have, in intellectual debate. And when change has occurred, one set of thematics (or one set of theories or one method) can be said to have 'shaded into' (IH, 162), to have turned into the other. In this way the modifications and emergent additions in a historical process of development are significantly *like* the mutual modifications that occur in an intellectual confrontation, a debate, between two competing accounts of a common practice (for example, the practice of physics over time).

It would be an intellectually satisfying solution to any such historic confrontation if we could identify one account as the best in view of all that went before. If such a task could be performed for the *whole* practice of physics over time, then we would have (presumably in the latest version) the best and deepest available account – as seen from the perspective of physics itself – of the practice overall.

Two clarifications are required, however, before we can regard this task as even minimally well defined. First, we need to consider whether the notion of a scale of forms undergoes any significant alteration in being transferred from the philosophical context (of EPM) to the historical context of a process of development (of IH and, by hypothesis, of EM). Then, second, we need to identify the main criteria by which one might plausibly arrange competing accounts of an entire science into a scale of forms. So far we have merely assumed that there are some such criteria, if scale of forms ordering is to be successful. But we have not identified any relevant criteria specifically. (At this stage, of course, this lapse is not really a point of failure. It is fully to be expected, since EPM is concerned simply with the abstract model of scale-of-forms analysis, one which will be invariant over the various specific subject matters – actual contents – to which it is applied.)

I will take up these two lines of clarification in turn. Let us start with the need, if any, to modify scale-of-forms analysis. The account in EPM makes certain important simplifying assumptions. Specifically, it is assumed there (for heuristic purposes) that the theories in a scale of forms are coincident, that the *instances* (or exemplifications) of each theory are precisely the same (see EPM, 48, 51). Clearly, this won't do in a historical process of development; for in such a process the competing theories are explicitly avowed to be in a temporal sequence such that elements present at one time are not present at another (and when present are due to the modification and emergent addition that itself happens *over time*). Thus, it would be impossible for the *instances* of such theories to be precisely the same ones.

Now Collingwood altered his own account of overlap in the course of EPM (see 91) to say, not that the theories were merely coincident in their *instances*, but to say that the theories 'overlapped' one another in confrontation, in mutual modification. And this new emphasis is much more compatible with the idea of a *historical* process of development.

However, to say that *all* the various theories overlapped one another in this way (which is what Collingwood's new version would require) is something one could say only from the perspective of some 'best available' version, where all the other stages, all the other versions had been pulled together – telescoped, as it were, and summed up. But it is not something one could say at just any point during the process itself, during the actual course of development over time. Thus, even the notion of an overlapping scale of forms (as we find it in EPM) is not apposite to a process of development, taken in flow.

We would need, then, to modify Collingwood's idea of a scale of forms (as we have it in EPM) in one important respect. We would need to drop the idea of overlap in order to put scale-of-forms analysis to work in a process of historical development. We would say, in this proposed modification, not that all the competing theories confronted and wholly 'overlapped' one another but, rather, that they all belonged as stages to the same process and that a predecessor stage turned into its successor stage through modifications (including mere fade-outs) and emergent additions in the predecessor stage and cumulative transmissions to the successor.

We have come up, then, with the idea of a *modified* scale of forms. Here the overlaps are partial and spread out over time. For, typically, the actual confrontation is not between *all* the relevant theories (as it is in the EPM idea of a scale of forms) but, rather, only between those standing in an immediate predecessor/ successor relationship. And the topmost (or best) theory in a *modified* scale of forms, then, usually comes far down the road (and with little or no direct overlap between it and its much earlier predecessor forms). This is in obvious contrast with the 'logical' model propounded in EPM, where all the theories confront one another, once we reach the final stage, on a point-by-point basis, and where the topmost theory emerges almost vertically and contains all that went before (though in modified form or as *expressly* suppressed).[31]

Interestingly, Collingwood actually employed something like what I have called a *modified* scale of forms at one well-recognized point in his later writings. I have in mind the analysis he provides in *The New Leviathan* (part I, 1-129) of the different levels of mental activity, ranging from mere feeling at one end to theoretical reasoning at the other.

My reason for calling the NL scale a *modified* scale of forms is that Collingwood explicitly said that in it there are 'primitive survivals' of instances from each predecessor level which persist in unmodified form throughout all the successor stages. Thus, the different stages do not overlap one another perfectly (even when the 'ultimate' stage is reached) nor are they then coincident with one another regarding instances, as would be the case in a standard scale of forms (as portrayed in EPM).[32]

I do not, I should add, want to say that Collingwood's reason for using a *modified* scale of forms here is that he regarded the differing levels of mental life as the exhibition of a historical process of development. He probably had a different inclination here; he wanted, I suspect, to preserve the idea of a radical separation between 'thought' and 'feeling' by continuing to allow for actions determined by *mere* impulse and appetite (see IH, 230-1).[33] But I leave off such speculations immediately; my object here is simply to show that Collingwood actually used something like a modified scale-of-forms analysis in his later writings.

However, we still stand in need of the other main clarification I mentioned earlier. We need to specify the material criteria that could in Collingwood's view be employed to assert, respecting a particular scientific practice over time (say, physics), that one of the competing accounts of that practice is better, from the perspective afforded by that practice, than another and, indeed, that it is the best available account among them all.

To take some steps toward specifying Collingwood's criteria for progressive improvement, I suggest we turn to one of his lesser-known (or, at least, less frequently cited) pieces, the short essay on progress that comes at the end of his *Idea of History* (see part V, ch. 7, 321–34). There Collingwood, talking about historical progress generically, identified two principal criteria.

> If thought in its first phase [at some first stage], after solving the initial problems of that phase, is then, through solving these, brought up against others which defeat it; and if the second solves these further problems [criterion 1] without losing its hold on the solution of the first, so that there is gain without any corresponding loss [criterion 2], then there is progress. (IH, 329)

He then proceeded to apply this analysis of progress (in the sense of improvement) specifically to science (see 332).

What is important about Collingwood's criteria is that they are given and their content is built up in the historical process itself. Presumably, the experience, the 'history,' of engaging in science (to stay with the practice we're crucially interested in) itself provides the relevant criteria.

The Collingwoodian historical metaphysician is interested in competing versions of a science, of a practice. These criteria make it possible to say about two competing versions of a science, about two stages in the development of one and the same science, that the science is better done at one of those stages than it was at the other. The fact that these are two stages in a historical process of development, that the science itself is changing over historical time, in no way precludes such judgements of progress (if the criteria for progress can be satisfied so as to achieve what I have called a *modified* scale of forms, one appropriate to historical processes of development).

Absolute presuppositions, the metaphysician's ostensible subject matter, are in a historical process of development (with all that that implies) simply because any given science is itself in such a process. Such presuppositions are implicit in the various phases (in the stages) of scientific development, implicit as their groundform. These basic conceptions cannot be divorced from the methods, the theories and the thematics they ground and in which they are, ultimately, wholly bound up. As groundforms, as ingredients, of going sciences, they are involved in the same processes of development that the sciences are involved in.

It stands to reason, then, if we can compare pre-Darwinian to Darwinian biology or Ptolemaic to Copernican astronomy or Newtonian to Einsteinian physics on the point of the betterment in knowledge and explanatory power of the one over the other, that we can compare the ingredient absolute presuppositions (the groundforms reached through philosophical analysis) of each pair, on the same point. Thus, just as we can say that one of these versions, one of these phases of scientific development, marked an improvement over an earlier, so we can say that one ingredient set of absolute presuppositions marked an improvement over another. The fact that these contrasting absolute presuppositions are found in different stages of a historical process of development in no way precludes such judgements of progress. Indeed, the very criteria by which we make such judgements are found *in* the process.

If such judgements are possible between two sets of absolute presuppositions in a discrete predecessor/successor relationship, then a scale of forms *could* be offered for the whole sequence of absolute presuppositions of a given science within the overall process of its development. There's nothing that rules such a result out in principle (if the criteria for progress can be satisfied so as to accomplish a scale of forms analysis).[34]

It would be a *modified* scale of forms, the prototype for which is principally developed in Collingwood's *Essay on Philosophical Method*. The point of such a scale would be to show that in this case the historical process of development was one of progressive improvement.

Of course, we understand that a historical process of development is not *necessarily* progressive. To say that such a process is progressive, certain criteria have to be satisfied. And when they are (and when we are at a fairly high level of abstraction, dealing with theoretical accounts of a scientific practice or the like), the analytical result is simply a *modified* scale of forms. We do not, ultimately, have two distinct things here, but only one: for when the criteria have been satisfied and when a suitable level of abstraction has been reached, there is no real difference between an actual scale-of-forms analysis (here a *modified* scale of forms) and an actual assessment of historical progress (as between two stages, for example, between differing accounts of a single, developmental practice).

Here we would understand the practice implicated in the process from the point of view of its best available version – an understanding we could have only by employing scale-of-forms analysis in which historically relevant criteria, themselves found in the process of development, were used. It is precisely such a denouement that Collingwood pointed to when he described the work of metaphysics, as part of science and of the 'labour of reason,' as 'progressive' (EM, 135).

## V

In short, the main consideration I would offer in support of my interpretation of Collingwood (and of his claim that metaphysics is a historical discipline) is his oft-stated view that science – and, by the same token, metaphysics – is progressive. Progressive, that is, in the sense given by the notion of *historical* progress.

It is the fact of historical progress in science, or at least Collingwood's assertion of progress as fact, that allows us to link Collingwood's essay on philosophical method with his later essay on metaphysics. For historical progress in such a case is to be understood, I have argued, by reference to the idea of a *modified* scale of forms, an idea that was introduced to account for the situation where the main elements in the scale – here various, successive constellations of absolute presuppositions of a given science – are themselves in a process of historical development and differentiation.

That Collingwood regarded absolute presuppositions *per se* as standing in a relationship of progressive improvement (within a process of development) is beyond doubt, in my view. For example, he regarded the presupposition of the science of history at an earlier stage (the presupposition that there is a constant and common human nature) as inferior to the basic conceptions characteristic of re-enactment in present-day history (though he did not, I hasten to add, make very clear what these latter conceptions are). And he regarded the monotheistic presuppositions of classical science as superior to the polytheistic ones of an even earlier proto-science, a point I will return to shortly.[35]

Now that I have laid out the main line of analysis and my reason for accepting it, some refinements in this account of Collingwood are called for before we can consider our preliminary reflections on it complete. Let me provide these in conclusion.

It is important to see clearly the context of all scale-of-forms metaphysical judgements. Collingwood believed, to cite an example mentioned earlier, that natural science (in particular, physics and astronomy) at some point in its development needed the idea of a cosmos, of a single order of natural things susceptible of coming under a select few explanatory principles and general laws. And this idea of a single natural order had as its precursor certain developments in the history of religion and was itself often expressed (even as an affirmation of science) in a theological idiom.

Thus, when the metaphysician says, for example, that the proposition 'God exists' accurately describes an absolute presupposition of classical Greek and, even more clearly, of Patristic science and that 'God is one' describes another, he is talking about science principally, not religion or theology. And when he says that the presupposition 'God is one and there is one God' marks an improvement over the prior presupposition of a plurality of gods, he is saying that, in the actual historical process of scientific development, better science – science that represented progress over what it had achieved previously – has 'one God' as its presupposition and inferior science, in that same process, had 'many gods' as its presupposition.

The Collingwoodian metaphysician is not saying that monotheism is absolutely better than polytheism, not even in the context of science. He is saying only that in the practice of science, with the history it actually has had and in the process of development it has actually undergone, the monotheistic presupposition goes with improved science in that particular process of development and, hence, can be regarded as superior in a (*modified*) scale of forms to the presupposition of polytheism.

There is nothing particularly odd in such scientific deployments of theology. Even contemporary science expresses some of its more controversial claims in a similar idiom. Witness Einstein's famous *mot* that God does not play dice with the universe –

meaning that causality at all levels is strict and not probabilistic.

The metaphysician as regards his locus of contrast or comparison – which is sometimes implicit (as in the Einstein *mot*), sometimes explicit – is interested, not with an entire way of life, but with something much more discrete – with a going science, presumably within that way of life. What he compares are different phases in the history of that science, compares them with each other but not with whole ways of life themselves. Indeed, he makes no attempt to compare whole ways of life at all, either with each other or with regard to the total effect within any one of them of a single line of development going on there (see IH, 325–9).

As the metaphysician approaches his own day, his characteristic task changes somewhat. He is, of course, still interested in providing an accurate formulation of some (or all) the presuppositions of the present-day science he is concerned with. And he probably will want to exhibit the *bona fides* of the present set of presuppositions by showing that they belong to a progressive version of science – progressive, that is, when contrasted with earlier versions of the same science.

I should add that I have assumed, for convenience, that the presuppositions involved (in both past and present) can be reduced to single, self-consistent (see EM, 66) and preferred sets (one for each past era, or several such eras, and one for the present). Things are often far messier than this, in that *alternative* sets are available in each case (or, worse, alternative sets no one of which is easily made self-consistent). But the doctrine of progress does not require the simplified assumptions I've been making. For, certainly, we could speak of progress even where the past (or both the past and the present) did afford alternative sets. None the less, we will stay with the simpler idea for purposes of illustration. Thus, we take the metaphysician to be attempting to show that a single, preferred version of a science (held in the present) is progressive in contrast with similar preferred versions of the same science held in earlier times.

But he may well want to go beyond this. The metaphysician may want to identify problems in present science and to suggest how these problems might be resolved. Sometimes, to do this, he may have to formulate for consideration presuppositions different from those being entertained now, presuppositions which would ground another version of science than the current version but one that could be reached from the here and now and, more important, one in which present problems, arguably, could be resolved.

Now suppose that scientists followed the metaphysician step by step here: they consciously entertained the *present* presuppositions of science (made available thanks to the work of that metaphysician) and they followed the line of reasoning he had developed in favour of change. What would happen?

Well, science wouldn't just change. For scientists couldn't simply start thinking about the world differently and then bring scientific practice into line with those new thoughts. That isn't the way things happen.

Neither the scientist nor the metaphysician can occupy a standpoint outside practice. And they can't just *will* changes into being there, changes that will then redound on the practice (rather than the reverse). Instead, they must stay within the practice; it is the only standpoint they, the scientist or the metaphysician, can occupy. And changes that occur there, in the practice, can become – usually in time they will amount to – changes in the very groundform of the practice.

So, if scientists gradually and carefully changed scientific practice itself – so that new methods and theories and thematics came to be employed and got institutionalized there – then it might shake out that the proposed conceptions of the metaphysician would be found *in fact* to be embedded in this new version of science.

It is not wholly accurate to say (as was said in section I) that the change here is 'unconscious'; it may in fact be conscious at a number of points. For the scientific community might have fairly clear ideas about what the current presuppositions are, what the current problems are, what the shape of successful change would look like. And the effecting of such change might be facilitated in virtue of such clarity.

But the point remains: the transformation of science, of its fundamental conceptions, is not a basic action: something one simply does or can do (like raising one's own arm intentionally). We do not even know exactly how to get from here to there; this is a matter on which consciousness is relatively opaque. We do know that we can only go *through* the practice itself, through something that is relatively massive, very complex and quite intractable.

If this is so, then we have the reason, I think, why Collingwood none the less called such changes 'unconscious' (EM, 48n.): they aren't like actions or the relatively direct and foreseen (or intended) results of actions; they are more like long-term historical processes of development, the proximate end terms of which are something we can be only dimly conscious of at best. (This is why, by the way, I put so much energy in section II into denying that re-enactment figures in our knowledge of absolute presuppositions in any significant way.) And we have as well the reason why Collingwood put, on the point of change, more weight on the practice itself (and the scientists who make it go) than on the metaphysician, however prescient he might be.

Even so, metaphysics is indispensable to science in a historical process of development (see EM, 224, 343). It is Collingwood's view that progress in science must be *organized* to some degree; progress here – in particular, sustained progress – isn't simply happenstance. Metaphysics may help in the work of forwarding scientific progress, as I've made clear. But its main task lies elsewhere. Its role is the essentially comparative one of *assessing* progress, of showing that it has occurred as between two stages in a historical process of development and differentiation.

In this role of assessing, metaphysics is indispensable to science. For the crucial judgement of improvement can be fully accomplished, at least between one version of a science and another, only by making explicit the presuppositions of each version, by subjecting these explicit presuppositions to scale-of-forms analyses, and by using the material criteria for progress afforded in the process of development itself. And these accomplishments, as I've tried to show, simply track the main programme of Collingwood's account of metaphysics as historical.

There is much that the metaphysician does, in his ordinary work, that is very like the work of any historian. The metaphysician studies records of science and, very likely, the analyses of other metaphysicians (see EM, 58–9). And he tries, like any historian, to give an accurate account of his subject matter (that is, certain particular absolute presuppositions). When he is assessing progress he must in fact have *two* such presuppositions, or sets of them, in view and each must satisfy standards of accurate representation and of fit (as between, for example, the practices themselves and that which in some sense 'gives rise' to them), if the metaphysician's work is to be given any degree of credit at all.

Here the work of historian and of metaphysician are very close and could be called, rather loosely, descriptive.

But the metaphysician does not, we have noted repeatedly, employ the standards of re-enactment in his work, contrary to what many historians characteristically do in theirs. What he does is much closer to conceptual analysis than it is to re-enactment or, for that matter, to any of the standard patterns of historical construction and explanation (as found today in departments of history or among the great historians in the past). Indeed, his crucial and characteristic project is nothing like what historians normally do.

At some points the metaphysicans's work is better described, again loosely, as normative rather than as descriptive. The formulations of the metaphysician are not simply reportorial in nature; rather, they are logical or dialectical conclusions to complex arguments. The metaphysician does not perceive absolute presuppositions, for they do not pre-exist as something that can be perceived, or introspected for that matter. One can become conscious of an absolute presupposition only by formulating it. More important, they must be argued to. For the task of metaphysics, on the conception Collingwood advanced, is to *reason to* the various sets of absolute presuppositions that are (respectively) ingredient in competing accounts of a scientific practice and (assuming both fit and accuracy of formulation) to show that one such account (hence one such set or, failing that, the set of *alternative* present versions) is the best of all those involved.

Thus, metaphysicians put their data into a scale of forms. Constructing such a scale is a philosophical activity, with a philosophical goal in view (the goal of providing the *background* of the judgement of betterment in knowledge and explanatory power, as we go up the scale), a goal as old as Plato. On the crucial points, then, the work of metaphysics is not descriptive (the term we emphasized in section I), but normative or, if you will, critical. The work of metaphysics is not *merely* descriptive.[36]

Metaphysicians are not simply historians; they are, in Collingwood's view, philosophers. But metaphysicians do study a subject matter (absolute presuppositions) which is wholly involved in historical processes of development and differentiation. Thus, metaphysicians are principally concerned, as Collingwood said, with 'propositions about the history of absolute presuppositions' (EM, 163). And their pattern of analysis, the modified scale of forms, is designed to capture and organize a subject matter that is itself historically enmeshed.

The 'historical plain method' (a phrase Collingwood liked and took over from Locke to describe what he was himself doing in *The New Leviathan*) is not the method of history, not the method of re-enactment.[37] Rather, that method is simply to look at history, at development, in an orderly way in order to determine its content. Its informing model, in so far as we are interested in particular in progress – in improvement – is the modified scale of forms.

If the interpretation I've advanced in this paper is a plausible one and well grounded in Collingwood's texts, we are in a position to draw some important conclusions. One is that Collingwood's thought did not undergo a radical change, at least between his *Essay on Philosophical Method* (1933) and his *Metaphysics* (1940). Donagan and Knox, as we have seen, thought otherwise; they argued that Collingwood changed his views about philosophy, about metaphysics, in a fundamental and radical way during this period. Donagan, for example, saw Collingwood's essay on method as a sort of programmatic statement for a conception of philosophy as the science of Being, a programme which Collingwood later came to reject (in his *Metaphysics*).[38] And Knox saw the *Metaphysics* as abolishing any real differentiation between history and philosophy, with the result that philosophy now became prey to the demons of scepticism and relativism.

My account is strikingly different. Rather than a doctrinal break between Collingwood's two treatises on metaphysics I see an unbroken continuity. Indeed if my account is accepted, the two essays (the one on method and the one named *Metaphysics*) afford a unified treatment of the nature of metaphysical analysis, for the idea that absolute presuppositions (the subject matter of metaphysics) are wholly involved in historical processes of development (the thesis of the *Essay on Metaphysics*) is comfortably integrated with the essay on method's idea of scale-of-forms analysis, suitably modified. And we can purchase this integration – at least Collingwood holds out the hope that we can – without paying the price of a debilitating scepticism and relativism that so offended and even horrified Knox.[39]

The claim that metaphysics is a historical discipline bids us keep in mind that the work of scale-of-forms analysis can fail, for historical processes of development and differentiation are not always or necessarily progressive. It is, though, the regulative ideal of philosophy historically – an ideal that Collingwood held out to us – that it will not fail. Or, at least, that the assessment of progress is a quite possible or even likely rational outcome. Accordingly, we can conscientiously strive to see that this ideal does not fail, strive to see that progress is established as the outcome of philosophical assessment. And believing this, that it makes sense so to strive, we can do the work of philosophy with zeal and with clear sight.[40]

## Notes

[1] R. G. Collingwood, *Essay on Philosophical Method* (Oxford, Clarendon Press, 1933); *An Essay on Metaphysics* (Oxford, Clarendon Press, 1940); *An Autobiography* (Oxford, Clarendon Press, 1939). Hereafter cited EPM, EM and A respectively.

[2] A number of people, following Collingwood's lead, have used the so-called logic of question and answer to ground Collingwood's claim that absolute presuppositions are not propositions, e.g., Louis O. Mink, *Historical Understanding*, ed. Brian Fay, Eugene O. Golob and Richard T. Vann (Ithaca, Cornell University Press, 1987) (hereafter: Mink, HU), 269–70; Lorraine Code, 'Collingwood's Epistemological Individualism', *Monist*, 542–67 (544).

[3] A. H. Donagan, *The Later Philosophy of R. G. Collingwood* (Oxford, Clarendon Press, 1962; reprinted with changes, Chicago, University of Chicago Press, 1985), 12 (hereafter: Donagan, LPC; all quotes and citations are from the 1985 printing). See also T. M. Knox, 'Editor's Preface' to R. G. Collingwood, *Idea of History*, x–xi (hereafter: Knox, Preface). In the preface to the revised version of LPC, Donagan says, 'In *The Later Philosophy of R. G. Collingwood* [1962] I did not dispute Knox's judgement that there was a radical discontinuity in Collingwood's work after 1933, but I maintained that it was confined to philosophy of mind and metaphysics' (viii; see also ix).

[4] See Donagan, LPC, 15, also 14.

[5] For Mink's idea, see Louis O. Mink, *Mind, History and Dialectic: the Philosophy of R. G. Collingwood* (Bloomington, Indiana University Press, 1969), 144–51. (The same idea can be found in Mink, HU, at 270, and in D. Rynin, 'Donagan on Collingwood: Absolute Presuppositions, Truth and Metaphysics', *Review of Metaphysics* 18 (1964–5), 301–33,

esp. sect.2, where absolute presuppositions are represented as conceptual commitments.) A second consideration telling against the idea that absolute presuppositions are *a priori* concepts has already been introduced, in effect. The formulation, as a statement, of an *a priori* concept would have truth value, and this value would derive directly from the concept that was formulated (presumably accurately). For the accurate formulation of any such concept would itself be an *analytic* truth (in so far as it was based simply on that *a priori* concept); thus, if the concept of event contains, as it were, the notion of a cause, then the formulation of that concept as a statement ('all events have a cause') is *analytically* true. It would be hard to escape the conclusion, then, that *a priori* concepts here are on all fours with the *a priori* propositions that formulate them – in that both can be said to have an intrinsic truth value (implicit in the former case, explicit in the latter). If this is so, then *a priori* concepts (contrary to Mink) cannot qualify as the equivalent of Collingwoodian absolute presuppositions, for to say that they are commits one to assigning *intrinsic* truth values to absolute presuppositions (which runs against Collingwood's initial hypothesis). See also below n.10.

[6] For the term 'preconscious,' see R. G. Collingwood, *The New Leviathan: Or Man, Society, Civilization and Barbarism* (Oxford, Clarendon Press, 1942), 38 (sects.5.9ff.). Hereafter cited NL.

[7] See A. Shalom, 'R. G. Collingwood et la métaphysique', *Les Etudes philosophiques* 10 (1955), 693–711 (710).

[8] See my book *Historical Explanation: Re-enactment and Practical Inference* (Ithaca, Cornell University Press, 1977) (hereafter: HE, chs.1 and 2, for discussion of Collingwood's critique of the idea of human nature (itself an absolute presupposition of the incipient social sciences being developed in the seventeenth and eighteenth centuries). Mink is quite right, then, to see Collingwood as offering a criticism and revision of that particular absolute presupposition (see Mink HU, 265).

[9] R. G. Collingwood, *The Idea of Nature*, ed. T. M. Knox (Oxford, Clarendon Press, 1945) (hereafter: IN); Collingwood, *The Idea of History*, ed. with an introduction by T. M. Knox (Oxford, Clarendon Press, 1946) (note: all page citations are to the printing of 1956: New York, Oxford University Press). Hereafter cited IH.

[10] Both Hurup Nielsen and Donagan make the point that Collingwood used this particular characterization of absolute presuppositions to deny that metaphysical statements are Kantian *a priori* propositions (and thus to deny *a priori* propositions in general). See Margit Hurup Nielsen, 'Re-enactment and Reconstruction in Collingwood's Philosophy of History', *History and Theory*, 20 (1981), 1–31 (19–20, also 21–2); Donagan, LPC, 210–11.

[11] The last item here is cited by Knox as being from 'a series of notes' for

Collingwood's manuscript, *Principles of History* (1939); this MS of 1939 was until recently unfortunately lost. (See Donagan, LPC, xi, and W. J. van der Dussen, 'Collingwood's Unpublished Manuscripts', *History and Theory*, 18 (1979), 287-315 (307-9).) It is perhaps worth noting that doubts about the reliability of Knox's editing of IH, at least on points of detail, have been raised. Van der Dussen says, for example, that a passage quoted by Knox as 'from a manuscript written in 1936' (Introd., xii) is actually from a private letter from Collingwood to Knox ('Collingwood's Unpublished Manuscripts', 307.) See also Hurup Nielsen, 'Re-enactment and Reconstruction in Collingwood's Philosophy of History (cited above n.10), 1n., 21; Donagan, LPC, xi; W. J. van der Dussen, *History as a Science: the Philosophy of R. G. Collingwood* (The Hague, Nijhoff, 1981), n.106 to ch.2; and W. J. van der Dussen, 'Collingwood and the Idea of Progress', *History and Theory* Beiheft, *Reassessing Collingwood* (no. 29 (1990)), 21-41, in sect.1. A considerably revised and expanded version of van der Dussen's paper appears in this volume.

[12] Donagan, citing Collingwood A, 66, also said that metaphysics is historical in that its statements are 'categorical and singular' (LPC, 262). It should be noted that the material cited here and in the text is identical in the two versions (1962 and 1985) of LPC. See, in addition, B. A. Haddock, 'Vico and the Problem of Historical Reconstruction', *Social Research*, 43.3 (1976), 512-19, (n.12 on p.516); L. Code, 'Collingwood's Epistemological Individualism' (cited above n.2), sect.III; and D. Boucher, 'The Quest for Civilization: an Introduction to the Social and Political Thought of R. G. Collingwood', MS published as *The Social and Political Thought of R. G. Collingwood* (Cambridge, Cambridge University Press, 1989). (Note: the passage in question was found on p.66 of the manuscript for this book, and I cite it with Boucher's permission; but the passage does not occur in the actual published text of the book.) Both Haddock and Boucher, unlike Code, are critical of Collingwood's linkage of metaphysical thought with re-enactment. Boucher puts the central point well in the passage – from MS p.66 quoted in the text (two paragraphs below).

[13] Hurup Nielsen treats Collingwood as a constructionist; see her paper, 'Re-enactment and Reconstruction in Collingwood's Philosophy of History' (cited above n.10), 1, 5, 11-15, and esp. 25-9 and sects. 6 and 8. She explicitly identifies re-enactment with reconstruction (or construction, if you will) on 5, 24, 28. In sect. 5 she treats re-enactment – correctly, I think – as an absolute presupposition. Thus, I single her work out for special attention because she advances a constructionist interpretation of Collingwood and is, at the same time, one of the few such commentators to tie the idea of re-enactment explicitly in with Collingwood's account of absolute presuppositions from EM. The

other main theorist who advances a constructionist interpretation of Collingwood is Leon Goldstein; see his articles, 'Collingwood on the Constitution of the Historical Past,' in M. Krausz (ed.), *Critical Essays on the Philosophy of R. G. Collingwood* (Oxford, Clarendon Press, 1972), 241–67, and 'Collingwood's Theory of Historical Knowing,' *History and Theory*, 9 (1970), 3-36. The same judgement of Collingwood has been expressed, in a quite incidental way, by P. H. Nowell Smith, 'The Construction Theory of History', *History and Theory* Beiheft, *The Constitution of the Historical Past*, 16 (1977), 1–28 (1–2), and by Mink, HU, 93. I should add that I do not find Goldstein's account of Collingwood, as regards Collingwood's constructionism, to be as clear-cut as Hurup Nielsen's. She states the claim that he is a constructionist quite unequivocally and makes explicit the crucial identification of re-enactment with construction from evidence.

14 The merits of constructionism have been set forth, most ably, by M. Oakeshott, *Experience and its Modes* (Cambridge, Cambridge University Press, 1933); by Jack Meiland, *Skepticism and Historical Knowledge* (New York, Random House, 1965); and by Leon Goldstein in his book, *Historical Knowing* (Austin, University of Texas Press, 1976), and in his article, 'History and the Primacy of Knowing', *History and Theory*, Beiheft 16 (1977), 29–52. For discussion and criticism of constructionism, see *History and Theory*, Beiheft 16 (1977): articles by Nowell Smith, cited above n.13, and W. H. Walsh; P. H. Nowell Smith, *What Actually Happened*, The Lindley Lecture (Lawrence, University of Kansas, Department of Philosophy, 1971); R. F. Atkinson, *Knowledge and Explanation in History: An Introduction to Philosophy of History* (Ithaca, Cornell University Press, 1978), ch.2; Dorothy Haecker, 'The Historical Way of Knowing' (Ph.D. dissertation, University of Kansas, 1981). For background, see Arthur C. Danto, *Narration and Knowledge* (New York, Columbia University Press, 1985), chs.3–5. My main reason for rejecting constructionism as a general account of historical knowledge is that I find the arguments against it decisive, particularly those developed by Haecker. My main reason for rejecting a constructionist account of Collingwood, in particular, is that I cannot square it with what he says about the historian's thinking the *same* thought as that of the agent under study (see IH, part 5, ch.4). For Collingwood's idea of a supposed identity at certain points, between the *content* of the historian's thought and that of a past person, strongly suggests that *two* things are involved here: the historian's construction and the independent past thought itself. For discussion of Collingwood's 'identity' thesis, see Donagan, LPC, 216–22; Martin, HE, 57–62; Heikki Saari, *Re-enactment: a Study of R. G. Collingwood's Philosophy of History* (Åbo, Finland, Åbo Akademi, 1984) (and note my review of Saari's monograph in *Theoria*, 51.2 (1985), 115–24); Saari,

'R. G. Collingwood on the Identity of Thoughts', *Dialogue*, 28 (1989), 77–89; and Hurup Nielsen, 'Re-enactment and Reconstruction in Collingwood's Philosophy of History' (cited above n.10), 26 and n.105 there.

15 The schema as suggested here is spelled out in my book HE, at 77–8 and 158–9.

16 The ideas set out in this section were first developed, in wider compass, in my book HE, esp. chs.3–5, 8. It should be emphasized, though the point is not often noted, that Collingwood had a *general* idea of re-enactment explanations (see EM, 192–3). Thus, he could be said to be committed to the sketch I've drawn as the *form* of such explanations.

17 See Martin, HE, 57 and ch.8, esp. 147–8.

18 The example of Darwin is taken from Collingwood, IH, 332. The references to fading and accentuation come from IH, 162; 'internal' modification is described in IH, 226 and 334.

19 See IH, 162. Thus, an accepted thesis in physics might require some novel addition to the stock of acquired thoughts; for example, it might require the idea that space was curved rather than Euclidean. This novel idea might be reached, not through modification of existing theories of physical space, but through a leap (through an idea that emerges, consistent with the practice of mathematical physics, as a way of accommodating and rationalizing this accepted thesis).

20 I think it is quite likely that Collingwood used the Darwinian theory of the evolution of species as the model for his idea of a process of development (see IH, 321). But Collingwood averred, significantly, that the origin of the whole evolutionary way of thinking 'must be sought in the historical movement of the late eighteenth century, and its further development in the growth of the same movement in the nineteenth' (IN, 10; see also 13). In other words, Collingwood thought that the idea of evolutionary development originated in the discipline of history and was borrowed by the theorists of natural evolution, not vice versa.

21 For Collingwood's idea of the 'living past', see IH, 225–6, and A, 97–100.

22 The notion of 'incapsulation' is found in A, 98. 100, 113; see also IH, 227.

23 For the phrases quoted see IH, 227 (for the first) and 216 (for the second). For the discussion of Collingwood's ideas of the mind-as-thought and of actions 'determined by thought', see my book HE, ch.2. Collingwood asserts that there is no mind *except* in 'historical process' and that 'it is only in the historical process, the process of thoughts, that thought exists at all . . .' (IH, 227). Collingwood's position here, if pushed to its logical conclusion, would either yield an infinite regress or require *some* human thinking which could not be accounted for

along the lines he suggested. However, these unaccounted-for thoughts would not very likely be deep, metaphysical ones but, instead, rather primitive and perhaps presently unnecessary ones (very early superstitions, perhaps). More important, what Collingwood says here may well be true of the sort of high-grade, disciplined thought he was concerned with in EM, the kind of thought he called 'scientific.'

24  In the first section of this chapter, absolute presuppositions were said to be the groundforms of social or corporate practices (specifically, the practices of science). Collingwood *explicitly* tied his process view of mind in with corporate or social practices (see IH, 83–5, 91, 220, 223, 226). Note that in EM, 60, Collingwood treats the assumption here (of the *social* sharing of absolute presuppositions) as merely a 'probable' one.

25  See IH, 90–1, 224, 239.

26  See IH, 210–11, 223, 248, 324, and NL, 285 (sect.34.63). The line of argument here is summarized in my book HE, 29–32.

27  The tension is there, admittedly, but it does not amount to a logical incompatibility (see my book HE, ch.11, and my paper, 'Collingwood's Doctrine of absolute presuppositions and the Possibility of Historical Knowledge,' in L. Pompa and W. H. Dray, eds., *Substance and Form in History: a Collection of Essays in Philosophy of History* (Edinburgh, Edinburgh University Press, 1981), 89–106, sects.3 and 4).

28  Mink, it should be noted, also emphasized processes of development in his account of what he called Collingwood's 'dialectic,' and this account of Mink's was specifically intended to include absolute presuppositions (see Mink, HU, ch.11). Mink's account of such processes, unlike my own, is drawn principally from works other than IH and A (from EPM and NL, in particular). This difference is significant, as will become clear shortly, for I regard the *kind* of development exhibited in history (as captured in the phrase 'historical process of development') as quite different from that discussed in EPM; the difference here is, largely, the difference between *logical* development (in EPM) and evolutionary or *temporal* development (in IH). More important, in so far as Mink had the latter kind of development in mind (as I believe he sometimes did), that sort of development is incompatible with his notion of absolute presuppositions as *a priori* concepts (see above n.5). For absolute presuppositions cannot be involved – changed – in such processes (or be their products) and still be *a priori* in any interesting sense.

29  Collingwood's best summary of his views here is found in EPM, 88–91, 100. My paper 'Collingwood's *Essay on Philosophical Method*', *Idealistic Studies*, 4.3 (1974), 224–50, can be referred to for general background (in particular, 234–5, 240, 244, and 249–50). Collingwood usually speaks in EPM, not of a practice and theories about it, but of a

genus and its species. My paper provides arguments for loosening up Collingwood's terminology (and, hence, for the direction I am taking in the present chapter).

[30] For Gallie's useful idea (of 'essentially contested concepts'), see W. B. Gallie, *Philosophy and Historical Understanding*, second edn (New York, Schocken Books, 1968), 157–91, esp. 161 and 168.

[31] Knox is quite wrong to equate an EPM scale of forms with a process of development (as he does in Introd., ix–x). They are not and cannot be the same *if* the process of development in question is *historical*. (See also above n.28.)

[32] Mink, in *Mind, History and Dialectic* (cited above n.5), 85, 106–7, treats the NL analysis (of the forms of consciousness) as a standard scale-of-forms analysis, of the EPM sort. Again, I think such conflation is a mistake. For, if the two analyses were the same – if the 'overlap' were complete, and point by point, for all the theories – there would be no such thing as 'primitive survivals' of instances, from one level of consciousness (a lower level) lying beside instances of another (a higher level), as we find throughout the NL discussion (see NL, 65 (sects.9.5ff.) and 103 (sects. 14.55 and 14.6)).

[33] I will grant, though, that Collingwood *said* he was giving a historical account in NL of the 'modern European mind' (NL, 62 (sects.9.2ff.)). But what he meant by 'historical' here is, of course, subject to interpretation. I suggest that he meant here, not the discipline treated in IH, but, rather, what Locke called the 'historical plain method' (see below n.37 and the text relevant to it). For a discussion of Collingwood's radical separation of thought from feeling, see my book HE, 32–7.

[34] My point, simply, is that if we can speak of progress at three points – the *methods*, the resultant substantive *theories* (or laws), and what I have called the *thematics* of a going science – and, I believe, Collingwood would allow that we could, then we can also speak of progressive modifications in the very groundform of such a science. (For the groundform is simply an analytic abstraction from things at those points, as something presupposed by them, and it stands or falls with them.) And in so far as we can identify the various stages of the implicit groundform of any ongoing progressive science, we would have a modified scale of forms. For additional discussion by Collingwood on progress, see NL, 64–5 (sects. 9.44–9.48). Also, see Collingwood, 'Croce's Philosophy of History' (1921, 3–22); 'The Theory of Historical Cycles' (1927, 76–89); 'Oswald Spengler and the Theory of Historical Cycles' (a review, 1927, 57–75); 'A Philosophy of Progress' (1929, 104–120). These essays are all reprinted, at the pages indicated, in William Debbins, ed., *Essays in the Philosophy of History by R. G. Collingwood* (Austin, University of Texas Press, 1965). For discussion of

these essays, see van der Dussen, 'Collingwood and the Idea of Progress' (cited above n.11), sects.4 and 5.

35 For Collingwood's idea of progress in the absolute presuppositions of the discipline of history, see IH, part 5, ch.1, and n.8 above. For Collingwood's discussion of monotheism as in a progressive relationship to polytheism, and of each as an absolute presupposition of physics, see EM, part 3, sect.A, 185–227.

36 Collingwood does not prefer the term 'normative,' introducing instead the curious term 'criteriological,' whereby he meant 'self-critical' or critical on internal standards (see EM, 108–9, 111, 115–16). At EM, 142, he identifies metaphysics as criteriological. Thus, it is clear that he doesn't regard it as a merely reportorial study. Accordingly, I would be reluctant to regard Collingwoodian metaphysical statements as essentially *descriptive* in nature, as Walsh and Atkinson, to cite two examples, have done. Such statements are more accurately viewed, I believe, as analytic constructs, as rational reconstructions. (See W. H. Walsh, 'Collingwood and Metaphysical Neutralism,' in Michael Krausz, ed., *Critical Essays on the Philosophy of R. G. Collingwood* (cited above n.13), ch.7, esp. 149; R. F. Atkinson, *Knowledge and Explanation in History* (cited above n.14), 93.)

37 For Collingwood's use of the phrase 'historical plain method,' see IH, 206, 220, and NL, 61 (sects.9.1ff.) and 62 (sect.9.2). Interestingly, Collingwood characteristically referred to the *method* of metaphysics as 'analysis.' He said at one point, 'The analysis which detects absolute presuppositions I call metaphysical analysis; there is no difference whatever between metaphysical analysis and analysis pure and simple as I have been hitherto describing it [in EM, 38–9]' (EM, 40; see also 92, 101, 149).

38 See Donagan, LPC, 6–8, 10, 13; also 11, 20, 253, 259, 260, 263–4.

39 I do not, of course, want to intimate that my suggested reading of Collingwood here is in any way obvious. The very opposite is true; for, so far as I know, no one has proposed anything like it before. And for many years it was not at all obvious to me. Indeed, I was puzzled about the relationship to one another of Collingwood's two main treatises on metaphysics. I thought there *ought* to be a connection (as I said at the beginning of this article); it's just that I couldn't discern any significant connecting line between them. But when, after having first worked out the idea of a modified scale of forms, I finally came to put the two treatises together (in a seminar in 1985), their connection along the lines I have proposed seemed altogether natural.

40 The present paper has drawn, at some points verbatim, on earlier writings of mine. Thus, a principal source for sect. 1 is my paper, 'Collingwood's Doctrine of Absolute Presuppositions and the Possibility of Historical Knowledge' (cited above n.27), sect.2. I should

add that the account of Wittgenstein in my book HE, 203–10, actually draws on an earlier version of this section of that paper on Collingwood. The important distinction between an absolute presupposition *per se* and an accurate *statement* of its content is found in Pierre Fruchon, 'Signification de l'histoire de la philosophie selon l'Autobiographie de Collingwood', *Les Etudes Philosophiques*, 13 (1958), 143–60 (158). The principal source for sect.2 is my paper. 'Collingwood on Reasons, Causes, and the Explanation of Action', *International Studies in Philosophy*, 33 (1991), 47–62. And the principal source for sect.4 is my paper, 'Collingwood's *Essay on Philosophical Method*' (cited above n.29). I am indebted to Michael Hinz, George Trey and Ted Vaggalis for their helpful and encouraging comments on the original draft of this chapter.

# Collingwood on the Ideas of Process, Progress and Civilization

## JAN VAN DER DUSSEN

### I

At the beginning of the chapter in his autobiography entitled 'The Need for a Philosophy of History' Collingwood claims that two branches of philosophical inquiry need special attention. Besides epistemological problems related to historical knowledge he mentions in this connection 'metaphysical problems, concerned with the nature of the historian's subject matter: the elucidation of terms like event, process, progress, civilization, and so forth' (A, 177).[1]

Looking back on the discussions within philosophy of history as they have developed since Collingwood wrote these words, it is striking that attention has almost exclusively been directed towards the epistemological aspects of history. It has become common to call this branch 'critical' or 'analytical' philosophy of history, this being put against its 'speculative' counterpart. It is also striking that the subjects dealt with by the latter do not correspond to the ones Collingwood mentions under the heading 'metaphysical problems'. For the usual questions discussed by speculative philosophy of history concern the possible patterns, mechanisms or purpose of history and not the type of concepts Collingwood cites as examples.

Collingwood himself, however, had a keen interest in these metaphysical questions, and this is especially true of the concepts of process, progress and civilization. In this essay the relation between these concepts, as seen by Collingwood, will be examined in more detail.

## II

It is not easy to come to grips with Collingwood's views on the concepts of process, progress and civilization. It is less difficult, however, to find the reason for this. For these concepts are a typical example of a philosophical concept as elaborated in *An Essay on Philosophical Method*. In that book Collingwood argues that the character of a philosophical concept is such that, unlike scientific or empirical concepts, no exhaustive definition can be provided. A philosophical concept is characterized by an overlap of its specific classes; these overlapping classes each embody the generic essence, but they make up a scale of forms differing from each other both in degree and kind and by opposition and distinction. A philosophical concept is therefore intrinsically unlimited in nature and 'leaks or escapes' out of the limits characteristic of non-philosophical concepts (EPM, 35).

The concept of civilization being dealt with at the end of this essay, I will start with discussing the concepts of process and progress. In achieving an understanding of the way in which these concepts are conceived by Collingwood one has also to bear in mind the way in which other related concepts are understood by him, for only in this way can their characteristics and specific problems be brought to the fore. One should mention in this connection in particular the concepts of change, development and evolution. In respect of these concepts one should further keep in mind the distinction Collingwood makes between nature and (human) history.

The difference between change, and development or process (Collingwood in fact does not make a distinction between these terms) is based on the one between matter and life. In a case of change there is always a substratum $x$ which is permanent and changes from one state into another, the cause being something from without. Water might be taken as an example. Though this exists in a solid, liquid or gaseous state, its essence, Collingwood writes, 'is represented by the formula $H_2O$', the variable in this case being 'something extraneous to the generic essence' (EPM, 59).

In a development, however, 'there is no substratum and no states of it, but always something turning into something else'.[2] This is typical of organic nature, and it was Aristotle who first worked this conception out. Collingwood is not always precise in his terminology, since he says of Aristotle that for him 'nature as such is process, growth, change' (IN, 82). After this he continues:

> This process is a development, i.e. the changing takes successive forms ... in which each is the potentiality of its successor; but it is not what we call 'evolution', because for Aristotle the kinds of change and of structure exhibited in the world of nature form an eternal repertory, and the items in the repertory are related logically, not temporally, among themselves. It follows that the change is in the last resort cyclical; circular movement is for him characteristic of the perfectly organic, not as for us of the inorganic. (IN, 82)

The same distinction is also made in *The Idea of History*, where Collingwood states that two views of natural process are possible: 'that events in nature repeat one another specifically, the specific forms remaining constant through the diversity of their individual instances... or that the specific forms themselves undergo change, new forms coming into existence by modification of the old. The second conception is what is meant by evolution' (IH, 321).

To use the language of *An Essay on Philosophical Method*, an evolutionary process differs both in degree and kind from a cyclical one. In Collingwood's view the idea of nature as an evolutionary process has been conceived since the end of the eighteenth century on the analogy of the study of human affairs, because by that time historians had begun to see history as a process instead of the succession of separate periods (IN, 9–10).

The great importance Collingwood attached to the idea of process may be gauged from the fact that he calls it in his *Autobiography* 'my first principle of a philosophy of history' (A, 97) as worked out in his essay '*Libellus de Generatione*' of 1920.[3] 'At the time I expressed this', Collingwood says, 'by saying that history is concerned not with "events" but with "processes"; that "processes" are things which do not begin and end but turn into one another' (A, 97–8). Collingwood also makes it clear that this conception of process is related to his well-known ideas of the past being alive in the present and also being somehow encapsulated within it as an unconverted residue (A, 140–1).

Though based on history the idea of process got its familiarity and even popularity within the ideas of biological and cosmic evolution. Collingwood was especially interested in modern cosmological theories, in particular those propounded by Alexander and Whitehead. His extensive 'Notes toward a Metaphysic' of 1933–4 – on which *The Idea of Nature* is partly based, and being part of his unpublished manuscripts – bear witness to this.[4]

Though Collingwood did not succeed in accomplishing a cosmological theory of his own, his studies in this field had a side-effect which was of great importance in the development of his ideas. For though he agreed that nature should be seen as a process, he was unwilling to conclude from this that the distinction between natural and historical processes should be considered as superseded. When considering a historical process Collingwood always refers to the history of mind, that is, to the history of the human past. This implies, in Collingwood's view, the all-important difference between a historical and a natural process: in the first there is no mere time-sequence as in nature, but the past conserves itself in the present, the historical process therefore being of a rational nature. In a historical series, Collingwood writes in his 'Notes toward a Metaphysic', the earlier continues with 'accumulation or enrichment of the existent by the sum of its own past'. 'For mind in general', he then concludes, 'this accumulation is called experience; for consciousness, it is called memory; for a social unity, it is called tradition; for knowledge, it is called history'[5].

So an important result of Collingwood's examination of cosmological problems was the development of a clear distinction between natural and historical processes. This distinction pervades *The Idea of History* – all manifestations of naturalism or positivism being severely criticized in that book.

Summarizing the preceding argument, it may therefore be said – using Collingwood's theory of philosophical concepts as elaborated in *An Essay on Philosophical Method* – that there is a scale of forms of overlapping classes from natural change with a permanent substratum undergoing various changes caused from without, to natural development of a cyclical nature, the forms remaining constant, to natural process or evolution where the forms change, and finally historical processes with their distinguishing feature of retaining the past in the present.

## III

Moving on to the concept of progress, one may observe as a preliminary that it includes the idea of development. It is a development, however, of a specific type, which may be described by saying that a later phase is conceived as an improvement upon an earlier. Though this conception is sometimes used in the evolutionary theory of nature as well, it is emphatically rejected by Collingwood. 'The archaeopteryx may in fact have been an ancestor of the bird', he says, 'but what entitles us to call the bird an improvement on the archaeopteryx? A bird is not a better archaeopteryx, but something different that has grown out of it. Each is trying to be itself' (IH, 322). He was also at times very critical of the idea of progress in history. For example, in 1921 he can be found criticizing Croce for his 'vulgar optimism' and for seeing all history as 'a change from the good to the better' (CPH, 16–17).

This was not, however, Collingwood's last word on the matter, since he later came back to the question on several occasions, developing rather different views. In this connection it should first of all be noted that he does not always use the concept of progress unambiguously. For though in his essay on the subject in *The Idea of History* (IH, 321–34) Collingwood indeed rejects the idea of progress in nature in the sense of being a process of improving states, in a preceding passage he maintains that 'in one sense, to call a natural process evolutionary is the same thing as calling it progressive' (IH, 321). He means by this that the modifications of the various forms of a natural process can only come into existence in a certain order: 'In this sense of the word "progress", progressive only means orderly, that is, exhibiting order.' In *The Idea of Nature* the term 'progressive' is used in a similar sense, as for example when Collingwood comments: 'where by progress I mean a change always leading to something new, with no necessary implication of betterment' (IN, 14). In his discussion of Kant in *The Idea of History* Collingwood even plainly states: 'All history certainly shows progress, i.e. it is the development of something' (IH, 104).

It is obvious that in these cases the concept of progress is used in a wide sense, equating it with the idea of development as an orderly process. In that sense even natural evolution as conceived by Darwin can be seen as progressive. Collingwood did not dwell on this aspect and preferred to concentrate on the idea of historical process, which is, as we have seen, of a rational nature. He considered it an achievement of the first order that in the eighteenth century history was conceived for the first time as making sense: 'It had a plot. It revealed itself as something coherent, significant, intelligible', and he described this as 'a genuine discovery' (PP, 111).

For Collingwood, seeing history as a plot means that it is conceived as a continuity consisting of the succession of problems confronting man and the various solutions found for them. 'Now such a course of events may be truly called a progress', he maintains, 'because it is a going forward; it has direction, everything in it proceeds out of what has gone before and could not have happened without the occurrence of its past' (THC, 86). He then continues: 'But though history is in this sense a progress and nothing but a progress, it cannot be so in any other sense. No one of the phases through which it moves is any better, or any worse, than any of the others' (THC, 86–7). The reason given for this position is that each generation is confronted by unique situations giving rise to unique problems.

So we find Collingwood here using the concept of progress in two different ways: one in the sense of history as an orderly and rational process (a 'going forward'), and one in the sense of each phase of the historical process as an improvement on the last. Progress in the first sense is accepted by Collingwood and even thought necessary, while he rejects progress in the second sense – at least in the passages so far considered. Since progress in the second sense should be seen as its proper meaning this is the sense on which we shall concentrate.

In order to assess the arguments developed by Collingwood concerning the idea of progress it is important to bear in mind certain relevant distinctions: such as, on the one hand, the distinction between history as an 'objective' process and history as conceived by a historian; and on the other, the distinction between history seen 'as a whole' and history seen only partially or under a certain aspect.

The latter distinction is discussed by Collingwood in *The Idea of History*, when he gives as an example a community of fish-eaters which develops a more efficient method of fishing, catching ten instead of five fish on an average day. He is reluctant to call this an 'objective' improvement, since the older generation is inclined to consider changes such as these as a form of decadence, while the younger one will see it as progress. The important point here is the reason Collingwood supplies for the impossibility of comparing the two practices within the fisher community. For the older generation will stick to the old method, thinking it better than the new, and this is not done 'out of irrational prejudice', but 'because the way of life which it knows and values is built round the old method, which is therefore certain to have social and religious associations that express the intimacy of its connexion with this way of life as a whole' (IH, 325).

The important distinction Collingwood makes here is that between change in respect of a certain activity within the fisher community (namely catching more fish) and change related to its 'way of life as a whole'. Though one could claim, of course, that the first type of change can be seen only as an improvement, he is not willing to take this possibility seriously, since it is generally the case that improvements have unforeseen (and often negative) side-effects or consequences and that it is precisely this which makes the idea of progress such a difficult one. Here one can only endorse Collingwood's position. A necessary condition of ascribing progress in any particular case is, therefore, that it is conceived as related to the whole of a community's way of life.

Collingwood not only points out that succeeding generations will disagree about alleged progress, but also rejects the idea that a historian might function as a neutral judge. For what is required in a case like this, Collingwood avers, is a comparison of different 'ways of life as a whole' and he is of the opinion that this is not possible. 'The task of judging the value of a certain way of life taken in its entirety is an impossible task', he says, 'because no such thing in its entirety is ever a possible object of historical knowledge' (IH, 327). The reason he gives for this is that 'there must be large tracts of life for which he has either no data, or no data he is in a position to interpret' (IH, 329).

Both in 'The Theory of Historical Cycles' and *The Idea of History* Collingwood is of the opinion, however, that historians can have knowledge of certain historical periods.[6] Since these are equated in *The Idea of History* with 'ways of life',[7] there is a certain inconsistency here in his argument. Collingwood denies, though, that forms of life can be compared, his main argument being that each one is to be characterized and judged in terms of its own problems and the solutions it finds to them (IH, 329).

## IV

This position clearly precludes the possibility that the historical process can be conceived as progressive. This, however, is not Collingwood's last word on the subject of progress, though his ideas on it are variegated and not always easy to grasp. It is possible to distinguish four different positions in his attitude to the concept of progress: (1) it is dependent on a point of view; (2) it is meaningless; (3) it is meaningful; (4) it is necessary.

(1) Collingwood's rejection of historical realism implies that any suggestion of historical progress being conceived as an 'objective phenomenon' is rejected accordingly. In this connection his usual reaction is to emphasize that not only the idea of progress, but also the idea of decay, is dependent on the point of view taken up by the historian. This emphasis is already to be found in his article of 1921 on Croce's philosophy of history (long before his elaboration of the principle of the ideality of the past in the 'Outlines of a Philosophy of History' of 1928)[8] in which Croce is criticized for his 'transcendent attitude' of 'asserting the existence of a criterion outside the historian's mind', which implies – at least in Croce's view – that history is seen as a purely progressive process. 'A change that is really a progress seen from one end', Collingwood retorts, 'is no less really a decadence, seen from the other. It is true to say that the decay of archery was the rise of firearms; but it is not less true to say that the rise of firearms was the decay of archery' (CPH, 16). In 'The Theory of Historical Cycles' the same argument is used, Collingwood this time giving the 'growth of the steamship' as an example, it being 'the passing-away of that splendid thing, the sailing-ship' (THC, 81).

(2) The concept of progress cannot be used in a meaningful way, according to Collingwood, in the realms of art, happiness and morality. For art he gives three reasons: 'every phase of art has its own beauty, which it is idle to assess in terms of a scale of degrees' (PP, 110–11); the various artists were not trying to do the same thing and we find their products differentiated by a difference of

the ideal aimed at (THC, 82); a work of art arises out of the artist's unreflective experience and the flow of that experience 'is not an historical process' (IH, 330).

The question whether human happiness has increased or decreased in the past is also considered meaningless (PP, 13). The reason given for this is that happiness cannot be measured, and there is therefore no such thing as 'the sum of human happiness': 'Different ages find happiness in different things' and 'the happiness of a peasant is not contained in the happiness of a millionaire', is the simple yet entirely adequate conclusion (PP, 114; IH, 330).

The reason that it is improper to speak of an increase in morality is that 'a man's moral worth depends not on his circumstances, but on the way in which he confronts them' (PP, 15). Collingwood therefore particularly objects to the view that certain circumstances such as the abolition of slavery render those living under those circumstances morally more worthy than those who do not (PP, 115–16).[9]

Although in *The Idea of History* Collingwood is of the opinion (as we will see) that progress in science is possible, in the manuscript called 'The Function of Metaphysics in Civilization' (1937-8)[10] he is sceptical of the idea. This manuscript was written in preparation for *An Essay on Metaphysics*, and it is here that the conception of metaphysics as a science of absolute presuppositions is developed for the first time. This conception is indeed of a relativistic nature and this is reflected in Collingwood's discussion in the manuscript of the question to what extent our science may be taken as superior to Greek science. He questions this alleged superiority in two ways. In the first place he points out that there is no real standard of comparison between them, though there exists a continuity and development. He suggests that Greek science has provided the spade-work 'preparing a soil out of which we moderns are winning our harvests'. If this is the case, 'is not the richness of these harvests a proof, not of our superiority to the ancients, but of the excellence of their pioneer work?'[11]

In addition, he gives another, more fundamental argument for questioning the superiority of our science over Greek science. Deciding which of two things is better, he argues, implies the possibility of choosing between them; but we cannot be in a position to choose between our science and Greek science, and the question is therefore meaningless. He calls it 'a nonsense question', because 'to ask it presupposes the existence of a situation which does not exist.'[12]

In 'The Theory of Historical Cycles' the idea of progress is also linked in a similar way to the possibility of practical choice, for Collingwood there makes the observation that the question whether we might prefer to live in a past period because we think it a better one 'cannot arise' as a problem, since 'the choice cannot be offered.' He therefore says that in speaking of the past 'we ought not to call it either better than the present or worse; for we are not called upon to choose it or to reject it, to like it or to dislike it, to approve it or to condemn it, but simply to accept it' (THC, 85). Comparison between historical periods is therefore considered to be both theoretically and practically meaningless.

In the 'Outlines of a Philosophy of History', the subject of comparing periods is discussed within the context of the historiographical principles involved in the narrative of a particular historical period. In describing a period, Collingwood contends, that period should be viewed from its own ideals and accordingly be seen as progressively revealing them. After this he continues:

> It does not follow that the next period will be still better according to the same standards. On the contrary, it will certainly be worse; and at the same time, according to its own standards, better. But to hold two periods together in this way side by side for comparison is bad history. If two periods are thought of together, they must be fused into one period and their common characteristics brought to light. If they have no common characteristics, it is idle even to compare them. No one would wish to compare any two things, unless he thought he detected something in common between them. But by bringing to light these common characteristics one is treating the two periods in question as articulations of one single period, and their ideals as modifications of a common ideal. (IH, 481)

The argument developed here by Collingwood is clarifying in the sense that it provides a criterion for making a distinction between using the idea of progress in a meaningful way – to be discussed hereafter – and using it in a way that is meaningless.

(3) 'In its crudest form', Collingwood avers, 'the idea of progress would imply that throughout history man has been working at the same problem, and has been solving it better and

better' (THC, 84). The identity of a certain problem serves Collingwood as a criterion for the meaningful application of the concept of progress. The absence of such an identity also provides him with his reason for denying the possibility of progress in art or morality, both activities being responses to contingent problems.

There are, however, certain problems which Collingwood does regard as having a continuous historical identity and which therefore allow the possibility of progressive solution. An example is engineering. Discussing the preference one may have for Norman or Gothic buildings he denies that this can be decided on rational grounds with regard to their aesthetic merits; but if judged by the standards of engineering, the transition from Norman to Gothic was 'definitely an improvement': 'The main purpose of the architect is to build; the Gothic architect built stronger and cheaper than the Norman' (PP, 110).

In the essay on progress in *The Idea of History* Collingwood maintains that science 'is the simplest and most obvious case in which progress exists and is verifiable'. He makes the qualification, however, that progress in science 'would consist in the supersession of one theory by another which served both to explain all that the first theory explained, and also to explain types or classes of events of "phenomena" which the first ought to have explained but could not' (IH, 332).[13]

Collingwood is of the opinion that philosophy and religion may also be seen as progressing, but he makes two reservations: first, any solution to a group of problems should retain the already achieved solutions of past problems. Secondly, it is only by historical thought that progress can be established: 'Whether it has actually occurred, and where and when and in what ways' (IH, 333). This means that progress cannot be postulated *a priori*, either generally or specifically, as has been done by so many progressivists in the past.

After this point there is a crucial shift in Collingwood's argument, for he now maintains that historical thought should not only *establish* whether there is any progress, but should *create* this progress as well: 'For progress is not a mere fact to be discovered by historical thinking: it is only through historical thinking that it comes about at all' (IH, 333). The argument he uses to justify this conclusion is consistent with his view of history as a rational process. For we have seen that this process is characterized by retaining its past phases in its present. With regard to science this implies that at a certain phase preceding achievements are kept 'by the retention in the mind' and that this is the only way in which progress can take place (IH, 333).

Collingwood's argument is not only convincing, but also fully consistent with his general view of history, as outlined above: both the aspect of continuity and the rational nature of the historical process are emphasized. His position does not, however, appear to be consistent with the theory of absolute presuppositions as expounded in *An Essay on Metaphysics*. We might put it more bluntly: it flatly contradicts that theory, for according to the theory of absolute presuppositions it is exactly the discontinuity between the various fundamental principles which is emphasized. These principles are seen by Collingwood as merely succeeding each other throughout history without displaying any rational transition.

It is difficult to conceive of any way in which Collingwood's theory of absolute presuppositions, with its implications of discontinuity, incommensurability and irrational change, can be reconciled with his essay on progress in *The Idea of History*, in which he expresses directly contradictory views on the development of science. This contradiction can only be resolved, in my opinion, by keeping in mind the different context within which each argument was developed, and especially the different questions each was intended to answer.

*An Essay on Metaphysics* (written in 1938–9) deals with Collingwood's conception of metaphysics. He was extremely concerned by the attacks on metaphysics, the latest of which was expounded with great force and clarity by A. J. Ayer, and he was convinced that these attacks were based on misunderstandings concerning the nature of metaphysics. For this reason he decided to make his own contribution to the theory of metaphysics. His theory should not, it is important to note, be considered as an original theory of Collingwood's own making within metaphysics, but rather as a description of what metaphysics in his view had always been. This at least was his expressed intention. Metaphysics is and was, he claims, a historical science, that is, a science describing the absolute presuppositions of a certain time or culture. A metaphysician, therefore, should be a neutral observer, who is not in a position to express judgement on the absolute presuppositions he surveys. This implies that any suggestion that any one system of absolute presuppositions is superior to any other is improper, and the possibility of progress in presuppositions is rejected accordingly. As science depends on a system of absolute presuppositions, the possibility of progress in science is also dismissed. As we have seen, Collingwood develops this argument explicitly in the manuscript 'The Function of Metaphysics in Civilization', coming to the conclusion that we do not have the right to consider our science better than Greek science.

The essay on progress in *The Idea of History* (written in 1936 and forming part of the lectures on the philosophy of history he gave in that year) deals with a completely different subject. Here the question is when and in what sense the concept of progress can be applied in a meaningful way. As we have seen, Collingwood is of the opinion that 'ways of life as a whole' cannot be compared by a historian for the purposes of evaluation. One could draw a parallel between such 'ways of life' and systems of absolute presuppositions in that both appear to be fundamental and all-embracing; and one could go on to conclude that ways of life and systems of absolute presuppositions cannot be judged by a historian, and accordingly cannot be seen as progressive. However, in discussing the possibility of scientific progress in *The Idea of History*, Collingwood does not deal with the assessments made by historians, but those made by scientists themselves. Historical thought is therefore involved, but it is not the historical thought of *historians*, but that of *scientists*: 'If Einstein makes an advance on Newton, he does it by knowing Newton's thought and retaining it within his own' (IH, 333). Collingwood therefore claims that in order to achieve scientific progress a scientist should be a historian of the subject he studies. Referring to Newton, Collingwood says: 'It is only in so far as Einstein knows that theory, as a fact in the history of science, that he can make an advance upon it' (IH, 334).

In this case the past is not viewed, therefore, in the detached way of a historian, but as a participant in the – or (better) a – historical process. In this way scientists see themselves as participants in the latest stage within the history of science, as historians do within historiography and philosophers within philosophy.

This brings us to the final aspect of the concept of progress – its necessary nature.

(4) Not only does Collingwood claim that in relation to certain

aspects of the past the historian is justified in employing the concept of progress, but he also considers that in relation to solving theoretical and practical problems it is necessary. These problems are always passed down from the past, and in order to solve them they have to be reconstructed and understood by historical thought. In this sense there is a real continuity between the past and the present, but Collingwood refers to it as a continuity 'of a peculiar kind' (IH, 333).

What he means is what he refers to in his autobiography as the encapsulation of past thought within present thought. This means that present thought is not completely encompassed by the rethought thought of the past, but is conscious of the act of rethinking. In this way a distinction is made between the 'primary series' of 'real' life and the 'secondary' series of the rethought thought of the past (A, 113). Collingwood furthermore holds the opinion that all thinking is critical thinking: 'the thought which re-enacts past thoughts, therefore, criticizes them in re-enacting them' (IH, 216). It is this critical capacity which allows the possibility of progress, and this is what lies behind Collingwood's remarks when he says of the thought of Newton as re-enacted by Einstein, that it is 're-enacted here and now together with a development of itself that is partly constructive or positive and partly critical or negative' (IH, 334).

The necessary function of historical thought in solving present problems applies not only to theoretical but also to practical problems: having discussed Einstein's advance on Newton, Collingwood observes: 'similarly with any other progress', giving the following example:

> If we want to abolish capitalism or war, and in doing so not only to destroy them but to bring into existence something better, we must begin by understanding them ... This understanding of the system we set out to supersede is a thing which we must retain throughout the work of superseding it, as a knowledge of the past conditioning our creation of the future. (IH, 334)

It should be noted in this connection that it was Knox who gave the essay on progress in *The Idea of History* the title 'Progress as Created by Historical Thinking', the title in the manuscript simply being 'Progress'.[14] Collingwood refers to this creative aspect only once, in his statement that there is, besides determining whether progress has actually occurred, 'one other thing for historical thought to do: namely to create this progress itself' (IH, 333). This statement should be interpreted to mean that historical thought is a necessary condition for any form of progress, since it is only from this that scientists, historians or philosophers can see their own work as an advancement. The idea of progress itself could then be understood as having the function of serving as a guiding principle in solving present problems. As such, its position is similar to the regulative function of 'ideas' in the Kantian sense (Kant's own *Idea for a Universal History from a Cosmopolitan Point of View* is a good example of this use).[15] This is made clear by the way Collingwood concludes his article on 'A Philosophy of Progress':

> The question whether, on the whole, history shows a progress can be answered, as we now see, by asking another question. Have you the courage of your convictions? If you have, if you regard the things which you are doing as things worth doing, then the course of history which has led to the doing of them is justified by its results, and its movement is a movement forward. (PP, 120)

## V

Summing up the discussion thus far, the following distinctions may be made within Collingwood's views on progress. The first meaning of the concept of progress is one used in a wide sense: when it is equated with the historical process being developmental and of an orderly nature. This is the way the past is dealt with by historians, that is, the events are described in such a way that they are connected both logically and temporally.[16] These logical and temporal relations can only be seen retrospectively, however. This means that it is not implied that they are prospectively determined. On the contrary, Collingwood clearly states in *The New Leviathan* that 'there are no laws of development or progress' (NL, 7.28) and he declares in the same book that in mental development 'there is nothing in A to necessitate B; nothing in A+B to necessitate C; nothing in A+B+C to necessitate D.' It is always possible that developments cease. This is called the Law of Contingency: 'the earlier terms in a series of mental functions do not determine the later' (NL, 9.48).

As we have seen, Collingwood is also against the idea of comparing historical periods or 'ways of life' in the sense of one being an advance on the other, that is, the use of the idea of progress in the strict sense, in contrast to the wide sense as used in historiography. In this connection he simply used to remark that the periods with which a historian is well acquainted are seen as luminous and progressive, while the periods with which he has little acquaintance are considered dark, primitive and irrational.[17]

In solving present problems, both theoretical and practical, the situation is different, however. For we have seen that, in Collingwood's view, in this context the idea of progress is necessary, and the relation between past and present is viewed accordingly. The difference is, as has been argued, that in this case the past is not viewed in the detached way of an historian, but as a participant. That is, in the theoretical field scientists, historians or philosophers necessarily see their own work as an advance on the past, the concept of progress being used as a guiding principle. This is exemplified, for instance, by Collingwood himself, when he closes his *Essay on Philosophical Method* by expressing the hope that through the methodological principles as outlined in that book 'philosophy may . . . set its feet once more on the path of progress'. (EPM, 226)

## VI

We have seen that Collingwood is of the opinion that the idea of progress also serves as a guiding principle in practical life. Collingwood spent a good deal of time illustrating this with regard to the idea of civilization. In the following this will be examined in more detail.

Though the concept of civilization is discussed extensively in *The New Leviathan*, the manuscript 'What "Civilization" Means', which was written in preparation for *The New Leviathan*, is of special interest here.[18] In both studies it is emphasized, however, that civilization should be seen as a process and that it cannot be separated from its opposite, barbarism.

In the manuscript Collingwood uses his conception of a scale of forms by saying that in an absolute sense civilization and barbarism are two ends of a scale, with many intermediate terms, which as such are not really existing conditions of any society. In a relative sense, however, a society 'is civilized as compared with one lower down in the scale, and barbarous as compared with one higher up' (NL, 488). Collingwood rejects, however, the conception of civilization in the absolute sense as the point towards which the civilizing process is directed, and barbarism as the one from which it is directed. For this implies the typical nineteenth-century idea that the civilizing process has always and everywhere been identical. This 'historical monism' should in his opinion be replaced by a 'historical pluralism', that is, the idea that there are different kinds of civilization, each with their own characteristics. The consequence is that each civilization has its own standards and will be inclined to consider the standards of other civilizations as barbarous.

This seems to imply a historical relativism. This suggestion is rejected, however, by Collingwood, since this would only be true, he argues, if merely the actual behaviour of people is taken into consideration. What is left out in this case is the element of certain ideals, which are considered by Collingwood a crucial aspect of the concept of civilization. He makes in this connection a distinction between three orders of ideals. The first one is the level of ideals within a society that are realized: this is the factual level which indeed shows a wide divergence, both within a society and between societies and various periods. The second order is composed of ideals which are recognized but not yet realized:

> Every man who is civilized in a certain way and up to a certain degree recognizes other ways and higher degrees in which he might be civilized and is not to that extent conscious of shortcomings in his own civilization. This implies that, in addition to the ideal of civilization which he both recognizes and realizes, he has another ideal of civilization which he recognizes but does not realize. (NL, 491–2)

These ideals of the second order differ less than the realized ideals of the first order.

Finally Collingwood distinguishes a third-order ideal in which all particularities of the ideals of various civilizations are left behind, that is, an ideal of universal civility or civility as such. This is the sense, Collingwood says in the manuscript, 'in which all civilizations, or ways of living in a civilized manner, are one' (NL, 494). In *The New Leviathan* the idea of three orders of ideals within a civilization is not discussed, but the third order is worked out, one could say, in the chapters 'What "Civilization" Means: Specifically' and 'The Essence of Civilization'. In the first he says that 'civilization has something to do with the mutual relations of members within a community . . . with the relation of these members to the world of nature; and . . . with the relation between them and other human beings not being members of the same community' (NL, 35.34).[19]

In the manuscript 'What "Civilization" Means' the second order of not realized, though recognized, ideals plays a vital role. The discrepancies between the achieved ideals of the first order and the non-achieved of the second are called by Collingwood the elements of barbarism within a civilization. His conception of barbarism is crucial for his argument, especially with regard to the idea of progress. For he rejects the conception that the civilization process should be seen as a sort of long-range plan in which certain aspects of barbarity are demolished in the course of time. Elements of barbarism should not be seen as relics of a past evolutionary stage, Collingwood argues, but as creations of the civilization process itself. He gives as examples the poverty resulting from the industrial revolution and the horrors of modern warfare from technological developments (NL, 496).

It is not accidental that the two examples of barbarous elements within the civilization process used by Collingwood are both in the sphere of technological developments. For of the three constituents of civilization mentioned in *The New Leviathan* (the relation between members of a community, the relation with the world of nature and the relation with members of other communities) the second is the only one where the concept of progress is explicitly mentioned, implying, as we will see, the possibility of regress. To learn to save one's muscles by using one's brains, Collingwood maintains, 'is to become civilized relatively to the world of nature: to progress in the second constituent of civilization' (NL, 35.53), and hereafter it is stated that 'a community that becomes relatively civilized becomes relatively good at exploiting the natural world in a scientific or intelligent way' (NL, 38.1).

A partial progress in civilization of that sort is not equated by Collingwood, however, with progress in civilization as such. On the contrary, he considers it only as a neutral opportunity inherited from the past, an opportunity which may also be used in a way leading to barbarism. The greater the achievements of a civilizing process, Collingwood avers,

> the more power it puts into the hands of men for evil as well as good. Every new advance in civilization, once achieved, has a double face. For those who wish to behave in a civilized manner it gives new opportunities for civilized behaviour; for those who wish to behave barbarously it gives opportunities to create new forms of barbarism. (NL, 496–7)

What is inherited from ancestry are certain facts, which make up the situation in which one has to act, Collingwood continues. Though the facts related to the control of nature, as mentioned by him before, are certainly the more concrete ones, he also refers to social and legal facts. What is not inherited, however, Collingwood emphasizes, is man's will: 'Every man has to make his will for himself' (NL, 497). 'Is there, then, no progress?' Collingwood asks. His answer is: 'certainly there is progress.' And after this he continues:

> What one generation inherits is not identical with what the last generation inherited. Our fathers have left us opportunities greater than those which their fathers left to them. Opportunities progress. What does not progress is the human will, which is just as capable of using its opportunities well or ill as it always has been: just as capable of recognizing and realizing ideals, just as capable of yielding to temptation. The greater the opportunities it inherits, the greater the temptation to abuse them. This temptation, which no progress can abolish, is the origin of barbarism. (NL, 497–8)

In *The New Leviathan* the same position is presented. Discussing mind, he observes, after saying that there are no laws of development or progress: 'Occasions arise when certain kinds of progress, certain steps in development are possible for a mind.' After this he continues: 'They are never necessary. Whether the mind takes the step that is possible for it depends entirely on the mind's practical energy' (NL, 7.28–7.29). This view is in line with the emphasis put by Collingwood further on in the same book on the role of the will in the civilizing process. In the chapter on 'The Essence of Civilization' he maintains that 'with the appearance of free will in human life, begins the process of civilization' (NL, 36.84) and that 'civilization is the process in a community by which the various members assert themselves as will: severally as individual will, corporately as social will' (NL, 36.89). His conclusion is that 'the will to civilization is just will':

> The members of any non-social community who, awaking to free will, decide no longer to drift with their emotions, but to take charge of the situation in which they corporately find themselves and do something with it, whatever in particular they decide to do, have embarked on the process of civilizing themselves. (NL, 36.93)

In contrast to this, the will to barbarism is described as a will to do nothing, 'a will to acquiesce in the chaotic rule of emotion' (NL, 36.94).

In summary, the essence of Collingwood's view on the process of civilization may be described by saying that though the aspect of the inheritance from the past (the 'factual' side) indeed is a necessary condition for it, the aspect of the human will is of primordial importance. It is neither inherited nor determined. As with the solution of theoretical and practical problems it is guided, though, by the idea of progress. This is made clear in the paragraph called 'The Dialectic of Discontent' in the manuscript 'What "Civilization" Means'. By discontent Collingwood means the awareness 'of a discrepancy between what is already realized in your own society and what you would wish to be realized there' (NL, 498). He equates this with the awareness of barbarous elements in one's civilization. Discussing in this connection the reforming attitude Collingwood says:

> Civilization and the advancement of civilization are one and the same. The will to be civilized is identical with the will to become more civilized. To go on thinking is to go on discovering and correcting your own errors; to go on being civilized is to go on detecting and eradicating the barbarous elements in your own civilization. (NL, 500)

Collingwood is of the opinion, however, that the factual side of the situation should not be neglected. A wise discontent, he says, 'does not cease to ask the question "What ideal do we want to realize?"'. But, studying the facts of social life and considering what opportunities they present, converts it into the question 'what ideal can we realize here and now?' This is a harder question to answer: but it is worth answering' (NL, 501).

Though it is not mentioned explicitly by Collingwood it is obvious that since the facts of social life are inherited from the past, it is only by historical knowledge that they can be known. Taking Collingwood's view on the character of civilization into consideration it is also evident, however, that it is in this case not correct to claim that progress is created by historical thought, as he does, as we have seen, with regard to the solution of theoretical and practical problems. For in the case of civilization it is human will that is pivotal: though itself not progressing, it is in Collingwood's view the basis for progress in civilization. This does not preclude, though, that historical knowledge plays a role as well. Its function should rather be seen, one could say, in more general terms, as described by Collingwood in his 'Lectures on the Philosophy of History' of 1926.[20] Collingwood makes in them the observation that 'history is nothing but the attempt to understand the present by analysing it into its logical components of necessity, or the past, and possibility, or the future; and this is an attempt that is made by everybody and at all times' (IH, 422). From this point of view the idea of progress in civilization, made concrete in certain ideals for the future, may indeed be seen as a guiding principle in deciding which possibilities, and consequently opportunities, should be realized.

## Notes

[1] In the text references to *The New Leviathan* and *The Idea of History* are made to the revised editions. The following abbreviations are used for essays from *R. G. Collingwood: Essays in the Philosophy of History*, ed. W. Debbins (Austin, University of Texas Press, 1965): CPH: 'Croce's Philosophy of History'; THC: 'The Theory of Historical Cycles'; PP: 'A Philosophy of Progress'.

[2] Quoted from the manuscript 'Notes toward a Metaphysic', in W. J. van der Dussen, *History as a Science: the Philosophy of R. G. Collingwood* (The Hague, Nijhoff, 1981), 269.

[3] A copy of this essay has recently been added to the collection of manuscripts deposited at the Bodleian Library in Oxford.

[4] See D. S. Taylor, *R. G. Collingwood: a Bibliography: the Complete Manuscripts and Publications, Selected Secondary Writings, with Selective Annotation* (New York and London, Garland, 1988), no.1.63.

[5] 'Notes toward a Metaphysic', DEP 15.

⁶ 'In point of fact, he [the historian] can only see it [history] in bits; he can only be acquainted with certain periods, and only be competent in very small parts of those periods'; '. . . we see history split up into disconnected episodes, each episode forming a relatively intelligible whole, separated from its neighbours by dark ages' (THC, 87, 88); 'Every period of which we have competent knowledge . . . appears in the perspective of time as an age of brilliance' (IH, 327–8).

⁷ 'The condition is that the person who uses the word [progress] should use it in comparing two historical periods or ways of life . . .' (IH, 328–9).

⁸ Collingwood's lectures under this title are part of the revised edn of *The Idea of History*, ed. by Jan van der Dussen (Oxford, Clarendon Press, 1993), 426–96.

⁹ The argument developed in this context is similar to the argument used in the discussion of the alleged intellectual superiority of Western civilization as against 'primitive' civilizations, for here too Collingwood is of the opinion that 'civilized man . . . mistakes the superiority of his tools for a superiority in himself' (quoted in van der Dussen, *History as a Science*, 191).

¹⁰ See Taylor, *Bibliography*, no.1.93.

¹¹ 'The Function of Metaphysics in Civilization', 36.

¹² Ibid., 37.

¹³ In the same vein Collingwood contends in the 'Outlines of a Philosophy of History' that 'progress relatively to a certain conception of that which is progressing is intelligible enough.' After this he continues: 'If I have a certain conception of what science is, then I may be able to say that science progressed in the nineteenth century; that is to say, my history of nineteenth-century science may show it as becoming more and more scientific. If I had a different conception of what science is, I might have been obliged to say that it was becoming less and less scientific' (IH, 479).

¹⁴ See Editor's Introduction in the revised edn of *The Idea of History*, xiii–xiv.

¹⁵ In the 'Outlines of a Philosophy of History' Collingwood says of this essay by Kant: 'he threw out the suggestion that the idea of cosmopolitan citizenship could be treated . . . as the subject-matter of an essay covering the whole of recorded history. And if it were so treated, he saw, and saw rightly, that the narrative would be a narrative of progress, of the gradual consolidation of an ideal whose presence in one form or another could be traced throughout that period' (IH, 481).

¹⁶ 'What I want to suggest here is', Collingwood says in his 'Notes toward a Metaphysic', 'that history is the coincidence of logical with temporal order. I mean that the successive events of history form an order which, so far as it is genuinely historical (not all chronological sequences of

events in human life are so), is a logical order as well as a temporal one. If it is temporal but not logical, the sequence is not historical but merely chronological – it is what Croce calls annals, or a mere series of events' ('Notes toward a Metaphysic', A 69).

17 In 'The Theory of Historical Cycles', for instance, Collingwood remarks:

Each period with which we are tolerably acqainted, each period which we understand well enough to appreciate the problems and motives of its agents, stands out as something luminous, intelligible, rational, and therefore admirable. But each period is an island of light in a sea of darkness. If we ask why it arose out of barbarism, and why it relapsed into barbarism, we cannot answer, and the reason is that if we knew enough to answer the question we should cease to ask it. (THC, 88)

18 The manuscript 'What "Civilization" Means' is printed in the revised edn of *The New Leviathan*, ed. David Boucher (Oxford, Clarendon Press,1992), 480–511.

19 In the manuscript 'What "Civilization" Means' a slightly different description is given of three senses of 'civilize': 'being civilized in relation to the material world means being able to master the forces of nature and use them for one's own ends'; 'the social definition . . . is that which concerns a man's relation to the world of human beings'; 'the legal definition . . . means a society governed by law', especially the civil law (NL, 502).

20 These lectures are part of the revised edn of *The Idea of History*, 359–425.

# The Place of Education in Civilization

## DAVID BOUCHER

> If we could suppose an agreement made between a statesman and a sage that one should make the laws of a nation and the other its schools, there would be no doubt which of the two would have the destiny of the nation in his hands.
>
> T. H. Green, *Works*, III, 413

## I

Collingwood's strong, and somewhat intemperate views, expressed in *An Autobiography* and in conversations with friends and students, on the English public school system, occasioned by his own unpleasant experience of the transition from an informal general education, which served to develop his inquisitive instincts, to a formal rigid system, which appeared to him to be designed to inhibit and suppress those very same instincts,[1] along with the view that he articulated in *The New Leviathan* that parents should assume the responsibility of educating their own offspring in order to save those children from the pernicious and iniquitous influence of professional educators, have tended to be viewed with incredulity or ridicule[2] and have thus tended to act as a barrier to serious discussion about his theory of education. However, I want to suggest that these views of Collingwood's are in fact important to his educational theory, but that concentration upon the tone rather than the spirit of what he says detracts from the very important place that education had in his philosophy as a whole. The fact that he sent his own son to public school may betray a certain insincerity, but what should be emphasized is Collingwood's focus in the first instance on who is being taught, that is the natural development of the child, rather than upon the formal subject matter of the curriculum. It is undeniable that Collingwood's views on the role of parents in education echo the modern move to transfer the authority of the teacher to the parent. In this respect he stands in the tradition of Rousseau and Dewey.[3] The question of how one might reverse the reliance upon the state occasioned by the deplorable and inadequate provision of education before the state made it compulsory is not a question I can pursue here.

It needs to be emphasized at the outset that to focus upon Collingwood's theory of education is not to isolate an aspect of his thought, but to look at the whole from the vantage point of the particular in which the whole is reflected. This holistic approach necessarily entails a good deal of scene-setting and a certain amount of self-denial in that hares are set running but often not pursued, in order to avoid being distracted from the main purpose of coming to an understanding of the role of education in civilization.

In this chapter I want to bring together Collingwood's various and scattered statements on education, from both his published and unpublished works, in order to show the extent to which he believed education to be crucial to the promotion of the ideals of civilization, and to the formation of the character of the individual. There are at least four aspects to Collingwood's educational theory: first, the process of learning; second, the purpose of teaching; third, the content of teaching; and, fourth, the manner of teaching. The first aspect entails a detailed exposition of Collingwood's philosophy of mind. Collingwood's philosophy of mind has received extensive consideration in the works of Alan Donagan, Louis Mink and Lionel Rubinoff, and the learning process has been explicitly linked to this philosophy by Sherman M. Stanage.[4] The detail of the process of learning and its relation to the levels of consciousness is beyond the scope of this chapter. It is imperative, however, to give an indication of Collingwood's philosophy of mind in order to illuminate the second, third and fourth aspects of Collingwood's educational theory. In short, then, this essay is principally concerned with the purpose, content and manner of teaching. The three aspects are integrally related, but nevertheless distinct. We may find the argument for the purpose and content of the teaching compelling, for example, while failing to be convinced by the manner of teaching proposed.

## II

For the British Idealists in general, education had a narrow institutional meaning, but also a broader sense in which the organized will of society was at once the exemplar and facilitator of virtue fulfilling the educative function of the state. In this respect they were inspired by Hegel and the Greeks in believing that the best education a person could have was to be born and brought up in a good state. We see throughout the *Elements of the Philosophy of Right*, for example, how the purpose of education is to liberate people from ignorance, expose as misconceived the idea that the law is externally imposed, and achieve the realization that in the good state law is the expression of one's own will, and a self-imposition.

Philosophical Idealism in general was premised upon the belief that a civilized or good life is indistinguishable from acting virtuously. Consciousness of freedom entails acknowledging that same attainment in others, and eliminating from one's conduct the use of force, physical or mental, in relations with them. Acting virtuously, which also meant rationally, required knowledge, and knowledge required education. Education was absolutely imperative for good citizenship. A democratic society required for rational political decision-making an educated and informed public, the responsibility for which was the duty of the whole citizen body. A developed degree of cognitive competence was the precondition of a civilized life.

In relation to the general role of education, in the broader sense, its importance for Collingwood in his theory of civilization cannot be overestimated. Education is the means 'by which a civilization keeps itself alive from one generation to the next' (NL, 39.18). It is the means by which the inheritance of civilization is passed on to succeeding generations.[5] European civilization has become such a complex affair that finding one's way about in it demands long 'educational preparation' (NL, 22.31). Educating pupils in the inheritance of civilization must equip and prepare them for practical adult life and at all times aim to bring about the betterment of human nature.[6] Education, then, is not the mere provider of such accomplishments as reading, writing and arithmetic. These are the external features of education, but more fundamentally there is an inner purpose to education and that is to develop the character of the individual and promote self-control over one's 'own lower nature . . . which is the best gift that a good education can impart'.[7]

Education, then, is meant to initiate the pupil into the inheritance of civilization, but at the same time facilitate the development of the capacity to enjoy such an inheritance. In other words, it is engaged in the business of 'helping a mind to create itself, to grow into an active and vigorous contributor to the life of the world' (SM., 316). One of the principal purposes of education for Collingwood is to develop the mind up to the level of mental maturity. What this means is that the mind must be nurtured into developing through various stages of consciousness, emerging in the end into the life of rational consciousness. The specifications of the number and nature of the levels of consciousness are articulated in *The Principles of Art* and modified in *The New Leviathan*. A brief characterization of the specifications is necessary in order to highlight the role Collingwood envisaged for education.

In *The Principles of Art*, *The Idea of History*, and also in *An Essay on Metaphysics*, Collingwood distinguishes between the psyche and the spirit, maintaining that the psyche is the proper domain of psychology.[8] Psychology, for Collingwood, is a non-criteriological science in that it does not concern itself with the self-critical aspects of thought. It can therefore only have appropriate things to say about the feelings and emotions which occur at the psychic level of experience. Psychology becomes transformed into a dangerous pseudo-science as soon as it permits itself to offer conclusions about thought. Thought is self-critical and to ignore this is to misrepresent the nature of thought (EM, ch.XI). The understanding of mind is the province of historical inquiry. In understanding the development of mind two important principles have to be acknowledged. First, the development is contingent and therefore cannot be predicted. To paraphrase Hegel, where the spirit is concerned the logic of the past does not enable us to foretell the future. Secondly, borrowing a notion from Tylor, 'primitive survivals' of previous levels of consciousness are to be found in the higher (NL, 9.43–9.55).[9]

In *The Principles of Art* Collingwood identifies a psychical level of feeling whose mode of expression is quite distinct from those associated with consciousness. 'Psychical expression' is physiological rather than linguistic. Facial distortions, for example, may express pain and the dilation of the pupils of the eye may be expressive of fear. The problem, in Collingwood's view is how we move from this psychical level of feeling to that of intellect. To bridge the gap between feeling and intellect, an explanation has to be given of how mind makes connections between the various sensa. In order to make such connections between fleeting and transitory sensations which have ceased to be sensed, a level of consciousness has to be postulated which recalls past sensations and relates them to those currently being sensed. In order to compare and distinguish sensations, they must be attended to. In other words, we must become conscious of them. Consciousness facilitates identification of what we hear, see, taste, smell and touch. The act of becoming conscious of feelings is not at the same time the act of relating one sensation to another. The sensa identified still have to be interpreted and related to other sensa. 'Imagination' enables us to recall and retain sensa which are no longer sensed. Consciousness and imagination both refer to the same level of experience within which the former converts sensa into the latter. 'Intellect' establishes the relations and makes the inferences between sensa which imagination has recalled and retained.

It is necessary to dwell a little here on the place of imagination in the life of the mind because, as we will see, its proper cultivation is of profound significance for personal development and for the survival of civilization. In *Speculum Mentis* Collingwood argues that art is 'pure imagination' (SM, 61), by which he meant that 'facts' and propositions, or assertions about reality, are absent from the 'world of imaginations' (SM, 61). Children and savages, Collingwood contends, are natural artists whose imaginations have a free rein. Civilized human beings can only achieve this artistic experience by shutting out the objects they see historically or scientifically in order to see them aesthetically (SM, 58). The mind is not a machine which manufactures artistic objects;

instead the mind 'creates itself as the activity of imagination by creating these works of art which are its imaginary objects' (SM, 65).

Thought in its most rudimentary form, in Collingwood's view, is art. Play is the counterpart of, and even identical with, art in that it is the form which the most rudimentary kind of action takes. Aesthetic consciousness has a theoretical side, which is art, and a practical side, which is play. The importance of the aesthetic consciousness is that in its innocence it allows us to have a foretaste of what condition a mind achieves, having faced its problems and overcome them. Art enables the mind to reach out into the unknown, whereas play treats the world as a place in which adventures can be perpetually enacted. Collingwood is quite emphatic that 'the spirit of play, the spirit of eternal youth, is the foundation and beginning of all real life' (SM, 107). Art, which is imagination, is the foundation upon which all other forms of experience are built,[10] and imagination is 'the first step in the growth of knowledge'.[11]

In *The Principles of Art* Collingwood argues not that art is pure imagination, but that it is the expression of emotion. In his view, language comes into existence with the emergence of imagination. It is consciousness, as we saw, which converts sensa into imagination. The function of language at the level of consciousness, or imagination, is to express emotion. Art and language are identical in that they are both the imaginative activity of expressing emotion (PA, 274). The ability to express one's emotions is particularly important in the development of consciousness. It is only in expressing an emotion that we become conscious of it. Consciousness of the emotion is an acknowledgement of what we are feeling. Selective attention to sensa makes it possible to divide emotional experiences into those we wish to acknowledge and those we do not. If we fail to express an emotion we effectively disown it, and repress it. Consciousness fails to convert psychic emotions into imaginative expression. In this 'corruption of consciousness' what intellect receives is a series of false emotional expressions upon which to build its thought (PA, 217-20, 251, 282-5 and 336).

Allied to Collingwood's theory of emotion, with art being its expression, is his idea that magic (or folk practices) is also a necessary vehicle of emotional expression and emotional arousal.

We look at magical practices in the lives of savages, and folk customs in the rituals of agricultural peoples and the uneducated classes, and conclude with disdain that they are the irrational and senseless acts of ignorant human beings. This, in Collingwood's view, is a total misconception: 'for magic, which sums up all that we dislike in savage life, is beginning to reveal itself as the systematic and organized expression of emotion'.[12]

Artistic activities, such as dancing, the singing of songs, drawing and modelling, are integral elements in magical rituals. Magic differs from art in that it is directed towards a preconceived end, and in this respect it is more akin to craft (PA, 65). The purpose of magic is to arouse in us certain emotions which are channelled into the inspired performance of our practical and necessary activities of life. Magic generates the emotional energy vital for the survival of any society. Collingwood contends that 'Magical activity is a kind of dynamo supplying the mechanism of practical life with the emotional current that drives it' (PA, 69). We tend to think that our own mental development has surpassed that in which magic has a positive and dynamic role, and in this respect we are deluding ourselves. Modern society includes within its customs numerous magical practices,[13] and without these practices emotional expression becomes artificially suppressed. A healthy society needs magical practices to channel its emotions into positive enterprises. To take just one example: dance is a magical practice and in its modern forms is, for the most part, a ritual associated with courtship. The emotion aroused and expressed is not fully expended in the dance, but is intended to bear fruit in the creation of a future partnership (PA, 76).

In summary, imagination, the level of consciousness at which art and magic express emotions, is an intermediary level between feeling and intellect. In imagination, Collingwood argues, 'the life of thought makes contact with the life of purely psychical experience . . . it is not sensa as such that provide the data for intellect, it is sensa transformed into ideas of imagination by the work of consciousness' (PA, 202–3). Imagination, it should be emphasized is present in the higher levels of consciousness, and enables the historian, for example, imaginatively to re-enact the past, on the basis of present evidence. We will see the importance of history in the curriculum in due course. Thus the development of imagination is imperative.

In *The New Leviathan* Collingwood reformulates his theory of mind. The psychic level of experience, or the level of feeling and sensa, no longer stands outside consciousness. This level is now termed simple consciousness, and that of which it is conscious is simple feeling. Feelings, however, remain transitory: they begin to fade as soon as they are experienced. Knowledge is alien to this level of consciousness and can only be attained when more sophisticated forms of consciousness arise. Second-order consciousness is the level at which conceptual thinking takes place. This involves attending to what is present to simple consciousness and subjecting it to questioning. After having identified the feeling, say a noise that emanates from without, the mind attempts to discover the origin by comparing it with similar noises it imagines or recollects that it has heard (NL, 4.3.–4.37). To evoke feelings which are not those to which you are attending is to arouse in yourself, through the medium of thought, feelings that are not immediately sensed.

The first-order object of the second level of consciousness is Appetite. It is an unsatisfactory feeling-state of the *actual self* which is contrasted with the satisfactory feeling-state of the *ideal self*. Hunger, one of the two forms which appetite takes, impels you toward an indeterminate feeling-state. The ideal-self is an idiomorphic God; 'the infinite satisfaction of man's hunger: man itself become omnipotent' (NL, 8.29). Hunger becomes modified by love. Love is the source of differentiating between the self and not-self.

Love postulates something other than yourself. Something that can satisfy the loneliness of your present dissatisfaction. The idiomorphic God is replaced in love by the heteromorphic God who is the object of love. Each lover is a heteromorphic God to the other. In love you create the object of your satisfaction and in doing so a relation is created between yourself and an other self. This is the origin of both the self and not-self. The not-self has the power to throw you into a passion by merely frustrating the satisfaction of your demands. All you can ascertain in reflecting upon the hindrance is that a not-self of indeterminate character has acted upon you and provoked a reaction. This is Passion, which manifests itself in the forms of fear and anger. Shame converts fear into anger, and it 'is in a larger sense a critical point in the whole development of mind: for unlike a man in a condition of appetite a man in a condition of shame knows what he wants: he wants to be *brave*; not devoid of fear, but triumphant over fear' (NL, 10.5). Anger forms the bridge from the lower levels of consciousness, in which thought receives what is given and conceptualizes abstractions from it, to the third and fourth levels. In the third, propositional thinking develops, and in the fourth, rational consciousness, or will, emerges.

Desire and happiness are the corollaries of the third level of consciousness. Desire differs from appetite in that it knows what it wants. In desire you face alternatives. To accept one alternative entails the rejection of the other. Truth and error emerge in relation to desire in that the alternative decided upon may be a true or false expression of the desire. Knowing yourself becomes possible in knowing 'what you want' (NL, 11.39). Desiring something bestows goodness upon the thing desired. We do not desire things because they are good; they are good because we desire them. What human beings desire is happiness, that is, being able to dominate circumstances rather than be dominated by them. Being at the mercy of your passions is to be unhappy. In relation to the not-self, unhappiness is being weak, that is, being dominated by others and by circumstances. In the twentieth century the manifestation of this unhappiness is the powerlessness with which we face the overwhelming power of economic, social and political forces.

Reason is absent from the three levels of consciousness discussed so far. For example, at the level of Desire we are not making choices. What we desire is not a matter of choice. Someone who prefers apples to bananas is not choosing between the two. That person 'suffers desire for *a* and aversion towards *b*'. The desire leads the person in one direction rather than in another (NL, 13.14). We can only make a choice when the alternatives are open. Freedom is not something attained by making a choice. To choose presupposes freedom, and freedom is achieved by an act of self-liberation. It involves breaking free of desire and making choices. In positive terms this means the free exercise of will, and in negative terms it is to be free from being dominated by desire. Why people liberate themselves is inexplicable because they are at the third level of consciousness incapable of appreciating the potential rewards of self-liberation.

Language is crucial to the development of the mind because

without language there is no thought, and without thought the mind cannot progress from the lowest to the highest stage of consciousness. You cannot confer upon a person the freedom presupposed in choice. Self-liberation from enslaving desires is what makes freedom possible, and it can only be attained by naming the desire. In refusing to let desire dictate to us we become conscious of our freedom and acquire a self-respect lacking in the three levels of consciousness prior to the fourth.

It is the role of education, both social and political, to promote in persons the consciousness of freedom. Education must ensure that those people who are only pre-consciously free, that is, capable of making choices but who are not yet aware of possessing freedom, are made conscious of their freedom and stimulated to develop their self-respect. Put simply, the role of education is the attainment of cognitive competence which will enable every potential citizen to achieve his or her potential and participate fully in the political and social life of the community.

It is the transition from the third to the fourth levels of consciousness that is crucial to Collingwood's social and political philosophy. Without freedom of the will no society and no civilization is possible. Education, although unable to confer freedom, facilitates the conversion from the stage of propositional to rational thinking, and promotes the development of the will from the lowest to the highest stage of rational activity. Having attained freedom of the will, rationality is a matter of degree. Within the fourth level of consciousness itself there are levels of rational action, all of which differ in progressive degrees from simple choice, which is completely capricious. Caprice is 'mere choice or mere decision, uncomplicated by any reason why it should be made in this way and not that' (NL, 13.12). Here we have a will, but not a rational will. We begin to leave caprice behind once we seek reasons, both for our choices and for why we believe that certain propositions are true. There are three types of reason, Collingwood suggests, given in answer to the question, 'why did you do that?' First, I did it because it was useful; second, because it was right, and third, because it was my duty. The initial stage of rational action is utilitarian, that is, the equation of means and ends; the second, regularian action which equates activity with the following of rules; and, the third, is dutiful action, the only form which is truly moral, and which is informed by your historical consciousness of what it is imperative for *you* to do given the circumstances. At each stage the element of caprice is gradually reduced. Duty, the highest form of practical reason, is in principle totally free of caprice and completely determinate.

In true Hegelian fashion, Collingwood believes that to think of oneself as free is correlative with thinking of others as being free, and as people between whom relations exist. To be conscious of being free entails association with other free agents. The association between free agents can only become manifest in the form of social relations. Rational and social consciousness are simply two sides of the same coin: Collingwood emphasizes this by saying that 'No man can think himself free except as integrated in a context of other free men constituting with himself a society' (NL, 21.76).

The idea of a society presupposes individuals who have attained the level of rational consciousness and who thus respect themselves. Self-respect generates respect for others. To be conscious of your own freedom is to be conscious of others as the possessors of freedom. Consciously free persons comprise a society whose members agree together to pursue joint enterprises. In a society, each mentally adult person recognizes that the freedom he, or she, claims to possess must also be possessed by others. Each person must acknowledge that the wills of others are the source of rules which are binding upon everyone: 'And this is not a mutual slavery, because the joint enterprises out of which these rules grow are pursued by each party of his own free will.'[14] Freedom and society, then, are inextricably related.

A society does not exist in isolation and must concern itself with matters of self-preservation and perpetuation. A society, for the most part, is an entity in a mixed community, the latter comprising non-social and social elements, that is, mentally immature and mentally mature persons, the one group devoid of consciousness of freedom of will and the other possessing it. A family, for instance, is a mixed community of temporary duration, and a body politic is one of permanent duration. In both forms of mixed community those of its members who lack the capacity of free will are incapable of ruling, because ruling presupposes freedom of choice. A non-social community cannot exist without being ruled, and cannot rule itself. A society, on the other hand, exercises self-rule, that is, it is self-determining; the rulers and the ruled are the same people. This is what Collingwood calls immanent rule. Where one group of people rule over another this constitutes a case of transeunt rule (NL, 20.37.– 20.39). A social community, by exercising joint will, is capable of bringing itself into existence, whereas a non-social community is not. The former, however, may bring into existence the latter, over which it exercises transeunt rule. The relation between the non-social community and the social community, which together comprise a mixed community, is one of force, which in this context means the mental superiority of one group over another (NL, 20.1– 20.6).

Education, without a doubt, is central to this whole theory. It is education which facilitates conversion from the non-social to the social element within the mixed community. The family, for instance, is a mixed community comprising mature adults who have, in principle, freely chosen to enter into the society of marriage. In producing offspring, these adults create a non-social community over which they exercise transeunt rule. In cultures less developed than those of modern Europe, puberty heralds the entry of the child into adult membership of the tribe. In modern Europe, however, the complexities of life, which are bound up with cultural practices, make it imperative that our children receive a longer 'educational preparation' (NL, 22.32) before becoming initiated into the social element of the family. Parents exercise transeunt rule over their children with the intention of helping them to achieve mental and physical maturity with a view to incorporating them into the 'family-society' (NL, 23.6). Such a process is achieved by education: partly by self-education, partly by the parents, and partly by others. There is no automatic transition to the family-society. Having reached a certain degree of maturity the child must be helped in the conversion process by being welcomed as an equal by the parents. The education which the child receives must always make clear the promise of future incorporation into the family-society, and of being welcomed as an equal when signs of mental maturity become evident. Once again, then, we see cognitive competence the goal of education.

Similarly, in the body politic there is a ruling social element and a ruled non-social element. One of the principal laws of politics, Collingwood claims, is that the barrier between the rulers and the ruled is at all times permeable.[15] Unlike the social element in a family, the social element in a body politic is a permanent society, the members of which are obliged to be constantly vigilant about replenishing their numbers. Indeed, 'political activity and political education are inseparable, if not identical.'[16] In Collingwood's view, 'The body politic, like the family, contains a nursery; in this case a ruled class which is a nursery of rulers as containing human beings in a process of education for the business of rule' (NL, 27.12). The rulers are concerned to induct into their ranks recruits from the non-social community, and this induction is in fact a process of education. What Collingwood means by induction is the inspirational effect that someone of a stronger will may have upon someone who is weaker in this respect. Rulers must set high standards in discharging their public duties in order to provide exemplars for the future rulers to emulate: 'The ruler as path-finder is the ruler as setter of examples.'[17] Inspiration of this kind can only be effective upon those who have just attained, or who are about to attain, the level of freedom of the will. For Collingwood, the 'inductive process often repeated is an important part of all education' (NL, 25.52). The qualities associated with good leadership are learned by responding to good leadership. Good leaders are careful at all times to teach their followers to be good leaders themselves. Rulers, or the social element in the body politic, are like parents concerned to convert what is not a society into a society 'by bringing about a capacity for free will in human beings which hitherto did not possess it, in other words educating them up to mental maturity' (NL, 32.31).[18]

If this were all that education aspired to do then social life would not have progressed very far. However, education seeks to attain more than the conversion of individuals from a non-social to a social condition. It is meant also to develop in people a social consciousness which gradually renounces eristic or adversarial methods of solving disputes, and adopts a dialectic or conciliatory approach to overcoming differences. In other words, education has the role of refining social relations and promoting mutual respect in order that society approximates to the ideal of civility.

Civilization is the name that Collingwood gives to the process of socializing a community towards the ideal of civility. To civilize and to socialize are in fact the same thing (NL, 37.22). Both are the education process directed at converting the non-social into the social, and encouraging the social to approximate to the ideal of civility. Education and civilization are integrally related in the thought of Collingwood. In an essay written in 1936 he makes the connection quite explicit. He says: 'What education is to an individual, civilization is to a people.'[19] In *The New Leviathan* education becomes the civilizing process itself: 'In the case of the family, the agent in this process is the parental society, and the name of the process is education' (NL, 40.63). In the case of the community at large the agent is the ruling, or social, element.

Civility can be understood from the perspective of three dimensions. First there are the civil relations which pertain between individuals who are members of the same mixed community. The process of education in relation to human conduct internal to a community is that of teaching members to 'behave "civilly" to one another' (NL, 35.4). Here we see how integrally related mind, society and civilization are. To act civilly is to refrain from doing anything that would throw someone into a passion, or stimulate a desire so strong that it diminishes that person's self-respect to such an extent that the person fears losing his or her power of choice and of becoming overcome by the passion of desire. Engendering such a breakdown of the will is to exercise force over that person. An absence of such force is the ideal of civility. A certain degree of force is necessary; the relation between the non-social and social elements is itself one of force and may be described as uncivil, but unnecessary force is uncivilized.

The second dimension concerns the community and its external relation with nature. A community is civil when its attitude towards nature is informed by a scientific understanding of the natural world. This relation is summed up in the idea of the intelligent exploitation of nature, where desires and needs do not outstrip one's ability to satisfy them. The kind of natural science to which Collingwood refers need not be complex, sophisticated and technical. In fact, he has in mind the sort of practical scientific knowledge that is handed down from generation to generation concerning such 'things which it is useful for a hunter or a shepherd or a fisherman or a farmer or a sailor or a miner or the like to know: things about the seasons, the weather, the soil, the subsoil, the habits of game and fish and domestic animals and vermin . . .' (NL, 36.32).[20]

The third aspect of civility is the community's external relations with other communities. To be civilized in this context means to adopt the same 'civil demeanour' towards members of another community as is afforded to members of one's own (NL, 35.6–35.63). We come to treat foreigners civilly when we engage in common action. Commerce, for instance, may facilitate such mutual respect. In the course of sustained common action a social consciousness may arise in one person towards a member of another community. This should be differentiated quite clearly from simply liking or having an affection for someone. Irrespective of whether a person is liked or disliked, civility is something to which a person is entitled by the mere fact that we acknowledge that he or she possesses a rational will.

Civility, then, is the relation between persons and persons, both internal and external to a community, and between persons and nature. It is what constitutes a community's civilization relative to the human world and makes possible that community's civilization relative to nature (NL, 36.51). Civilization is both the process of handing on the common heritage of a community and the name given to that heritage: it is both the process of education and the content of that education. In summary, the purpose of education is to facilitate the development of mental maturity by first, ensuring that emotions are identified and expressed; secondly, to encourage the process of conversion from a non-social to a social condition, without which no civilization is possible; and thirdly to develop social relations to a point where they approximate to the ideal of civility and make rational political decision-making possible. The first aspect of education would predominantly concern itself with developing proficiencies in the media of artistic expression, including dance and play, and the second and third concern themselves with 'inducing habits of orderly and systematic thinking' (EM, 134).

## III

What should be the content of education? This is not a question which Collingwood systematically addressed, except in relation to the place of art in education. We can, however, construct an answer from his many and varied comments on such matters. Education should attempt to provide an understanding of all the forms of experience. In *Speculum Mentis* these forms of experience were art, religion, science, history and philosophy, all of which constituted a linked hierarchy, and each of which represented a different stage of mental development. In his later writings, philosophy and history became much more closely allied than they had been earlier, and at times appear to have been identified with each other.[21] All of the forms of experience, including the historical sciences, were seen by Collingwood to be important features of the civilizing process. Each has an important place in the education of a civilized community.

Art, because it is the 'initial state' in the 'formation of knowledge',[22] is particularly important in the education of children. Out of art, the primary activity of the mind, all others grow.[23] Art is imagination,[24] and 'imagination is a fundamental mode of mind's activity, and the right training of imagination is therefore a fundamental part of education'.[25] It is imperative, then, that small children in particular should become 'more proficient in imagination than in anything else'.[26] The importance of developing the aesthetic faculty necessitates careful educational planning that neither discourages nor allows to run riot the imagination of the child. When we learn to draw, for instance, we learn to see; painting itself 'consists in an attempt on the part of the painter to force upon himself a habit of precise observation'.[27] Education of the aesthetic faculty should not aim to make artists better artists, but instead be designed to improve men and women generally.[28] Art is not a luxury of the mind. It is necessary to the expression of emotion, and hence to knowing those emotions. It is in fact a form of self-understanding. The concern of art education must be 'that the child should become able to speak its mind, to utter itself clearly and accurately in every medium it handles'.[29]

Just as art is a form of self-understanding, so too is the study of magic and ritual, because coming to know the savages, with whom we associate these activities, enables us to come to know the savage within ourselves.[30] To immerse ourselves in the magical themes which so thoroughly imbue and permeate the fairy tales of traditional cultures facilitates a temporary liberation from our scientific preoccupations with nature by means of transporting us into a world of make-believe.[31] The importance of being aware of the magical element in life and of engaging in its practices to express emotions has become more imperative as our civilization gradually develops a self-image of itself as being eminently rational and confidently scientific. Our own civilization has attempted to suppress magic, first by means of force – which betrayed the fact that we actually believed in the witches we were burning – and secondly, in order to purge such irrational beliefs from society, ridicule replaced persecution. We have 'developed a whole system of education and social life',[32] which emphasizes that magic is folly.

We live in a utilitarian society in which everything is justified in terms of its usefulness. Those things which are not scientific, rational, sensible and businesslike are dangerous and have to be suppressed. Emotions are dangerous and have to be repressed because they are hostile forces which, if allowed free expression, would destroy civilized life. The problem to which this utilitarian obsession gives rise is that we conceive of civilization not as it is, that is coloured through and through by magical practices, but as we would like it to be. Our false sense of intellectual superiority leads us to despise savages and those people whom we think less intelligent. This is because we recognize in the savage something that we are desperately trying to suppress in ourselves, and deny in their cultures something that we refuse to acknowledge in our own. To suppress emotions, to deny their existence, as I have already suggested, is to corrupt consciousness, that is to pass on to intellect from the realm of imagination false data upon which to build its rational life.

To allow consciousness to be corrupted at such a fundamental level by denying the expression of emotion through magical practices is to pervert the life of the mind and to generate 'illusions about the nature of our own civilization'.[33] The emotional life of the child and adult must be allowed the freedom to develop through the media of art, including poetry and prose,[34] and through play. Similarly we must acknowledge the magical expression of emotions in the rituals associated with all of our activities. For children especially, fairy tales incorporate the magical elements in life which serve to liberate their minds and open up for them a world of imaginative fantasy. This imaginative facility, as we have seen, is crucial throughout the development of consciousness.

Religion and science, in addition to art and magical practices, are both necessary to the education of the young. It is science that has brought about the great material advances of twentieth-century communities, but wealth in itself cannot make us happy. Science can provide the externals of a civilization, but only 'the *religious* element in our nature'[35] can bring us inner happiness. Religion is an inward flame burning in our hearts making us conscious of the universe in all its infinite mystery and of our personal relation to it. To be in harmony with the universe, and to be content, knowing that despite everything, successes, failures and discomforts, nothing can undermine that harmony between you and the whole nature of things, is to be happy. To be civilized, Collingwood contends, 'means to be happy', and because happiness is a result of the flame of religion burning inwardly in your heart, that flame must always 'be kept burning in the heart of civilization'.[36] Religion is the 'vital warmth at the heart of civilization'.[37] A people possessed of 'religious energy can overcome all obstacles and attain any height in the scale of civilization'.[38] Religion, and Christianity in particular, has given us most of the values we cherish. The idea of freedom itself, and the associated freedom of speech, thought, inquiry and discussion have been derived from Christian practice. Indeed, Christianity was the source of the views of human nature (and not the empirical researches of anthropologists and psychologists) upon which liberal or democratic political practices were premised (EM, 133–42). It follows from this that religion is an essential element in the civilizing process, and that it is the business of parents within the family-community, and of society, or the rulers, within the body politic, to keep the inner light of religion burning.

Religion without science, however, would not be religion. It would be the mere superstitions of irrational beings. Conversely, without the inner peace born of religion, the material benefits that science can bring 'would be dust and ashes to a mind'.[39] Natural science, like religion, is of immense importance to the civilizing process. It is what enables us to develop an intelligent approach to the exploitation of nature. The body of traditional scientific knowledge relating to all aspects of life must be passed on to future generations if society is to develop and flourish. The conservation of such knowledge is important, but it is vital that it be adapted and developed to correspond to growing needs and expectations: 'The gradual building-up and storing of all this knowledge . . . is the gradual building-up and garnering of human civilization relatively to the natural world' (NL, 36.45). The whole process is facilitated by the spirit of agreement, persons interested and willing to learn seeking out those willing and happy to impart their knowledge. In Collingwood's view we have a natural passion for learning, and a 'natural desire to impart knowledge' (NL, 36.64). If we ever lose this will to teach future generations the traditional inheritance to which they are heir, 'then of all the civilization our ancestors have left us they will inherit nothing' (NL, 36.61).

Scientific thinking should not, however, be exclusively related to natural science. Science, more generally speaking, 'means a body of systematic or orderly thinking about a determinate subject-matter' (EM, 4). Education should therefore 'be predominantly a method for inducing habits of orderly and systematic thinking' (EM,176), whether the subject matter be the natural or historical sciences, that is, metaphysics, logic, ethics and historical inquiry itself. These so-called historical sciences, unlike psychology, are criteriological: they are at once descriptive and critical, and should therefore not be confused with any crude notion of historicism. They have developed criteria, or standards, of judgement by which each participant in an activity, or each thinker, can judge the success of his or her act or thought (EM, 109). The criteriological sciences, as we will see, are descriptive in that they articulate the criteria in terms of which individuals judge their thoughts and actions a success: they are critical in that they denounce those attempts at articulation that wrongly characterize the criteria operating at a particular time. Thus, for example, when Collingwood discusses the various approaches to anthropology he is critical of the common tendency to apply modern scientific standards to the role and function of magic in primitive societies because by necessity it leads to the ridiculous conclusion that magical practices are irrational, and that the savage is mentally ill (EM,188; PA, 62–9).[40]

History's place in the education of the child and the maturing adult is of particular significance. History is the means by which we achieve self-understanding, and 'the self-understanding of my mind is nothing else than historical knowledge' (IH, 174). Mind has created European civilization, and in order to understand its creation we must come to understand the mind whose creation it is. The attainment of self-knowledge enables us to understand the present. Contrary to what we commonly think, the 'ultimate aim of history is not to know the past but to understand the present'.[41] In knowing the present we prepare ourselves for future action. For Collingwood the achievement of historical knowledge is a prime duty which is 'essential to the maintenance' of reason. (IH, 228). Reason only exists in the historical process, and reason is only knowable through history. Civilization, or the civilizing process, cannot even begin until mind has reached the level of reason, and without the revelation of reason in historical knowledge there can be no civilization. Collingwood expressed what he was trying to get at in a letter to F. G. Simpson dated 6 October, 1922:

> Now the truth seems to me to be that only the historian sees things from the point of view of eternity: because the evolutionary biologist, the astronomer, the mathematician etc. only see from the point of view of the momentarily fashionable biological or other theory: the scientist never sees *himself*. But the historian sees from the point of view of eternity because his history is the history of himself, and he achieves eternity not by ignoring time but just by recognizing time and recognizing himself as the heir of the past. Therefoe to understand history is to understand oneself, which is the Delphic oracle's formula for salvation. (letter now in the Bodleian Library among the Collingwood Papers)

The value of the historical or criteriological science of metaphysics in the education of mankind may not be immediately apparent. It is, however, of crucial importance. Metaphysics has both a historical and critical dimension. It is historical in that it asks what absolute presuppositions were absolutely presupposed at a particular time, and critical in that it takes to task metaphysicians who misunderstand the nature of metaphysical inquiry, or who make mistakes about what absolute presuppositions were being absolutely presupposed.[42] About absolute presuppositions we ask no questions concerning their truth or falsity. In order to detect absolute presuppositions we work backwards from relative presuppositions, which are both answers to questions logically prior to themselves and questions logically prior to their subsequent answers. When we reach a presupposition that is not an answer to a question it is absolute and not susceptible to questions of its truth status.

The manner, or *modus operandi*, of detecting absolute

presuppositions is of general applicability. Knowing whether a presupposition is relative or absolute is important to all forms of enquiry in so far as such knowledge circumscribes those things which we confirm or deny, and those things which we have to take as given if the activity, or mode of life, is to continue to flourish. All analysis has this in common with metaphysical analysis: there is a common *modus operandi*. The scientific character of science rests upon its mode of analysis, a mode which it has in common with metaphysics. Both are, 'inextricably united, and stand or fall together . . . As long as either lives the other lives; if either dies the other must die with it' (EM, 41). Both science and metaphysics have important places in the civilizing process. Without metaphysics and the *modus operandi* it entails there is no science, and without science there is no civilization. That metaphysical analysis be passed on to future generations is imperative in that it can detect absolute presuppositions upon which the most treasured values of society are based, and also expose the logical fallacies perpetrated by those thinkers who demand proofs, refutations or justifications of absolute presuppositions. These misguided thinkers undermine the whole moral and social heritage of Europe.

The historical or criteriological science of logic has its place in the educating process in order to make explicit to modern society the principles of valid thought to which it subscribes. Logicians like Mill and Jevons, in Collingwood's view, formulated as good accounts as they could of the principles of valid thought which operated in their own historical epoch. The inductive logic of which they gave accounts was that which informed the work of their contemporary positivist scientists. However, Collingwood seriously questions to applicability of the logic of the nineteenth to the twentieth century. The historical civilization which is gradually superseding the utilitarian civilization of the nineteenth century brings with it its own principles of valid thought. Indeed, Collingwood's theory of the logic of question and answer is such an attempt to uncover the principles of valid thinking applicable to the historical civilization emerging in modern Europe (A, ch.V).

The historical or criteriological science of ethics is concerned to make explicit the principles of action which are applicable within particular societies. Ethics attempts to portray the type of life that a society aspires to pursue. Politics and economics, for example, are ethical sciences which 'describe the political and economic principles accepted at the time and place'.[43] However, they do not merely describe what political and economic principles are, but also attempt to discover what these principles ought to be.[44] In Collingwood's view, 'teaching in moral philosophy' or ethics, is designed to 'improve your own practice; and its appeal is an appeal to confirmation or disproof by reference to your practical experience'.[45] In *An Autobiography*, for instance, the Realists are criticized for teaching that philosophy makes no difference to the known object. Collingwood maintains that moral philosophy had from the time of Socrates 'been regarded as an attempt to think out more clearly the issues involved in conduct for the sake of acting better' (A, 35–6). This was the case until the end of the nineteenth century and exemplified by the school of Green, which gave students 'ideals to live for and principles to live by' (A, 36). Students who thought carefully about what they were doing, or were about to do, would on the whole become more likely to do it better. This is the message that Collingwood himself tried to impart to his students. In the 'Lectures on Moral Philosophy' for 1933 Collingwood ends by emphasizing the value of moral philosophy for future conduct. He does not, however, recommend any course of action, nor does he present any list of ethical principles to follow. Instead he offers a cautionary note about thinking clearly before acting. The more clearly one thinks about moral action, Collingwood suggests, the more likely it is that one will act wisely. Indeed, this echoes the point relentlessly pursued throughout *Speculum Mentis* that a false conception of one's activity is bound to have adverse implications for its practice.[46]

## IV

As well as seeing education in the broader sense as a civic duty, most social reformers were in favour of greater state interference in the institutional provision of education. The extension of the franchise in the 1867 Reform Act made it imperative in the eyes of many to ensure that a voting population exercised its will rationally. It is true to say that before 1870 governments interfered less in school than they did in industry. A school was closed down only if it was an incubator of contagious diseases or the location of serious crime. The 1870 Education Act facilitated the provision of elementary schools within the reach of all children, giving the power to local boards, where new schools were required, to make education compulsory throughout England and Wales. The immediate aim was to combat illiteracy, reduce juvenile crime and determine a standard curriculum.

Such British idealists as T. H. Green, Henry Jones and R. B. Haldane looked to the German school system which distinguished between academic and technical state-provided education at secondary level. The government itself in 1895 produced a report on the German system written by Michael Sadler, educated at Oxford and deeply influence by T. H. Green. H. A. L. Fisher, the President of the Board of Education in the 1916–22 coalition government was himself an Idealist sympathizer, and like them a great believer in the socially levelling powers of education. Fisher justified the provisions of the 1918 Education Act in thoroughly Idealist terms. The extension of the school-leaving age, provision for continuing education, and restrictions on the employment of children were presented not as a restriction upon liberty, but as as an enhancement of individual freedom.[47]

The experience of the First World War and the exemplar of a patriotic state-educated population inspired the British government to emulate the German achievement. Philosophical Idealists saw the Act as rather less concerned with education for its own sake, and more directed to the needs of industry than they would have liked. They were particularly disappointed about the scaling-down of the proposals for continuing education after the formal school-leaving age. They nevertheless saw the Act as a decisive step on the way to attaining a system which, in the words of Green nearly forty years earlier, 'would heal the division between those who angrily look up to others as having the social reputation which they themselves have not, uniting both classes by the freemasonry of common education'.[48] Green was not here romaniticizing about the proletariat. The proletariat for him was the measure of the failure of education.[49] The education of a gentleman was to be extended and not diluted in dissolving the insidious class barrier.

Collingwood never fully and formally presented his ideas on the content of education, but he did write a remarkable account of its manner. He claimed that one of the principal faults of modern civilization was that it had entrusted the education of children in its intellectual and practical heritage to professional educators. One of the remedies to revitalize modern life was to entrust parents with the education of their own children. Parents have the advantage over specialist educators in that they exercise a good deal more power over the child. In dividing the power between parents and educators, each has his or her strength greatly diminished. Further, a parent as educator, being a non-specialist, has a greater degree of versatility than a specialist. For these two reasons the parent is able to stimulate the child to do well, constantly finding, and letting the child find on its own initiative, new subjects to study. The emphasis here is upon developing the cognitive competence of the child by stimulating the imagination with things that are at least partially familiar.

Such a responsibility would not be burdensome, in Collingwood's view, as long as we dispense with the ridiculous deference that has developed towards specialists. If the parent gets little enjoyment out of keeping the children clean, then the parent should let them run about dirty. Similarly, if the children are getting on their nerves, Collingwood suggests that they 'neglect them a bit; don't take them so seriously; be irresponsible about them' (NL, 37.94).

This intense distrust of the specialist is echoed in modern political theory. Like Collingwood, Hans-Georg Gadamer and Ronald Beiner, for example, take the technological revolution not as evidence of liberation from the drudgery of everyday life, but as the rejection and denial of our vital human capacities. For them, and for Collingwood, our ever-increasing reliance upon experts or technocrats subdues our critical faculties, and leads to the denial of the importance of emotions in our civilization.[50]

Professional educators, in Collingwood's view, would still have a role to play in society. They would be available to teach parents and children who go to them for tuition in special subjects. Their expertise would be solicited rather than imposed. Further, professional educators should be allowed to go on researching because every civilized society needs to ensure that research is being conducted into the various sciences and branches of learning. We should keep educational institutions partly for teaching all those who wish to attend, and 'partly as institutions of research where science and learning shall be kept alive instead of being, as they too often are in our educational institutions of today, dead' (NL, 37.98).

In what remains of this chapter I would like to make some brief observations without wishing to offer at this stage detailed criticism of Collingwood's theory as a whole.

It goes without saying that the seriousness with which Collingwood's own parents undertook the education of their children instilled in him a blind optimism with regard to the capabilities of all parents, and demonstrates the extent to which Collingwood, unlike many of his Idealist predecessors, was divorced from the poverty and deprivation, ignorance and misery, that were prevalent among large sections of the community, and to which the notion of education, let alone educational responsibility, was still largely alien. He does, however, strike a chord that resonates in current educational theory. Too strong a reliance upon the authority of the teacher had diminished the role of the parent to that of an observer, whose interest in the progress of the child was regarded as little more than an intrusion into what was essentially a professional matter. Parental choice and involvement is certainly a step in the direction in which Collingwood pointed.

Collingwood refused, however, to look at England in terms of social classes. Such a view implied to him the notion of an eristic, that is confrontational, view of social relations, rather than the dialectic view, that is, the idea that agreements are reached through compromise, implied in the European strand of liberalism to which he was passionately attached. There can be no question about the sincerity with which he attacked fascism and nazism, but the war for him was 'a war of ideas'.[51] For all his protestations concerning bringing about a rapprochement between theory and practice, Collingwood was far less sensitive to the social condition of England than were, for example, T. H. Green, D. G. Ritchie, Bernard Bosanquet and Henry Jones. Green, to take one illustration, showed himself to be far more perceptive than Collingwood in matters of the practical difficulties of broadening education when he said, 'all questions of education are complicated by class.'[52] With one stroke of his pen, Collingwood swept away the educational gains, such as they were, of the past century, with no regard for the practicalities of his scheme. A rather idyllic view of a rural England uncorrupted by industrialization informed his thinking on educational issues. One of the reasons for the decline in the rural way of life and the disregard of its ancient traditions was, in Collingwood's mind, the implementation of the 1870 Education Act which imposed on the 'countryman an education modelled on town-dwellers' standards' (PA, 102).[53]

Green, of course, had been critical of the 1870 Act for not going far enough. It had not extended the school board system sufficiently, and should have restricted denominationalism to schools that had already been established. Less reliance upon religious denominations and more upon the collective organized will of society through the instruments of the state was what was needed. What was clear in his mind was that parental responsibility was simply not feasible:

> In an ideal society, perhaps the education of all families might safely be left under the control, in each case of the parents. In the actual state of English society, however, no one pretends that it can be left, and it is doubtful whether under the modern system of labour in great masses, which draws all who have to work for their living more and more away from their homes, the fate of the children can ever with safety be left solely in the hands of the parents.[54]

We need to dig deeper to get at what Collingwood was complaining about. We have already seen that Collingwood had a marked respect for folk practices and skills, and that compulsory education (which had developed by 1880), based upon the regulation of the clock rather than the season, would undermine the imparting of these skills. More fundamentally, I think, he saw the school system as part of a wholescale destruction of the countryside by the town-dwellers, the significance of which for him was the sustained erosion of our traditional and profound emotional attachment to the land, a religious attachment, which was being eradicated by the values of a utilitarian civilization. Collingwood argues that 'The sanity of man as civilized depends upon the health in him of the emotions fundamental to his type of civilization.'[55] Our own civilization, he contends, depends upon the health of our emotions towards the land. It is not an aesthetic love of the beauty of nature. The country landscape as we know it is not a product of nature but of human endeavour, whose character is moulded into the hillsides, valleys and glens. For our civilization nature is our 'divine mother', and 'upon the vitality of this religious feeling, depends the vitality of our civilization as a whole.'[56] The imposition of the standards of the town by a uniform education system, was for Collingwood a threat to the emotional foundations of our civilization.

While Collingwood displayed genuine insights in warning of the dangers of a technocratic and utilitarian civilization, and the consequent denial and suppression of the emotional elements in our lives, his answer to the problem was, to say the least, rather extreme.

If we disregard the apparent naiveté of Collingwood's optimism about the capacities of parents, and his apparent ignorance of the social conditions that would render his scheme ineffective, there are still questions to be asked about his proposal. For example, how much of the content of education specified above could we reasonably expect to be passed on by ordinary people to their children? It would in fact be remarkably little. Certainly in the case of the historical or criteriological sciences people would have to rely almost totally upon professionals like Collingwood for their education. Out of the total number of specialist teachers in Britain, very few would be engaged in research. Those who were, would on the whole tend to work in the universities. In other words, Collingwood is implicitly emphasizing the importance of people like himself in the civilizing process and securing the future of the type of work they do. A population, however, which under his scheme would probably be semi-literate, superstitious and largely ignorant of the value of the things which Collingwood himself valued, would hardly be likely to appreciate the existence of such institutions.

I do not wish to labour the inadequacies of Collingwood's idea of the manner of education any further. However, this aspect of his educational theory is not the logical consequence of his ideas on the purpose and content of education. There is much, as I hope I have demonstrated, that is worthy of serious consideration in Collingwood's theory of the purpose and content of education.

*Notes*

[1] R. G. Collingwood, *An Autobiography* (Penguin, Harmondsworth, 1944), ch.2; Tom Hopkinson, *Of This Our Time: a Journalist's Story*

*1905–50* (Hutchinson, London, 1982), 86. In the latter of the references Collingwood is reported to have said, 'I went to Rugby, where we thought winter a time for playing football – and summer a time for thinking about playing football'.

2. See, for example, the reviews of *The New Leviathan* by George Catlin in *Political Science Quarterly*, LVII (1943), 436; John Laird in *Philosophy*, XVIII (1943), 79; Willoughby Dewar in *Time and Tide*, 15 August 1942, 660; and, anonymous reviewer in *The Scotsman*, 20 August,1942. Also see T. M. Knox, *Dictionary of National Biography 1941–1950*, 168.

3. I am indebted to Marnie Hughes for suggesting to me this parallel, and for persuading me that Collingwood's ideas on pedagogy are rather more central to his eductional thought than I was once willing to admit. I have also modified other aspects of the chapter in the light of her comments.

4. Alan Donagan, *The Later Philosophy of R. G. Collingwood* (Oxford, Clarendon Press, 1962); Louis O. Mink, *Mind, History and Dialectic* (Bloomington, University of Indiana Press, 1967); Lionel Rubinoff, *Collingwood and the Reform of Metaphysics* (Toronto, University of Toronto Press, 1970); Sherman M. Stanage, 'Collingwood's Phenomenology of Education: Person and the Self-Recognition of the Mind' in *Critical Essays on the Philosophy of R. G. Collingwood*, ed. M. Krausz (Oxford, Clarendon Press, 1972).

5. Diderot, for instance, was well aware of this when he said, 'Instructing a nation is the same as civilizing it; stifling learning in it means leading it back to the primitive state of barbarity ... Ignorance is the lot of the slave and the savage' (quoted in Lucien Febvre, *A New Kind of History*, ed. Peter Burke (London, Routledge, 1973), 233).

6. R. G. Collingwood, 'The Place of Art in Education', *Hibbert Journal*, 24 (1926), 435.

7. R. G. Collingwood, 'Science, Religion and Civilization', Collingwood MS, DEP 1 (1930), 135.

8. R. G. Collingwood, *The Principles of Art* (Oxford, Oxford University Press, 1977), 164; R. G. Collingwood, *The Idea of History* (Oxford, Oxford University Press, 1946), 231; R. G. Collingwood, *An Essay on Metaphysics* (Oxford, Clarendon Press, 1940), 110.

9. Cf. Edward B. Tylor, *Primitive Culture: Researches into the Development of Mythology, Philosophy, Religion, Art and Custom*, two vols. (New York, Gordon Press, 1974: first published, 1871), 85.

10. R. G. Collingwood, 'Outlines of a Philosophy of Art', reprinted in *Essays in the Philosophy of Art*, ed. Alan Donagan (Bloomington, University of Indiana Press, 1965), 55.

11. R. G. Collingwood, 'Aesthetic' in *The Mind*, ed. R. J. S. McDowall (London, Longmans, 1927), 240.

12. R. G. Collingwood, [Fairy Tales] 'IV Magic', Collingwood MS, DEP

¹² 21, 16, 14–19, which I have titled 'The Utilitarian Civilization', appear as ch.18 of R. G. Collingwood, *Essays in Political Philosophy*, ed. David Boucher (Oxford, Clarendon Press, 1989).
¹³ Ibid., MS, 21.
¹⁴ R. G. Collingwood, 'Rule-Making and Rule-Breaking', sermon preached in St Mary the Virgin's Church, Oxford, 5 May 1935, Collingwood MS, DEP 1, 10.
¹⁵ See, for example, R. G. Collingwood, 'The Three Laws of Politics', L. T. Hobhouse Memorial Trust Lectures, no.11 (London, Humphrey Milford for Oxford University Press, 1941), 7.
¹⁶ R. G. Collingwood, 'Man Goes Mad' (1936), Collingwood MS, DEP 24, 17. Pages 16–28, titled 'Modern Politics', appear as ch.16 in Collingwood, *Essays in Political Philosophy*, ed. Boucher. Cf. 'The Life of politics is the life of political education', NL, 32.34.
¹⁷ Collingwood, 'The Three Laws of Politics', 10. For a comprehensive discussion of Collingwood's political philosophy see my *The Social and Political Thought of R. G. Collingwood* (Cambridge, Cambridge University Press, 1989).
¹⁸ The importance of public exemplars of good political conduct was, of course, something that Hegel highlighted when he spoke of the Estates Assemblies (Hegel, *Elements of the Philosophy of Right* (Cambridge, Cambridge University Press, 1991), §315).
¹⁹ Cf. Collingwood, 'Science, Religion and Civilization', 2.
²⁰ Cf. Collingwood, *The Principles of Art*, 59, and Collingwood, 'Man Goes Mad', 30.
²¹ R. G. Collingwood, 'Notes on HISTORIOGRAPHY', Collingwood MS, DEP 13, 1–19 passim. On Collingwood's final unequivocal rejection of relativism see my introduction to *The New Leviathan* and Jan van der Dussen's contribution to this volume.
²² R. G. Collingwood, 'Aesthetic', 238.
²³ Collingwood, 'Outlines of a Philosophy of Art', 55.
²⁴ See Collingwood, *Speculum Mentis*, 58–63; R. G. Collingwood, 'The Place of Art in Education', *Hibbert Journal*, 24 (1926), 439–43; Collingwood, 'Outlines of a Philosophy of Art', 52–5 and 125–8.
²⁵ Collingwood, 'The Place of Art in Education', 442.
²⁶ Collingwood, 'Aesthetic', 240.
²⁷ Collingwood, 'Outlines of a Philosophy of Art', 129.
²⁸ Collingwood, 'The Place of Art in Education', 435.
²⁹ Collingwood, 'Art and the Machine', Collingwood MS, DEP 25, 14.
³⁰ R. G. Collingwood, [Fairy Tales] 'C:III The Historical Method', Collingwood MS, DEP 21, 3 and 11.
³¹ R. G. Collingwood, [Fairy Tales] 'A', Collingwood MS, DEP 21, 14.
³² Collingwood [Fairy Tales] 'IV Magic',15. Cf. *Principles of Art*, 57–77.
³³ Ibid., 18. Cf. 'We have fabricated an altogether mistaken idea of our

own civilization. We flatter ourselves that it is everywhere based on scientific knowledge whereas at every point it is riddled with magic', R. G. Collingwood [Fairy Tales] 'F: The concluding chapter', Collingwood MS, DEP 21, 4. Cf. *Essay on Metaphysics*, 46.
34 Collingwood, 'The Place of Art in Education', 442. Collingwood says, for example: 'Poetry is pure imagination, prose is imagination as controlled by and consciously expressive of thought'.
35 Collingwood, 'Science, Religion and Civilization', 16.
36 Ibid., 16.
37 R. G. Collingwood, 'Fascism and Nazism', *Philosophy*, 15 (1940), 168.
38 Ibid., 176 .
39 Collingwood, 'Science, Religion and Civilization', 13.
40 For a full discussion of this theme see R. G. Collingwood, [Fairy Tales] 'B II: Three Methods of Approach: Philological, Functional, Psychological', Collingwood MS, DEP 26,1–51.
41 R. G. Collingwood, 'History As the Understanding of the Present', Collingwood MS, DEP 16, 1.
42 R. G. Collingwood, 'Function of Metaphysics in Civilization', Collingwood MS (1937–8), DEP 19, 47.
43 Ibid.
44 This is implied in the following statement: 'aesthetic tries to discover not merely what art is, but what art ought to be. This again is true of all philosophical sciences' (R. G. Collingwood, 'Aesthetic Theory and Artistic Practice', Collingwood MS, DEP 25, 40).
45 R. G. Collingwood, 'Goodness, Rightness, Utility: Lectures delivered in H.T. 1940', Collingwood MS, DEP 9, 10. Published in *The New Leviathan*, revised edn, 401.
46 R. G. Collingwood, 'Lectures on Moral Philosophy' (1933), Collingwood MS, DEP 8, 127–30. Cf. *Speculum Mentis*, 241 and 250.
47 H. A. L. Fisher, *Educational Reform Speeches* (Oxford, Clarendon Press, 1918), 48.
48 T. H. Green, *Works* (London, Longmans Green, 1888), III, 460.
49 See John MacCunn, *Six Radical Thinkers* (London, Arnold, 1910), 252.
50 Hans-Georg Gadamer, *Reason in the Age of Science* (Cambridge, Mass., MIT Press, 1981); and Ronald Beiner, *Political Judgment* (London, Methuen, 1983). Collingwood's concerns are best expressed in a number of unpublished manuscripts already referrred to in this paper, 'Man Goes Mad' and 'Art and the Machine'.
51 R. G. Collingwood, letter to T. M. Knox, 6 January 1940, Knox MS, University of St Andrews, MS no.37524/430. In a letter to von Leyden Collingwood argues that 'It comforts me a little to reflect that the present war is not a war between nations but a war between men, who want to stamp out thought and men who want to go on thinking' (20 July 1940), Bodleian Library, Oxford.

52 T. H. Green, *Works*, III, 403. Cf. 'we have a people which in common phraseology is divided into the educated few and the uneducated many. Much as we may dislike the phrase, we must confess that it represents the truth' (ibid., 456).
53 This appears to be a firmly held conviction. In the unpublished manuscripts Collingwood argues that the 1870 Education Act turned the peasantry 'away from their old fairy-tales' (Collingwood, [Fairy Tales] 'F: The Concluding Chapter', 9).
54 Green, *Works*, III, 431–2.
55 Collingwood, 'Man Goes Mad', 32.
56 Ibid., 32–3.

# Civilization and the Open Society: Collingwood and Popper

## A. J. M. MILNE

## Introduction[1]

In their respective books *The New Leviathan* and *The Open Society and Its Enemies*, R. G. Collingwood and Sir Karl Popper were fellow labourers in the same vineyard. Collingwood described his book as 'an inquiry into civilization and the revolt against it' (NL, 1.92). Popper in his introduction also referred to 'the revolt against civilization' (OS, I, 4) and identified the enemies of the open society with it. Both had Western civilization in mind, and more especially the civilization of modern Europe whose survival was at stake in the Second World War. Their common aim was to delineate the character of that civilization, to identify ways of thought hostile to it, and thereby to understand the fundamental issues underlying the war. In carrying out this aim, each was making his own contribution as a philosopher to the war effort and to post-war reconstruction. But there was no collaboration between them. They worked independently, neither being aware of what the other was doing. Collingwood died in 1943, the year following the publication of *The New Leviathan*. *The Open Society* was first published in 1945 and was written in New Zealand, where Popper spent the war.

This chapter is a comparative study of what they accomplished. So far as I know, it has not been undertaken before. Of the two, Popper's book is far better known. Indeed the name 'Open Society' has been adopted by not a few politicians and some academics as a synonym for 'liberal democracy'.[2] Collingwood's work in other areas of philosophy, such as metaphysics and the philosophy of history, is also well known, and in recent years has been attracting increased attention. But only a few political philosophers have taken much interest in *The New Leviathan*. One way of stimulating greater interest is to compare what Collingwood has done in that book with Popper's better-known work. Their shared aim provides the basis for such a comparison, and notwithstanding their different approaches, there is much which is complementary in their work.

The chapter is divided into three sections. Of these, the first two are mainly expository, one dealing with Collingwood and the other with Popper. The third is devoted to a comparative assessment of what they have respectively achieved. Such an assessment must involve criticism. It is necessary to consider not only how well each has achieved what he set out to do, but also the merits and limitations of their respective approaches. The latter is the task of the third section. But it presupposes the former, and in order to provide for that, I have added a brief critical commentary to each of the first two sections. Finally, some qualifications: my comparative assessment is not exhaustive. It is no more than an initial attempt. There are issues which I have passed over, which others might wish to include and emphasize. I claim only that those which I have raised should find a place in any fuller treatment. It is now more than fifty years since Collingwood and Popper wrote their books, and during that time Western civilization has survived, albeit precariously. A contemporary inquiry into it, into what threatens it, and into what in it is worth preserving, might well have a different emphasis from theirs. But it would do well not to neglect them. At the very least, their work is a fruitful point of departure.

## I – Collingwood

(1) According to Collingwood, civilization is 'a process of approximation to an ideal state' (NL, 34.5) The process occurs in a community and is one 'whereby a community approaches nearer to an ideal state which I will call "civility" and recedes further from . . . an ideal state which I will call "barbarity"' (NL,

34.5–3.51). For reasons which we shall examine in a moment, civility can never be completely attained and barbarity never wholly eliminated. The process necessarily remains one of approximation. About the nature of the process Collingwood says: '. . . civilization has something to do with the mutual relations of the members within a community, something to do with relations of these members to the world of nature, and something to do with the relations between them and other human beings not being members of the same community' (NL, 35.34). The key to what this something is, so far as the first and third sets of relations are concerned, lies in the idea of civil behaviour.

> Behaving civilly to a man means respecting his feelings, abstaining from shocking him, frightening him, annoying him, or briefly arousing in him any passion or desire that might diminish his self-respect, i.e. threaten his consciousness of freedom by making him see that his power of choice is in danger of breaking down and passion or desire likely to take charge. (NL, 35.41)

Collingwood then characterizes being civilized positively thus. 'Being civilized means so far as possible living *dialectically*, i.e. in the constant endeavour to convert occasions of non-agreement into occasions of agreement' (NL, 39.15).

The idea of dialectic invoked here is Plato's. Collingwood attached great importance to the Platonic distinction between *eristic* and *dialectic* which he characterizes thus:

> What Plato calls an eristic discussion is one in which each party tries to prove that he was right and the other wrong. In a dialectical discussion you aim at showing that your own view is one with which your opponent really agrees even if at one time he denied it, or conversely that it was yourself and not your opponent who began by denying a view with which you really agree. (NL. 24.58)

In eristic, there is disagreement which can be resolved only if one party gives in and concedes victory to the other. In dialectic there is non-agreement which may be resolved by further discussion which brings out the common ground between the parties. The mutual relations between the members of a community are civilized to the extent that they are able and willing to try to find common ground to overcome their differences. To the extent that they are unable or unwilling to do this and adopt the eristic attitude towards their differences so that non-agreement hardens into disagreement and potential conflict, their mutual relations are uncivilized. The same holds of their relations with foreigners, with the rider that only to the extent that the latter reciprocate the dialectical attitude can relations with them be civilized. So far as relations with the world of nature are concerned, civilization means 'a spirit of intelligent exploitation' (NL, 36.25). This is possible only to the extent that the members of a community treat one another civilly, and therefore so far as possible live dialectically. The dialectical attitude is necessary for the development, conservation and transmission of the knowledge and experience which makes the intelligent exploitation of nature possible.

To see why the process of civilization can never be more than an approximation, we must turn to Collingwood's theory of the body politic. He says of a body politic that its members always consist of two classes. 'The first class is a society and rules itself. Its members are *persons* or agents possessed of free-will. It also rules the second class which is a community only because it is ruled. Members of the second class are devoid of free-will' (NL, 25.13–25.16). He calls the first class the council of the body politic, the second class its nursery. 'It [sic] the body-politic, recruits the council by promotion from the nursery. It recruits the nursery by breeding babies and taking the consequences' (NL, 25.17, 25.18). We can now begin to see why the process of civilization can never be more than an approximation to civility. Babies and young children are not yet capable of the dialectical living which constitutes civility. Hence in every body politic there is always a class of members who are not yet civilized. In Collingwood's words, 'In the body-politic new babies are always being born, the nursery is always being replenished and the work of imposing order upon it is never concluded' (NL, 25.24). But this is only part of the story. To understand more fully, we must go to his account of freedom.

Collingwood says that 'The freedom of the will is positively freedom to choose, freedom to exercise a will, and negatively freedom from desire: not the condition of having no desires but the condition of not being at their mercy' (NL,13.25). If you are at the mercy of your desires, you can act from preference, but this is not free action. 'A man who prefers A to B does not choose at all. He suffers desire for A and aversion towards B, and goes where desire leads him' (NL, 13.14). Freedom of the will is achieved by an involuntary act of self-liberation. 'Liberation from what? From the dominance of desire. Liberation to do what? To make decisions' (NL, 13.22). Voluntary acts are those which issue from decisions. The act of self-liberation which makes voluntary acts possible, cannot itself be a voluntary act. It is not an act which anyone can decide to perform. But while the act of self-liberation is involuntary, its occurrence is not inevitable.

> It marks the stage at which in modern Europe a man is supposed to reach intellectual maturity. If anything interferes with the course of his mental development, this step may never happen. He will then become a man who is incapable of growing up, perhaps a man who hates the thing (mental maturity) he does not possess. (NL, 13.57–13.58)

The freedom of the will which any man can achieve is, however, always a matter of degree. 'On certain questions and in certain circumstances, an agent may be capable of decision or free. On other questions or in other circumstances the same agent may be utterly unable to prevent a certain passion or a certain desire from taking charge' (NL, 21.8). Collingwood calls this breakdown of freedom a 'crack of the will' and adds: 'for any man there are, I suppose, certain conditions under which a crack of the will would happen' (NL, 21.81).

This means that the nursery of a body politic, the second class whose members are devoid of free will, consists not only of babies and children but of mentally immature adults. The former have not yet reached the self-liberation necessary for making choices and decisions, the latter will never reach it. They can act only from preference and cannot meet the demands of dialectical living which constitute civility. In any body politic there are always likely to be mentally immature adults, which is a further reason why the process of civilization can never be completed. The members of the first class, the council of a body politic, are agents possessed of free will. They constitute a society which rules itself. Collingwood calls this 'immanent rule' and says that 'It is immanent when that which rules, rules itself, the same thing being both agent and patient in respect of the same activity' (NL, 20.38). Members of the second class, because they lack free will and are at the mercy of their passions and desires, are incapable of immanent rule. If they are to be ruled, it must be through what Collingwood calls 'transeunt rule'. He says of ruling that: 'It is transeunt when that which rules, rules something other than itself, when in respect of the same activity of ruling, there is one thing which is agent, the ruler, and another thing which is patient, the ruled' (NL, 20.37–20.39). Because transeunt rule is exercised over people who are at the mercy of their passions and desires, it can operate only through those passions and desires. This it does by means of punishment and reward. These are forms of what Collingwood calls 'mental force'. Such force operates through the passions and desires of those to whom it is applied. 'When a man suffers force the origin of the force is always something within himself, some irresistible emotion which makes him do something he does not intend to do' (NL, 20.59).

The *raison d'être* of a body politic is to provide within a community for the exercise of transeunt rule over those members who are incapable of immanent rule by those members who are capable of it. So far as the latter, the council, are concerned, the body politic is a social community or society. 'A society is a self-ruling community' (NL, 20.36). But so far as the former, the nursery, is concerned, a body politic is a non-social community. 'A nonsocial community needs for its existence to be ruled by something other than itself' (NL, 20.36). Collingwood is equating the capacity for social living with the capacity for immanent rule. In virtue of its *raison d'être*, a body politic is always a mixed community: social with respect to its council, non-social with respect to its nursery. The capacity for social living is also the capacity for initiating and carrying on partnerships. Collingwood says that: 'People become partners by deciding to behave like partners', and he goes on: 'A society or partnership is constituted by the free-will of the partners, an act of free-will whereby the person who thereby becomes a partner decides to take upon himself a share of the joint enterprise' (NL, 20.22).

But Collingwood not only equates the capacity for immanent rule with the capacity for social living. He equates both with the capacity for dialectical living and hence for civility. 'Civilization is a process in a community by which the various members assert themselves as will, severally as individual will, corporately as social will the two being inseparable' (NL, 36.89). The members assert themselves severally as individual will by individually achieving the self-liberation necessary to make choices and decisions, and thereby becoming capable of immanent rule. They assert themselves corporately as social will by deciding to behave as partners in a social community, each deciding to take upon himself a share in this joint enterprise. These are inseparable because the decision to behave as partners in a social community presupposes the achievement by each member of the self-liberation necessary to make choices and decisions. It follows that the *raison d'être* of the body politic must be widened to include the protection and development of the process of civilization already going on within it. That means admitting to the social community as full partners in their own right every member of the non-social community who has achieved enough self-liberation to be capable of immanent rule. It also means regulating and protecting the many forms of partnership initiated and carried on by the members of the social community. In addition to exercising transeunt rule over the non-social community, the council must constantly attend to these matters.

Collingwood distinguishes between lack of civilization and the rejection of civilization. Lack of civilization he calls 'savagery' and says 'Savagery is a negative idea. It means not being civilized and that is all. In practice I need hardly say there is no such thing as absolute savagery. There is only relative savagery, i.e. being civilized up to a certain point and no more' (NL, 41.11). Hence, *qua* social community, a body politic is civil, *qua* non-social community, savage. As a mixed community its condition is always one of relative civility and relative savagery. The non-social community is never in a condition of absolute savagery because it is always turning into a society and its members grow up and join the council. But as we have seen, this conversion can never be completed. New babies are always being born, the nursery is always being replenished, and there are likely always to be mentally immature adults who are incapable of immanent rule and who can act only from preference. Whether a given body politic is as civilized as it could be, depends upon how well its council is doing its job of protecting and developing the process of civilization already going on within it. It is less civilized than it could be to the extent that there are mentally mature adults who are not admitted to the social community as full partners in their own right, and to the extent that there are arbitrary restrictions upon the kinds of partnership which it is open to the members of the social community to initiate and carry on.

Concerning 'Barbarism', the rejection of civilization, Collingwood says: 'By *Barbarism* I mean hostility towards civilization, the efforts conscious or unconscious to become less civilized than you are, either in general or in some special way, and so far as in you lies, to promote a similar change in others' (NL, 41.12). He describes the will to barbarism as 'the will to acquiesce in the chaotic rule of emotion which it began by destroying. All it does is to assert itself as will and then deny itself as will' (NL, 36.94). A barbarian in Collingwood's sense is not a mentally immature adult, although he may inspire mentally immature adults to follow him. He is an adult who having become capable of immanent rule by achieving the necessary self-liberation, deliberately renounces what he has achieved. He decides to let the passions and desires which he has mastered determine his conduct, or if he is trying to become less civilized in a special way, to let his conduct be determined by specific passions and desires. According to Collingwood there have been several barbarisms or revolts against civilization in the course of European history, the latest being that of the Germans. The Nazis have successfully promoted the desire to become less civilized in all too many of their fellow countrymen, with the result that the German body politic has been transformed into a belligerent horde bent upon conquest.[3] Those Germans who might have been expected to resist, the professional and business classes, have mostly suffered a 'crack of the will' in the face of the new barbarism and thrown in their lot with it. Hence for Collingwood what was at stake in the second World War was the preservation of European civilization. The new barbarism had to be destroyed, which meant the military defeat of the Nazis by those bodies politic which had not yet succumbed and still retained a grip on the process of civilization.

(2) Collingwood equates being civilized with living dialectically (NL, 39.15). But he also says that politics itself is dialectical. 'The world of politics is a dialectical world in which non-social communities, communities of men in what Hobbes called a *state of nature*, turn into societies' (NL, 24. 71). What makes politics dialectical is the character of the body politic as a mixed community. 'Such a community might be described by attending

to its positive element as a society, by attending to its negative element as a non-social community. Yet it might be one community which was being so described, the difference being only a difference in point of view, a dialectical difference' (NL, 24.67). But granted that the non-agreement between these points of view can be converted into agreement by coming to understand the character of a body politic as a mixed community, that does not mean that politics is itself dialectical. It involves transeunt rule which, according to Collingwood, is a form of force, and to use force is not to discuss with the aim of converting non-agreement into agreement. On the contrary, the use of force puts an end to discussion. In both a body-politic and a discussion, a process of development is going on. But in the first case the process is one of mental development both intellectual and emotional, in the second, one in which the understanding of whatever is under discussion develops. Collingwood runs these two processes together, perhaps misled by the fact that the capacity to understand develops in the course of the mental process. But they need to be kept distinct. Politics is not as such dialectical. There is, however, scope for dialectic within it in the form of practical deliberation.

But there is also scope for eristic in the form of advocacy. This is nowhere more apparent than in party politics, which together with free elections is an integral part of the politics of representative government. In an election each candidate tries to show that he is right and his opponents wrong. His aim is not to convert non-agreement into agreement but to win enough votes to get elected. He is an advocate for his party and himself. Representative political institutions historically developed in Europe, and by the early twentieth century had become the basis for much of modern European politics. They are the distinctive political achievement of modern European civilization, and this needs to be acknowledged in an account of that civilization. Collingwood, however, has little to say about representative government, perhaps because of his disillusionment with British politics occasioned by the attitude of the Chamberlain government towards the Spanish Civil War (*Autobiography*, ch.8). But if the adversarial character of party politics is not to get out of hand, advocacy must be tempered by deliberation. No party has a monopoly of wisdom or virtue, hence the value of free elections. Away from the hustings, each party must be prepared to listen to and learn from its opponents. Many public issues cut across conventional party divisions and need to be approached in a collaborative, not an adversarial spirit. Collingwood neglected the positive role in politics of advocacy with its eristic attitude. But advocacy uninformed by deliberation is only rhetoric, at best innocuous, at worst destructive. He was therefore right in emphasizing the priority of dialectic to eristic but wrong in supposing that eristic could be dispensed with altogether.

The second part of a body politic's *raison d'être*, providing for the protection and development of the process of civilization already going on within it, roughly corresponds to the situation in modern European nation-states. Social life in these states is largely a life of private enterprise, not only in economic activity but in cultural, leisure, and not least political activity. It embraces many forms of partnership or voluntary associations, carried on within a framework of law maintained and enforced by government. The first part, providing for the transeunt rule of those incapable of immanent rule by those capable of it, incorporates what Collingwood took to be the *raison d'être* of criminal law: providing for the conviction and punishment of perpetrators of culpable harmful acts in order to deter would-be perpetrators. This rests on the controversial assumption that all criminals are mentally immature because no one capable of immanent rule would commit a culpable harmful act. There is, however, a more serious objection to Collingwood's whole theory of the body politic. This is that in his conception of the social community he commits the fallacy of composition, i.e. the fallacy of assuming that because each of the parts of a whole individually possesses a certain characteristic, the same characteristic must be possessed by the whole as a corporate entity. According to Collingwood, each member of a social community is capable of immanent rule, i.e. can master his passions and desires and make choices and decisions. This does not entail that the social community of which they are the members, the whole of which they are the parts, is capable of immanent rule. As a corporate entity, it is logically different in type from its members. Unlike them, it does not have passions and desires, and its will can only be the joint or common will of its members, i.e. the will of each of them to keep it in being as a social community.

The trouble lies in Collingwood's account of ruling. 'Immanent rule' covers both personal self-rule or self-discipline and social self-rule or self-government, the logical difference between them being ignored. He has repeated Plato's error of regarding the state as 'the individual writ large'. This prevented him from seeing that political rule is necessarily transeunt in the sense that there is always one thing which rules, the government, and another which is ruled, the governed. But not all transeunt rule is a form of force. The governed in a modern European state number many millions, many of whom are mentally mature adults. The latter obey not from fear of punishment but because, as members of the community, they have an obligation to do so, provided that the government as the community's agent does not betray its trust. Representative institutions make the government accountable to them, and this in an intelligible sense makes them self-governing. Collingwood's conception of the council of a body politic is not even in an embryonic sense a conception of representative government because it leaves unanswered the question of how the council is to govern itself. With the exception of what is implied in the first part of a body politic's *raison d'être*, there is no account of government properly so called, much less of self-government. His theory is not so much one of a modern European body politic as of a modern European body social. My comments in this and the three preceding paragraphs, or something like them, are likely to occur to any reader of *The New Leviathan* who studies Collingwood's argument carefully. They do not, however, mean that there is nothing of value in his account of civilization and the revolt against it. But more about that in a moment. First we must consider Popper.

## II – Popper

(1) Popper develops his account of the open society seriatim in the course of a running fight, extending through two volumes, with those whom he takes to be its enemies. Four definitive characteristics of the open society emerge which Popper calls respectively *Critical Dualism, Critical Rationalism, Piecemeal Social Engineering* and *The Protectionist State*. As he makes clear, the latter has nothing to do with economic protectionism. I shall summarize

them briefly in turn before saying something about the enemies, and in particular one school of thought which he regards as the most dangerous, and to which he gives the name *Historicism*.

Critical Dualism is Popper's name for his modernized version of the ancient Greek distinction between *nature* and *convention*.

> It is the distinction between A., natural laws or laws of nature such as the laws describing the movements of the sun, the moon, and the planets, the succession of the seasons etc., or the law of gravity, or say, the laws of thermodynamics, and on the other hand B., normative laws or norms, or prohibitions or commandments, i.e. such rules as forbid or demand certain modes of conduct. Examples are the Ten Commandments, or the legal rules regulating the procedure for electing members of Parliament, or the laws which constitute the Athenian constitution. (OS, I, 57)

The crucial difference is this: 'A law of nature is unalterable. There are no exceptions to it' (OS, I, 58). And 'since laws of nature are unalterable, they can neither be broken nor disobeyed' (OS, I, 58). But 'a normative law whether it is a legal enactment or a moral commitment, can be disobeyed by men. Also it is alterable' (OS, I, 58).

For critical dualism, the significance of this difference is that it is up to human beings to decide what norms they are to live by.

> Critical Dualism merely asserts that norms and normative laws can be made and changed by man, more especially by a decision or convention to observe them or to alter them and it is therefore man who is morally responsible for them, not perhaps for the norms which he finds to exist in society when he first begins to reflect upon them but for the norms which he is prepared to tolerate once he has found out that he can do something to alter them. (OS, I, 61)

Popper emphasizes this human responsibility, 'Norms are manmade in the sense that we must blame nobody but ourselves for them, neither nature nor God' (OS, I, 61). Because norms are man-made it does not follow that they are arbitrary. Popper says that 'We can compare the existing normative laws or social institutions with some standard norms which we have decided are worthy of being realised' (OS, I, 61). However, he concedes that 'even these standard norms are of our own making in the sense that they are our own decision and that we alone carry the responsibility for adopting them' (OS, I, 61). Popper insists that while decisions pertain to facts, they cannot be derived from facts.

> If we consider a fact to be alterable, such as that many people are suffering from diseases, then we can always adopt a number of different attitudes towards this fact. More especially we can decide to make an attempt to alter it, or we can decide to resist any such attempt, or we can decide not to take action at all. (OS, I, 62)

He goes on: 'All alterable facts of social life can give rise to many different decisions, which shows that the decisions can never be derivable from these facts or from descriptions of these facts' (OS, I, 62).

In an open society, critical dualism is widely understood. In a closed society, this understanding is conspicuous by its absence.

> It is one of the characteristics of the magical attitude of a primitive, tribal, or closed society, that it lives in a charmed circle of unchanging taboos, of laws and customs, which are felt to be as inevitable as the rising of the sun, or the cycle of the seasons, or similar regularities of nature, and it is only if this magical closed society has actually broken down that a theoretical understanding of the difference between nature and society can develop. (OS, I, 57)

This development culminates in critical dualism. 'The starting point can be described as a "Naive Monism" (OS, I, 59). It may be said to be characteristic of the closed society. The last step which I describe as "critical dualism" or "critical conventionalism", is characteristic of the open society' (OS, I, 59). It is not Popper's view that religion is characteristic only of the closed society and has no place in the open society. Referring to the view that norms are man-made, he says: 'It must be admitted, of course, that this view is an attack upon certain forms of religion, namely on the religion of blind authority, of magic and tabooism' (OS, 1, 65). He then adds: 'But I do not think that it is in any way opposed to a religion built upon the idea of personal responsibility and freedom of conscience' (OS, I, 65).

Popper distinguishes between 'critical' and 'uncritical' or 'comprehensive' rationalism. Both embody an attitude which he says 'is an attitude of readiness to listen to critical argument and to learn from experience' (OS, II, 225). He goes on: 'It is fundamentally an attitude admitting that 'I may be wrong and you may be right, and by an effort we may get nearer to the truth' (OS, II, 225). This emphasis upon argument has a major moral and political implication.

> The fact that the rationalist attitude considers the argument rather than the person arguing is of far-reaching importance. It leads to the view that we must recognise everybody with whom we communicate as a potential source of argument and reasonable information. It thus establishes what may be described as 'The rational unity of mankind'. (OS, II, 225)

Uncritical or comprehensive rationalism however claims too much for argument. Popper says that it is the attitude of a person who is not prepared to accept anything which cannot be defended by argument, and goes on: 'We can express this also in the form of the principle that any assumption that cannot be supported either by argument or by experience is to be discarded' (OS, II, 230). He comments: 'Now it is easy to see that this principle of uncritical rationalism is inconsistent, for since it cannot in its turn be supported by argument or by experience, it implies that it should itself be discarded' (OS, II, 230). Then summing up, he concludes: 'Since all argument must proceed from assumptions, it is plainly impossible to demand that all assumptions should be based upon argument' (OS, II, 230).

This conclusion applies to rationalism itself.

> The rationalist attitude is characterised by the importance it attaches to argument and experience. But neither logical argument or experience can establish the rationalist attitude, for only those who are ready to consider argument or experience, and who have therefore adopted this attitude already, will be impressed by it. (OS, II, 230)

Concerning the adoption of this attitude, Popper says: 'We may describe it as an irrational faith in reason' (OS, II, 231). Critical rationalism recognizes this, uncritical or comprehensive rationalism does not. Whether we adopt the rationalist attitude is up to us. The decision to adopt it is a moral decision, i.e. a decision to adopt and be bound by the norms of logical argument and respect for evidence. It is a decision which implies an understanding of critical dualism. It implies a practical as well as an intellectual commitment. 'We have not only to listen to arguments but we have a duty to respond, to answer where our actions affect others'

(OS, II, 238). Popper says that adopting critical rationalism and accepting its commitments 'will deeply affect our whole attitude towards other men and towards the problems of social life' (OS, II, 232). According to him, critical rationalism and the attitude it engenders, have their roots in what he takes to be the fundamental values of Western civilization. 'I too believe that our Western civilization owes its rationalism, its faith in the rational unity of mankind and in the open society, especially its scientific outlook, to that ancient Socratic and Christian belief in the brotherhood of all men, and in intellectual honesty and responsibility' (OS, II, 243–4).

Popper contrasts 'piecemeal social engineering', the third of the four definitive characteristics of the open society, with what he calls Utopian or wholesale social engineering. He characterizes the attitude of the Utopian social engineer thus.

> Only when the ultimate aim is determined in rough outline at least, only when we are in possession of something like a blueprint of the society at which we aim, only then can we begin to consider the best ways and means for its realisation and to draw up a plan for practical action. (OS, I, 169)

He comments that: 'At present the sociological knowledge necessary for large-scale engineering simply does not exist' (OS, I, 162). He points out that 'The social world must continue to function during any reconstruction' (OS, I, 167). He concludes that 'this is the simple reason why we must reform its institutions little by little . . .' (OS, I, 167). Such 'little by little' reform is the method of piecemeal social engineering: 'Blueprints for piecemeal engineering are comparatively simple. They are blueprints for single institutions, for health and unemployment insurance for instance, or arbitration councils, or anti-depression budgeting, or educational reform. If they go wrong, the damage is not very great and the readjustment not very difficult' (OS, I, 159). Popper stresses that 'In all methods we can only learn by trial and error, by making mistakes and by improvements' (OS, I, 167). In Utopian social engineering, with its single blueprint and masterplan, there is little scope for such learning. 'But the piecemeal method permits repeated experiments and continuous readjustments' (OS, I, 163). According to Popper, 'This and not Utopian planning and historical prophecy, would mean the introduction of scientific method into politics since the whole secret of scientific method is a readiness to learn from mistakes' (OS, I, 163).

In an open society, 'the state would be considered as a society for the prevention of crime, i.e. of aggression ...'(OS, I, 111) That it should be so considered is entailed by the answer given by a humanitarian, i.e. a partisan of the open society, to the question: 'Why do we prefer living in a well-ordered state to living without a state, i.e. in anarchy?' (OS, I, 109). According to Popper, a humanitarian's reply is:

> I do not wish to live at the mercy of anybody who has the larger fist or the bigger gun. In other words, I wish to be protected from aggression by other men. I want the difference between defence and aggression to be recognised and defence to be supported by the organised power of the state. (OS, I, 110)

Such organized power entails some restriction upon personal freedom. A humanitarian acknowledges this but insists that it should be minimal and equal.

> But I demand that the fundamental purpose of the state must not be lost sight of. I mean the protection of that freedom which does not harm other citizens. Thus I demand that the state must limit the freedom of the citizens as equally as possible and not go beyond what is necessary for achieving an equal limitation of freedom. (OS, I, 110)

Commenting on this demand, Popper says: 'It is a demand which permits the social technologist to approach political institutions rationally, i.e. from the point of view of a fairly clear and definite aim' (OS, I, 110).

This 'Protectionist' state, as Popper calls it[4] is not identical with the 'Nightwatchman' state of classical liberalism. State action which creates conditions necessary for or favourable to the freedom of all citizens, is justified. Education is a case in point.[5] 'A certain amount of state control, for instance in education, is necessary if the young are to be protected from a neglect which would make them unable to defend their freedom and the state should see that all educational facilities are available to everybody' (OS, I, 111). Popper comments that 'It is certainly difficult to determine exactly the degree of freedom that can be left to the citizens without endangering that freedom whose protection is the task of the state', but he thinks that 'Something like an approximate determination of that degree is possible', and adds: 'In fact this approximate determination is one of the main tasks of legislation in democracies' (OS, I, 110). Democratic political institutions provide protection from the abuse of state power and enable freedom to be reconciled with security. This is why the Protectionist state must be a democratic state.

> Viewed in this light, the alleged clash between freedom and security, i.e. a security guaranteed by the state, turns out to be a chimera, for there is no freedom unless it is secured by the state and conversely only a state which is controlled by free citizens can offer them any freedom at all. (OS, I, 111)

This is in line with his contention in the Introduction to *The Open Society* that 'only democracy provides an institutional framework that permits reform without violence and so the use of reason in political matters' (OS, I, 4).

It follows that any philosophy which explicitly or implicitly is hostile to the use of reason in political matters, is *ipso facto* hostile to the open society. According to Popper, there are many such 'Oracular' philosophies (OS, II, ch.24, p.224). But there is one which he believes to be especially dangerous and to which he gives the name of 'historicism'. 'It is an old idea, or rather a loosely connected set of ideas, which have become unfortunately so much part of our spiritual atmosphere that they are usually taken for granted and hardly ever questioned' (OS, I, 8). The central historicist doctrine is 'the doctrine that history is controlled by specific historical or evolutionary laws whose discovery would enable us to predict the destiny of man' (OS, I, 8). There are different forms of historicism. 'A naturalistic historicism, for instance, might treat the developmental law as a law of nature. A spiritual historicism would treat it as a law of spiritual development, an economic historicism as a law of economic development' (OS, I, 8). Holism or collectivism is another feature of historicism. 'Tribalism is an element which we shall find in many forms of historicist theory. Other forms which are no longer tribalism, still retain an element of collectivism. They still emphasise the significance of some group or collectivity without which the individual is nothing at all' (OS, I, 9). It is this group or collectivity which, according to the historicist developmental law, will eventually inherit the earth. According to Popper, there is in every form of historicism, some version of the doctrine of the 'Chosen People'. This may be theistic or secular. In its secularized form, it is the doctrine of the chosen race, the chosen nation, or the chosen class (OS, I, 9).

Popper reminds his readers that he has criticized the central historicist doctrine elsewhere.

> In the *Poverty of Historicism* I have tried to argue against these claims and to show that in spite of their plausibility, they are based on a great misunderstanding of the method of science and especially on a neglect of the distinction between scientific prediction and historical prophecy. (OS, I, 3)

Referring to historicist prophecies, he says that he has been led to the conviction that 'Such sweeping historical prophecies are entirely beyond the scope of scientific method' (OS, I, 3). He then adds: 'The future depends upon ourselves and we do not depend upon any historical necessity' (ibid.). This recalls critical dualism with its emphasis upon our human responsibility for our norms and social institutions. That responsibility is incompatible with historical necessity, and belief in such necessity is incompatible with commitment to the open society. This is why Popper devotes so much of his book to historicism. 'The story of the rise and influence of some important forms of historicism is one of the main topics of the book which might even be described as a collection of marginal notes on the development of certain historicist philosophies' (OS, I, 2). According to Popper, both nazism and communism are historicist in spirit, the former inspired by Hegel, the latter by Marx (OS, I, 10). The fact that during the Second World War their respective adherents were on different sides may obscure, but does not alter, what was fundamentally at stake in that conflict, the preservation of the open society.

(2) According to critical dualism, normative laws, unlike natural laws, can be broken and can be changed. About the first of these characteristics, there can be no doubt. A norm which it is logically impossible to disobey would be pointless, something which Popper himself emphasizes (OS, I, 58). What about the second? Consider the familiar moral norms of truth-telling and promise-keeping. One way in which they could be changed is for their

excusing conditions to be altered: i.e. for what counts as an acceptable reason for not telling the truth or not keeping a promise to be modified, certain kinds of reasons hitherto excluded now being included or vice versa. This could happen through changes in social practice, through legal enactment, or both. But could they be changed in the sense of being given up altogether? If they were, and there were no longer obligations to be truthful and to keep faith, the conditions necessary for rational communication and systematic co-operation would cease to exist and organized social life would cease to be possible.[6] Popper seems to have thought that because norms can be disobeyed, they can be changed. But if *changed* means *given up*, this is not always the case. Nor is he wholly consistent about alterability. As we have seen, after saying that norms are man-made, he concludes that 'It is man who is morally responsible for them' and that 'We must blame nobody but ourselves for them' (OS, I, 61). This moral responsibility is a norm which we cannot alter, much less give up, although we may fail to understand it or refuse to acknowledge it.

Popper employs the term 'moral' but there are two questions which he does not consider: 'What distinguishes moral from non-moral norms?' and 'Why do there have to be moral norms at all?' The answer to the first is that moral norms are those which there is an obligation to comply with. In Kantian language they are *categorical* or unconditional imperatives, non-moral norms being *hypothetical* or conditional imperatives. Truth-telling and promise-keeping are categorical, not hypothetical imperatives. Unlike the hypothetical imperatives of expediency, economy and prudence, they are not conditional upon convenience, desire or self-interest. The answer to the second is that without the moral norms which constitute morality, there could be no social life. This is because morality is what makes trust possible, and without trust there could be no social life. People cannot live together without trust. They need to be able, for the most part at least, to rely upon one another to be truthful, to keep promises, to refrain from unprovoked violence, from theft, from deception and from taking unfair advantage of one another. This mutual reliance is possible only between people, each of whom acknowledges that it is right to act in such ways and believes that the others acknowledge it too. They must, that is to say, be moral agents who share, and are aware that they share, common standards of right and wrong conduct. This does not mean that morality is instrumental. It is not a means to the end of social living but part of what is involved in living socially. A person becomes a moral agent as he grows up in and becomes a member of his native community. Early in his life, he learns that he cannot simply do what he likes. Certain ways of acting are right, others wrong, and he is morally required, i.e. has a general obligation, to do whatever is right and to refrain from doing whatever is wrong.

But while these considerations show that critical dualism needs amending, they leave its central thrust substantially intact. It will be recalled that after saying that norms are man-made and that man is morally responsible for them, Popper continues: 'not perhaps for the norms which he finds to exist in society when he first begins to reflect upon them, but for the norms he is prepared to tolerate once he has found out that he can do something to alter them' (OS, I, 61). The core of truth in this is that no one is irrevocably committed to the particular values and institutions of his native community. Critical reflection upon them is always possible. This can lead a person to abandon some of what he has been brought up to believe and practise because of the errors, inconsistencies and anomalies he has found in it, and to turn instead to ways of thought and action in which he finds no such defects. But Popper's emphasis upon the role of decision in relation to norms is misleading. It fails to bring out the role of the social and cultural context in all critical reflection. That context necessarily includes moral norms such as truth-telling, promise-keeping and refraining from violence, without which social life would not be possible. Commitment to them is presupposed in critical reflection upon particular values and institutions. Unlike the norms of a religious creed, of a code of sexual ethics, of medical practice or of social welfare provisions, they cannot be abandoned in favour of others. They are not on the agenda for decision in the way in which these are.

Finally, a brief comment on two other matters. The first concerns the 'irrational faith in reason' (OS, II, 231). 'Non-rational' would surely be better, as 'irrational' implies latent if not overt self-contradiction. It also implies hostility to reason, i.e. an attitude which is anti-rational. 'Non-rational' carries no such implications. It is confined to the proposition that the possibility of giving reasons is logically excluded. This preserves Popper's central point, that reasons cannot be given for being rational. The second concerns piecemeal social engineering. The analogy between 'reform' and 'engineering' is misleading for two reasons. One is that it assumes that there is no difference in kind between the natural and the social sciences, that the logic of social inquiry is the same as the logic of natural inquiry. This is questionable in such fields as anthropology, sociology and political science, which yield little in the way of natural laws although much in the way of understanding. The other is that social reform involves considerations which have no place in engineering. Reforms in industrial relations, in race relations or in social welfare provision require understanding and co-operation from the people concerned if they are to be successful. But while an engineer must shape his plans in the light of the physical properties of his materials, he does not have to enlist their understanding and co-operation. They are incapable of understanding and therefore of either supporting or opposing his plans. He has only to manipulate them, not to convince them.[7] This is not to deny that proposals for social reform can be informed by insights drawn from the social sciences. But while such insights increase understanding, they cannot yield technical procedures with invariant outcomes.

## III

According to Collingwood, 'Being civilized means living, so far as possible, dialectically, i.e. in the constant endeavour to convert occasions of non-agreement into occasions of agreement' (NL, 39.15). This is Popper's rationalist attitude of 'I may be wrong and you may be right, and by an effort we may get nearer to the truth' (OS, II, 225). It is this attitude, and more especially critical rationalism, which informs thought and action in an open society. What for Popper makes a society open, for Collingwood makes it civilized. They have reached the same central thought, although they have come to it in different ways. They both go back to classical Greek thought. But for Collingwood it is the *dialectic–eristic* distinction which is significant, for Popper the *nature–convention* distinction. Collingwood incorporates the former into a philosophy of mind in the light of which he interprets Hobbes's conception of 'the state of nature' and the transition from that state into 'Civil Society'. Popper's approach is through the philosophy of science which he brings to bear upon the latter distinction. These two approaches are not incompatible. But notwithstanding certain defects in his development of it, Collingwood's is the more fruitful and enables some shortcomings in Popper's to be overcome.

Popper has nothing to say about the origins of the rationalist attitude beyond misleadingly describing it as 'an irrational faith in reason (OS, II, 231). Collingwood has something to contribute here (NL, 13.22 and 13.57). The origins of the rationalist or dialectical attitude lie in the involuntary act of self-liberation which makes choice and decision possible (OS, II, 230, 238). The capacity for decision and for rational thought and action develop together, their joint development being made possible by the involuntary and non-rational act of self-liberation. There can indeed be a decision to maintain and develop the rationalist attitude, but only if its development is already underway.

However, there can also be a decision to abandon it in favour of desire and emotion, a decision which, for Collingwood, is the rejection of civilization. Collingwood's emphasis on development and his insistence that the process of civilization can never be completed, suggests an amendment to Popper's account of the open society (NL, 41.12 and 36.94). This is that no society can ever be completely open. Every society is always necessarily at least partly closed because it must contain children, and probably also mentally immature adults who are incapable of the rationalist attitude. A society can, therefore, become more open than it is, perhaps even a predominantly open society, but never completely open. Popper's comment that 'We are still in the midst of the transition from the closed to the open society' (OS, I, 58) suggests that the amendment might be acceptable. It entails equating the closed society with the non-social community. But more about that in a moment.

As we have seen, Popper does not distinguish between the irrational and the non-rational. Nor, except by implication in his distinction between critical and uncritical rationalism, has he anything to say about degrees of rationality. Here too Collingwood has something to contribute. The involuntary act of self-liberation is a non-rational, not an irrational act. A mentally immature person who can only act from preference is not irrational. He may be capable of enough instrumental rationality to attain the ends he desires, but such rationality is less than, and inferior to, that of which a mentally mature person who can make choices and decisions is capable.[8] Again, a person who can think and act eristically but not dialectically is not irrational. But he is less rational than a person who can think and act dialectically. It is the attitude of the barbarian which is irrational. Having liberated himself from the dominance of emotion and desire, he decides to let emotion and desire determine his conduct. Having become capable of rational thought and action, he rejects what he has become capable of. This is the attitude of hostility to reason, the anti-rational attitude. According to Collingwood it was the attitude of the Nazis, which is why they were the enemies of modern European civilization.

For Popper, Nazism is simply one more case of an *oracular philosophy* (OS, II, ch. 24). Marxism is another, and to adopt either Marxism or Nazism is to reject the rationalist attitude, and along with it, the open society, in favour of irrationalism. But while Popper himself has convincingly shown that Marxism is philosophically unacceptable, this is not because it is hostile to reason (OS, II, 81, chs.13–17 (135), chs.18–21 (199) and ch.22). It attempts to give a scientific account of society and politics which will provide a programme for rational political action. The attempt is a failure owing to an inadequate understanding of the logic and methodology of scientific inquiry, including the error of confusing prediction with prophecy. But Marxism, unlike Nazism, at least aspires to be rational even though its aspiration is only imperfectly fulfilled. To adopt it is not to adopt irrationalism but a defective form of rationalism. An objection on behalf of Popper is that so far as the open society is concerned, the difference between Marxism and Nazism is only academic. To adopt either, is to reject the open society in favour of a closed society. But granted that both a Marxist and a Nazi society are closed, the sources of their hostility to the open society are different. On the principle of 'Know your enemy', friends of the open society need to understand the difference. Here the dialectic–eristic distinction has something to contribute, although it must be said that Collingwood did not himself take it up.

A Marxist society is comparable to a secular theocracy. Marxist doctrine takes the place of theological orthodoxy, and a ruling party, the place of a ruling priesthood. Thought and action are predominantly eristic because they have to conform to the *correct* interpretation of Marxism laid down by the party. Dialectical thought, for which no *correct* interpretation is sacrosanct, may be permitted in such fields as scientific and technological research which are regarded as uncontentious. But in all doctrinally sensitive areas, it can only be carried on underground in defiance of party orthodoxy.[9] The 'correct' interpretation together with a political programme based upon it, gives a monolithic stability to a Marxist society. In a Nazi society, with its hostility to reason, there can be no such stability. There is no political programme, only the caprice of the leader, and what that will move him to do in the future, neither he nor anyone else can tell. In a Marxist society the process of civilization is arrested but not, as in a Nazi society, rejected. Collingwood's conception of *barbarism* brings out the difference and highlights the danger which in 1941 threatened not only the relatively advanced civilizations of the Western democracies but the arrested civilization of the Soviet Union as well. Popper's conception of *oracular philosophy* cannot do this, owing to its failure to distinguish between the irrational and the non-rational, and to take account of degrees of rationality.

The justification for equating Popper's conception of the closed society with Collingwood's of the non-social community is that each is the conception of a society, or in Collingwood's case, a community, in which the same characteristic is lacking. This is what Popper calls the rationalist attitude, Collingwood the dialectical, and as we have seen, they are different names for the same attitude. According to Collingwood, the attitude is lacking either because the members are incapable of choice and decision and can act only from preference, or because, as in barbarism, those among them who are capable of choice and decision, reject what they are capable of, deciding to let emotion and desire determine their conduct. According to Popper it is lacking either because the members do not understand critical dualism and accept all values and institutions uncritically, or because, while understanding that they are not irrevocably committed to the particular values and institutions of their society, many members adopt irrationalism in the form of some oracular philosophy. Popper's account needs amending in the light of the discussion of the preceding paragraphs. In adopting an oracular philosophy, the members are not necessarily adopting irrationalism. They may be adopting a defective form of rationalism such as Marxism which, because of the eristic attitude it engenders, is largely incompatible with the rationalist attitude. But Collingwood's account also needs amending because of the implications of the dialectic–eristic distinction which he did not develop. As we have seen, these show that in a Marxist society civilization is arrested but not rejected. Another reason, therefore, why the dialectical attitude may be lacking in a community is that those of its members who are capable of choice and decision have committed themselves to eristic thought and action by committing themselves to a comprehensive doctrine such as Marxism. With these amendments, the two conceptions can be equated. Equating them justifies my earlier amendment to Popper: every society is necessarily always at least partly closed because it must contain children and probably mentally immature adults.

I have criticized Popper for failing to distinguish between moral and non-moral norms. Collingwood has something to say about this, but it is not very illuminating. He says of *Duty* that 'A man's duty on a given occasion is that act which is both possible and necessary, the act which at the moment character and circumstance combine to make it inevitable that if he has a free will he should freely will to do it' (NL, 17.8). Decisions about what duty requires are not, however, incorrigible. The most that a man can say is: 'I have considered X, Y, and Z, as claimants for the title of my present duty. X is a better answer than Y and Y than Z. But there may be a better answer than any which I have overlooked' (NL, 17.81). This recalls the deontological intuitionism of Collingwood's Oxford colleagues, Prichard, Ross and Carritt.[10] None of them raised the question of why there should be duty at all, and neither did Collingwood. Both he and they ignored the social basis of morality. To the question which he did not ask, 'How can a man identify claimants for the title of his present duty?', Collingwood might have answered in terms of his account of partnership. The claimants will be those acts by doing which he can make the best contribution in the circumstances to the various partnerships which he has entered into, among which will necessarily be the social community or council of his body politic. His present duty will then be to do what, in his judgement, is the most urgent of these acts. But this is only conjecture.

Collingwood should have said more about morality in general and the moral requirements of a social community in particular. These are matters which must be dealt with in an account of what makes a community civilized, or a society open. Neither Collingwood nor Popper dealt with them satisfactorily.

I criticized Collingwood's theory of the body politic on the grounds that it contains no account of government properly so called, much less of democratic representative government. Popper is not open to this criticism. His protectionist state is recognizable as being in broad outline, the modern European democratic state. A protectionist state must be democratic to prevent abuses of state power and to enable politics to be conducted in the spirit of critical rationalism. On this topic, the state in a civilized or open society, it is Popper who corrects the defects of Collingwood. But Popper did not inquire systematically into the logic of democratic procedures and of democratic political controversy.[11] As we have seen, although Collingwood did not appreciate it, the dialectic–eristic distinction has something to contribute to such an inquiry. There is scope for dialectic in the form of deliberation, and for eristic in the form of advocacy in party politics, notably at elections. But if the adversarial character of party politics is not to get out of hand, advocacy must be tempered by deliberation, and hence eristic by dialectic.[12] Both then have something to contribute to understanding the kind of politics appropriate to a civilized or open society. Popper's contribution is explicit, Collingwood's implicit and inadvertent, but Popper's contribution needs to be supplemented by Collingwood's, notwithstanding its inadvertent character. The perspective of critical rationalism is that of dialectic, not eristic. Popper seems to have missed the significance of advocacy, as distinct from deliberation, in democratic politics.

Popper's failure to distinguish between Nazism's irrationalism and Marxism's defective rationalism does not detract from the merits of his philosophical critique of Marxism, and especially his exposure of its scientific pretensions. Through this he has contributed much to the understanding of the issues at stake between communism and the West in the years after the Second World War. But as we have seen, it was Collingwood rather than Popper who was able to show that what was at stake during that war was the survival of modern European civilization. Nor if he had lived to see it, is it likely that he would have dissented from Popper's critique of Marxism. There are passages early in *The New Leviathan* which show that he had grasped the essentials of Popper's philosophy of science with its emphasis upon falsifiability and the provisional status of all scientific claims to knowledge (NL, 1.3–1.61). Concerning piecemeal social engineering, what Collingwood had to say in *The Idea of History* about the possibility of progress in human affairs suggests that he would have accepted Popper's case against Utopian or wholesale social reform, although probably not the engineering analogy. For him, what was important in any attempt at reform, was not to lose what had already been achieved but to build upon it.

Referring to capitalism, Collingwood says:

> That system has solved a good many problems and therein lies its economic value. But it gives rise to a good many others which as yet it has failed to solve. A better economic system, one whose substitution for this would be a progress, would continue to solve the same problems which are solved by individualist capitalism and solve these others as well. (IH, 333)

Later he says:

> If we want to abolish capitalism or war and in doing so, not only to destroy them but to bring into existence something better, we must begin by understanding them, seeing what the problems are which our economic or international system succeeds in solving and how the solution of these is related to the other problems which it fails to solve. This understanding of the system we set out to supersede is the thing we must retain throughout the work of superseding it. (IH, 334)

He adds a warning:

> Our hatred of the thing we are destroying may prevent us from understanding it, and we may love it so much that we cannot destroy it unless we are blinded by such hatred. But if that is so, there will once more, as so often in the past, be change but no progress. We shall have lost our hold on one group of problems in our anxiety to solve the next, and we ought by now to realise that no kindly law of nature will save us from the fruits of our ignorance, (ibid.)

Collingwood would almost certainly have objected to Popper's treatment of Plato and Hegel in *The Open Society*.[13] He would not have denied that, in his political dialogues, Plato was an intellectual paternalist and no friend of Athenian democracy. What he would have objected to can be epitomized in the comment, which must have occurred to many readers of *The Open Society*, that when Popper likes it he says that it is Socrates, when he does not, that it is Plato, ignoring the fact that the Socrates whom he likes is the Platonic Socrates of whom Plato said in the *Phaedo*, when describing his death, putting the words into the mouth of Phaedo, 'Of all the men I ever knew, he was the wisest and the best.' To judge by the tone and temper of the many comments on Plato scattered through his philosophical works, Collingwood would have found Popper's treatment misleading and distasteful. Concerning the latter's treatment of Hegel, he might well have endorsed G. R. G. Mure's comment that it is 'almost meaninglessly silly' (IH, 334).[14] If he had so reacted, he would have been right. Notwithstanding the interest and vigour of his own thought, Popper is an unreliable guide to the thought of others.[15] In his criticisms of past philosophers, his approach is eristic in spirit. He is not interested in learning from them but in showing that they are wrong. Not so Collingwood. In the many critical discussions of past philosophers in his works, he makes it clear that he is interested in learning from them. His approach is both historical and dialectical: historical in that he always does his best to understand the problem with which a past philosopher was concerned as that philosopher understood it; dialectical in that, in his criticism, he is concerned not only with the formulation of that problem and the solution offered to it, but also with the contribution of both to advancing the philosophical inquiry in the course of which they have arisen.

To judge by the *Idea of History* Collingwood would not have wished to defend historicism from Popper's criticisms. But while agreeing that prediction must not be confused with prophecy, and that neither is the business of history, he would have found Popper lacking in appreciation of the difference between scientific and historical understanding, and of the distinctive character and significance of the latter.[16] He could with justice have accused Popper of 'throwing out the historical baby with the historicist bathwater'. But this is a matter which cannot be pursued further here. Suffice it to say that in writing *The New Leviathan*, Collingwood had at his disposal greater knowledge and understanding than had Popper in writing *The Open Society*. But despite the disparity in their intellectual and scholarly equipment, their respective books must be assessed on their merits. I have tried to do that in this chapter.

*Notes*

[1] All quotations from Collingwood, unless otherwise stated, are from R. G. Collingwood, *The New Leviathan* (Oxford, Clarendon Press, 1947). All quotations from Popper are from K. R. Popper, *The Open Society and its Enemies* (London, Routledge and Kegan Paul, fifth edn, revised 1969), hereafter OS. In giving references to NL, I have followed Collingwood's own system of numbering

[2] An example of the latter is the economist P. T. Bauer; see his essay 'The Grail of Equality' in W. Letwin, ed., *Against Equality: Readings on Economic and Social Policy* (London, Macmillan, 1983).

[3] The remark usually attributed to Goering, 'When I hear the word "culture" I reach for my gun', exemplifies Nazism and barbarism.

[4] Popper makes it clear that 'Protectionism' as he uses it has nothing to do with tariffs, import controls or any kind of economic protection.

[5] This is very much like T. H. Green's view of state action as removing obstacles to individual freedom which, if left to voluntary action, either would not be removed at all or only imperfectly removed.

[6] Cf. Peter Winch's essay 'Nature and Convention', in *Ethics and Action* (London, Routledge, 1972). If I understand him correctly, his criticism of Popper is essentially along the same lines.

[7] Cf. Rush Rees, 'Piecemeal Social Engineering', in his *Without Answers* (London, Routledge, 1959).

[8] In saying that the rationality of the mentally immature is less than and inferior to that of the mentally mature, I am invoking Collingwood's contention in his *Essay on Philosophical Method* that in the philosophical treatment of a concept, in this case the concept of 'rationality', differences of degree are also differences of kind. The key idea in his contention is that of a concept specified in a scale of forms. Although he does not discuss it in NL, Collingwood makes use of it especially in parts 1 and 2, as he does also in *The Principles of Art* in connection with the difference between 'art' and 'craft'. I have not the space to pursue this matter here. For an attempt to apply it to the concept of 'rationality', see my *Freedom and Rights* (London, Allen and Unwin, 1968), ch.3.

[9] Marxism claims to be dialectical, but not in the Platonic sense which Collingwood connected with civilization.

10. Cf. H. A. Prichard, *Moral Obligation* (Oxford, Clarendon Press, 1949), W. D. Ross, *The Right and the Good* (Oxford, Clarendon Press, 1930) and E. F. Carritt, *Morals and Politics* (Oxford, Clarendon Press, 1935). Deontological Intuitionism was the dominant school of moral philosophy at Oxford, if not in Britain, between the wars.
11. I exclude his *Paradox of Democracy* which rests upon the oversimplified characterization of democracy as majority rule. The core of truth in it is that if a significant proportion of citizens, not necessarily a numerical majority, cease to care for and are unwilling to abide by democratic procedures, democracy will break down.
12. Also see my *The Right to Dissent*, ch.5, 'Politics and Controversy' (Aldershot, Avebury Press, 1983)
13. He would almost certainly also have taken exception to Popper's treatment of Aristotle, but for the sake of brevity, I pass over that here.
14. See G. R. G. Mure, *A Study of Hegel's Logic* (Oxford, Clarendon Press, 1951).
15. A partial exception is Marx, to whom in OS Popper accords a more sympathetic treatment. I should add that my comment on his criticism of past philosophers is primarily concerned with what he says in OS.
16. I have in mind especially parts 1–4 of *The Idea of History* and *The Idea of Nature*. As examples of philosophical discussions of Plato and Hegel with which Collingwood would have sympathized, I cite the following, both of which were written many years after the publication of OS. R. K. Cross and A. D. Woozley, *Plato's Republic: a Philosophical Commentary* (London, Macmillan, 1964), and C. Taylor, *Hegel* (Cambridge, Cambridge University Press, 1975).

# A Baconian Revolution: Collingwood and Romano-British Studies[1]

## MARGOT BROWNING

I

During the last three decades, scholarship on R. G. Collingwood's philosophy of history has expanded its horizons from a solely philosophical focus to considering Collingwood's historical writings as well.[2] To a certain extent, this extension parallels what Stephen Toulmin has described as a shift from 'form to function' in the philosophy of science since the 1960s, as philosophers have increasingly incorporated the previously ignored dimension of the history of science.[3] However, Collingwood scholars have not fully taken this further step of placing Collingwood's philosophy of history in its historical context, of incorporating the history of history in analyses of his philosophy of history. In addition to any general interest accruing to such a historical contextualization, the history of history is especially appropriate to Collingwood's philosophy of history, because – as I will argue – his philosophy of history aimed to codify recent developments in historical method. Collingwood observed these methodological developments specifically in his practice as a historian and archaeologist of Roman Britain, and considered these developments, more generally speaking, to effect changes of such magnitude as to warrant being called a 'Baconian revolution'. Aligning himself with the Baconian tradition, Collingwood developed a theory of scientific revolutions and acted as its proponent in Romano-British studies. From a reconstruction of this theory and its exemplification in Romano-

British archaeology, Collingwood's philosophy of history gains an empiricist component overlooked by traditionally idealist interpretations.

The Baconian tradition has fathered numerous reforms in scientific method since Bacon's time; a 'herald of the new science' for the seventeenth-century scientific revolution, his philosophy of science has consequently also served as a standard for theorists seeking methods for investigating humanity.[4] As a founding figure for these subsequent reforms, Bacon is credited – among other contributions – with advocating a new method of investigating nature: the inductive method.[5] As Michel Foucault remarks while discussing the methodology of the human sciences: 'On the threshold of the classical age, Bacon, lawyer and statesman, tried to develop a methodology of investigation for the empirical sciences.' According to Foucault, this methodology for the sciences of nature was born to some extent from the 'practices of investigation' that were invented in the Inquisition; the Inquisition's 'politico-juridical, administrative and criminal, religious and lay, investigation' was no doubt the 'operating model' for the 'great empirical knowledge that covered the things of the world and transcribed them into the ordering of an indefinite discourse that observes, describes and establishes the "facts"'.[6] Collingwood likewise imputes juridical roots to Baconian induction: 'It was Bacon who insisted that the science of nature begins when man begins "putting nature to the question" (that is, the torture; Bacon was a lawyer and knew what "the question" meant in his own profession), extorting from her an answer to the questions he chose to ask, instead of contenting himself with noting down whatever she elected to reveal.'[7]

Contrasting the older sciences of nature with the recently born sciences of man, Foucault asks: 'What Great Observer will produce the methodology of examination for the human sciences?'[8] Collingwood's philosophy of history provides one answer to this question, not for the particular human sciences Foucault had in mind (namely, political economy, biology, and philology) but for history in conjunction with archaeology.[9] Since Collingwood conceived of history as the medium for analysing human affairs, both past and present,[10] his philosophy of history can be apprehended as a candidate for this methodology of examination for the human sciences. While subsequent developments in the human sciences have no doubt disqualified this candidacy, it none the less suits his aspirations as both a philosopher and a historian. He proposed this Baconian methodology for historical science in philosophical and historical terms, which are examined here in his theory of scientific revolutions, his codification of Baconian principles for historical science, and their application to Romano-British archaeology.

In returning inquisitional method to the study of human affairs,[11] Collingwood's codification of this revolution in historical method reflects the cross-fertilization between science and history that had already taken place during the nineteenth century. On the one hand, the advance of historical method had contributed to the concurrent development of the sciences of nature and the sciences of man.[12] During the nineteenth century, according to Collingwood, 'history stood forth the unmistakable queen of the sciences and biologists like Darwin and Huxley, philosophers like Hegel, theologians like Baur and Newman, and economists like Marx explicitly resolved the problems of their special sciences into historical problems.'[13] Toulmin likewise asserts: 'Whether we consider geology, zoology, political philosophy or the study of ancient civilizations, the nineteenth century was in every case the Century of History – a period marked by the growth of a new, dynamic world-picture.'[14]

On the other hand, historical method had itself benefited from these scientific developments. Historical understanding was extended by developments in these other disciplines, as historians adapted principles of 'evolution', 'progress', or 'uniformitarianism' to human affairs. In importing such principles, history acquired empirical methodologies and aims whose ramifications for the study of humanity were as yet unconsidered. As Collingwood discovered, these ramifications could be studied in the emergent discipline of archaeology. Like history, archaeology was subject to the influences of science; like science, it was subject to the influences of history. In Romano-British studies, which was the field of Collingwood's historical specialization, archaeology's methods and its objects were 'historicized' first by natural scientific disciplines and then historicized again by scientific history.

## II Collingwood's Theory of Scientific Revolutions

As a philosopher and historian of both history and science,[15] Collingwood compared these recent transformations of historical method with the seventeenth-century revolution in scientific method, and found in Bacon a herald once again, in this case not for reforms in natural scientific method but for the revolution in historical method that made history a science.[16] As he compares these two Baconian revolutions, he recurrently discusses the elements and dynamics of scientific revolutions.[17] Under analysis, these comparisons from various of his books and articles yield what I am calling his 'theory of scientific revolutions'. This theory has philosophical, historical and archaeological elements, in keeping with the theoretical and practical concerns of his philosophy of history. Philosophically speaking, it distinguishes between the respective roles of theory and technique in a scientific revolution. In historical terms, this theory demarcates definitive conceptual change without radical discontinuities. Finally, archaeology contributes examples of different stages and kinds of scientific thinking and practice.

When considered together, these elements and dynamics compose an unusually broad conception of change in the history of science. To characterize this breadth, Collingwood's theory of scientific revolutions is analysed here with reference to several heuristic models for the history of science. In histories of science, as historian Robert Richards has argued, certain basic characteristics of historical change usually inform fundamentally different historical perspectives on science, and these perspectives serve (explicitly or implicitly) as heuristics for historians of science.[18] Compared with these heuristic models, Collingwood's theory of scientific revolutions incorporates a greater breadth and depth of change on a conceptual dimension than any one of these models by itself encompasses.

Collingwood's theory most resembles what Richards terms the revolutionary model, but it also combines characteristics of the evolutionary model – understood in a non-specialized sense – as well as aspects of the growth model. For example, like the growth model, Collingwood comprehends 'science' not solely as a phenomenon of modern history but within the broader scope of two and a half millennia of Western civilization. In accord with this continuity of 'science', and akin to the evolutionary model, his concept of 'revolution' posits conceptual change in which old and new methods do exist at the same time and in which new techniques alter only in part how a scientist proceeds in his work. These characteristics of the growth and evolutionary models set the conditions of conceptual development for his theory of scientific revolutions, as can be seen with regard to his concepts of 'science', 'revolution', 'progress' and 'rationality'.

Because Collingwood's concept of 'science' is inclusive of all kinds of knowledge in its definition, it allows for a continuity in the history of science more commonly associated with an evolutionary model than a revolutionary one. In his terms, scientific thinking originated with the ancient Greeks, not with the first Baconian revolution in natural science and even less with the hegemonic claims of modern positivist science. 'The word "science"', he asserted, 'in its original sense . . . means a body of systematic or orderly thinking about a determinate subject-matter' (EM, 4). In the seventeenth-century Baconian revolution, according to his interpretation, science changed from a 'science of observing' to a 'science of questioning'; this major revolution in thought did not transform the knowledge of nature from a completely unscientific status to a radically new scientific status. What the first Baconian revolution did accomplish was the creation of a new type of science, whose 'more sophisticated or mature attitude' raised science 'to a level of efficiency which previously would have seemed quite impossible' (EM, 276–7). Whereas 'pre-Baconian science' typically proceeds by first observing facts and then by asking 'what, if anything, they prove,' Baconian science is 'the kind of science in which the first stage is to ask a question and the second stage is to get it answered' (EM, 278).

Just as Collingwood accords to pre-Baconian thinking the status of 'science', he also rejects the exclusive claim of modern natural science to the name of 'science': 'There is also a slang sense of the word, unobjectionable (like all slang) on its lawful occasions, parallel to the slang use of the word "hall" for a music-hall or the word "drink" for alcoholic drink, in which it stands for natural science' (EM, 4). However, as his opposition implies here and elsewhere in his philosophy of history (IH, 228),[19] this very 'slang' sense of 'science' was indeed the reigning one, in which generally speaking one part of the whole of knowledge was substituted for the whole. Such a positivist stance raised 'the methodology of natural science to the level of a universal methodology: [it was] natural science identifying itself with knowledge' (IH, 134). The public authority of the *Encyclopaedia Britannica* illustrates this positivist definition of 'science': in its eleventh edition (1910–11) the article on 'science' acknowledged the 'broadest sense' of the word in which 'science' is 'synonymous with learning and knowledge,' but adopted 'a more restricted meaning,' 'which differentiates "science" from other branches of accurate knowledge'. The article then defined 'science' in the very fashion which Collingwood had denigrated as 'slang': 'science may be defined as ordered knowledge of natural phenomena and of the relations between them; thus it is a short term for "natural science," and as such is used here technically in conformity with a general modern convention.'[20] In claiming that history was indeed a science, and not a positivist one either, Collingwood was assailing this general modern usage.

Like his concept of science, Collingwood's concept of 'revolution' also partially resembles the evolutionary model, in this case because he posits the relative slowness of conceptual change. He analyses two causes of scientific revolution: namely, revolutions in method or revolutions in technique. Although he did not specify the precise relation between the two causes, by implication they respectively bring about changes of a greater or lesser order of magnitude. To take the scientific revolution of greater magnitude first: in such a revolution change is caused by method, yet not by method *per se*; to cause a revolution, method had to have been codified in a form that made it accessible to the ordinary intellect. For this reason, while revolutionary periods in science might appear to be cataclysmic to those undergoing them, in fact the new method had already been in use by individuals and became gradually widespread. In the cases of the Baconian revolution in natural science and the Baconian revolution in historical science, a new method changed each inquiry from a science of observing to a science of questioning: this new method was the method of inquisition, or, in Collingwood's phrase, the 'logic of question and answer'. His analogy between these two revolutions in scientific thought exemplifies the evolutionary role of methodological change:

> Even if the revolution by which history has become a science is only about a half-century old, we must not be deceived by the word 'revolution'. Long before Bacon and Descartes revolutionized natural science by expounding publicly the principles on which its method was based, people here and there had been using these same methods, some more often, some more rarely. As Bacon and Descartes so justly pointed out, the effect of their own work was to put these same methods within the grasp of quite ordinary intellects. When it is said that the methods of history have been revolutionized in the last half-century, this is what is meant. It is not meant that examples of scientific history will be sought in vain before that date. It is meant that whereas, earlier, scientific history was a thing of rare occurrence, hardly to be found except in the work of outstanding men, and even in them marking moments of inspiration rather than the even tenor of study, it is now a thing within the compass of everyone; a thing which we demand of everybody who writes history at all, and which is widely enough understood, even among the unlearned, to procure a livelihood for writers of detective stories whose plot is based upon its methods. (IH, 320)

Thus in Collingwood's view of the first scientific revolution, the philosophy of science played an essential role; by analogy, the Baconian revolution in historical method requires similar methodological codifications. His own philosophy of history exemplifies this premise in its history of the idea of history: best known in *The Idea of History,* his philosophy traces the development of the idea of history in the theories of philosophers (for the most part) and of some historians, and proposes his own codification of Baconian method for history. With regard to archaeology, as we shall see, he propounded his philosophical codification of Baconian method for archaeological theory and practice in Britain, in effect assuming the role of a modern-day Baconian revolutionary.

On a lesser order of magnitude, the scientific thinking of specific fields of knowledge can also be revolutionized by the introduction of a new 'technique'; as examples, Collingwood cites the astronomer's telescope and the archaeological technique of excavation. Such powerful techniques provide the scientist with a new 'weapon' (presumably for the better prosecution of his inquisition). In this case as well, his theory of scientific revolutions stresses the continuous character of conceptual change. When scientific thinking was changed by the incorporation of a new technique, what changed was only one aspect of scientific practice: the 'order of facts'. On the one hand, Collingwood recognizes that this change had a major impact on the scientist's activities: because the business of the scientist is 'to theorize on a basis of fact,' a change in the order of facts required him 'to reorganize his whole world'. In this reorganization,

> The old theories are superseded; the old controversies become meaningless; the old problems become unimportant. In such a landslide, it is difficult for any scientist to keep his head; impossible perhaps, were it not that revolutions of this kind (like all revolutions, when you understand their true history) happen very gradually.

Hence, on the other hand, whereas this landslide might tempt a scientist to think 'that such a revolution changes everything,' in fact the new technique 'changes only one thing – the materials which in his theorizing the scientist has to use'. In this new order of facts, 'the starting-point of the work of theorizing has changed.' However, Collingwood insists, 'the ways in which he can use them remain unchanged' – 'the nature of that work [of theorizing] itself is unaltered.'[21]

Consequently, Collingwood's theory of scientific revolutions is similar to the growth model for the history of science, since his theory maintains that the development of historical thought has consisted of steady, long-term progress. Moreover, it claims that this development is fundamentally rational. First, with regard to such a conception of progress in the history of science, this steady advance is illustrated in his histories: namely, both his history of history as a kind of knowledge in general and his history of the specific field of Romano-British studies. In each case, he characterizes the stages of history's advance in epochs; and in these accounts, these stages correspond for Western history in general and for Romano-British history in particular. In his periodization of Western civilization, the idea of history originated in Greco-Roman historiography; it was influenced by Christianity from early Christianity to the Enlightenment; it reached the threshold of scientific history from Romanticism to Positivism; and finally achieved scientific status in theories of history beginning at the start of the twentieth century. Likewise, in his periodization of Romano-British archaeology, the history of the problem of the Roman Wall divides into similar stages: the ancient authorities (the Roman historians), the native historians (medieval scholars), the period of surface inspection of ancient remains from the Elizabethan age to the Enlightenment, the beginning of scientific excavation during the early nineteenth century, and finally the period of scientific excavation which commenced during the 1890s.[22]

With regard to the second issue of whether scientific development is rational or irrational, Collingwood defends the fundamentally rational character of such conceptual development as an assumption on which the 'very possibility' of 'all science and all history depend'. One such defence epitomizes his interdisciplinary interpretation of science, history and archaeology; it appears in his second article on the history of the problem of the Roman Wall. In his view, what is at stake in this assumption of rationality is the reality of scientific ideals of method and of truth: 'If the facts of nature and of human history are nonsense facts, obeying no law, forming no intelligible whole, connected by no rational relations, then scientific and historical thought are folly, and their ideals of method and of truth are delusions.' To an audience of historians and archaeologists, he outlined the success of science in this respect, and upheld it as a goal for history to achieve in its own right:

> The real service which natural science does to the human mind lies in the assurance which it gives, by the forward march of its discoveries, that no part of nature can remain finally impenetrable to human understanding. Science achieves this result by taking a special portion of nature and thinking about it until the object becomes, as it were, incandescent in the flame of thought, and is revealed as wholly intelligible. If there is any residue of unintelligibility left over at the end of the process, when science has done all it can, the whole process is in vain.

He next exhorted his colleagues to consummate the Baconian revolution in history:

> In the same way, history can only demonstrate its own right to exist by demonstrating the rationality of its subject-matter; and this it must do, not by showing that certain points or tracts, scattered here and there in the abyss of time, shine with the light of rationality, but by showing that any tangle of human facts, patiently unravelled, makes sense.

Finally, he used this principle to justify his own history of the problem of the Roman Wall: 'If the real is rational, it is possible, by intense and methodical thought, to see the mass of facts accumulated by the blind or half-blind industry of generations of archaeologists, as a luminous whole, out of which rises the truth.'[23]

Thus, Collingwood's theory of scientific revolutions places them in this broader context of continuous, slow, progressive and rational change. Within this context of conceptual change, his theory resembles what Richards calls the revolutionary model: the most essential feature of this model is that 'a revolution in thought, a decisive overthrow of distinctly ancient modes of conception, is necessary to set a discipline on the smooth course of modern science.'[24] That Collingwood preferred a revolutionary model can be inferred in several regards. His concepts of scientific revolution and political revolution are similar, and at one point, in speaking of the former, he parenthetically makes reference to the latter.[25] In addition, he often criticizes the use of organic models for human history[26] because they imply biological development rather than the civilizational analogue implicit in 'revolution'.

Furthermore, from Collingwood's philosophical and historical writings, his references to revolutions in historical thought can be recovered; and the composite concept that emerges satisfies this essential feature of the revolutionary model (as quoted above). In historical thinking, the ancient modes of conception were 'scissors-and-paste history' and 'critical history,' both prevalent during the nineteenth century (IH, 269); he compares this condition of historical studies with that of natural science before Galileo (A, 79). In contrast, by the end of the nineteenth century, 'historical thought had been achieving an acceleration in the velocity of its progress and an enlargement in its outlook comparable to those which natural science had achieved about the beginning of the seventeenth century' (A, 87). With this acceleration and enlargement of historical studies, its ancient modes of conception were overthrown: 'in scientific history, or history proper, the Baconian revolution has been accomplished' (IH, 269). This revolution was indeed decisive: 'It would be an understatement to say that since 1800 history has passed through a Copernican revolution. Looking back from the present day [1938] one sees that a much greater revolution has been accomplished than that associated with the name of Copernicus' (A, 79n.).

Collingwood's archaeological writings describe a revolution of a lesser order of magnitude, one brought about by the new technique of excavation. To contrast it with a revolution of greater magnitude, such as the Baconian revolution in historical method, we can interpolate that this lesser revolution involves the overthrow of ancient techniques rather than modes of conception, and occurs distinctively in different fields of knowledge, such as archaeology or astronomy, rather than occurring once for an entire division of knowledge. Prior to what Collingwood termed the 'archaeological revolution of the nineteenth century,'[27] English antiquaries had employed such techniques as literary interpretation of ancient texts and surface inspection of the remains to formulate theories about the Roman Wall in England.[28] During the nineteenth century, antiquaries began to excavate the remains which previously had only been viewed on their surfaces. Collingwood locates the cause of this revolution in the high level of theoretical thinking that preceded it:

> Repeatedly, in the history of science, you will find that the best theoretical thinking is done just before a revolution. It is, in fact, the high quality of this thinking, the finality of its conclusions on the basis of existing evidence, that necessitates the revolution, by convincing men that nothing more can be done until we have learnt to explore a new region of facts.

The technique of excavation brought to light 'a new region of facts' that forced Romano-British theoreticians of the Wall to reconsider their facts in a new order. Yet such a revolution in technique could also lead scientists to ignore the role of theory:

> They become engrossed in the use of their new method, and accumulate fact upon fact, forgetting that to the scientist facts are useless except so far as they become a basis for theories. Absorbed in the excitement of hunting new facts, they neglect the discipline of theoretical thinking, and in consequence an advance in scientific technique is often accompanied by a falling-off in the quality of scientific thought.[29]

In Collingwood's view, how were these two kinds of revolutions – of method and of technique – linked together? Although not stated in the texts from which I have reconstructed this theory, the connection of these two kinds of revolutions can be inferred from his histories. On a greater order of magnitude, Collingwood's reflexive history of the idea of history culminates with the Baconian revolution in historical method (i.e. in *Idea of History*). Likewise, within the microcosm of Romano-British studies, his history of the problem of the Roman Wall in England finds its resolution with the application of Baconian method to the relatively new technique of archaeological excavation.

These two revolutions contributed to one another. On the one hand, the technical revolution in archaeology added to the accelerated progress and enlarged outlook of nineteenth-century history, thereby contributing to the Baconian revolution in method: 'the whole apparatus of archaeological research' was one source of 'a vast increase of detailed historical knowledge' from the 'compilation of vast masses of carefully sifted material' (IH, 127).[30] On the other hand, the Baconian revolution in historical method brought badly needed 'theoretical discipline' (as Collingwood termed it) to antiquarian excavations. After all, nineteenth-century excavation was 'pioneer work, and inevitably destroyed much evidence which to-day would be valuable': it was not 'what we call scientific digging'.[31] Beginning in the 1890s, principles and methods of scientific archaeology were developed through the unusual conjunction of academics and antiquaries working together on the problem of the Roman Wall. As a consequence, the new theory about the Wall's history would stand on a 'somewhat different footing from any which preceded it': it would be 'tested throughout by the spade'.[32]

Thus, the second Baconian revolution consisted of methodological and technical advances in history and archaeology analogous to the kinds of developments that caused the first Baconian revolution. In both of these two Baconian revolutions, according to Collingwood, each science – a science of nature as well as a science of humanity – adopted a method of questioning; its subject of knowledge was fundamentally rational; and its development was progressive. In these several ways, Collingwood's theory emphasizes similarities between the first Baconian revolution in natural science and its counterpart in historical science. In so doing, his theory incorporated an empirical dimension into historical science.

Yet in characterizing this second revolution in historical method as Baconian, does Collingwood controvert his customary critique of positivistic models for historical knowledge by using natural science as a model for historical theory and practice?[33] How could the method of inquisition be applied to a human science, an inquiry which took not 'nature' as its object but 'humanity'? Generally speaking, Collingwood defines a Baconian revolution as a 'revolution which converted a blind and random study into one where definite questions are asked and definite answers are insisted upon' (A, 124). On this common ground he compares the seventeenth-century revolution in natural science with the nineteenth-century revolution in historical science. Unlike other modern philosophies of history whose positivist tendencies he critiqued,[34] however, Collingwood returned this empirical method of inquisition to the sphere of studying human affairs in accordance with Idealist philosophical principles.[35]

## III  Archaeology Historicized

Whereas Collingwood's theory of scientific revolutions emphasizes the similarities between scientific history and natural science, his codification of Baconian principles for historical method differentiates knowledge of nature from knowledge of humanity. On the one hand, as we have seen, the likeness between scientific history and natural science lay in the method of inquisition which he advocated for scientific history. In returning this 'operating model' (as Foucault termed it) to its original sphere of human affairs, Collingwood's theory transformed the Baconian inquisitional investigation of nature into a mode of scientific knowledge of humanity. According to his reformulation of Baconian method for history, 'the historian puts his authorities in the witness-box, and by cross-questioning extorts from them information which in their original statements they have withheld, either because they did not wish to give it or because they did not possess it' (IH, 237). On the other hand, however, Collingwood's codification of Baconian methodology for history distinguishes the objects and methods of historical science from those of natural science. This codification reflects the reciprocal influences of historical and archaeological studies on each other, as they both underwent synchronous Baconian revolutions: for history, a revolution in methodology; and for archaeology, a revolution in technique.

According to Collingwood's analysis, the broader Baconian revolution in historical method (in distinction from the Baconian revolution in natural scientific method) consisted not only in the application of the method of inquisition to history, which he termed the 'principle of question and answer' (A, 122–6)[36] but also comprised two additional principles. A second principle differentiates the object of historical science from that of natural science by asserting its internality: 'since history proper is the history of thought, there are no mere "events" in history: what is miscalled an "event" is really an action and expresses some thought (intention, purpose) of its agent; the historian's business is therefore to identify this thought' (A, 127–8). A third principle of the Baconian revolution in history makes history itself a methodological tool for the formulation of theory: 'no historical problem should be studied without studying what I called its second-order history; that is, the history of historical thought about it' (A, 132). These three principles constitute Collingwood's codification of the nineteenth-century developments in historical method that culminated by century's end in 'scientific history.' By the late 1930s, he described these principles as 'more or less unconsciously, common ground among historians'; though historians might not consciously recognize them, he argued that they were 'principles by which the historian ought to stand firm through thick and thin' (A, 121–2).

In Collingwood's codification of principles for Baconian history, archaeology played a crucial role, as he recounted in his *Autobiography*. Archaeology served as a 'laboratory' in which he conducted 'experiments' in historical epistemology in particular as well as epistemology in general; from these thought-experiments he developed his 'logic of question and answer' (A, 24–5, 30). By 1914, as Collingwood related, 'I had made myself an expert in a certain kind of research, and had found out how to use it as a laboratory for testing epistemological theories' (A, 28). While archaeology informed his epistemology, at the same time his philosophical inquiries also influenced his theory and practice of archaeology.[37] In pursuit of philosophical issues, he was attracted to 'obscure provinces' of knowledge, such as Roman Britain, in which 'you have to invent new methods for studying them, and then you will probably find that the cause of their obscurity is some defect in the methods hitherto used' (A, 86).[38] Finally, archaeology served as the model for his codification of Baconian principles:

> In describing these researches into historical method, I am taking most of my examples from archaeology (that is, history in which the sources used are 'unwritten' sources, or, more accurately, are not pre-existing narratives of the events into which the historian is inquiring). But this is not because my results did not equally apply to history whose sources are 'written'. The reason I am talking so much about archaeology is that in archaeology the issue raised by the project of a Baconian revolution is unmistakable. (A, 133)

As these quotations attest, Collingwood's *Autobiography* provides direct testimony of the mutual influence among archaeology, history and philosophy in his thinking; his other writings also illustrate how he connected his epistemological concerns and archaeological research. For instance, in making a distinction between a 'science of observing' and a 'science of questioning' in *An Essay in Metaphysics*, he noted how his historical and archaeological research had given him personal experience of these two kinds of science: in British history and archaeology, the differences between these two kinds of science had divided 'researchers into two camps. There has been a kind of war between the two camps, in which I have taken part' (EM, 276).[39] On the other hand, from the archaeological trenches, Collingwood reminded his colleagues of the epistemological implications of their research for historical science at the close of an article on Hadrian's Wall:

> It is only by the determined attempt to make sense of a collection of historical data which at first seem nonsense, that we can discover whether we are right, as historians, to assume that the real is rational and the rational real, or whether the story of human affairs is 'a tale told by an idiot, full of sound and fury, signifying nothing'.[40]

While Collingwood thereby apprehended archaeology as an epistemological laboratory, and as a science of observing or a science of questioning, what in fact was the status of archaeological knowledge during Collingwood's lifetime? In the Introduction to Collingwood's *Autobiography*, Toulmin recalls for us that when Collingwood first encountered ancient history, it was 'in some disarray. The work of Schliemann at Troy, and of Arthur Evans at Knossos, had made the recovery of Antiquity a matter of popular interest, a craze, even "big business". In the excitement of discovery, serious intellectual questions were thrown into shade.' Archaeology needed to be put in order:

> Against this background, Collingwood's historiographical arguments represent a necessary return to the concerns of science and scholarship. The primary business of archaeologists and historians is not to dig up art objects for display in museums . . . so much as to formulate and answer significant questions about past modes of human life and thought.[41]

As Collingwood put it, ancient monuments must be treated 'not as objects of sentimental pilgrimage but as potential sources of historical knowledge' (A, 127).[42] In order to reorient ancient archaeology to historical scholarship, he became a self-avowed 'preacher' for the conjoined Baconian revolutions in historical method and archaeological technique.[43]

In claiming archaeology for historical science, Collingwood acquired for Baconian history a field of knowledge that had already undergone an earlier stage of historicization. During the nineteenth century, archaeology originated as a 'scientific' discipline from principles developed in geology and in evolutionary theory, which themselves had recently benefited from a temporal perspective. From this historicized study of nature, archaeology adopted for the study of humanity a set of principles that visually interpreted time: the principles of uniformitarianism, stratigraphy and the vastly extended age of the earth.[44] From these geological principles new excavation techniques were invented. As Toulmin asserts, 'the application of geological techniques to the study of human history was adding "the testimony of things" to the evidence of documents and archives, so creating the beginnings of archaeology.'[45] Concurrently, evolutionary theory contributed to the interpretation of archaeological artefacts; new testimony was elicited from 'things' when they were classified and ordered in temporal sequences according to their characteristics.[46]

As an ancillary science of history, archaeology contributed qualitatively more to Romano-British history than merely the acquisition of a new body of specialized knowledge, like numismatics. Because -- unlike epigraphy or palaeography – archaeology's sources were unwritten, providing the 'testimony of things,' archaeology made historical science empirical in a distinctively objective fashion. Collingwood recognized this differentiation between the objects of historical and archaeological research when he defined archaeology as 'history in which the sources used are "unwritten" sources, or, more accurately, are not pre-existing narratives of the events into which the historian is inquiring'. However, he didn't press this distinction and acknowledge that archaeological examples made the Baconian revolution in history 'unmistakable' especially because the objects of archaeological knowledge were not texts but things (A, 133). (To have done so, I suggest, would have run counter to his larger goal of differentiating historical science from natural science.)

Like the acquisition of Baconian method for historical science, this acquisition of archaeology for historical science reoriented it from the study of nature to the study of humanity. In so doing, as Toulmin indicates, Collingwood provided archaeology with a methodology of inquiry that it had previously lacked. To make Romano-British archaeology useful to history, Collingwood reconceived the object of archaeological inquiry in terms of Baconian principles of historical method. Historicized once through its adoption of temporal principles from the natural sciences, archaeology was historicized a second time with the aim of making it a human science. Viewing historical knowledge itself as an autonomous realm of scientific knowledge independent of natural science, Collingwood subsumed archaeology to history as a species of historical knowledge.

When Romano-British archaeology was historicized a second time, undergoing a Baconian revolution in historical method, it acquired a methodology of inquiry from the application of Baconian-cum-Collingwoodian principles.[47] In keeping with Collingwood's codification of these three principles, this archaeological methodology employed 'inquisition,' imputed 'purpose' to its object of knowledge and required the use of theory. These new methodological principles contributed to making archaeology 'scientific' because they trained the archaeologist's vision and informed his conception of what he saw. Intended in this sense, 'science' assumed that the 'knower' and the 'known' were related, that the knower contributed to the constitution of his object of knowledge (A, 25–6). This assumption was a central tenet of Collingwood's epistemology more generally, one that led him to argue against positivistic conceptions of methodology in several arenas, including the philosophy of history.[48] Thus Collingwood's methodology for Baconian archaeology not only dismissed the antiquarian craze to which Toulmin refers, but also superseded a positivistic understanding of archaeological knowledge, thereby bringing archaeology up to date with other similar, earlier efforts in epistemology.[49]

If and when the Baconian revolutions in historical method and archaeological technique were combined, the result for archaeology was a dialectical inquiry between questions that posed definite problems, and answers that contained historical content. Archaeologists then became inquisitors in the service of historical knowledge; in Collingwood's terms, they developed a method of excavation that selected its site and plan for digging in line with outstanding historical questions, and sought to answer or modify these questions as the dig proceeded. Thus, the Baconian archaeologist guided his dig not solely according to the site at hand, following its character to determine how the excavation proceeded, but also according to the problems he needed currently to solve. Collingwood had discovered this principle as he experimented in his 'laboratory of knowledge'; his account of this discovery is worth quoting in full because it contrasts a method of questioning with a method of observation. Experimenting in his 'laboratory of knowledge,' he asked himself a number of questions:

> at first . . . a quite vague question, such as: 'was there a Flavian occupation on this site?' then dividing that question into various heads and putting the first in some such form as this: 'are these Flavian sherds and coins mere strays, or were they deposited in the period to which they belong?' and then considering all the possible ways in which light could be thrown on this new question, and putting them into practice one by one, until at last I could say, 'There was a Flavian occupation; an earth and timber fort of such and such plan was built here in the year a+/-b and abandoned for such and such reasons in the year x+/-y.' Experience soon taught me that under these laboratory conditions one found out nothing at all except in answer to a question; and not a vague question either, but a definite one. That when one dug saying merely, 'Let us see what there is here', one learnt nothing,

except casually in so far as casual questions arose in one's mind while digging: 'Is that black stuff peat or occupation-soil? Is that a potsherd under your foot? Are those loose stones a ruined wall?' That what one learnt depended not merely on what turned up in one's trenches but also on what questions one was asking: so that a man who was asking questions of one kind learnt one kind of thing from a piece of digging which to another man revealed something different, to a third something illusory, and to a fourth nothing at all. (A, 24–5)[50]

This principle of question and answer differentiates between what Collingwood characterized as the two 'warring camps' of British historical and archaeological research: with this inquisitional method, scientists practice a 'science of questioning'; without it they are consigned to a 'science of observing' or even to mere observation. Whereas the latter researchers might insist that they approached a site with a problem in mind such as 'Let us see what we can find out about this site,' Collingwood countered that such a problem was only a 'pseudo-question' which covered 'a multitude of possible questions' without 'precisely expressing any of them' (A, 122). Such a vague question could not motivate a logic of inquiry.

In Baconian archaeology, what kind of object is the researcher to subject to such torture? In Collingwood's analogy between Baconian inquisition in natural science and in historical science, he put the historian's 'authorities in the witness-box' (IH, 237); then, what kind of testimony could and should the archaeologist elicit from artefacts? Applying Collingwood's second principle of historical methodology (that 'history proper is the history of thought'), the artefact should be compelled to witness to its 'purpose'. To force artefacts to testify, the archaeologist must ask two questions of any object: first, 'What was it for?' and secondly, 'Was it good or bad for it? i.e., was the purpose embodied in it successfully embodied in it, or unsuccessfully?' (A, 128).

Collingwood distinguishes the use of such questions in archaeological inquiries from their use in geological research, thereby historicizing the archaeological object a second time as well. To differentiate this use he argues:

> There is a certain analogy between the archaeologist's interpretation of a stratified site and the geologist's interpretation of rock-horizons with their associated fossils; but the difference is no less clear than the

similarity. The archaeologist's use of his stratified relics depends on his conceiving them as artifacts serving human purposes and thus expressing a particular way in which men have thought about their own life. (IH, 212)

To the archaeologist, his artefacts are not (only, I would add) stone, clay or metal; they are (also) 'building-stone and potsherds and coins; debris of a building, fragments of domestic utensils, and means of exchange, all belonging to a bygone age whose purposes they reveal to him' (A, 108). These questions about purpose historicized the artefact for two reasons: first, because the historian must himself supply historical evidence to answer them definitively (A, 128); and secondly, because purpose was essential to historical understanding: the archaeologist could use artefacts 'as historical evidence only so far as he understands what each one of them was for' (A, 108). Like a prosecuting attorney or a laboratory scientist, in order to complete his inquiry the archaeologist had to bring information to bear on his witness that in itself it did not provide.

How would the prosecuting archaeologist know what specific questions to ask of a site, or indeed for what reasons to select a particular site in the first place? And what evidence would provide the necessary context for interpreting the purpose of an artefact or a site? In order to practice the first two principles of Baconian methodology, the archaeologist must possess historical knowledge. Collingwood's third principle of Baconian methodology locates the inquiry from which the archaeologist would gain this knowledge: the archaeologist must be knowledgeable about the history of the problem he is studying, that is, about 'the history of historical thought about it' (A, 123). This principle adds a final historical dimension to archaeological method and the object of archaeological knowledge. It implies several criteria for archaeological interpretation: first, that archaeological interpretation of evidence should involve previous thinking about the evidence at hand; second, that the previous thought relevant to archaeological evidence was historical thinking; and finally, that this historical thought constituted the problem to which the archaeologist's inquiry addressed itself. While obvious to us, these criteria established that archaeologists should interpret their finds in terms of theory. These criteria were correctives to kinds of archaeology that paid little or no attention to theory at all, or related archaeological evidence to aesthetic, political or religious concerns extraneous to the historical problem at hand; as well as to archaeology that focused less on historical theory than on evolutionary theory.

For Romano-British archaeology and history, Collingwood put this third principle into practice as the field's historiographer. Especially in his two articles on the historiography of Hadrian's Wall, he gave a history of the problem of the Wall, a problem that concerned when the Wall had been built. From Collingwood's historiographical viewpoint, past investigations into the history of this problem were theories that offered possible solutions to the problem. Although the main protagonists of this history were relatively minor English antiquaries, the German historian Theodor Mommsen also contributed to the solution of this problem, so that recent historical thinking was included in formulating this archaeological problem.[51] In addition, Collingwood simultaneously presented the history of these theories as a progressive development of archaeological method that culminated in both the invention of scientific techniques of archaeological excavation and the definitive solution of the problem of the Wall: this culmination had occurred when archaeological inquiry had recently identified its builder as the Emperor Hadrian rather than Severus.[52]

Moreover, in these articles Collingwood also assessed the purpose for which the Wall had been built and how well it had fulfilled that purpose. According to his interpretation of current scholarship, the Wall's purpose was not primarily military but more 'in the nature of a police work,' designed 'not to repulse hostile armies, but to keep out raiders and reivers'.[53] Additionally, the Wall was determined to have been adequately constructed and competently designed for this purpose: 'it never fell in fair fight, and when properly manned it was always perfectly able to do the work for which it was designed.'[54] True to his mission as a preacher, then, Collingwood used these historiographical articles about Hadrian's Wall to exemplify, explicate and finally to justify Baconian principles in history and archaeology: 'A single highly complex problem like that of Hadrian's Wall, just because of its richness in apparently pointless and fruitless minutiae of evidence and interpretation, offers a perfect field for that experimental work without which no scientific method can be devised.'[55]

For the practising archaeologist, these three Baconian principles of historical method implied the kind of scientific knowledge he ought to seek. Here again, the differences between a positivist and a Baconian-cum-Collingwoodian conception of 'science' formed the terms of discussion. Just as Collingwood called for a more powerful scientific method than the 'science of observing' could provide, he likewise insisted that archaeological knowledge should aim for more than knowledge of 'the general and the particular'. For the Baconian archaeologist, his methodology included knowledge of the general and the particular, but its aim was, rather, knowledge of the individual. In this fashion Baconian methods of inquiry harnessed archaeology and history together in a logic of inquiry; according to Collingwood's analysis, the steps of this logic alternated constantly between 'the general and the individual, the individual as end and the general as means'. For example, generalizations available from the inductive study of pottery might enable an archaeologist to recognize from stray artefacts on a site the presence of a Roman villa; in such a case, generalizations would have served as a means to the knowledge of the individual (i.e. a Roman villa). Alternately, archaeological evidence might question historical interpretation: 'this inductive study [of pottery] is itself based on ascertained facts; but these facts in their turn are never at any given moment finally ascertained.' Thus, historical research proceeds by 'using its own previous results as materials upon which to generalize in order thereby to help itself in the determination of fresh facts.'[56]

Because the Baconian revolution in historical method was a recent achievement, in Collingwood's view historical and archaeological research were still threatened by this positivistic misconception of scientific knowledge which would limit it to making generalizations from particular instances. Despite the fact that history had 'created within itself new bodies of generalised thought'; and even though historians were tending 'to group themselves into what seem to be independent sciences' (such as archaeology, numismatics, palaeography etc.), he insisted that these bodies of generalized thought as well as these 'independent' sciences should still be subordinated to history: to history's 'own supreme end, the determination or interpretation of individual fact,' 'the reconstruction of historical narrative.' An archaeologist should aim for conclusions that individualize rather than generalize: he should reach conclusions not in the form 'we can now assert that Samian bowls of shape 29 went out of use about AD 80,' but in the form 'we can now assert that Agricola built this fort.'[57] Only with this aim would archaeological knowledge fully realize its Baconian revolution.

Thus, as historiographer for Romano-British studies and methodologist for archaeology and history more generally, Collingwood effected 'a necessary return to the concerns of science and scholarship,' as Toulmin has described. As we have seen, Collingwood claimed archaeology for historical ends, and defined these ends as 'scientific' in a broader sense of the term than the narrower model of 'natural science' would provide. As a historical science, the object of archaeological knowledge was humanity, conceived not as 'nature' but as 'thought.' In order for the object of archaeological knowledge to be constituted as 'humanity-as-thought' according to Collingwood's codification, archaeological methodology had had to undergo historicization in the practice of his predecessors.

## IV  Excavations in Romano-British Archaeology

This historicization of archaeology – or the lack of it – can be illustrated by contrasting two Romano-British excavations at the start of the twentieth century: the excavation of the Roman Wall and the excavation of Roman Silchester. Important milestones in Romano-British archaeology in their own right, these two excavations also figure in Collingwood's critique of 'Baconian' versus 'antiquarian' archaeology.[58] The respective success and failure of these two excavations exemplifies how Baconian revolutions in technique and method did not necessarily occur together, as was the case at Silchester; and by contrast, how the conjunction of the two Baconian revolutions empowered the advance of archaeological and historical knowledge, as occurred at the Roman Wall.

Because each of these archaeological projects employed the technique of excavation, they both had progressed beyond earlier stages of antiquarian field-work or mere speculation: at the very least, their methods were empirical. None the less, although these excavations took place during the same two decades (the 1890s and 1900s), at the Silchester site neither the method nor the objects of archaeological study was historicized: the excavation failed to record any temporal dimension to the site of this Roman town. By contrast, at sites on the Roman Wall, both archaeological method and objects were historicized, and these sites successfully determined the hard-won answer to a centuries-old controversy over when and by whom the Wall had been built. What differences account for the failure of the one and the success of the other?

These two contemporaneous excavations exemplify how archaeological techniques developed under the respective influences of natural scientific methods and theories versus historical methods and theories. At Roman Silchester, the excavators were influenced by the evolutionary and stratigraphical archaeology of General Pitt-Rivers; considered the 'father of scientific excavation' in England, Pitt-Rivers historicized archaeological method by incorporating principles from geology and evolutionary theory.[59] Under the aegis of the Society of Antiquaries of London, the Silchester excavation adopted Pitt-Rivers's innovative method of total excavation and his procedures for recording its results; since the site of Silchester covered one hundred acres, the goal of total excavation presented an unprecedented challenge. Undertaken with Pitt-Rivers's personal involvement at its inception, the total excavation of this site took twenty years (1890–1909) of seasonal digging to complete, and produced maps of the town and plans of its buildings which were detailed and highly accurate.[60]

However, despite the thorough and meticulous record the site's published reports provided, they proved to be of little or no historical use: the town's excavators had omitted stratigraphical principles from their methodology. The excavation's methodology did not attain the status even of a 'science of observing' (to use Collingwood's term) but was – at best – merely observation. As we might expect, Collingwood's criticism was scathing:

> The result was that, although museums were choked with the finds, amazingly little (as it now appears) was discovered about the history of the site. The Society of Antiquaries had excavated Silchester in this style for twenty years running; and although long before the end of that time the principles of stratigraphical digging were familiar even to the

general public, and the dating of strata on Roman sites by coins and pottery was a well-established practice, the Silchester excavations fixed the date neither of the town's beginning nor of its end, nor of the walls nor of the street-plan, nor of a single house or public building, nor even of any alteration carried out to a house or public building. The analysis of the bath-building into work of several different periods remains a model of its kind, except for the fact that not one of these periods was dated; so that the whole analysis is historically useless. Phases in the occupation of this or that house which can now be dated, on the evidence of parallels elsewhere, to the fourth century or even the third, were ascribed by pure guess-work to 'wandering herdsmen' of the Dark Ages. (A, 125–6)[61]

Assessed in Collingwood's terms, the results of the Silchester excavation could be characterized as achieving only the first stage of a combined archaeological and historical inquiry: the excavation did recover particulars about the town, but its reports neither made generalizations about these particulars, nor utilized them further for comparative study, nor inferred historical knowledge about this individual town or its buildings from them.[62] Consequently, the excavation of Silchester illustrates how the first historicization of archaeology (by geology or evolutionary theory) was a precarious achievement.

If the concurrent excavation of the Roman Wall had employed the method of total excavation, it too would have been unsuccessful in maintaining the historicization of archaeology. The drawbacks of conceptualizing a site in only this way are graphically illustrated by the problem of how to excavate the Roman Wall in northern England. Collingwood succinctly poses the problem of how to conceive of this Wall as an archaeological site:

> The peculiarity of the problem depended on the fact that the site to be studied was 73 miles long by, say, a quarter of a mile broad. The strongest staff in the world, backed by all the financial resources at the disposal of British archaeology, could never have excavated these sixteen square miles in the way in which the Society of Antiquaries excavated Silchester. The excavation of Silchester took twenty years; at that rate, to excavate the Wall would have taken two thousand.[63]

The solution to this problem lay in the confluence of historical theory and archaeology that had been initiated by nineteenth-century German historiography on the Roman provinces. Led by the scholar Theodor Mommsen, this historiography provided a model for both criticizing sources (such as Latin inscriptions) and using these sources to compose histories, as well as a comparative perspective on the different Roman frontiers.[64] This innovative historiography was transmitted to Romano-British studies in part by an English disciple of Mommsen's, the Oxford professor F. J. Haverfield,[65] and under his leadership was developed further by English academics and antiquaries at the Roman Wall – among them, R. G. Collingwood, who had been Haverfield's student at Oxford. For English historians and antiquaries, this model overturned traditional practices whereby historians were unlikely to create their own materials, and antiquaries were unlikely to write histories (as the Silchester excavation demonstrated).

In contrast to Pitt-Rivers's method of total excavation, the newly forged archaeological partnership of English academics and antiquaries invented what Collingwood called a method of 'selective excavation'.[66] Whereas the method of total excavation proceeded according to the excavator's conception of a physically defined site, the method of selective excavation delimited a physical site according to a conception, the historical problem at hand. In relation to a historical problem, selective excavation applied a 'science of questioning' to archaeological technique, in which the inquisitor mediated between historical theory and archaeological evidence in order to produce historical narrative. According to Collingwood, Haverfield and his colleagues of the Cumberland Excavation Committee used this method to excavate the Wall: they were

> consciously and completely Baconian in their methods. They never dug a trench without knowing exactly what information they were looking for; they knew both that this information was the next thing they needed for the progress of their study, and also that this trench would give it them. That is why they could settle highly intricate and abstruse problems at a cost of never more, and often much less, than thirty or forty pounds a year. And their successors in the north adopted and continued to apply their principles. (A, 124)

As Collingwood deftly put the difference: applied to archaeology, Lord Acton's maxim 'study problems, not periods' would be changed to 'study problems, not sites' (A, 125).

At the Roman Wall, therefore, the method of selective

excavation combined the revolution in archaeological technique with the revolution in historical method: its excavators practised Baconian archaeology. Collingwood recounted how this method had developed from a slowly evolving integration of observation, theory and excavation:

> The whole sixteen square miles of the site [i.e., the Wall] were first of all intensively studied on the surface [by eighteenth and nineteenth century antiquaries]. . .Tentative theories were then put forward to explain the whole complex of works: and finally these were tested by bringing the problems to a focus at particular points where they could be solved, or at any rate advanced, by some quite small piece of excavation, planned and supervised and recorded with the utmost care.[67]

Under the direction of Haverfield's successors at the Wall, this centuries-long inquiry reached a successful conclusion in 1911 when generalizations from archaeology, numismatics and the study of pottery combined to ascertain historical knowledge of the individual: the Roman Wall in England had indeed been built during Hadrian's principate.[68] In the resolution of this inquiry, the Romano-British scholars' pursuit of a 'logic of question and answer' transformed the disciplines of archaeology and history: archaeology acquired temporality from historical method, while history became empirical through the use of archaeological evidence.

As we have seen, then, Collingwood participated in this contemporary Baconian revolution as a Romano-British historian and archaeologist as well as its historiographer and philosopher. His codification of Baconian principles and his theory of scientific revolutions were grounded in his own experience of how historical and archaeological knowledge were advanced by empirical methods. At the same time, according to his own theory of scientific revolutions, he recognized that revolutions of technique tended to focus on amassing new facts to the detriment of theory; and that revolutions in methodology required codification in order to be secured. As a proponent of Baconian revolution, he tackled these problems on two fronts: in archaeology and in philosophy. As a member of archaeological societies, he lobbied for Baconian archaeology with other like-minded colleagues; as a result, he could claim that by 1930 'the principle of question and answer had been officially adopted by British archaeology' (A, 126). As a philosopher, his codification of Baconian principles for historical knowledge proposed a 'new organon' for the scientific knowledge of humanity, akin to Bacon's *New Organon* for the science of nature.

This historical contextualization restores an empiricist dimension to Collingwood's philosophy of history. Like the studies of science that Toulmin has described, which integrate the philosophy and the history of science, Collingwood's studies of scientific history were both philosophical and historical. This combination of theory and practice helped to keep his work 'on track' and 'honest,' as Toulmin has noted: Collingwood tested the worth of his philosophical arguments in historical investigations, and relied on his philosophical concern with method to do history and archaeology.[69] Thus, while Collingwood's philosophy of history was Idealist in its orientation, this Idealist orientation was counter-balanced by his experience of the history of history, which supplied an empiricist perspective.

## Notes

[1] I am indebted to Professor George Stocking of the University of Chicago for his comments on an earlier version of this paper.

[2] As the philosopher Leon Goldstein declared in an article published in 1972: 'Nothing is rarer in the critical literature on Collingwood's philosophy of history than consideration of his actual work as a historian; indeed, one almost never sees even the slightest citation on his historical writings' (Leon J. Goldstein, 'Collingwood on the Constitution of the Historical Past,' in M. Krausz, ed., *Critical Essays on the Philosophy of R. G. Collingwood* (Oxford, Oxford University Press, 1972), 254. Due to W. J. van der Dussen's book, *History as a Science: the Philosophy of R. G. Collingwood* (The Hague, Nijhoff, 1981), history has been restored to a central place in the interpretation of Collingwood's philosophy of history. Yet neither van der Dussen's book nor a more recent article by Charles Salas on 'Collingwood's Historical Principles at Work', *History and Theory*, 26 (1987), 53–71, place Collingwood's philosophy of history in its historical context.

[3] Stephen E. Toulmin, 'From Form to Function: Philosophy and History of Science in the 1950's and Now', *Daedalus*, 106 (1977), 143–5.

[4] For example, Giambattista Vico; see Benedetto Croce, *The Philosophy of Giambattista Vico*, transl. R. G. Collingwood (New York, Russell and Russell, 1964; first published in translation, 1913), 33–5, 74.

[5] I. Bernard Cohen, *Revolution in Science* (Cambridge, Mass., Belknap Press of Harvard University Press, 1985), 147–8.

[6] Michel Foucault, *Discipline and Punish* (New York, Vintage Books,

1979), 226; Hubert L. Dreyfus and Paul Rabinow, *Michel Foucault: Beyond Structuralism and Hermeneutics* (Chicago, University of Chicago Press, 1982), 162.

7. R. G. Collingwood, *An Essay on Metaphysics* (Chicago, Henry Regnery, First Gateway edn, 1972; first published in 1940), 239. Collingwood continued, noting: 'and Kant took care to acknowledge his debt by using a quotation from Bacon as the motto of the Critique'. Kant's motto was a quotation from Bacon's *The Great Instauration*.

8. He continued: 'Unless, of course, such a thing is not possible' (Foucault, *Discipline and Punish*, 226).

9. In *The Order of Things* Foucault examines the relationship of the discipline of history to the human sciences. This relationship is problematic: 'Perhaps history has no place, in fact among the human sciences, or beside them: it may well be that it maintains with them all a relation that is strange, undefined, ineffaceable, and more fundamental than any relation of adjacency in a common space would be' (Michel Foucault, *The Order of Things: an Archaeology of the Human Sciences* (New York, Vintage Books, 1973), 367). Later, in another regard, he includes history among the human sciences, 371.

10. R. G. Collingwood, *An Autobiography* with an Introduction by Stephen Toulmin (Oxford, Clarendon Press, first published 1939, paperback 1970, reprinted with Introduction 1978, 1982), 95–106, 148–9.

11. In *The Idea of History*, Collingwood defines the object of historical knowledge as '*res gestae*: actions of human beings that have been done in the past', 9 (Oxford, Clarendon Press, 1946; London, Oxford University Press paperback, 1956; reprint, 1970).

12. According to Foucault, this historicization began 'in the great upheaval that occurred in the Western episteme' at the beginning of the nineteenth century, when 'it was discovered that there existed a historicity proper to nature' (Foucault, *The Order of Things*, 367).

13. R. G. Collingwood, *Speculum Mentis or The Map of Knowledge* (Oxford, Clarendon Press, 1924), 53. With regard to the concept of nature in particular, Collingwood stated in *The Idea of Nature* that 'The historical conception of scientifically knowable change or process was applied, under the name of evolution, to the natural world' (*The Idea of Nature* (Oxford, Clarendon Press, 1945; Oxford, Oxford University Press, paperback, 1960; reprint, 1976), 13).

14. Stephen Toulmin and Jane Goodfield, *The Discovery of Time* (Chicago, University of Chicago Press, Midway reprint, 1977; Phoenix edn, 1982; first published Harper and Row, 1965), ch. 10, 'History and the Human Sciences', 232.

15. See Collingwood, *Idea of History* and *Idea of Nature*.

16. Although I am not aware of any other Oxford scholar who put Bacon to this use, Collingwood's interest in Bacon may have developed from

his education at Oxford. According to the handbook *Oxford: Its Life and Schools*, for the study of logic in the Honour School of Literae Humaniores 'the only book absolutely prescribed is part of the *Novum Organum* of Bacon' (ed. A. M. M. Stedman (London, George Bell and Sons, 1887), 249). An article by G. R. G. Mure, 'Oxford Philosophy', offers this historical glimpse of Bacon's importance in the Literae Humaniores examinations: 'During the next ten years the influence of J. S. Mill becomes obvious, and in 1865 there appears the name of Bacon. Bacon had died nearly two and a half centuries before, but now that he had come into his own he was destined to survive in every logic paper until the Great War' (*Philosophy*, 12, 47 (July 1937), 298). Since Collingwood was an undergraduate at Oxford from 1908 to 1912, and then became a Fellow there, he would have encountered this Baconian influence at Oxford.

[17] Although Collingwood's idea of scientific revolution is briefly and partially discussed by van der Dussen, to the best of my knowledge the theory I reconstruct here has not previously been presented and analysed in the context of models for history of science. Van der Dussen, *History as a Science*, 238–9, 409; also see Alan Donagan, *The Later Philosophy of R. G. Collingwood* (Oxford, Clarendon Press, 1962), 179–80.

[18] In discussing various historians of science, Richards identifies six models: the static model, the growth model, the revolutionary model, the gestalt model, the social-psychological model, and the evolutionary model. To analyse these five models, he discusses them in terms of specific historians' historiographies. For example, for the static model he cites early modern thinkers such as R. Bostocke and Olaus Borrichius; for the growth model, William Whewell and George Sarton; for the revolutionary model, Alexander Koyre and others; for the gestalt model, Norwood Russell Hanson, Thomas Kuhn and Michel Foucault; for the social-psychological model, J. D. Bernal and others; and for evolutionary models of scientific development, Karl Popper, Stephen Toulmin, Donald Campbell, Imre Lakatos and his own work. See Robert J. Richards, *Darwin and the Emergence of Evolutionary Theories of Mind and Behavior* (Chicago, University of Chicago Press, 1987), appendix I: 'The Natural Selection Model and Other Models in the Historiography of Science', 559–93.

[19] 'Throughout this essay ['Human Nature and Human History'] it has been necessary to engage in a running fight with what may be called a positivistic conception, or rather misconception of history, as the study of successive events lying in a dead past, events to be understood as the scientist understands natural events, by classifying them and establishing relations between the classes thus defined.'

[20] *Encyclopaedia Britannica*, 11th edn. (1910–11), s.v. 'science,' 398.

[21] R. G. Collingwood, 'John Horsley and Hadrian's Wall', *Archaeologia Aeliana*, fourth ser., 15 (1938), 39–40.
[22] Collingwood, *Idea of History*, Table of Contents; R. G. Collingwood, 'Hadrian's Wall: A History of the Problem', *Journal of Roman Studies*, 11 (1921), 37–66.
[23] R. G. Collingwood, 'Hadrian's Wall: 1921–30', *Journal of Roman Studies*, 21 (1931), 62–3. See van der Dussen, *History as a Science*, 280.
[24] Richards, *Darwin and the Emergence of Evolutionary Theories*, 567.
[25] See van der Dussen, *History as a Science*, 238–9, 279–81; Collingwood, 'John Horsley and Hadrian's Wall', 1–42.
[26] See Collingwood's analyses of Arnold Toynbee and Oswald Spengler in *Idea of History*, where he criticizes their use of naturalistic conceptions of history; also see Collingwood's *Idea of Nature*, 174–7.
[27] Collingwood, 'John Horsley and Hadrian's Wall', 40.
[28] Collingwood, 'Hadrian's Wall: a History of the Problem', 45–54.
[29] Collingwood, 'John Horsley and Hadrian's Wall', 40.
[30] Other such sources that enriched history included 'calendars of close and patent rolls, the corpus of Latin inscriptions, and new editions of historical texts and sources of every kind'.
[31] Collingwood, 'Hadrian's Wall: A History of the Problem', 55.
[32] Ibid., 66.
[33] Stephen Toulmin, Introduction in Collingwood, *An Autobiography*, xiii–xiv.
[34] Collingwood, *The Idea of History*, part IV: 'Scientific History'; in his view, only Croce's philosophy of history fully achieves a non-positivist position. Broadly speaking, Collingwood defined positivism in the following way: 'Positivism is the name of a philosophy greatly favoured in the nineteenth century whose motives were a good deal like those of eighteenth-century materialism. Its central doctrine was that the only valid method of attaining knowledge is the method used in the natural sciences, and hence that no kind of knowledge is genuine unless it either is natural science or resembles natural science in method' (*An Essay on Metaphysics*, 143).
[35] He also returned Baconian theory to the practical sphere of human affairs, in line with Bacon's principle that 'knowledge is power'; but that is another story. See *Autobiography*, ch. IX, 'Foundations of the Future', especially 90–2, 95, 106.
[36] On the broader issue at hand here, namely, the history of archaeological practice and theory as it was transformed into a science, Collingwood's *Autobiography* is especially pertinent. As Toulmin notes in his Introduction, the *Autobiography* provides clues to the historical context in which Collingwood developed his philosophy of history: 'Chapters X and XI of the *Autobiography* are a better statement of Collingwood's historical principles, in this respect, than the longer and more complex essays in *The Idea of History* . . .' (xviii).

37 While I. A. Richmond (Collingwood's student and a scholar of Roman Britain) criticized the role he saw philosophy had played in Collingwood's archaeological research, the philosopher Alan Donagan absolves Collingwood's methodology of these failings, if not all of his practice. See I. A. Richmond. 'R. G. Collingwood', *Proceedings of the British Academy*, 29 (1943), 478–9; Alan Donagan, *The Later Philosophy*, 196–200; also Collingwood, 'Hadrian's Wall: 1921–1930', 62–3.

38 He continued: 'When these defects have been removed, it will be possible to revise the generally accepted opinions about other, more familiar, subjects, and to correct the errors with which those opinions are perhaps infected.' Elsewhere he described the field of Roman Britain as 'ripe for intensive cultivation' (120).

39 He didn't need to indicate on which side he had taken part. W. J. van der Dussen, author of *History as a Science: The Philosophy of R. G. Collingwood*, first suggested to me the significance of this note for my history of Romano-British archaeology.

40 Collingwood, 'Hadrian's Wall: 1921–1930,' 63. Collingwood's correspondence with his colleague F. Gerald Simpson, a Romano-British archaeologist, shows similar connections between his epistemological concerns and his archaeological research. I am indebted to Dr Grace Simpson of Oxford for permitting me to read this correspondence.

41 Toulmin, Introduction in Collingwood, *Autobiography*, 17–18.

42 Although Collingwood does not explicitly refer to the pilgrimages to Hadrian's Wall, his language here certainly suggests them.

43 Collingwood, *An Autobiography*, 126.

44 Glyn Daniel, *A Hundred and Fifty Years of Archaeology*, second edn (London, Duckworth, 1975), 25–8.

45 Toulmin and Goodfield, *The Discovery of Time*, 237.

46 For example, see John Evans, *The Ancient Stone Implements, Weapons, and Ornaments of Great Britain* (New York, D. Appleton, 1872) and *The Ancient Bronze Implements, Weapons, and Ornaments of Great Britain and Ireland* (New York, A. Appleton, 1881).

47 An issue arises here which is (unfortunately) beyond the purview of this chapter: namely, once Collingwood has used the Baconian philosophy of science to codify a methodology for scientific history, to what extent can these principles still be called 'Baconian', if at all?

48 In positing his own philosophy of history, Collingwood described how he engaged necessarily 'in a running fight with what may be called a positivistic conception, or rather misconception, of history. . .' (IH, 228). In his discussion of the contrast between sciences of questioning and observing, for example, he distinguishes between two views of how facts are known: according to the first view, 'facts are things which

present themselves to our senses,' which he defines as a medieval conception with which modern positivists misconstrue the character of natural science; according to the second view 'facts are things which give us answers to our questions,' which he describes as the view of modern science, from Bacon onwards (EM, 277). He indicated that his critique of positivism lay not in 'the importance it attaches to natural science, but its errors as to what natural science is like'.

[49] For example, see Reba N. Soffer, *Ethics and Society in England: the Revolution in the Social Sciences 1870–1914* (Berkeley, University of California Press, 1978), chs. 1 and 2.

[50] Since Collingwood's first question included a historical characterization of time from the term 'Flavian', the element of time was included in his inquiry from the start.

[51] Collingwood, 'Hadrian's Wall: a History of the Problem', 57.

[52] Ibid., 62.

[53] Collingwood, 'Hadrian's Wall: 1921–1930', 51.

[54] Ibid., 61.

[55] Ibid., 62.

[56] R. G. Collingwood, 'The Nature and Aims of a Philosophy of History' (first published in 1925) in *Essays in the Philosophy of History*, ed. William Debbins (Austin, University of Texas Press, 1965), 35–6.

[57] Ibid., 31.

[58] This comparison of these two excavations was suggested by Collingwood's use of them when he discusses the Baconian revolution in historical method in ch. XI on 'Roman Britain' in his *Autobiography*.

[59] Daniel, *A Hundred and Fifty Years of Archaeology*, 172–4; R. G. Collingwood, *The Archaeology of Roman Britain* (London, Methuen, 1930; revised edn by I. A. Richmond, London, 1969), 153. Writing fifty years later in 1930, Collingwood lauded 'the genius of a single man,' praising him for his attitude towards excavation and for his methods: Pitt-Rivers had approached excavation 'from a rigidly scientific point of view,' and had directed his excavations 'by methods, far in advance of his time and still appreciably in advance of ours.'

[60] *Encyclopaedia Britannica,* tenth edn (1902), s.v. 'Silchester', by F. J. Haverfield, 625–6; Kenneth Hudson, *A Social History of Archaeology: the British Experience* (London, Macmillan, 1981), 59–61; Joan Evans, *A History of the Society of Antiquaries* (Oxford, Oxford University Press, 1956), 343.

[61] Other critics have agreed with Collingwood. According to the Society of Antiquaries' official history by Joan Evans, the excavation 'almost ignored' the scientific use of stratigraphy and was 'carried out with no systematic technique'. Its accomplishment lay in revealing for the first time 'the consecutive story of a Roman city in Britain' (Evans, *A History of the Society of Antiquaries*, 372, 378). Two later archaeologists

of Roman Silchester similarly credit the first excavation with 'a town-plan to most intents complete,' yet 'of all the eighty houses, Forum-Basilica, Baths, temples, and other buildings uncovered, and the street-plan in which they were set, not a single one was dated, nor were the successive occupations of the town identified.' These authors excuse the excavation's ahistorical results on the mistaken grounds that at the time 'excavation techniques did not admit of precise dating' (M. Aylwin Cotton, Introduction and George C. Boon, in Boon, *Roman Silchester: the Archaeology of a Romano-British Town* (London, Max Parrish, 1957), 16–17, 27).

62 The directors of the Silchester excavation published annual reports that noted the year's discoveries and provided 'the record of the systematic excavation of the site'. These reports were written to the executive committee of the Silchester Excavation Fund. See W. H. St Hope, *Excavations on the Site of the Roman City of Silchester, Hants in 1896* (Westminster, Nichols and Sons, 1897), 1. Also, see Haverfield, 'Silchester', 626.

63 Collingwood, 'Hadrian's Wall: 1921–1930', 37.

64 F. Haverfield, 'Theodor Mommsen', *English Historical Review*, 19 (1904); 'Theodor Mommsen', *Biographisches Jahrbuch und Deutscher Nekrolog* (1904), 482; G. P. Gooch, *History and Historians in the Nineteenth Century* (London, Longmans, Green, 1913; second edn, 1952; new impression, 1967), 467.

65 Haverfield was the Camden professor of Ancient History at the University of Oxford from 1907 to 1919.

66 Collingwood, 'Hadrian's Wall: 1921–1930', 37. Haverfield and the Cumberland Excavation Committee conducted annual excavations at the Wall from 1894 to 1903. Haverfield wrote reports on the results of the excavations which were published annually in the Cumberland and Westmorland Antiquarian and Archaeological Society's *Transactions*.

67 Collingwood, 'Hadrian's Wall: 1921–1930,' 37–8. According to Collingwood, Haverfield's reports on the Wall excavations were 'the classic instances of this procedure': 'It is chiefly to Haverfield that we owe this method.'

68 Developed by Haverfield, the method of selective excavation was successfully applied in later excavations by J. P. Gibson and F. Gerald Simpson. With this 'Mural Controversy' solved, during the next four decades Simpson led the reconstruction of the Wall's history. During the interwar years, Collingwood was Simpson's partner in archaeological and historical research on Hadrian's Wall (Collingwood, 'Hadrian's Wall: a History of the Problem', 61–2; Collingwood, 'Hadrian's Wall: 1921–1930', 51, 61).

69 Toulmin, 'Introduction' in *An Autobiography*, xvii–xviii.

# *Of Mice and Men: Collingwood and the Development of Archaeological Thought*

## IAN HODDER

I will argue below that Collingwood's own failure to provide consistently convincing interpretations of archaeological data contributed to the general rejection by the archaeological community of the types of philosophical and theoretical positions with which he was most clearly associated. In other words, because archaeologists were suspicious of many of his interpretations of the past, they did not buy his theoretical programme. At least that was true of the 1950s, 1960s and 1970s. Why now, in the 1980s, and 1990s is there renewed archaeological interest in Collingwood's philosophical and interpretative enterprise? Why is Collingwood as a historical thinker important to many archaeologists, and particularly to prehistorians, today?

### I   Collingwood and Archaeological Theory in the 1980s

Collingwood is currently at the centre of archaeological debate (e.g. Binford, 1987; Lane, 1987; Nowakowski, 1987; Hodder, 1986; Cuyler Young, 1988). Indeed, his theories are probably being discussed now to a greater extent than they ever have been, since his views on history were largely discounted in archaeology until the present day. The renewed contemporary interest partly results from a growing emphasis in archaeology on explicit theory-building, deriving from the New Archaeology of the 1960s and

1970s. Initially, however, the theories espoused by New Archaeologists (Binford, 1962; Flannery, 1967) had a dogged materialist and natural-science orientation. There was no room in this world for Collingwood. Indeed, the New Archaeology developed specifically in reaction to the type of stance that Collingwood had taken.

The situation is not clear-cut since, paradoxically, there was much in the science of the New Archaeology that recalled the historical science of Collingwood. Collingwood reacted against realist philosophers in much the same way that Binford reacted against a theoretical, intuitive archaeology. Collingwood's emphasis on question and answer is close to Binford's notion of hypothesis-testing, and the notion that scientific excavation is a method which approaches a site with a specific question in mind, now termed problem-oriented research design, is common to both. Nevertheless, in most respects, Collingwood's idea of history was diametrically opposed to the anthropological and natural-science agenda of the New Archaeology, and his work was hardly, if ever, mentioned.

The renewed interest in Collingwood results from the collapse of the theoretical programme of New or Processual Archaeology (Flannery, 1982; Hodder, 1982; Shanks and Tilley, 1987) and the search within what I have termed post-processual archaeology (Hodder, 1986) for historical precedents. The quest for historical legitimation through Collingwood has been particularly strong in those strands of contemporary archaeological thought which wish to incorporate yet maintain a certain distance from Marxism. Of course the current developments within archaeology are closely tied to wider changes within the social sciences. But whether archaeologists are reading contemporary anthropologists (e.g. Bourdieu, 1977; Geertz, 1973; Sahlins, 1981), contemporary human geographers (e.g. Gregory, 1978) or contemporary historians (e.g. Ladurie, 1979), they cannot help but be struck by certain similarities with aspects of Collingwood's work. And in the legitimation process, Collingwood has the advantage of being an archaeologist. It is thus to Collingwood that current archaeological theory frequently turns, not only as a legitimation for their current endeavours, but also to learn from his experience, from his successes and failures.

Collingwood's work is important to a number of related

components of contemporary debate. The first component is the *opposition between the historical and natural sciences*. In common with many anthropologists (e.g. Boas 1940 and Kroeber 1963) and archaeologists of his time, Collingwood made categorical distinctions between the natural and human sciences. In the natural sciences, 'objective' events are classified, relationships are sought between the categories, and laws developed (Collingwood, 1946, 228). The human sciences, including history, systematize by seeing the particular more and more fully in context, among other facts structurally related to it. Because history is the history of thought rather than a natural process, it does not search for invariable causes or timeless universals and it does not use the comparative method. Collingwood rejects the positivism or naturalism which he sees in the copying of the methods of natural science in historical science (van der Dussen, 1981, 353–5).

The emphasis on archaeology as a form of history is widely found in the period up to the 1960s in America and Britain. In Britain Clark (1939), Daniel (1962), Hawkes (1954) and Piggott (1959) all emphasized the historical dimension of archaeological inference and discussed artifacts as embodiments of ideas, thoughts and intentions. In America, Taylor (1948) emphasized the analysis of the 'inside' of cultural units, and for Willey (1984, 13) 'the archaeologist must be immersed in the culture-historical contexts pertinent to the problems at hand.' Even with the advent of the New Archaeology in America, the importance of history continued to be argued forcefully by Trigger (1978). The New Archaeologists specifically rejected history and the related notion that culture could be described as a set of normative ideas (e.g. Flannery 1967). Instead they embraced anthropology, cross-cultural comparison, general laws and a natural-science perspective. Even Trigger's spirited and important defence of history was materialist in emphasis. In contrast, Deetz (1977) showed that at least in historical archaeology (by which is meant the archaeology of periods with historical records), material culture change was as much part of changes of thought and attitude as it was the result of adaptive processes.

The current return to a historical perspective in archaeology is thus by no means new, especially in Europe where the New Archaeology was never so readily accepted as it was in America. And neither can it be claimed that all contemporary archaeologists concerned with historical approaches find Collingwood equally relevant to their work. For example, much of the contemporary archaeological interest in history derives from a Marxist perspective (e.g. Rowlands, 1980). But for those archaeologists concerned with links to types of history or ethnohistory in which the interpretation of meaning plays a central role (e.g. contributors to Hodder, 1987a, b), Collingwood's work is relevant, whether it is his writing on the theory of historical cycles (Collingwood (1927) or his general outlines in *The Idea of History* (1946) and *An Autobiography* (1939). Problems concerning the relationships between the general and the particular, between the material and the ideal, and between the object and the subject remain at the forefront of archaeological debate.

A second aspect of Collingwood's work which is of renewed interest today is his *theory of action*. Collingwood's emphasis on actions as opposed to events, mechanisms or behaviour was clearly stated (e.g. in *An Autobiography*). He conceived of an action as incorporating some thought, intention or purpose expressed by the agent. Thus it is neither a behavioural response to a stimulus, nor a mere instance of the agent's normative disposition. Rather, action is situation-specific and context-dependent. Thus it would be impossible to have a full rule-book of behaviour. Action involves 'improvising, as best you can, a method of handling the situation in which you find yourself' (A, 105). Cultural rules are seen as being manipulated and negotiated in relation to strategy, and they are increasingly reproduced and transformed through action.

Collingwood's contemporaries in archaeology held similar views, although they rarely referred directly to his work. For example, Hawkes (1942, 125) claimed that cultures have both an extension in space and time, and an intention in the social and economic field. New Archaeologists, on the other hand, rejected any attempt to recover action in Collingwood's sense in two respects. First, they denied the possibility of, or explanatory interest in, evaluating the thoughts of past actors. Second, they embraced a deterministic position in which individual action was the result of external forces plus random effects. This probabilistic viewpoint was neatly summed up by Flannery (1967) in his statement that archaeologists should not try to reach the Indian behind the artefact, but the system behind the Indian behind the artefact. Material culture came to be seen as a passive adaptive tool – a mechanism to allow the system to survive.

In their reactions against behaviourist tendencies in archaeology, and against the equally determinist tendencies of structuralist archaeology (Hodder, 1986), some contemporary archaeologists have turned to social theorists who are concerned both with culture as involving thought and intention and with a recentring of the individual. The first of these two components of social action theory is by far the strongest in archaeology, since the role of the individual in long-term social change is widely argued (Shanks and Tilley, 1987). But it is clear that much of the discussion by Bourdieu (1977), Giddens (1979) and Sahlins (1981) of social-action theory has similarities with Collingwood's own account of action. For example, these authors, and the archaeologists using their work, acknowledge that thoughts, intentions and symbolic meanings are central to discussions of material culture change. They also, like Collingwood, accept that many of the relevant thoughts and meanings may be unconscious (van der Dussen, 1981, 326–9), and that cultural change is the result of practical, non-discursive activity. They see culture as both the medium and the outcome of action. Like Collingwood, they see action as taking place within conditions of uncertainty and limited knowledge, and therefore resulting in unintended consequences.

It would be wrong, however, to claim that archaeologists have yet produced a more sophisticated account of the relationship between individual action and social whole than that provided by Collingwood. The debate has been returned to, but as in Collingwood's own writings, it remains a debate with uncertain outcome. As van der Dussen notes (1981, 324), it has been claimed that Collingwood was a methodological individualist, and indeed at times he was critical of concepts such as the 'spirit' of Roman Britain, the 'corporate mind' or 'society'; but he frequently referred to the important influence of unconscious traditions on social action. For example, in *The New Leviathan* (1942, 149) he argues that an actor engaged in a joint enterprise has a general idea of the enterprise as a whole, but that this general knowledge need only be very vague. The actor must only know that there is a whole to which his own part, more precisely known, is linked. Thus the social whole and the individual act are interrelated, and

Collingwood avoids being either methodologically individualist or holistic; but problems concerning the individual and the whole remain. For example: how do 'wholes' change? can individual acts transform the whole? to what extent do different conceptions of the whole coincide? are not wholes simply the products of common material interests produced by a common situation in relation to social and economic resources? These questions have yet to be fully discussed in archaeology.

A third component of the contemporary archaeological interest in Collingwood concerns *generalization*. It is often assumed that Collingwood argued against all forms of generalization. Indeed, some New Archaeologists would have gone further and claimed that history was by its very nature antithetical to generalisation. Neither of these views is correct. Collingwood in fact thought archaeology to be aiming at generalizations which could be used in order to interpret specific types of evidence (van der Dussen, 1981, 339). He frequently used generalizations, for example concerning the organization of the Roman army, in order to interpret particular actions such as the building of military frontier lines.

The New Archaeology, too, was interested in generalization. In its most extreme form, this tendency involved the use and construction of universal laws (Schiffer, 1976). The reaction against this 'law-and-order brigade' has been widespread (Flannery, 1973). And yet it is still the case that many archaeologists would define explanation as the identification of an individual case as an instance of a general principle. The task of archaeology is seen as building general statements (for example within ethnography or ethnoarchaeology) which can be used to interpret the archaeological record. The remains from the past are seen as essentially static items which have to be placed within dynamic processes understood in general and in the present (Binford 1983). The aim of studying the past is to contribute knowledge about these generalizations.

Despite nearly thirty years of research since the onset of the New Archaeology, it remains difficult to identify examples of widely accepted generalizations which are not either trivial (of the sort that Flannery (1973) called Mickey Mouse Laws) or concerned merely with natural depositional and post-depositional processes of the survival and recovery of remains. There is an increasing realization that interpretation of material culture involves not only the use of generalizations, but also a moment of creative understanding in which attempts are made to grasp the 'otherness' of particular historical sequences (Hodder, 1986). As Collingwood argued, general terms and concepts need to be evaluated critically in relation to contextual data. He accepted that other rationalities could be interpreted precisely because they were, in their own terms, rational. And he believed that, by careful consideration of contextual data, other principles of rationality could, by trial and error, be approached.

But how can the *validation* of particular historical interpretations be achieved? This is a fourth area in which Collingwood's work is of contemporary interest. Archaeological accounts of validation have tended to see-saw between objectivist and subjectivist positions, and most archaeologists would place Collingwood firmly in the latter camp. However, it can be claimed (van der Dussen, 1981, 352) that Collingwood was neither one nor the other. He certainly rejected the idea of final or complete knowledge. There could be no possibility of knowing with any final certainty that one's interpretations of the past were correct. But this view did not result in an absolute relativism in which 'anything goes.' Rather, he was concerned with the careful and critical linking of theory to data through the procedures of question and answer. Thus a particular theory could be validated in relation to a set of data, but only in terms of the questions asked.

Collingwood's emphasis on evidence and the asking of explicit questions is similar to the New Archaeological stress on explicit theory-building and hypothesis-testing (Binford, 1977; Binford and Sabloff, 1982). Indeed, as already noted, both Collingwood and the New Archaeologists were reacting against a world which tended to avoid explicit theorizing, and was thus both blind to its own implicit theories and displayed a lack of critical concern with evidence. On the other hand, New Archaeologists sought an unambiguously objectivist position in which certain knowledge could be obtained (Binford, 1983). In the early years of the New Archaeology, both the data and the rules for interpreting the data were often seen as secure and absolute. In later years (e.g. Binford and Sabloff, 1982) it came to be accepted that the data were not neutral items, but theory-laden; none the less it was still felt that secure Middle-Range Theories, derived from studies of the modern world, could be used to make rational objective choices between paradigms.

In reaction, many archaeologists today (e.g. Shanks and Tilley, 1987; Leone, 1982) have emphasized the flaws in the objectivist account and have argued, in ways similar to Collingwood, that the past is always provisionally and socially interpreted. Charges of subjectivism and relativism have been raised (Binford, 1987) against this position in archaeology, and one begins again to ride the see-saw of objectivist and subjectivist positions. But as Rowlands (1984) has cogently argued, the current debate must try to rise above this tired dichotomy. We need to follow Collingwood in allowing that the data are both objective and subjective, and we need to develop methods of validation that incorporate these two dimensions. Thus once again Collingwood's work is vital to contemporary debate within archaeology, and I will discuss further his experience with validation in a discussion below of his archaeological practice.

Perhaps the clearest indicator of a contemporary reaction against the New Archaeology is the increased discussion of archaeological *knowledge as political*. This provides the final comparison I wish to draw between Collingwood and contemporary archaeological theory. Collingwood said that his work was 'a political struggle' (IH, 167). In general, the emphasis should be on understanding meanings rather than obtaining truth or falsity (IH, 260). 'We study history . . . in order to attain self-knowledge' (IH, 315), and this self-knowledge has the power to be emancipatory. Indeed, the whole aim of the historical approach was to liberate humanity from the potential dominance of the natural-science perspective. Collingwood (1935–8) wanted to establish that war, for example, was not an unavoidable human instinct. Rather, it was a creation of the human will. A historical approach could establish it as such and could therefore provide the hope for remedy (Collingwood, 1934a).

The objectivist stance of the New Archaeology resulted in a total lack of interest in the social and political dimensions of archaeological interpretation. Where one's ideas came from was thought to be irrelevant, since the emphasis was placed on objective testing of theory against data. Methodology ruled. It can be argued, however, that the New Archaeological emphasis on systems, laws and objective methods encouraged the types of attitudes to life in the present that Collingwood's humanist spirit so feared. Their work encouraged a vision of planned systems of control, of centralized administrative authority and of social wholes reacting in ways that only computer-aided intellectuals could predict, according to complex universal laws (Hodder, 1984). The current reaction against such unreflective and uncritical archaeology is widespread (Trigger, 1978). There is increased interest in the use of archaeology to further the rights of ethnic minorities in Australia, North America and Europe (Hodder, 1986). There is an increased interest in the different perspectives on the past provided by feminist writers (Conkey and Spector, 1984; Gero, 1985), and in working-class reactions to presentations of the past in museums and heritage displays (Leone et al., 1987). In addition, attempts are now being made to find theoretical arguments within which those new concerns can be couched, and the new emphasis on power, ideology and text play a major role here (Miller and Tilley, 1984; Shanks and Tilley, 1987). Much of the contemporary debate is influenced by Marxist writings, albeit with a heavily humanist bent, and I am uncertain that Collingwood would have played a major role in encouraging the current degree of reflexive thinking. It cannot be claimed that his work has much to offer in terms of either specific methodology or specific theory in this archaeological domain. On the other hand, his overall emphasis on the past as present and on historical knowledge as provisional and open to debate and change, provides an appropriate springboard for the current archaeological debate.

I have identified five ways in which Collingwood's work is relevant to theoretical debate in contemporary archaeology. Collingwood was not only a theoretician but also a practising archaeologist. His contemporary importance is not only that his theories are relevant to current theoretical debate, but also that he tried out his theories in archaeology. Present attempts to widen archaeological debate to include the dimensions of history discussed by Collingwood are not only legitimated by his precedent. They can also refer to his practical applications as models and as examples of how to carry out his programme. But his archaeological practice also has a wider relevance. When applied, how does his philosophical stance fare? Do the applications reveal serious flaws in the philosophy? What can we learn from Collingwood's archaeological experience?

## II  Collingwood as an Archaeologist

Despite the current archaeological interest in Collingwood's philosophical and theoretical writings, these sides of his work have been largely ignored in archaeology until recently. The degree to which his more general contribution was rejected can be made clear by the contrast with his reception as a synthesizer and organiser of primary data.

For example, Collingwood, in his preface to *The Archaeology of Roman Britain* (1930), described the book as strictly a handbook of archaeology, not a history, and the content of the book is largely classificatory and heavily descriptive. The first edition of the book was reviewed in no less than twelve journals dealing with archaeology. It was generally received as a sound, critical and scholarly synthesis. *Roman Britain* (1932) was reviewed in five such journals, and *Roman Britain and the English Settlements* (1936) also in five journals. Collingwood's (1933) review of prehistoric data in Cumberland, which he described (p.163) as aiming 'to sum up, in the briefest possible outline, the present state of knowledge about the prehistory of our district', was reviewed by O. G. S. Crawford in *Antiquity* (1934) in very positive terms, pointing to the scientific description and rigorous fieldwork methods provided by Collingwood.

Overall, it is undoubtedly the case that, until recently, Collingwood was best known within archaeology as a result of his archaeological syntheses, and to a lesser extent as a result of his field-work. He was also most highly evaluated in these terms. Thus, in Richmond's (1943) appreciation of Collingwood as an archaeologist, considerable emphasis is placed on Collingwood's skill as a draughtsman and on his corpus of inscriptions. His excavations at Ambleside are highly praised, as are his works of synthesis. 'His first edition of Roman Britain was a masterpiece' (p.476). His annual synthesis of work on Hadrian's Wall, his 'Handbook to the Roman Wall' (1934), his *Archaeology of Roman Britain*, and his (with Myres) *Roman Britain and the English Settlements* are all discussed positively. In summary, Richmond suggests that the value of Collingwood's work to archaeology lies first and foremost in his research on Roman inscriptions, second his earlier papers of definition and synthesis, and finally his personality.

No mention is made in Richmond's obituary of *An Autobiography* (1939), despite the fact that the book contains substantial discussions of archaeology. Indeed this book and *The Idea of History* (1946) were rarely reviewed in archaeological journals, in contrast to the archaeological syntheses discussed above. According to van der Dussen (1981) neither of these books, still less his other philosophical works, were reviewed in any archaeological journal. However, *Antiquity* for 1948 did contain a review article on *The Idea of History*. But the article (Slotkin, 1948) was by an American, it does not discuss archaeology, and it rejects Collingwood's approach because of its perceived Idealism and because of Collingwood's dichotomy between mind and nature. Unusually, the editor of the journal, provides no editorial comment. Overall, Collingwood's theoretical and philosophical writings were ignored by archaeologists.

Why this silence? It would be easy to argue that the lack of reference to Collingwood by New Archaeologists was the result of the fundamental differences in perspective that I outlined in the first part of this chapter. But why was there so little discussion of his work prior to the growth of the New Archaeology in the 1960s? Indeed, we have seen that many archaeologists in the 1930s to 1950s held similar views to Collingwood. They held that artefacts were embodiments of ideas, they saw archaeology as fundamentally historical, they were wary of generalization, and some accepted the need to discuss intentionality and purpose. It could even be argued that the title for Daniel's (1962) *The Idea of Prehistory* was derived from Collingwood's *The Idea of History*. But Daniel does not even refer to Collingwood in his book. Given the overall interest in Collingwood as a synthesizer, and given the similarity in theoretical perspective between Collingwood and archaeologists from the 1930s to 1950s, the lack of explicit archaeological reference to, and discussion of Collingwood's theoretical and philosophical writings is striking. The silence is deafening.

I think the main answer to this problem lies in the area of methodology. Archaeologists have always been heavily empiricist. They have always wanted to stay close to the data in order to establish themselves, in opposition to antiquarians, as scientists (members of a rigorous disciplined discipline). Although they, in abstract, saw the need for historical interpretation, in practice they shied away from statements which could not be grounded in hard data. They would have liked to follow Collingwood along his interpretative path, but they were frightened when it appeared to them that Collingwood's feet no longer touched the ground. Richmond (1943) talks of Collingwood's flights of fancy and of his ideas marching ahead of those held by field-workers.

It is unfortunately true that many of Collingwood's applications in archaeology did not inspire confidence in his theory and philosophy. In line with Richmond's comments, Wheeler (1939, 87–8) argues that Collingwood does not sufficiently distinguish between objective data and subjective interpretation. 'Mr. Collingwood has adopted a personal and subjective attitude towards history . . . it admits no compromise. He interpolates motives, builds characters, constructs episodes with a liberality or even licence that is great fun, but is liable to shock the pedant. Fact and speculation stand shoulder to shoulder.' Much of this criticism concerns Collingwood's later work, and particularly his contribution to *Roman Britain and the English Settlements* (1936).

Indeed, this book contains much lively imaginative writing, particularly in the sections dealing with both historical and archaeological sources. There is much 'thinking oneself into' Roman Britain in terms of both motives (why Caesar invaded Britain, for example) and reasoning (what plans were in Caesar's mind, for example). At times the writing is more worthy of a historical novel. For example, in discussing the reaction of the British chiefs to Caesar's invasion, Collingwood writes (1936, 39) 'In hurried whispers they exchanged an oath to raise the tribes once more . . . One by one, they slunk sway from the camp.' Caratacus is described (ibid., 89) as 'a man of fiery and overbearing temper, totally unsuited to the work of begging help from princes who thought themselves his equals and looked on him as a discredited exile'. As a reviewer commented in relation to Collingwood's account in this book of the Claudian invasion, 'there is so much which is not to be found in the only extant authority, that the reader who is familiar with the text of Dio is inclined to wonder if Professor Collingwood has not rediscovered the lost books of the "Annals"' (Reynolds, 1937, 451).

But it is not only in Collingwood's latest work that one finds a certain looseness in the question-and-answer re-enactment procedures. In his survey of Lake District prehistory, Collingwood

(1933, 176) gives Bronze Age stone circles a non-sepulchral, ceremonial function. 'The nature of the ceremonies we do not know; but we can hardly doubt that they included those sacred dances which play a great part in the social life of savages.'

At times, therefore, it becomes difficult to draw the line between dramatic licence and the careful interpretation of purpose. It seems to me that doubts arose concerning Collingwood's methodology for three reasons. First, as we have seen, his interpretations often wandered too far from the data. Second, his use of generalizations was sometimes uncritical. Third, he did not adequately entertain alternative hypotheses.

The uncritical use of generalisations is clear in his 1933 article on Cumberland prehistory, where it is assumed that monuments which are spatially close are also close in date. On *a priori* grounds, quite the opposite could of course be argued since contemporary monuments are often dispersed across landscapes. But Collingwood's uncritical espousal of what might be termed a 'law of spatial and temporal coincidence' leads to an unhappy logic. For example, he suggests that if we want to know where the builders of megalithic circles buried their dead, we need to find contemporary burial places, which will be those near the megalithic circles. We are thus sure to find, by a circularity of logic, that the builders of megalithic circles buried their dead near their circles! Elsewhere, Collingwood adopts the generalization that 'the more skilled agricultural races have a denser population than the less skilled agricultural races' (1929, 263). Some link between agricultural technology and population density is certainly widely accepted by archaeologists, but the route from this statement to the view that the Romano-Britains had a low density and therefore 'practised a primitive form of agriculture' (ibid.) is tortuous and weakly supported. Neither is the generalization itself critically evaluated.

The failure to entertain alternative hypotheses is also frequently found. For example, in several cases (e.g. 1933; 1936) Collingwood adopts Cyril Fox's 'law' that because of environmental differences between upland and lowland Britain, new cultures from Europe tend to replace or be imposed upon those in the lowlands, but to be fused or absorbed in the highlands. Collingwood frequently interprets the data in these terms without considering alternative possibilities. In other words, he simply imposes the theory on the data. For example, in his 1933 account of prehistoric Cumberland he argues that thin-butted axes, megalithic circles and Beaker pottery arrived later in his area than in lowland England because of the slower absorption in highland regions. There is no consideration of the possibility that innovations might have been adopted more readily in peripheral areas, or that the innovations were created indigenously within the highland zone.

The failure to examine varied, opposing views, giving Collingwood the reputation of being rather too rigid a theorist, is seen most clearly in his excavations of the circular ditched monument of King Arthur's Round Table (1938). Earthworks of similar type elsewhere in England were known to have contained wooden circles or stone circles from which the stones had been removed. Following question-and-answer procedures, Collingwood (ibid., 10) says, 'the purpose of the work, however, was to test the generally accepted hypothesis that the Round Table was a prehistoric monument, and more particularly to test the writer's conjecture that it had carried a wooden structure.'

But Collingwood did not follow a careful question-and-answer policy, questioning whether the data could have had alternative meanings. Rather, he imposed his view that the monument contained wooden circles on the evidence, and he imposed his experience of the Roman Wall on this prehistoric site. Indeed, he 'imported' (ibid., 10) a Mr Cruddas as foreman on the Round Table excavation because his previous field-work on the Roman Wall was thought relevant. In sites on the Roman Wall, Collingwood had found floors of a material termed 'Sammel', and he found floors of the same material within the prehistoric enclosure. To demonstrate that there were circles of post-holes within the enclosure he excavated circular trenches, plus some trenches on a radial axis which found entrances into the circle. Thus Collingwood had answered his question. The Round Table contained a prehistoric wooden circle.

Collingwood may have been hard-pressed for time, but he made no attempt to consider alternative hypotheses. Indeed, his layout of trenches ensured that he found what he wanted to find. In contrast, two years later, excavations on the same site were conducted by G. Bersu (1940). First, he dug trenches not only inside the monument, but also outside, where he found the same

'Sammel' 'floors'. In fact the 'floors' were simply layers of glacial outwash gravel, formed by natural processes. Second, Bersu extended rectangular trenches over larger areas of the interior. He found 'post-holes' everywhere. And when he dug the 'post-holes' he found galleries branching off them. The 'post-holes' were really animal burrows. 'Since mouse-holes and mole-galleries always fall into groups, these structures are sometimes densely and sometimes thinly distributed' (ibid., 142).

Of course all archaeologists make mistakes, and Collingwood was only a man, as liable to mistakes as any, and perhaps particularly frail towards the end of his life. But the Round Table example reinforced existing archaeological doubts about the viability of Collingwood's methodology, and thus about his whole interpretative enterprise. Archaeologists saw in his work too many instances of imaginative insight unlinked to data, uncritical use of generalizations, and failure to consider alternative hypotheses. Interest in his theoretical and philosophical writings was thus not encouraged by successful and attractive interpretations within archaeology. In fact the opposite was more true, and archaeologists remained uninterested in the whole programme.

The problem was compounded by a superficial reading of Collingwood's theoretical writings. Because there were doubts about his position, his writing was not read carefully, it was misunderstood and thought to be failing. As a result, doubts about his position intensified. A good example is provided by Childe (1949, 24) who suggested that 'Collingwood tells me in effect to empty my mind of all ideas, categories, and values derived from my society in order to fill it with those of an extinct society.' This view is so far from Collingwood's own that one wonders if Childe had read Collingwood at all. But on the other hand it would have been supported by a knowledge of, for example, some of Collingwood's archaeological writings. Archaeologists most commonly rejected Collingwood's approach through knowledge of his archaeological work and through a vague, often incorrect, understanding of his theoretical and philosophical writings.

It is perhaps only now, as Collingwood's archaeological work and syntheses have themselves become out of date and been replaced by more recent studies, that archaeologists can return to his more general writings with an open mind. It is also possible to see that Collingwood's archaeological failings resulted less from a shaky philosophical position and more from loose practice. We need to discuss his guidelines rather than his own applications of them.

That the re-enactment and question-and-answer principles can be applied successfully is clear in Collingwood's own work on the motives behind the construction of the Hadrianic and Antonine Walls. The purpose of the walls is a theme to which he regularly returned throughout his life. Hadrian's Wall was interpreted more as an elevated sentry walk than as a fortification (Collingwood 1926), partly by comparison with more strongly fortified walls elsewhere in the Empire, and partly because the wall was too narrow to allow large numbers of soldiers to move easily along it. In regard to the Antonine Wall, Collingwood (1936, 140) began with questions such as 'Why was the Antonine Wall so different from Hadrian's? Why were there no milecastles and turrets, and why were the forts along the wall smaller and much closer together than on the earlier walls?' Examination of the evidence suggested that a smaller force was placed on the Antonine Wall, that the Antonine Wall had been made of clay and turf instead of stone, and that it was smaller and the forts simply constructed. As a result, Collingwood interpreted the purpose of the wall. 'Both in construction and in organisation, then, the Antonine Wall bears the marks of a deliberate effort after cheapness, at the cost of a serious decrease in efficiency' (ibid., 142).

These arguments about the purposes of the two walls are carefully argued, the interpretations being closely linked to the data. There is careful and critical use of generalization, concerning the Roman army, and there is consideration of alternative views about the wall which are tested and excluded by excavation (van der Dussen, 1981, 232). The whole procedure has been successfully applied to the purposes of prehistoric walls by Merriman (1987). The guidelines are not at fault. But they do need to be applied critically.

## III Conclusion

The present awakening of archaeological interest in Collingwood as a historian, philosopher and theorist needs to examine both the failures and successes of Collingwood's archaeology in order to learn from them. There is concern today about how to interpret past meanings and purposes. It is thus natural to turn to Collingwood's methodology. It would be easy to be dismayed by some of his failures and by the reaction he received to some of his archaeological work. But a critical appraisal of his archaeology allows insight to be gained into the limitations and potential of his approach. I have outlined above some of the ways in which his archaeological methodology needs to be clarified. We can learn something from Collingwood the man, grappling with the realities of archaeological data.

The main general failing that can be identified in Collingwood's archaeological work is that he was insufficiently self-critical. He frequently uses generalizations that are not carefully examined, and fails to entertain alternative hypotheses. The methodology of question and answer can too easily be restricted to asking limited questions and providing stock answers. The method becomes a licence for the free play of the imagination, without sufficient regard to evidence. It is as if Collingwood had too much confidence in his own rationality, and insufficient awareness of the possibility of radical alternatives. A critical approach was often not followed in practice.

Indeed, in Collingwood's theoretical writings a self-reflexive position is not enunciated with force. A critical position in which one's own writing is examined as ideologically related to self-interest is not examined in full. Certainly, Collingwood accepts that each age writes its own history, and that historical writing is political. But from the perspective of the modern theoretical archaeologist, Collingwood pays insufficient attention to self, to power and to ideology. These components of contemporary archaeological theory were introduced through influences deriving in part from Western Marxism. It would be interesting to speculate on Collingwood's possible reactions to contemporary, 'humanist' Marxism. But the success of his own archaeological work would have been enhanced by a critical perspective. Through a rigorous appraisal of Collingwood's methodology, his full potential in archaeology as a historian and philosopher can be achieved.

*Note.* I am grateful to Richard Reece for stimulating discussions on Collingwood's role in Romano-British archaeology.

## Bibliography

Bersu, G. 1940. 'King Arthur's Round Table', *Transactions of the Cumberland and Westmorland Antiquarian and Archaeological Society*, 40, 169–206.

Binford, L. R. 1962. 'Archaeology as Anthropology', *American Antiquity*, 28, 217–25.

——1977. *For Theory Building In Archaeology* (New York, Academic Press).

——1983. *In Pursuit of the Past* (London, Thames and Hudson).

——1987. 'Data, Relativism and Archaeological Science', *Man*, 22, 391–404.

——and Sabloff, J. A. 1982. 'Paradigms, Systematics and Archaeology', *Journal of Anthropological Research*, 38, 137–53.

Boas, F. 1940. *Race, Language and Culture* (New York, Macmillan).

Bourdieu, P. 1977. *Outline of a Theory of Practice* (Cambridge, Cambridge University Press).

Childe, V. G. 1949. *Social Worlds of Knowledge* (Oxford, Oxford University Press).

Clark, G. 1939. *Archaeology and Society* (London, Methuen).

Collingwood, R. G. 1926. *A Guide to the Roman Wall* (Newcastle-upon-Tyne, Andrew Reid).

——1927. 'Oswald Spengler and the Theory of Historical Cycles', *Antiquity*, 1, 311–25.

——1929. 'Town and Country in Roman Britain', *Antiquity*, 3, 261–76.

——1930. *The Archaeology of Roman Britain* (London, Methuen).

——1932. *Roman Britain* (Oxford, Clarendon Press).

——1933. 'An Introduction to the Prehistory of Cumberland, Westmorland and Lancashire North of the Sands', *Transactions of the Cumberland and Westmorland Antiquarian and Archaeological Society*, 33, 163–200.

——1934a. 'The Present Need of a Philosophy', *Philosophy*, 9, 262–5. Reprinted in R. G. Collingwood, *Essays in Political Philosophy*, ed. D. Boucher (Oxford, Clarendon Press, 1989).

——1934b. *Handbook to the Roman Way* (Newcastle upon Tyne, Andrew Reid).

——1935–8. List of unpublished manuscripts of Collingwood in van der Dussen 1981.

——1936 (with J. N. L. Myres). *Roman Britain and the English Settlements* (Oxford, Clarendon Press).

——1938. 'King Arthur's Round Table', *Transactions of the Cumberland and Westmorland Antiquarian and Archaeological Society*, 38, 1–31.

——1939. *An Autobiography* (Oxford, Clarendon Press).

——1942. *The New Leviathan* (Oxford, Clarendon Press).
——1946. *The Idea of History* (Oxford, Clarendon Press).
Conkey, M. and Spector, J. 1984. 'Archaeology and the Study of Gender', in M. Schiffer, ed., *Advances in Archaeological Method and Theory*, 7 (New York, Academic Press).
Crawford, O. G. S. 1934. Review of R. G. Collingwood, 'An Introduction to the Prehistory of Cumberland Westmorland and Lancashire North of the Sands', *Antiquity*, 8, 361–3.
Cuyler Young, T. 1988. 'Since Herodotus, has History been a Valid Concept?, *American Antiquity*, 53, 7–12.
Daniel, G. E. 1962. *The Idea of Prehistory* (Harmondsworth, Penguin).
Deetz, J. 1977. *Small Things Forgotten* (New York, Anchor Books).
van der Dussen, W. J. 1981. *History as a Science: the Philosophy of R. G. Collingwood* (The Hague, Nijhoff).
Flannery, K. V. 1967. 'Culture History v. Culture Process: a Debate in American Archaeology', *Scientific American*, 217, 119–22.
——1973. 'Archaeology With a Capital S', in C. Redman, ed., *Research and Theory in Current Archaeology* (New York, Wiley).
——1982. 'The Golden Marshalltown: a Parable for the Archaeology of the 1980s', *American Anthropologist*, 84, 265–78.
Geertz, C. 1973. *The Interpretation of Cultures* (London, Hutchinson).
Gero, J. 1985. 'Socio-politics and the Woman-of-home Ideology', *American Antiquity*, 50, 342–50.
Giddens, A. 1979. *Central Problems in Social Theory* (London, Macmillan).
Gregory, D. 1978. *Ideology, Science and Human Geography* (London, Hutchinson).
Hawkes, C. 1942. 'Race, Prehistory and European Civilisation', *Man*, 73, 125–30.
——1954. 'Archaeological Theory and Method: Some Suggestions from the Old World', *American Anthropologist*, 56, 155–68.
Hodder, I. 1982. 'Theoretical Archaeology: a Reactionary View', in I. Hodder, ed., *Symbolic and Structural Archaeology* (Cambridge, Cambridge University Press).
——1984. 'Archaeology in 1984', *Antiquity*, 58, 25–32.
——1986. *Reading the Past* (Cambridge, Cambridge University Press).
——ed. 1987a. *The Archaeology of Contextual Meanings* (Cambridge, Cambridge University Press).
——ed. 1987b. *Archaeology as Long-term History* (Cambridge, Cambridge University Press).
Kroeber, A. L. 1963. *Anthropology: Culture, Patterns and Processes* (New York, Harcourt Brace Jovanovich).
Ladurie, E. Le Roy 1979. *The Territory of the Historian* (London, Harvester Press).
Lane, P. 1987. 'Re-ordering Residues of the Past', in I. Hodder, ed.,

*Archaeology as Long-term History* (Cambridge, Cambridge University Press).

Leone, M. 1982. 'Some Opinions about Recovering Mind', *American Antiquity*, 47, 742–60.

Potter, P. B. and Shackel, P. A. 1987. 'Toward a Critical Archaeology', *Current Anthropology*, 28, 283–302.

Merriman, N. 1987. 'Value and Motivation in Prehistory: the Evidence for "Celtic Spirit"', in I. Hodder, ed., *The Archaeology of Contextual Meanings* (Cambridge, Cambridge University Press).

Miller, D. and Tilley, C., eds., 1984. *Ideology, Power and Prehistory* (Cambridge, Cambridge University Press).

Nowakowski, J. 1987. 'Staddle-stones and Silage Pits: Successional Use in an Agricultural Community', in I. Hodder, ed., *Archaeology as Long-term History* (Cambridge, Cambridge University Press).

Piggott, S. 1959. *Approach to Archaeology* (Cambridge, Mass., McGraw Hill).

Reynolds, P. K. B. 1937. Review of R. G. Collingwood and J. Myres, *Roman Britain and the English Settlements*, *Antiquaries Journal*, 17, 451–3.

Richmond, I. A. 1943. 'Appreciation of R. G. Collingwood as an archaeologist', *Proceedings of the British Academy*, 29, 476–85.

Rowlands, M. 1980. 'Kinship, Alliance and Exchange in the European Bronze Age', in J. C. Barrett and R. Bradley, eds., *Settlement and Society in the British Late Bronze Age* (Oxford, British Archaeological Reports, 83).

——1984. 'Objectivity and Subjectivity in Archaeology', in M. Spriggs, ed., *Marxist Perspectives in Archaeology* (Cambridge, Cambridge University Press).

Sahlins, M. 1981. *Historical Metaphors and Mythical Realities* (Ann Arbor, University of Michigan Press).

Schiffer, M. B. 1976. *Behavioral Archaeology* (New York, Academic Press).

Shanks, M. and Tilley, C. 1987. *Reconstructing Archaeology* (Cambridge, Cambridge University Press).

Slotkin, J. S. 1948. 'Reflections on Collingwood's *Idea of History*', *Antiquity*, 22, 98–102.

Taylor, W. 1948. *A Study of Archaeology* (New York, Memoirs of the American Anthropological Association, 69).

Trigger, B. 1978. *Time and Tradition* (Edinburgh, Edinburgh University Press).

——1986, *Archaeology and the Future* (Montreal, McGill University Faculty of Arts).

Wheeler, R. E. M. 1939. 'Review of R. G. Collingwood and J. Myres, *Roman Britain and the English Settlements*, *Journal of Roman Studies*, 29, 87–93.

Willey, G. 1984. 'Archaeological Retrospect 6', *Antiquity*, 58, 5–14.

# Index of Persons

Acton, Lord 355
Alexander, Samuel 5, 94, 103, 249
Andre, Carl 74
Anselm 23, 81, 82, 89, 90
Aristotle 81, 84, 89, 122, 248
Augustine, St 89
Austin, J. L. 6, 8, 16–17, 25, 116, 127
Ayer, A. J. 6, 7, 8, 25, 206–7, 257

Bacon, Francis 331, 333, 336, 357
Barker, Ernest 5, 6
Barth, Karl 81
Baur, F. C. 332
Beiner, R. 292
Bentham, J. 126
Berkeley, G. 86, 88, 116, 118
Bersu, G. 377–8
Binford, L. R. 364, 365, 369, 370, 371
Blackburn, S. 19–20
Blakeway, Alan 84
Boas, F. 366
Bosanquet, B. 293
Boucher, D. 211–12
Bourdieu, P. 365, 368
Bradley, F. H. 86, 89, 90, 101, 117, 120, 125–6, 170–1
Buchanan, J. M. 19
Bultmann, R. 17

Caesar 185
Caird, Edward 87, 89
Carritt, E. F. 98, 324
Childe, V. G. 378
Clark, G. 366

Clark, G. N. 7
Code, L. 211
Cohen, T. 15
Collingwood, Ethel 5
Collingwood, W. G. 1, 4
Conkey, M. 372
Cook Wilson, J. 7, 84, 90
Cowling, M. 23
Crawford, O. G. S. 373
Croce, Benedetto xv, xvi, 8, 57, 92, 94–9, 101–3, 104, 107, 108, 111, 117, 118, 119–20, 124, 125–7, 130, 131–3, 138, 139, 144, 152, 155–62, 198, 250, 253
Cuyler Young, T. 364

Daniel, G. 366, 374
Deetz, J. 366
Descartes, René 63, 81–2, 131, 133, 336
Dewey, J. 270
Dilthey, W. 20, 198
Donagan, A. 218, 251, 332
Dray, W. H. 16
Ducasse, C. J. 46
Dunn, J. 16
Dussen, Jan van der 6, 366, 368, 369, 370, 374, 379

Edwardes, Kathleen 3, 5
Einstein, A. 231, 258–9
Evans, Sir A. 345

Feyerabend, P. 14

## Index of Persons

Fisher, H. A. L. 291
Flannery, K. V. 365, 366, 367, 369
Foucault, M. 331
Fox, C. 376
Frege, G. 83
Freud, S. 118, 121, 123, 124, 126

Gadamer, H.-G. 17, 18, 56, 292
Geertz, C. 365
Gentile, Giovanni xv, xvi, 8, 92, 96, 98, 100, 101, 103–7, 111, 115, 116–17, 118, 119, 120, 122, 124, 125, 126, 127, 132, 152, 155–65
Gero, J. 372
Giddens, A. 368
Goldstein, L. J. 20
Green, T. H. 269, 290, 291, 293–4
Greenleaf, W. H. 16
Gregory, D. 365
Grotius, H. 145

Haddock, B. 211
Haldane, R. B. 291
Hanson, N. R. 14
Harnack, A. von 85
Haverfield, F. J. 355
Hawkes, C. 366, 367
Healy, M. J. R. 12, 13–14
Hegel, G. W. F. 33, 87, 89, 120, 121, 122, 123, 125, 135, 145, 160, 161–2, 170, 198, 271, 317, 326–7, 332
Heller, Agnes 16
Herodotus 198
Hobbes, T. 116–17, 118, 120, 122, 123, 126, 195, 307
Hodder, I. 365, 367, 368, 370, 372
Hogan, J. P. 17
Hume, David 63, 108–9, 136, 171, 204
Huxley, T. H. 332

James, William 118
Jevons, W. S. 289
Joachim, H. H. 6, 93
Jones, H. 291, 293
Joseph, H. W. B. 6, 7, 80, 97, 98

Kant, I. 2, 33, 34, 63, 81–2, 83, 84, 87, 88, 89, 123, 125–6, 173–4, 195, 198, 210, 250, 259
Kennick, K. E. 72, 75
Kipling, Rudyard 70
Knox, T. M. 3, 5, 6, 19, 20, 21, 22, 25, 80, 130, 182, 206, 210–11, 213, 236, 259

Koyré, A. 82
Krausz, Michael xv
Kroeber, A. L. 366
Kuhn, T. S. 14

Ladurie, E. le Roy 365
Lane, P. 364
Leibniz, G. W. 88
Leone, M. 371, 372
Levenson, J. 12, 13
Lindsay, A. D. 7
Linklater, A. 12, 13
Locke, John 115, 120, 236
Loisy, A. 85
Lonergan, Bernard 17, 18
Luard Selby, Revd R. B. 4
Luther, Martin 79

Mabbott, J. D. 6, 25, 100
Martin, Rex 16, 190, 193–5
Marx, Karl 134–5, 184, 198, 199, 317, 332
McCallum, R. B. 4, 5
McGinn, Colin 19, 20
Mead, G. H. 119
Merriman, N. 379
Mill, J. S. 122, 289
Miller, D. 372
Mink, L. O. 184, 190, 195–7, 208, 270
Momigliano, A. 92–3, 103
Mommsen, T. 350
Moore, G. E. 71, 118
Mother Teresa 48, 50
Mure, G. R. G. 327
Myres, J. N. L. 373

Newman, J. H. 332
Newton, I. 258, 259
Nielsen, M. H. 212
Nowakowski, J. 364

Oakeshott, Michael 12, 13

Pannenberg, W. 17
Patrick, James 6
Peirce, C. S. 119, 127
Piggott, S. 366
Pitt-Rivers, A. L.-F. 353, 355
Plato 43, 62, 80–1, 123, 124, 195, 203, 302, 326, 327
Pocock, J. G. A. 16
Pompa, L. 16
Popper, K. R. xvii, 14, 16, 20, 199, 300–1, 310–28

Price, H. H. 8, 116
Prichard, H. A. 6, 7, 8, 98, 127, 324
Pufendorf, 145

Relton, Revd F. 23
Reynolds, P. K. B. 375
Richards, R. 333
Richmond, I. A. 3, 373, 374, 375
Ricoeur, P. 17, 18
Ritchie, D. G. 293
Robbins, M. 4
Ross, W. D. 6, 7, 97, 125–6, 324
Rousseau, J.-J. 270
Rowlands, M. 367, 371
Rubinoff, Lionel 23, 83, 85, 190, 270
Ruggiero, Guido de xv, 8, 92, 96, 98–9, 102, 103, 104, 107–8, 111, 123, 155
Ruskin, John 1
Russell, Bertrand 83, 87
Ryle, Gilbert, 6, 8, 9, 80, 81, 83–4, 88, 97, 100, 116
Rynin, D. 196–7

Sabloff, J. D. 370
Sahlins, M. 365, 368
Santayana, G. 6
Sartre, J. P. 120
Schiffer, M. B. 369
Schiller, F. 123
Schliemann, H. 345
Selden 145
Shanks, M. 365, 368, 371, 372
Shaw, G. B. 70
Simmel, G. 198
Simpson, F. G. 4, 24, 288
Sisam, K. 5, 6
Skinner, Q. 16

Slotkin, J. S. 374
Smith, J. A. 6, 93, 98, 103
Smith, Teresa 2
Socrates 327
Spector, J. 372
Spengler, O. 200
Spinoza, B. 124
Stanage, S. M. 270
Stevens, C. E. 5
Strauss, Leo 16
Suetonius 178

Tacitus 178
Taylor, W. 366
Taylor, M. V. 3, 24
Thucydides 198
Tilley, C. 365, 368, 371, 372
Toulmin, Stephen, xvi, 14, 182, 183, 192–5, 330, 332, 344–7, 357
Toynbee, A. J. 123
Trigger, B. 366, 372

Vico, Giambattista xv, 96, 101, 119, 124, 126, chapter 7 *passim*, 130–49, 198
Voltaire 135

Webb, C. C. J. 6, 90
Weldon, T. D. 7
Wheeler, R. E. M. 375
Whitehead, A. N. 86, 88, 249
Wilcox, Canon 4,
Willey, G. 366
Windelband, W. 156
Wittgenstein, Ludwig 8, 9, 10, 45, 64, 68, 75, 76, 195–6

# Index of References to Collingwood's Writings

## Books

*An Autobiography* 2, 5, 6, 7, 14, 15, 18, 57, 79, 80, 82, 84, 85, 86, 92, 93, 94, 95, 96, 97, 98, 99, 104, 105, 106, 108, 109, 130, 131, 132, 135, 138, 140, 141, 142, 146, 149, 152, 153, 154, 160, 184, 195, 203, 204, 217, 220, 246, 248, 259, 269, 289, 290, 308, 309, 310, 339, 340, 342, 343, 344, 345, 346, 347, 348, 349, 353, 354, 355, 356, 367, 374
*An Essay on Philosophical Method* 11, 12, 21, 22, 39–46, 52, 53, 54, 55, 72, 73, 83, 89, 98, 110, 132, 203, 223, 224, 225, 226, 227, 229, 247, 248, 249, 261
*An Essay on Metaphysics* 7, 11, 12, 14, 17, 22, 80, 84, 85, 86, 87, 88, 89, 118, 142, 146, 190, 191, 192, 194, 195, 203–10, 223, 225, 230, 232, 234, 236, 254, 257, 272, 283, 286, 287, 288, 289, 334, 344
*Essays in Political Philosophy* 19
*Handbook to the Roman Wall* 373
*Outlines of a Philosophy of Art* 63, 284
*Religion and Philosophy* 9, 22, 79
*Roman Britain and the English Settlements* 187, 373, 375, 376, 379
*Roman Britain* 187–8, 373
*Speculum Mentis* 11, 37, 38, 39, 43, 48, 53, 55, 63, 85, 86, 99, 100, 108, 118, 132, 144, 153, 184, 272, 273, 274, 284, 290
*The Archaeology of Roman Britain* 373
*The Idea of History* 6, 15, 17, 18, 19, 20, 21, 57, 71, 131, 132, 133, 135, 136, 137, 138, 139, 142, 145, 149, 152, 159, 160, 161, 170, 171, 172, 173, 174, 184, 185, 186–7, 188, 189, 190, 194, 197, 198, 199, 211, 219, 220, 221, 225, 227, 228, 232, 248, 249, 250–60, 266, 272, 287, 288, 326, 327, 334, 336, 339, 341, 342, 348, 349, 366, 367, 371, 374
*The Idea of Nature* 8, 20, 21, 22, 79, 86, 194, 196, 197, 199, 248, 249, 250
*The New Leviathan* xv, 7, 8, 9, 18, 19, 20, 21, 24, 55, 57, Chapter 6 (115–29) *passim*, 185, 227, 236, 260, 261, 262, 263, 264, 265, 269, 271, 272, 273, 276, 277, 278, 279, 280, 281, 282, 283, 286, 287, 292, 293, 300, 301, 302, 303, 304, 305, 306, 307, 308, 320, 321, 324, 327, 368
*The Principles of Art* 15, Chapter 3 (62–78) *passim*, 97, 102, 117, 118, 130, 143, 144, 272, 273, 274, 275, 287, 294

## Articles and pamphlets

'Aesthetic' 284
'A Guide to the Roman Wall' 379
'Can the New Idealism Dispense with Mysticism?' 96, 99, 103
'Croce's Philosophy of History' 96, 103, 250, 253

'Economics as a Philosophical Science' 110
'Faith and Reason' 80, 84
'Fascism and Nazism' 286
'Hadrian's Wall: 1921–1930' 338–9, 344, 350, 354–6
'Hadrian's Wall: A History of the Problem' 338, 341, 350
'Human Nature and Human History' 103, 107
'An Introduction to the Prehistory of Cumberland, Westmorland and Lancashire North of the Sands' 373, 375, 376
'John Horsley and Hadrian's Wall' 337, 340
'King Arthur's Round Table' 377, 378
'Nature and Aims of a Philosophy of History' 351–2
'Philosophy of Progress' 251, 254, 256, 260
'Plato's Philosophy of Art' 63
'Political Action' 110, 111
'Reason is Faith Cultivating Itself' 80, 82, 86, 87
'Review of Philosophy and History: Essays Presented to Ernst Cassirer' 105–6, 160
'The Present Need of a Philosophy' 371
'The Place of Art in Education' 284, 285, 286
'The Theory of Historical Cycles' 200, 251–6, 367
'Town and Country in Roman Britain' 376

[Fairy Tales] 'A' 284
[Fairy Tales] 'I', 1936–7, 189
[Fairy Tales] 'III The Historical Method' 284
[Fairy Tales] 'IV Magic' 275, 285
[Fairy Tales] 'F: The Concluding Chapter' 285
'Goodness, Rightness, Utility' 290
'History as the Understanding of the Present' 288
Lectures on Moral Philosophy (1933) 79, 88
Lectures on the Philosophy of History (1926), 266
'Libellus de Generatione' 92, 99, 102, 108–10, 248
'Man Goes Mad' 281
'Notes Towards a Metaphysic' 160, 162, 249
'Notes on Historiography' 284
'Notes on the History of Historiography and Philosophy of History' 103, 107
'Outlines of a Philosophy of History' ['Die' MS] 106, 255
'Rule-making and Rule-breaking' 279
'Science, Religion and Civilization', 272, 282, 286
'The Function of Metaphysics in Civilization' 254, 258, 288, 290
'The Principles of History' 6, 15, 18, 88
'What Civilization Means' 261–4, 265–6

## Unpublished manuscripts (including recently published MSS)

'Art and the Machine' 284
Correspondence with Gilbert Ryle, 83